THE CRAFT OF CONTEMPORARY COMMERCIAL MUSIC

D1710536

In the contemporary world, the role of the commercial composer has grown to include a wide range of new responsibilities. Modern composers not only write music, but also often need to perform, record, and market their own works. *The Craft of Contemporary Commercial Music* prepares today's music students for their careers by teaching them to compose their own music, produce it professionally, and sell it successfully.

The textbook integrates three areas of concentration—music theory and composition, audio engineering, and music business—allowing students to understand and practice how to successfully navigate each stage of a score's life cycle from concept to contract. Students will learn how to:

- Translate musical ideas into scores utilizing music theory and composition techniques
- Transform scores into professional audio through the production stages of tracking, sequencing, editing, mixing, mastering, and bouncing
- Market works to prospective clients

The textbook assumes no prior knowledge of music theory or audio topics, and its modular organization allows instructors to use the book flexibly. Exercises at the end of each chapter provide practice with key skills, and a companion website supports the book with video walkthroughs, streaming audio, a glossary, and printable exercise pages.

Combining a grounding in music notation and theory concepts with a foundation in essential technologies, *The Craft of Contemporary Commercial Music* offers an innovative approach that addresses the needs of students preparing for music careers.

Greg McCandless is Assistant Professor of Music Theory at Appalachian State University.

Daniel McIntyre is Department Chair of Music Composition at Full Sail University.

THE CRAFT OF CONTEMPORARY COMMERCIAL MUSIC

GREG McCANDLESS AND DANIEL McINTYRE

Routledge
Taylor & Francis Group

NEW YORK AND LONDON

First published 2018
by Routledge
711 Third Avenue, New York, NY 10017

and by Routledge
2 Park Square, Milton Park, Abingdon, Oxon OX14 4RN

Routledge is an imprint of the Taylor & Francis Group, an informa business

Library of Congress Cataloging-in-Publication Data
Names: McCandless, Greg, author. | McIntyre, Daniel, author.
Title: The craft of contemporary commercial music / Greg McCandless
    and Daniel McIntyre.
Description: New York ; London : Routledge, 2017.
Identifiers: LCCN 2017005837 | ISBN 9781138930612 (hardback) |
    ISBN 9781138930629 (pbk.)
Subjects: LCSH: Sound recordings—Production and direction. |
    Composition (Music) | Digital audio editors. | Music trade.
Classification: LCC ML3790 .M39 2017 | DDC 781—dc23
LC record available at https://lccn.loc.gov/2017005837

ISBN: 978-1-138-93061-2 (hbk)
ISBN: 978-1-138-93062-9 (pbk)
ISBN: 978-1-315-68033-0 (ebk)

Typeset in Berkeley Oldstyle
by Apex CoVantage, LLC

Visit the companion website: www.routledge.com/cw/McCandless

Printed and bound in the United States of America by Sheridan

For our wonderful wives Meghan McCandless and Carrie McIntyre, who created three beautiful children—Dillon McCandless, Kian McIntyre, and Miles McIntyre—while we created this book.

CONTENTS

ACKNOWLEDGMENTS

A project of this size requires the assistance of a great many people, and we are indebted to each of them. Our gratitude must first be extended to assistant editor Denny Tek, who initially served as our contact with Routledge and proposed the idea of creating a new kind of music textbook. Without her interest and enthusiasm, we would not have had the opportunity to work with senior editor Constance Ditzel, whose experience and sincere support of the project has given us the confidence and audacity needed to create something without a blueprint. Special thanks also go to editor Genevieve Aoki for patiently guiding us through the manuscript and production processes.

We would like to acknowledge the substantial contributions of our third team member, Brittany Self, who, as a graduate assistant at Appalachian State University, served as our organizational director and contributed to several aspects of this work, including the formatting and delivery of the final manuscript. Brittany also provided support for the project in the area of copyright permissions requests, and her success in this area has been enormously helpful in creating a book that addresses recent music and production technologies. Along with Brittany, we would like to acknowledge the assistance of Hao Do (Full Sail University) and Greg Ondo (Steinberg North America) in the area of copyright permissions.

Our own collaboration as co-authors has been inspiring and often fun despite the time and effort. For this, we would like to acknowledge the staff of Habaneros in Winter Park, FL, our unofficial brainstorming location for the first two years of the project. We appreciate that you always allowed the two of us to sit in the largest booth so that we could spread out chapter printouts with our computers at the ready, as obnoxious a scene as that was.

We also thank Eric Brook (Full Sail University) for his many contributions and especially his exciting pedagogical approaches to a variety of musical concepts. Other sources of inspiration whom we greatly appreciate include Jane Piper Clendinning (Florida State University), Elizabeth West Marvin (Eastman School of Music), Ralph Turek (University of Akron), Stefan Kostka (University of Texas at Austin), Dorothy Payne (University of South Carolina), Bryn Hughes (University of Lethbridge), Kris Shaffer (University of Mary Washington), Brian Moseley (University at Buffalo), Joseph Straus (the Graduate Center, CUNY), Nicole Biamonte (McGill University), Walter Everett (University of Michigan), Chris Latham (Full Sail University), Timothy Stulman (Full Sail University), Christopher Endrinal (Florida Gulf Coast University), and Brad Osborn (University of Kansas).

The credit for the performance, sequencing, and engineering of many of the musical examples included in this textbook goes to a few of our colleagues at Full Sail University: Steve Cox, Stephen Wheeler, and Michael Schiciano. We also thank you for your collaborations throughout the years, as well as for your excellent production insights.

Special thanks are also due to our colleagues and students for their encouragement and inspiration. In particular, we acknowledge Keith Lay (Full Sail University), Russ Gaspard (Full Sail University), and particularly Jennifer Snodgrass (Appalachian State University), whose recently completed textbook project served as a constant reminder that it can, indeed, be done.

Finally, we would like to express gratitude to our wives Meghan McCandless and Carrie McIntyre for their support and hard work guiding us through this project, which came at a time when our lives were changing at a very rapid pace. We truly could not have accomplished this without you.

Introduction

The Contemporary Commercial Composer and the Digital Audio Workstation

As technology has continued to develop, the role of the modern commercial composer has evolved to include many responsibilities that reach far beyond the duties of past composers. Indeed, today's composer is not only expected to compose, but often perform, record, edit, and master his or her own work. With each new generation of music creators, more and more technological aptitude is necessary to remain competitive; those who desire a career in the commercial side of the industry, in particular, need to be fluent in many aspects of the current technological tools available to them. With such a wide skill set required, the original title of *composer* hardly seems fitting. Others may choose the term *producer*, but a producer isn't necessarily a musician in the traditional definition of the term, which can cause even more confusion. In this textbook, we use the terms *composer* and *producer* interchangeably. It is our position that since contemporary *composers* are often accountable for *producing* music from start to finish, both terms justly reflect their responsibilities.

This book provides you with a path toward understanding the many functions of a contemporary producer. It proceeds from fundamental music concepts through advanced media composition and production techniques, all within the context of music technology and practical commercial situations. Such a book requires an in-depth treatment of music notation and music theory, which provides the modern musician with a solid foundation for musical communication and is paramount to a successful career in the industry. Understanding how music is put together on a page provides fluidity, efficiency, and professionalism to a contemporary composer's workflow. Facility with music software and technology are also imperative, and this book equally focuses on notated composition and production within the digital audio environment in order to provide you with a multifaceted skill set in support of your success as a contemporary composer.

The starting point of a composer's musical workflow has evolved to include many options. Some composers still prefer to begin with a notated score, while others favor working out their ideas directly into a piece of recording software, which we will refer to as a digital audio workstation or DAW in this book. A DAW provides an environment designed to consolidate the workflows related to the many stages of production into a single location. A producer using a DAW has the option of playing in his or her ideas with a keyboard, inputting ideas with a mouse, recording live instruments, editing work, and mixing and mastering all within a single setting. You will learn about notation essentials in Parts I and II of this book, and they will be used throughout its remaining chapters. For now, we'll proceed to an introduction to the DAW, which will be integrated into the discussion of notation starting in Chapter 1.

DIGITAL AUDIO WORKSTATIONS

The DAW is the central tool for any studio. There are many great DAWs on the market, and while each offers slightly different workflow alternatives, they all generally work the same way: they allow you to see a piece of music's structure in score form as well as other forms, adjust the way it sounds, add effects to it, edit out performance errors, adjust volume levels, and export it so that it can be heard and stored. A DAW works by manipulating two main parameters, audio and MIDI, which you will learn about in Chapter 5. Most DAWs share common view windows for handling different aspects of audio and MIDI, although they may refer to them by slightly different names. They also tend to possess similar design features, but the workflow strategies, layouts, and aesthetic schemes nonetheless distinguish one program from another. In the next few figures, you can explore some of the main working environments found in current, industry-leading DAWs. Keep in mind that the end product (the finished track) is far more dependent upon the user than it is on the software.

DAW DESIGN AND ANALOG EQUIPMENT

DAWs are designed to look and feel as much like analog equipment as possible. Many users in the early days of digital audio workstations were transitioning from a world of tangible equipment where they could touch, feel, and manipulate sound by turning dials and pushing faders, etc. The introduction of DAWs needed to be as straightforward as possible, allowing professionals the ability to make the change from analog to digital environments seamlessly. Play, record, and stop functions within DAWs clearly illustrate the tendency of software manufacturers to closely recreate the look of analog hardware in their designs. Figure 1 shows transport/control bar windows from Cubase Pro, Logic Pro X, and Digital Performer 9.

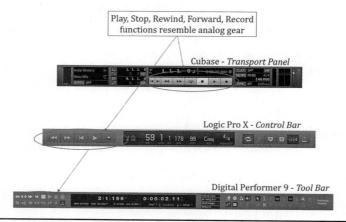

Fɪɢ. 0.1   Transport control windows from leading digital audio workstations

Tracks View Windows

Another common visualization used in a DAW is the tracks view window. These layouts indicate the instruments involved in an arrangement (audio and MIDI) and show when and where they are playing over the course of time.

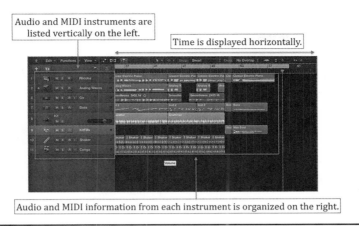

Fig. 0.2   Tracks view window in Logic Pro X

Compare Digital Performer 9's tracks view with Logic Pro X's. The same basic information is present in both windows, but it is displayed a little differently.

Digital Performer 9 - *Track View*

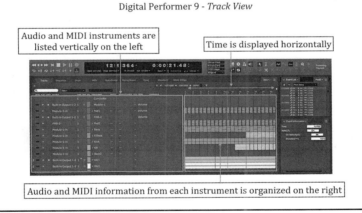

Fig. 0.3   Tracks view window in Digital Performer 9

Piano Roll Editors

One of the strongest features of any DAW is the piano roll editor, which may have a different name depending on the software in question. A **piano roll editor** presents a piano keyboard rotated 90 degrees such that the bottoms of the keys are facing right. Immediately to the right of the keyboard image is a graph made up of vertical and horizontal lines. The horizontal lines aid in the representation of pitch and run parallel to the keys of the keyboard. You'll learn more about pitch in Chapter 1. The lines running vertically across the graph relate to duration or rhythm (introduced in Chapter 2), and are divided into time segments that can be calibrated by the user. The small blocks found within a graph (called MIDI events) are composed of pitch and duration information; that is, each MIDI event indicates that a specific note will be articulated at a given temporal location and held for a prescribed amount of time, creating a specific rhythm.

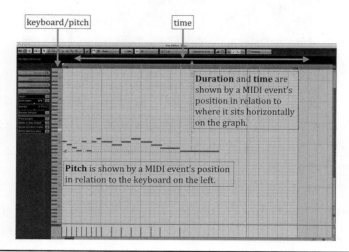

Fig. 0.4 Key Editor (piano roll editor) view in Cubase Pro

Notation Editors

Most DAWs also feature a window wherein a user can see a music notation score of the events taking place in the arrangement. Altering the MIDI events will alter the score in real time, and altering the score will likewise affect the MIDI events. Again, the exact name of the notation window will vary from software to software.

Fig. 0.5 QuickScribe (notation editor) view in Digital Performer 9

Virtual Mixing Boards

DAWs additionally include a mixing environment that displays the volume of each sonic element of an arrangement separated into discrete channels within a virtual mixing board. When labeled properly, it is easy to organize the sounds within a mix and discern the channels from which they originate. Virtual faders are used to raise and lower the volume of each channel.

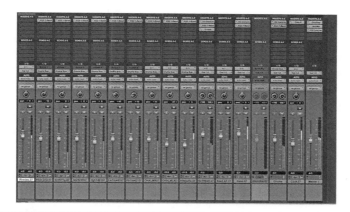

Fig. 0.6 Mix window in Pro Tools 11

Each *channel* column represents a different audio or MIDI track. The mix window affords producers a wide range of functions within a single view. These functions are covered in detail in Parts Ib and IIb in this book.

ARRANGE/OVERVIEW WINDOWS

DAWs also feature a layout that offers a broad view of the entire project, allowing for multiple window sets to be viewed at once while focusing on the arrangement of music as it unfolds through time. The user can typically define the exact windows he or she wishes to view within an overview window, providing personalized workflow possibilities.

Logic Pro X *Main View*

Fig. 0.7 Main View (overview window) in Logic Pro X

MIDI EVENT LIST

A MIDI event list is simply a detailed list of events that take place in an arrangement. The information within a list ranges from simple data (e.g., pitches being performed) through complex descriptions of musical expression. The far left column indicates *when* something is taking place, followed by more details about exactly *what* is happening at that specified time. Time is expressed in terms of measures, which you will learn about in Chapter 2.

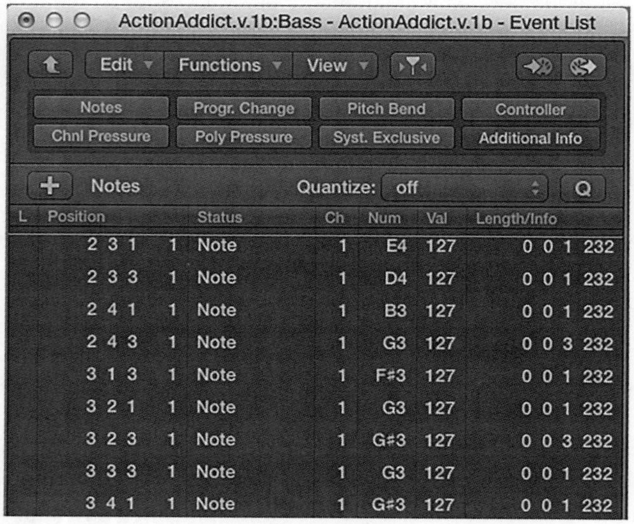

Fig. 0.8   MIDI event list in Logic Pro X

✶ ✶ ✶ ✶ ✶ ✶

As you progress through this textbook, you will investigate musical structure and audio/MIDI manipulation in Parts I and II, toward the development of a professional skill set that can be utilized in the creation of music for a variety of media. In Part III, you will learn how to compose and produce music for film, television, and production libraries as well as create jingles, sonic brands, and scores for other forms of media. You'll additionally receive practical business tips to help get your career underway in Part IV. The overall goal of this book is to prepare you for the real world of today's commercial composer by providing comprehensive training that addresses marketing, audio engineering, MIDI sequencing, and most of all, the creation of great music.

PART I
FUNDAMENTALS OF MUSIC AND AUDIO

PART IA
FUNDAMENTALS OF MUSIC

Chapter 1
Introduction to Pitch

Even the most complex subjects can be reduced to a series of far less intricate components. In learning to read and write in English, you first learned the letters of the alphabet, how these letters combine to form words, how words combine to form sentences, how sentences combine to form paragraphs, and how paragraphs combine to form compositions. The same process applies to the study of music. In this chapter, you will concentrate on the smallest elements of the Western musical language, and these elements will be combined in later chapters to form more elaborate structures.

Music is often described as being composed of four major elements: melody, harmony, rhythm, and form. In order to discuss melody and harmony, you first need to understand the primary element of pitch. A **pitch** is a musical sound occurring at a point along the continuum of audible frequencies from low to high. Pitches are traditionally named using the seven letters A through G, which combine to form the musical alphabet. It may be helpful to view the musical alphabet—an infinitely repeating series of seven letters—on a clock face diagram, as shown in Figure 1.1. Counting "up" in pitch involves moving clockwise through the diagram, such as the move from C to D, or from G to A, or, notably, from B up to C. Conversely, counting "down" in pitch is associated with counterclockwise moves.

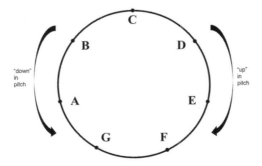

Fig. 1.1 Clock face diagram of the musical alphabet

THE KEYBOARD AND THE PIANO ROLL EDITOR

Though Figure 1.1 can be helpful in understanding pitch relationships abstractly, this book more frequently uses a diagram of the piano keyboard. This is because the keyboard provides us with the clearest visual representation of pitch organization of any instrument. It is also a very common instrument in a variety of musical contexts. Indeed, basic keyboard skills are essential for any serious musician today, regardless of one's primary instrument, and they are assumed in most professional situations. Moreover, the keyboard is the primary tool used for entering MIDI information in sequencing projects and is directly related to the main method of displaying pitch in today's digital audio workstations—the **piano roll editor**, which was first discussed in the Introduction (see Figures 1.2a and b). Note that pitches sound lower on the keyboard as you move to the left, while they sound higher as you move to the right. As you may recall, this left/right relationship is simply rotated 90 degrees in the formation of the piano roll editor, allowing you to view pitches in a down/up manner that more directly relates to the auditory experience and staff notation.

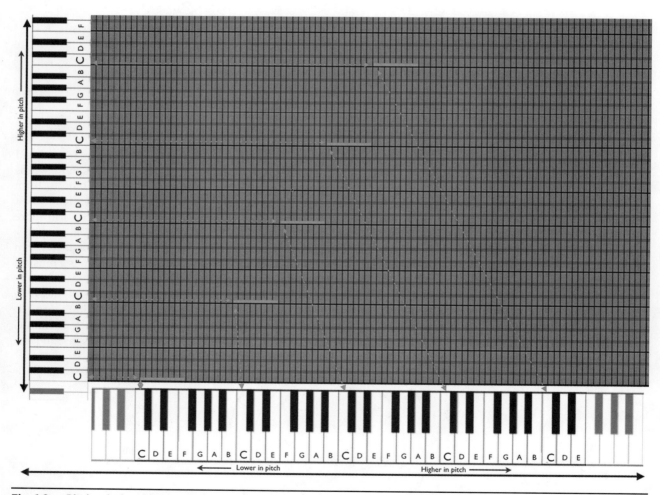

Fig. 1.2a Pitch relationships between the keyboard and the piano roll editor

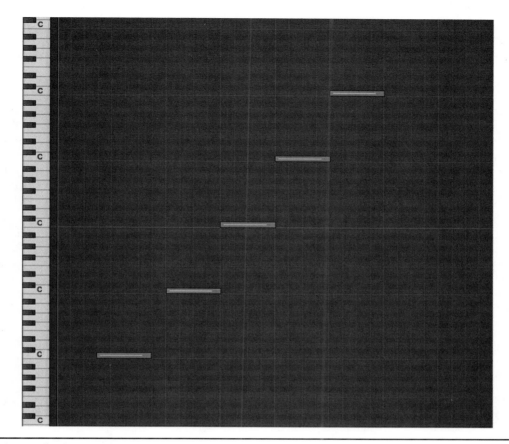

Fig. 1.2b Piano roll editor in Apple's Logic Pro X software

PITCH AND PITCH CLASS

The pitches represented in Figures 1.2a and 1.2b share the same letter name, C, and sound quite similar to one another. This is because they are members of the same **pitch class**—a group of pitches possessing the same letter name and similar sounds that are separated by octaves. An **octave** is the **interval**—or distance—from one pitch of a given letter name to another with the same letter name that is heard in a different pitch region, or **register**. Octaves are seven positions away from one another in the musical alphabet, for a total covered distance of eight positions—hence the term "oct-ave."

Pitch class members that are separated by one or more octaves do not sound *exactly* the same, as they possess differences in both tone "height" and tone color, or **timbre**. However, they do sound similar, and can be considered roughly equivalent in many musical contexts. This principle is known as **octave equivalence**. Pitches sharing the exact same sound and letter name are called **unisons**.

In many cases, it is necessary to be able to discuss a given pitch very precisely, taking into account its specific register. To accomplish this, it is common to label pitches with numbers relating to the octave in which they reside. These numbers, or **octave designations**, follow the labeling system created by the Acoustical Society of America (see Figure 1.3). Notice how each member of pitch class C begins a new octave, with **middle C**, the pitch performed nearest the center of the 88-key keyboard, labeled as C4. It is important to note that octave designations are not internationally standardized, and indeed, some music production software and hardware labels middle C as C3 instead of C4. This book, however, will consistently follow the Acoustical Society of America standard.

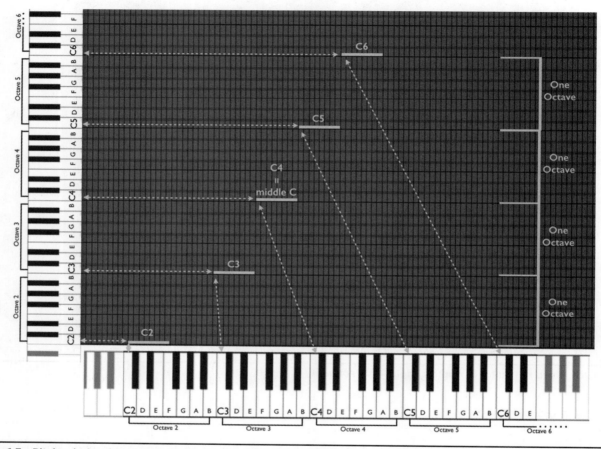

Fig. 1.3   Pitch relationships between the keyboard and the piano roll editor with octave designations

HALF STEPS AND WHOLE STEPS

All of the adjacent pitches in Figure 1.3 are members of the same pitch class, C, and are separated by exactly one octave, which is a relatively large interval. It is also necessary to discuss smaller intervals between members of different pitch classes. The smallest distance between two different pitches is called a **half step** or **semitone**, which is the interval between adjacent keys on the keyboard. For example, the distance from a black key to a white key on either side is always a half step interval. There are also half steps between some white keys—B and C as well as E and F. Each octave interval is made up of 12 half steps.

A **whole step** or **tone** is an interval that is twice the size of a half step. In other words, two half steps equal one whole step. This is the second smallest distance found on the keyboard. A whole step above A is B because it spans two half steps and skips a key on the keyboard. A whole step below F is performed on the black key directly to the left of E, as E would be only a half step below F. Each octave interval is made up of six whole steps (see Figure 1.4).

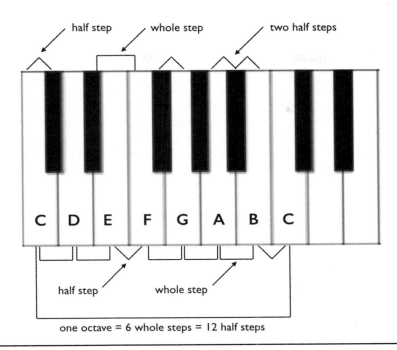

Fig. 1.4   Half and whole steps on the keyboard

ACCIDENTALS

Thus far, you have learned the seven letters of the musical alphabet: A, B, C, D, E, F, and G. These letters are associated with pitches performed on the white keys on the keyboard. In order to refer to the pitches that are played using the black keys on the keyboard, accidentals are used. An **accidental** is a symbol used to alter the pitch of a note in a given direction without changing its letter, creating a **chromatic alteration**. The most common accidentals are sharp signs and flat signs. A **sharp sign** raises a note by a half step, while a **flat sign** lowers a note by a half step. Another common accidental is the **natural sign**, which typically directs the performer to one of the "natural" notes (A, B, C, D, E, F, or G) and has a "canceling effect" in music notation that is discussed in further detail later in this chapter. Less common accidentals include the **double sharp sign**, which raises a note by two half steps (or a whole step), and the **double flat sign**, which lowers a note by two half steps (or a whole step). A summary of accidentals is provided in Figure 1.5.

Sharp sign	♯	A symbol that raises a pitch by a half step
Flat sign	♭	A symbol that lowers a pitch by a half step
Double sharp sign	𝄪	A symbol that raises a pitch by two half steps
Double flat sign	♭♭	A symbol that lowers a pitch by two half steps
Natural sign	♮	A symbol that cancels a previous chromatic alteration and restores the unaltered pitch, usually creating one of the seven "natural" notes

Fig. 1.5   A summary of accidentals and their effects

ENHARMONIC EQUIVALENTS

Although the majority of the notes that include sharp signs and flat signs are performed on the black keys, a few are actually played on the white keys, in the same positions as "natural notes." Examples include E♯, B♯, C♭, and F♭, which are performed using the same keys as F, C, B, and E respectively (see Figure 1.6). Additionally, most notes that include double flat signs and double sharp signs are played on the white keys. Indeed, every note can actually be named in a few different ways. For example, a G♯ and an A♭ within the same octave will produce the same pitch and use the same key on the keyboard. Notes like these, which sound the same but are named differently, are called **enharmonic equivalents**. Other examples of enharmonic equivalents include E♭ and D♯, D♭ and C♯, G♭ and F♯, and B♭ and A♯. Though enharmonic equivalents involve the same frequencies and thus "sound the same," they are not often treated as musical synonyms. In fact, you'll learn later in this textbook how two notes that sound the same in isolation can have drastically different functions in music.

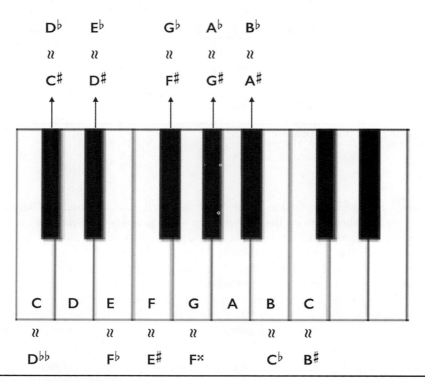

Fig. 1.6 Enharmonic equivalents on the keyboard

THE STAFF

Pitches are notated on a staff using ovular noteheads. A **staff** is composed of five parallel, horizontal lines that are equally spaced. Notes can either be notated directly on the lines of the staff, or in the spaces between them. Notes placed lower on a staff sound lower in pitch, whereas notes placed higher on a staff sound higher in pitch. Overall, you can think of the staff as being similar to a graph, with the X-axis representing time and the Y-axis representing pitch. Pitch is thus similarly represented on the staff and in the piano roll editor (see Figure 1.7).

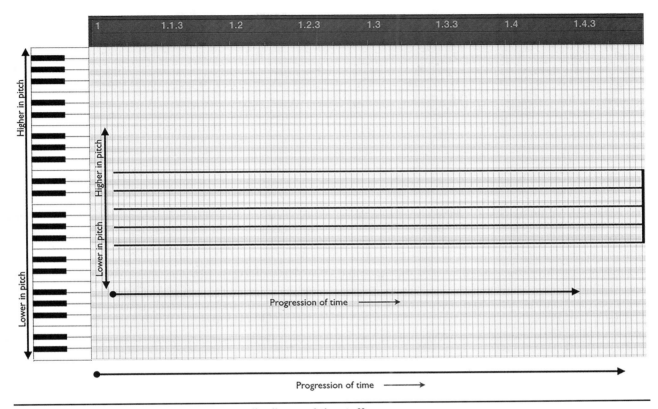

Fig. 1.7 Relationships between the piano roll editor and the staff

THE TREBLE CLEF

A staff requires a **clef** to orient the reader or performer to a specific note. All clefs thus identify a note on one line of a staff as a point of reference. The **treble clef** is also known as the G clef, as it looks like a stylized letter G. This clef features a spiral around the second line, which identifies it as a G (specifically, G4). Music for instruments that play higher pitches (such as the violin, flute, trumpet, or soprano voice) is written using the treble clef.

An easy way to remember note letter names on the staff is with mnemonics. For example, one of the many mnemonics for the letter names on the lines on the treble clef staff—E, G, B, D, and F—is "Every Good Boy Does Fine." The spaces of the treble clef staff spell out the word "FACE."

Notes that fall above or below the staff are written using **ledger lines**, which extend the staff vertically and allow for a range of multiple octaves to be notated using a single clef. On the treble clef, there are two octaves covered from the note positioned one ledger line below the staff—middle C, or C4—to the note positioned two ledger lines above the staff, C6 (see Figure 1.8).

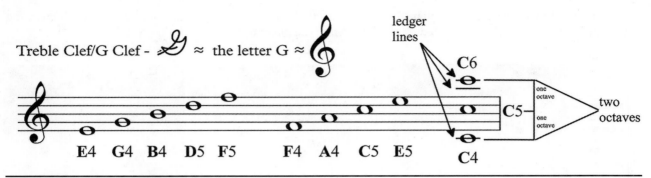

Fig. 1.8 Pitches on the treble clef staff

THE BASS CLEF

Another very common clef is the **bass clef**, which is sometimes called the F clef. Notice the two dots around the fourth line, which help form a stylized letter F and identify this line as the position for the note F (specifically F3). Music for lower-pitched instruments (such as the trombone, tuba, and, of course, the bass voice) is written using the bass clef.

To remember the note letter names on the lines on the bass clef staff (G, B, D, F, and A), you can use a variation of the treble clef mnemonic with its "good boys" theme: "Good Boys Do Fine Always." For the notes in the spaces on the bass clef staff (A, C, E, and G), it is common to employ the mnemonic "All Cows Eat Grass."

The note C2 is written two ledger lines below the bass clef staff. C3 is found in the second space on the staff, and C4, middle C, is located one ledger line above the staff (see Figure 1.9).

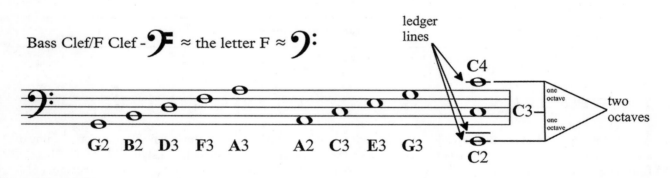

Fig. 1.9 Pitches on the bass clef staff

THE GRAND STAFF

The **grand staff** (or **great staff**) covers a very large pitch range by joining the treble clef and bass clef staves together with a bar line and a brace. Remember that middle C is notated one ledger line *below* the treble clef staff and one ledger line *above* the bass clef staff, which can help you to relate the staves in your mind by serving as a point of reference. Figure 1.10 reproduces the grand staff in relation to both the keyboard and piano roll editor and features five members of pitch class C notated on the grand staff that are labeled with octave designations. The notes span from C2 below the bass clef staff to C6 above the treble clef staff, covering the pitch range used in most music.

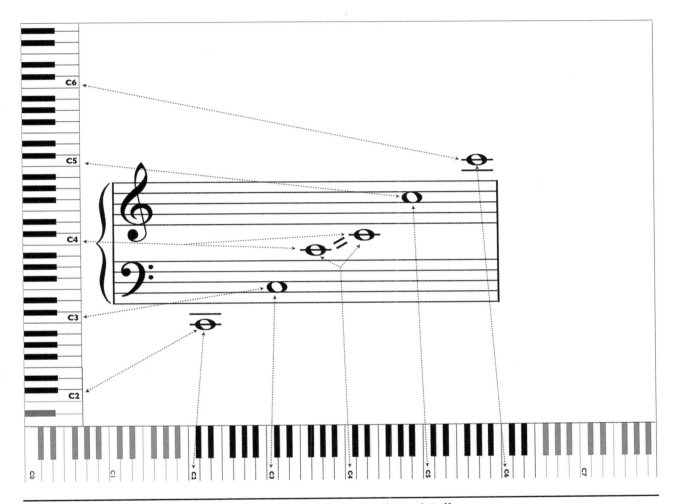

Fig. 1.10 Relationships between the keyboard, piano roll editor, and grand staff

C CLEFS

In addition to the treble and bass clefs, there is a group of clefs used in music called **C clefs**, each of which assign middle C (C4) to a different line on a staff with a distinctive symbol that can appear to be a stylized letter C (see Figure 1.11). The most commonly used C clefs today are the **tenor clef**, which assigns middle C to the fourth line of the staff, and **alto clef**, which assigns middle C to the third line of the staff. Tenor clef is used when writing for instruments such as the trombone, cello, and bassoon when their parts are written too high in pitch to be read in their native bass clef without an excessive amount of ledger lines. The alto clef is used primarily by the viola, which is typically played in a range that is slightly lower than that which is covered by the treble clef staff.

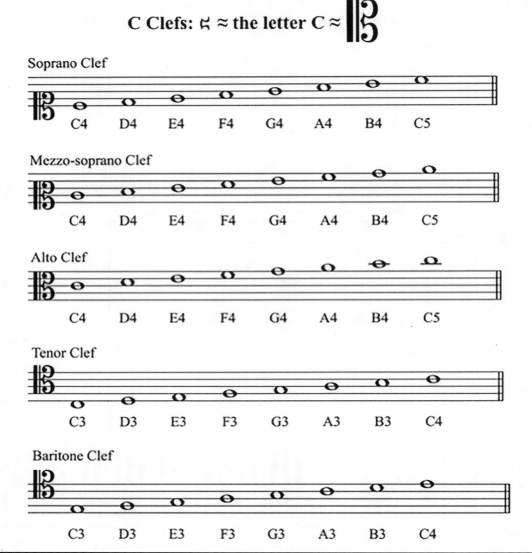

Fig. 1.11 Summary of C clefs

RELATING THE STAFF AND THE KEYBOARD

Regardless of the clef being used, the five-line staff represents pitch relationships in a visual format that is more "compressed" and efficient than the entire 88-key keyboard or a piano roll editor. For example, an octave interval is represented by 12 keys on a keyboard, but spans only eight positions on a staff. One general relationship that can elucidate the similarities and differences between staff notation and the keyboard is that of the step versus the leap.

On a staff, a **step** interval—such as a half step or whole step—is indicated either with noteheads that are on adjacent lines and spaces, or with noteheads on the same line or space with one or more chromatic alterations. Note that in staff notation, accidentals are always placed before noteheads, despite the fact that we label pitches with accidentals after the letter names (e.g., we say "C sharp" for pitch class C♯, but we place the sharp sign before the notehead on C when notating it). On a keyboard, however, half and whole steps always involve moves from one key to another that is either one or two keys away, respectively (see Figure 1.12).

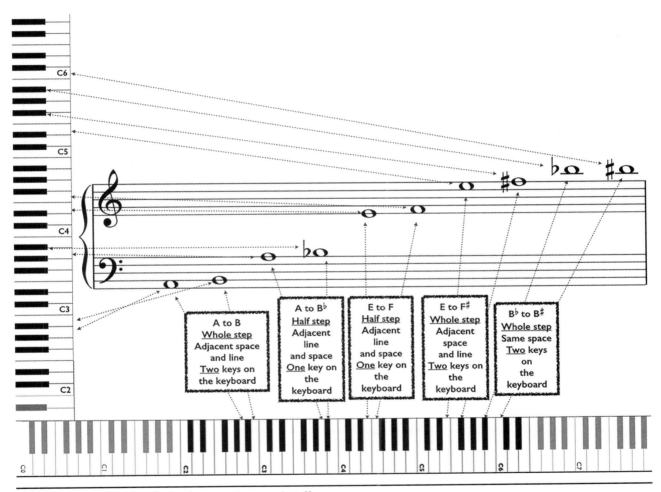

Fig. 1.12 Examples of melodic steps on the grand staff

On the other hand, a **leap**—which can be defined as any melodic distance that is greater than a step—is always indicated by noteheads that are more than one position apart on the staff, and by distances that are three or more keys apart on the keyboard (see Figure 1.13).

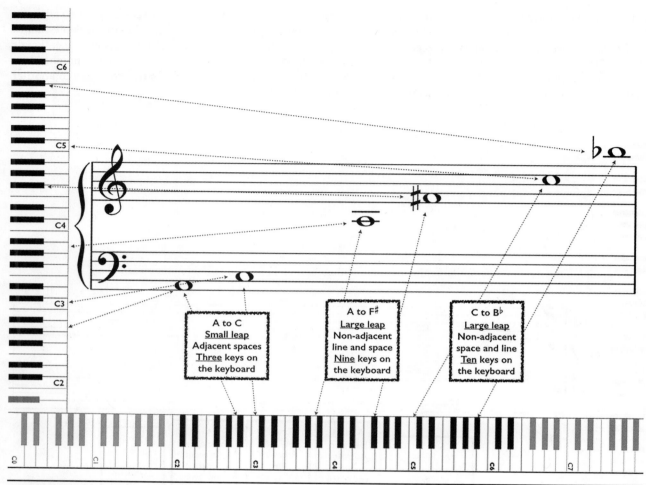

Fig. 1.13 Examples of melodic leaps on the grand staff

ENHARMONIC EQUIVALENTS ON THE STAFF

As mentioned previously, enharmonic equivalents are pitches that sound the same and are played with the same key on the keyboard, but are spelled differently. On the staff, these enharmonic equivalents are written with noteheads that are always at least one position away from one another, reflecting their differing spellings (see Figure 1.14). This obscures the enharmonic relationship in a way, but it is actually important to do so, as notes with different letter names behave differently in a tonal context.

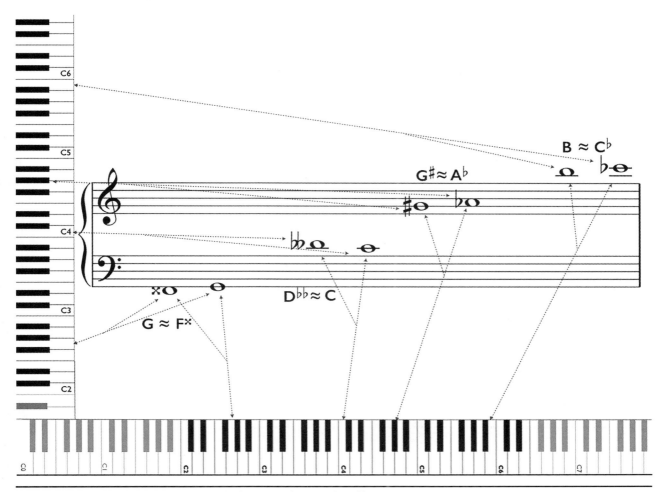

Fig. 1.14 Examples of enharmonic equivalents on the grand staff

NATURAL SIGNS IN STAFF NOTATION

In staff notation, accidentals are said to "carry through the measure"; that is, they continue to affect a given note until the end of a bar (see Chapter 2 for more on rhythmic notation). This saves composers from having to rewrite the same accidental over and over when a chromatically altered note recurs, which could make a score very difficult to read. Within a measure, the natural sign is most often used to cancel the effect of an accidental that was previously altering a given note, directing the performer back to one of the seven "natural" pitch classes—A, B, C, D, E, F, or G. Notice the placement of the natural sign in the example below, which is an excerpt from the first movement of

Mozart's Piano Sonata No. 16 in C Major (see Figure 1.15). The natural sign in the first notated bar cancels out the previous sharp sign, lowering the pitch of the note C#4 by a half step to the natural note C4, or middle C. Natural signs can also cancel the effects of flat signs in the same manner. However, the result is that the pitch becomes raised by a half step to a natural note, instead of being lowered to a natural note as in this example.

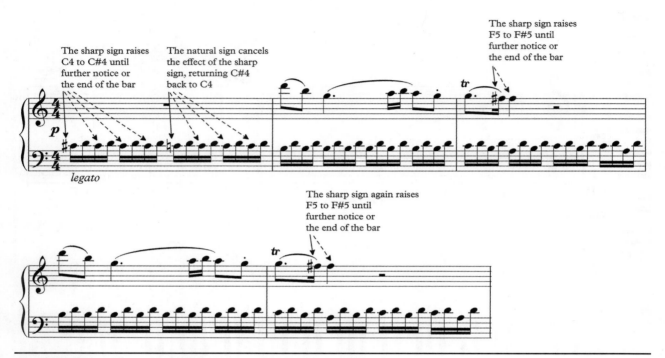

Fig. 1.15 Mozart, Piano Sonata No. 16 in C Major mvt. 1, mm. 13–17

SUMMARY OF TERMS FROM CHAPTER 1

pitch	middle C	staff
piano roll editor	half step/semitone	clef
notation	whole step/tone	treble clef
pitch class	accidental	ledger lines
octave	chromatic alteration	bass clef
interval	sharp sign	grand staff/great staff
register	flat sign	C clef
timbre	natural sign	tenor clef
octave equivalence	double sharp sign	alto clef
unisons	double flat sign	step
octave designations	enharmonic equivalents	leap

CHAPTER 1—EXERCISES

1. Place an X—or a line to an X, in the case of a note performed on a black key—on the key(s) in the diagram below for each octave of the following pitch classes:

    a. All Cs, Es, and Gs

    b. All Fs, As, and Cs

    c. All Gs, Bs, and Ds

    d. All Es, Gs, and Bs

    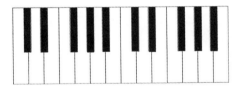

    e. All Ds, Fs, and As

    f. All C♯s, E♯s, and G♯s

    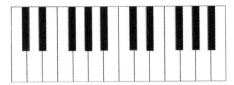

    g. All E♭s, G♭s, and B♭s

    h. All Bs, D♯s, and F♯s

    i. All Fs, A♭s, and C♭s

    j. All F♯s, A♯s, and C♯s

2a. Use lines to connect the indicated pitches to the appropriate keys on the keyboard in the diagram below.

b.

C3   E3   A3   B3   D3   D4   F4   A4   B4   F3

C♯3   D♯3   F♭3   A♯3   B♭3   B♯3   C♭4   E♭♭4   G×4   A♭4

3. Write one enharmonic equivalent for each indicated pitch class in the space provided.

E♭ _____

F♯ _____

C♯ _____

B♭ _____

A♭ _____

C♭ _____

F♭ _____

B♭♭ _____

F× _____

G♯ _____

4a. Analyze the piano roll editor diagrams below and indicate the specific pitch—including octave designation—signified by each MIDI event in the space provided. If an accidental is given in the space, it must be used as part of the pitch label.

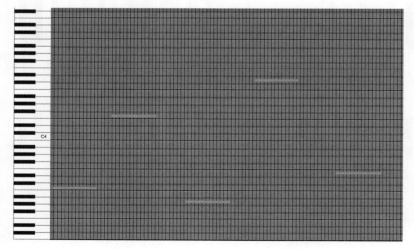

_____   _____   _____   _____   _____

b.

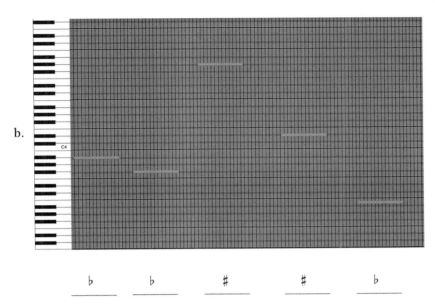

    ♭   ♭   ♯   ♯   ♭

_____   _____   _____   _____   _____

5a. Analyze the piano roll editor diagrams below and indicate an *enharmonic equivalent* to the specific pitch signified by each MIDI event in the space provided. If an accidental is given in the space, it must be used as part of the pitch label.

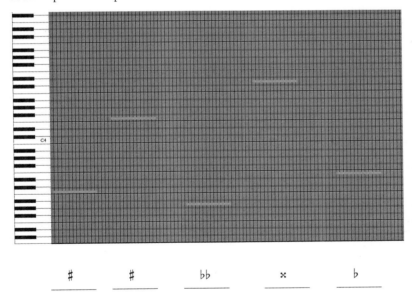

    ♯   ♯   ♭♭   ×   ♭

_____   _____   _____   _____   _____

b.

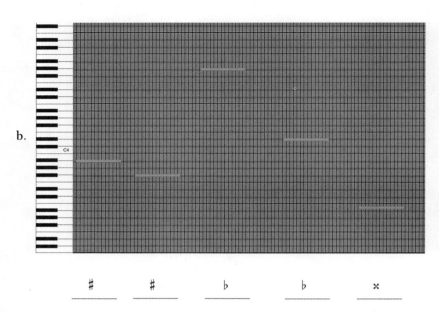

    ♯   ♯   ♭   ♭   𝄪
    ____   ____   ____   ____   ____

6a. Analyze the piano roll editor diagrams below and fill in each space provided with the interval type indicated by the pair of MIDI events. Choose from the following interval types: half step, whole step, leap, octave, or unison.

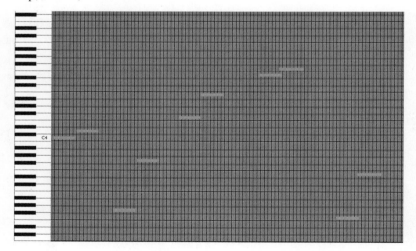

    ____   ____   ____   ____   ____

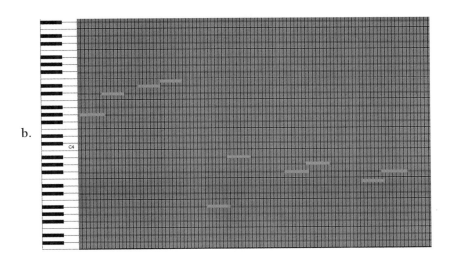

b.

___ ___   ___   ___   ___   ___   ___

7a. Analyze the notation below and label the pitches indicated by noteheads in the spaces provided. Include octave designations.

___ ___ ___ ___ ___ ___ ___ ___ ___

b.

___ ___ ___ ___ ___ ___ ___ ___ ___

8a. Analyze the notation below and label the pitches indicated by noteheads in the spaces provided. Include octave designations.

___ ___ ___ ___ ___ ___ ___ ___ ___

b.

9a. Notate each of the indicated pitches on the grand staff provided. Notate pitches C4 and higher on the treble clef staff.

C3   B3   B2   D4   G2   F4   E5   A5   C6   G4

b.

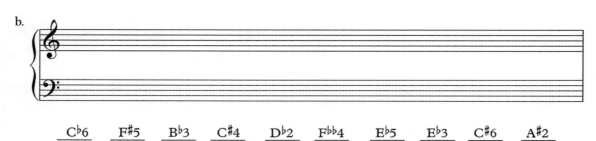

C♭6   F♯5   B♭3   C♯4   D♭2   F♭♭4   E♭5   E♭3   C♯6   A♯2

10a. Circle the pair of pitches that are enharmonically equivalent.

b.

c.

d.

11a. Analyze the notation on the grand staff below and fill in each space provided with the interval type indicated by the pair of noteheads. Choose from the following interval types: half step, whole step, leap, octave, or unison.

_____ _____ _____ _____ _____

b.

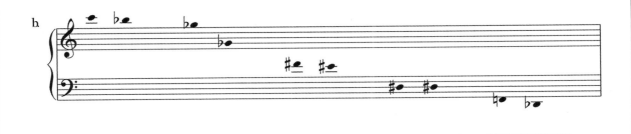

_____ _____ _____ _____ _____

12a. Melody analysis. Place a box around all melodic octaves, circle all other melodic leaps, and label the pitches with colored-in noteheads using pitch class names below the staff for the following examples.

John Williams, "Imperial March" from The Empire Strikes Back, *mm. 5–8*

_____ _____ _____ _____

_____ _____

b. *J. S. Bach, Fugue No. 16 in G Minor, mm. 20–23*

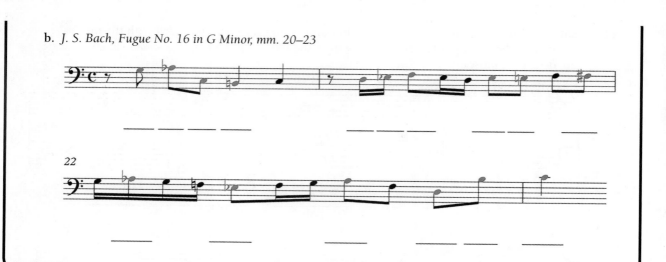

Chapter 2
Introduction to Rhythm

This chapter focuses on **rhythm**, a general term used to describe the time-based or temporal organization of music. More specifically, however, rhythms can be defined as durations of sound and silence in music. Perceptually speaking, rhythms give rise to a phenomenon known as **meter**, a perceived grouping of strong and weak stresses in music that themselves are called pulses or **beats**. While meter does not typically exist without rhythms, it can be difficult to understand rhythm (especially rhythmic notation) without first comprehending the variety of common meters. This "meter first" method is echoed in the workflows used within digital audio workstations. As you may recall from the Introduction, rhythms are cast against a duration-based grid in a DAW; as you'll learn in Chapter 6, one of the very first setup tasks you'll need to complete when creating a session is to establish the meter, which in turn allows musical events to be aligned visually with the recurring stresses in the music.

METER

The stresses or accents that engender meter arise from a multitude of musical sources. They can be created by moments of relative loudness, of highness or lowness in pitch, of durational length, etc. Notational symbols such as dynamic markings and articulations are commonly used in scores to help create such phenomena; these are discussed later in this chapter. Accents can also arise from changes in musical domains such as timbre, **texture** or density, harmony, rhythmic or melodic pattern, and more. Regardless of the sources of such accents, they can usually be felt quite readily. For example, it is common to tap your foot along with a piece of music. When you tap your foot, you're usually embodying the piece's primary pulse or beat, which is also called its *tactus*. Meters are categorized and named according to two parameters associated with beats: how they are divided and how they are grouped.

BEAT DIVISION AND SUBDIVISION

The first term used in the name of a meter relates to how its beats are divided. If they are divided into two equal parts (or **beat divisions**), we call the meter a **simple meter**. These meters are often described as having a "straight" feel. If its beats are divided into three equal parts, the meter is referred to as a **compound meter**. Compound meters are thought of as possessing a "lilt" or "swing" to them. Below the level of the beat division is that of the **beat subdivision**. At this level, the beat divisions themselves are typically split into two equal parts regardless of whether the meter is simple or compound. Confusing the matter is the common practice of musicians discussing the act of "subdividing the beat," which usually means counting beat *divisions* rather than the beats themselves in order to perform more accurately.

BEAT GROUPING

The second term used to describe a meter refers to how its beats are grouped. **Duple meters** involve groups of two beats, **triple meters** involve groups of three beats, and **quadruple meters** involve groups of four beats. While meters exist that possess five beats (quintuple), six beats (sextuple), seven beats (septuple), and so on, these are less common than duple, triple, and quadruple meters. Regardless, each grouping of beats typically involves a specific pattern of accentual strength, starting with the first, strongest beat (which is called the **downbeat**) and ending with the last beat, a very weak beat called the **upbeat**. Figure 2.1a is a visualization of the accentual profiles of six common meters. Each beat is indicated by the top row of colored blocks, while beat divisions are given in the bottom row. These colored blocks resemble MIDI events (which are discussed in Chapter 5). The accentual strength of each beat or beat division is portrayed via differences in shading, with darker shades representing stronger accents and lighter shades signifying weaker ones. This also relates to MIDI sequencing in the DAW, as the coloring and shading of MIDI events is often directly influenced by note intensity or "velocity," a term discussed in Chapter 8.

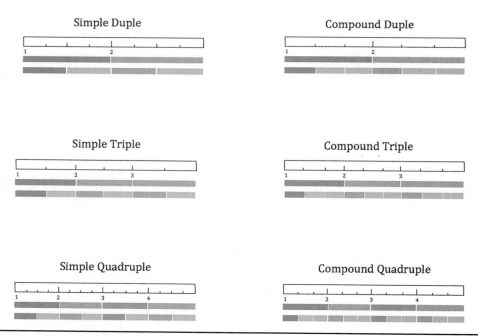

Fig. 2.1a   Accentual profiles of common meters

Conductors emphasize the weightiness of the downbeat in their physical patterns by moving their hand and arm downward into it; conversely, they demonstrate the weak and anticipatory nature of the upbeat by conveying it in a higher position than the rest of the beats and adding a lift motion immediately prior to the subsequent downbeat. Figure 2.1b reproduces the same example as before, adding the related conducting pattern of each meter. The dots in the patterns represent each beat, while the lines connecting the dots indicate the pathway of the conductor's arm or baton.

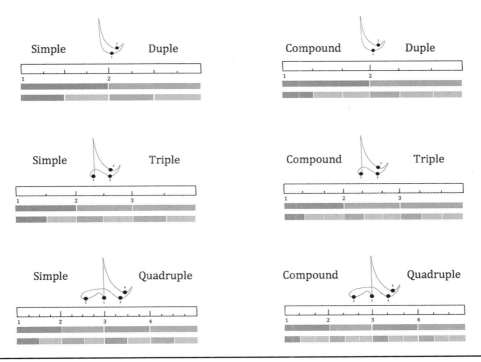

Fig. 2.1b   Accentual profiles and conducting patterns of common meters

TEMPO

While there are only a handful of commonly used meters in music, there are hundreds of unique musical "feels" or characters that can be created by the combination of meter and **tempo**, the speed of a piece of music or rate at which its beats are perceived. For example, the combination of a relatively fast tempo and a duple meter can create a lively march feel for a piece of music. Figure 2.2 lists common tempo markings in Western music (in Italian), and associates each with a range of metronome markings in "bpm" or "beats per minute," a more common and specific way to quantify tempo.

Tempo	Translation	Metronome Marking (in bpm)
Grave	Slow and solemn	Less than 40
Largo	Very slow and broad	40-60
Lento	Slow	60-66
Adagio	Slow and stately	66-76
Andante	At a walking pace	76-96
Moderato	Moderately	96-108
Allegretto	Not quite allegro	108-120
Allegro	Fast and bright	120-160
Vivace	Lively and fast	132-140
Presto	Very fast	168-200
Prestissimo	Extremely fast	More than 200

Fig. 2.2   Common tempo markings

Music cognition studies show that as listeners, we tend to hear beats that are between about a quarter second to two seconds in length, with a preference for beats that are slightly over a half second in length. As a result, tempo has a profound effect on what we perceive as the *tactus* and, accordingly, the meter of a piece of music. For example, "The Star-Spangled Banner" is typically performed at a moderate tempo and notated in simple triple meter. However, if the tempo were doubled, it would most likely be felt in compound duple (or even compound single) meter, with the original beats being recast as beat divisions in the new feel. Try singing this national anthem to yourself in both tempi (the plural of "tempo," though "tempos" is also used) to understand the different resultant meters.

Composers don't always stick to a specific meter or tempo when writing a piece of music. Varying these and other musical parameters helps create contrast and can aid in the delineation of a piece's formal sections, for example. Transitioning between sections of differing tempi can sometimes be jarring but is achievable via the use of a *ritardando* or *accelerando*. The *ritardando* (abbreviated as *rit.* in a score) tells the performer(s) to gradually slow the music down, while the *accelerando* (abbreviated as *accel.*) serves the opposite purpose. These devices can be used in a variety of other ways, as well, such as creating a "dying off" lament at the end of a piece (via the *ritardando*) or, conversely, a feeling of ever-increasing frenzy (via the *accelerando*).

RHYTHM IN SIMPLE METER

On the notated staff, numbers are used to indicate the meter of a piece of music, and each instance of the metric pattern is typically contained within a **bar** or **measure**, whose boundary is the **bar line**. The fraction-like notational symbol at the beginning of a passage that includes these numbers is a **meter signature**, or, more commonly, a **time signature**. The time signature includes a top number, which in simple meters shows the number of beats that make up the metric pattern, and a bottom number, which relates to the note value of the beat in these meters. Commonly used note values—which are used to visually represent various rhythmic durations—include **whole notes**, **half notes**, **quarter notes**, **eighth notes**, and **sixteenth notes**, though quarter notes and eighth notes predominate in time signatures as these note values tend to be assigned to beat and beat division levels most regularly. Figure 2.3 shows the proportional relationships between these common rhythmic units in the context of simple quadruple meter, and additionally indicates the common components of rhythmic values (the **notehead**, the **stem**, and the beam). Note that a whole note represents the same total duration as 2 half notes, 4 quarter notes, 8 eighth notes, 16 sixteenth notes, and so on. The *breve*, which is seldom used, represents a duration that is twice as long as that of a whole note. A traditional syllable assignment scheme for rhythms (or rhythm solmization) used by many American instrumentalists is also provided to show how each set of rhythms can be counted vocally. **Rests**, which signify moments of silence in music, are shown in Figure 2.3 as well. Rests are notated with special symbols that relate to equivalent durations of note values. Notice how the half rest looks similar to a whole rest, but with the filled-in section facing upward rather than downward. On the staff, both of these rests can be thought of as being directed into the third space. Though rhythms and rests need to combine to yield the same total duration as that which is indicated by the time signature for every bar, the whole rest is often used to denote a full bar of silence regardless of meter.

Fig. 2.3 Common note values and rest values in simple meter

The note values in each row of this figure combine to fill one measure of the most common representation of simple quadruple meter, $\frac{4}{4}$, a time signature that designates the quarter note as the beat unit (hence the "4" as the bottom number). Time signatures for simple quadruple meters always use 4 as the top number. $\frac{4}{4}$ is the most common time signature used in music notation, as simple quadruple meter is the most common meter used in music. As such, simple quadruple meter is commonly referred to as "common time," and is often indicated with a stylized "C" instead of $\frac{4}{4}$. Figure 2.4 features the famous melody from Jeremiah Clarke's "Trumpet Voluntary," which exemplifies simple quadruple meter and is notated here in "common time."

Fig. 2.4   Clarke, "Trumpet Voluntary," mm. 1–8

Included in Figure 2.5 are a few other, less common examples of time signatures that can be used instead of $\frac{4}{4}$ for the notation of music exhibiting quadruple meter: $\frac{4}{2}$, indicating four beats per bar but with a half note beat unit, and $\frac{4}{8}$, with four beats per bar and an eighth note beat unit.

Meter Type	Meter Signature	Number of Beats per Measure	Beat Value	Division Value	Full Measure Value
Simple Duple	2/4	2			
Simple Duple	2/2 or ₵	2			
Simple Duple	2/8	2			
Simple Triple	3/4	3			
Simple Triple	3/2	3			
Simple Triple	3/8	3			
Simple Quadruple	4/4 or C	4			
Simple Quadruple	4/2	4			
Simple Quadruple	4/8	4			

Fig. 2.5   Chart of simple meters and their related time signatures

Time signatures with a 2 as the top value refer to simple duple meters. Figure 2.5 includes a few time signatures reflecting simple duple meter: $\frac{2}{2}$, indicating two beats per measure with the half note getting the beat; the commonly used $\frac{2}{4}$, indicating two beats per measure with the quarter note getting the beat; and $\frac{2}{8}$, indicating two beats per measure with the eighth note getting the beat. The time signature $\frac{2}{2}$ is also known as *alla breve* or "cut time," and it is often substituted with a special symbol that resembles the "cent" sign used in currency. This time signature is used very often in marches, as is the case in the excerpt reproduced in Figure 2.6, taken from Julius Fucik's 1897 piece "Entrance of the Gladiators."

Fig. 2.6   Fucik, "Entrance of the Gladiators," mm. 13–20

STEM DIRECTION

Observe the stems attached to the noteheads in the previous example. Some of them are pointing upward, while many others point downward. Stems typically point upward if the notehead is at or below the second space on the staff, and point downward when it is above the third line. Noteheads appearing directly on the third line can face either upward or downward depending on the situation. Notice, for example, how the B4's stem in the second bar is facing downward, while the B4's stem in the second to last bar is facing upward. Other guidelines exist for specific situations, such as when pitches share the same stem or when multiple parts for different voices or instruments are notated on the grand staff; these guidelines are addressed when such situations arise in later examples.

BEAMING

As you might have noticed in the "Entrance of the Gladiators" excerpt, rhythmic durations represented by eighth notes and sixteenth notes can be notated in a couple of different ways. One way to notate these rhythms involves **flags**, which visually separate individual notes, as in the fifth and sixth bars of Figure 2.6 (when an eighth note is followed by an eighth rest). This practice is pervasive in the notation of older vocal music, where shorter rhythmic values (such as eighth and sixteenth notes) that correspond to each syllable of text are given their own flags to clearly align the music and text. However, it is generally easiest to read and play such rhythms if they are grouped together with beams (as is the case in the last two bars of the example), as this allows performers to more clearly understand where the beats fall within each measure. Single beams are used to group eighth notes, while double beams are used for sixteenth notes. (Triple beams are used for thirty-second notes, and so on.) Generally speaking, you should avoid beaming across beat boundaries, as beams are used to clarify the position of beats within measures. However, it is common to beam four eighth notes together in $\frac{4}{4}$ or $\frac{2}{2}$ (as in the previous example) if the group begins on the downbeat or the next strongest beat, beat 3. A summary of beaming guidelines is shown in Figure 2.7, which demonstrates a few common combinations of quarter, eighth, and sixteenth notes that are used in simple meters. Note this example's use of the **rhythm clef**, a clef used to notate non-pitched music such as percussion parts (hence its alternate name, the percussion clef).

Fig. 2.7 Summary of beaming guidelines

　　　Time signatures with a 3 as the top value indicate simple triple meters. Included earlier in Figure 2.5 are a few time signatures used to represent simple triple meter: $\frac{3}{2}$ indicating three beats per bar with a half note beat value; the frequently used $\frac{3}{4}$, indicating three beats per bar with a quarter note beat value; and $\frac{3}{8}$, indicating three beats per bar with an eighth note beat value. A relatively recent example of triple meter notated in $\frac{3}{4}$ comes from Klaus Badelt's music from the 2003 film *Pirates of the Caribbean: The Curse of the Black Pearl.*

Fig. 2.8 Badelt, "The Medallion Calls" theme

ANACRUSIS

Notice the unusual beginning of this excerpt: while the time signature is $\frac{3}{4}$, the initial group of rhythms does not "add up" to a full bar, and the first numbered measure comes afterward. While most music begins right on the downbeat, some works begin slightly beforehand with what is known as a "pick-up." This typically functions in creating momentum into the initial downbeat, which is often heightened by an increase in texture and/or harmonic movement that signals a strong arrival. Another name for this "pick-up" is **anacrusis**. An anacrusis is typically the length of a beat or two (as is the case here); however, it can truly be of any length that is less than a full measure. When counting music with an anacrusis, count as if the pick-up is the end of "measure 0."

Traditionally, composers "make up for" the duration of the anacrusis's incomplete measure by notating another incomplete bar at the end of the piece. This final bar would create a full measure when combined with the anacrusis, which is particularly important when repeat signs are used—doing otherwise would disrupt the meter. Not all notated music adheres to this convention of "balancing" the duration of the anacrusis with the final measure, however. The most important thing for you to do as a composer when choosing how to handle the notation of your music is to ensure that your scores are clear and easy to read for your performers.

RHYTHM VS. METER

In most music, the rhythmic "surface" does not completely conform to the neat, metric "grid" laid out by the meter signature or implied by the perceived beat pattern. Indeed, one of the simplest ways that composers generate musical interest is by deviating from the regular, anticipated pattern of beats, divisions, and subdivisions. Four common rhythms used to achieve this goal are dotted notes, tied notes, syncopations, and tuplets.

DOTTED NOTES

Dotted notes represent elongated values relative to their undotted counterparts, as the **dot** (or augmentation dot) increases the duration of the original note by 50%. For example, a dotted quarter note signifies the value of a quarter note combined with an eighth note, or one and a half quarter notes. Figure 2.9 provides a summary of dotted rhythms, featuring several commonly used values. Note that the double dot adds "half again" as much duration as that which is implied by the first dot, or a quarter of the original value. Dots are always notated on a space, even if a pitch's notehead is on a line (in which case the dot goes in the space immediately above the line).

TIED NOTES

Ties are notated arcs used to link and combine the durations of equally pitched notes, often from one measure to the next. Tied notes are also used in place of dotted notes to clarify the notation for the performer, as notes that are

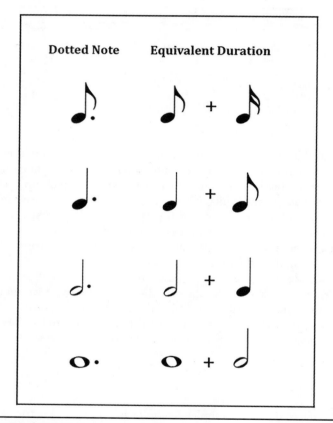

Fig. 2.9   Summary of common dotted notes

connected by ties can better show the positions of beats within the measure (even if they aren't articulated by rhythmic attacks as a result of being tied). Since they do not require a strict 3:2 durational relationship, ties can be used to create a much wider variety of rhythms than dots. Figure 2.10 recreates the previous example while including corresponding tied values.

Slurs look very similar to ties, but are used to create performance articulations, and involve two or more different pitches. Slurs and other types of articulations are discussed in more depth later in this chapter.

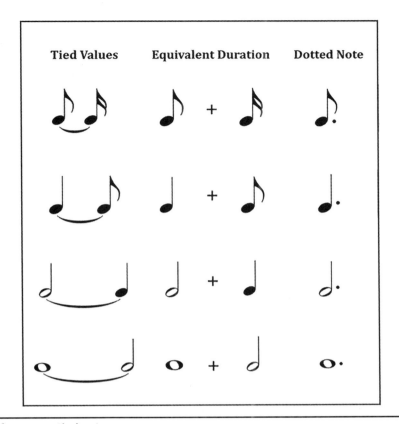

Fig. 2.10 Summary of common tied notes

SYNCOPATION

As noted previously, meters have a fixed pattern of strong and weak stresses. Typically, the strongest pulse in any meter is the downbeat. The next strongest pulses are the subsequent beats within the bar, with the upbeat normally feeling the weakest among them. Each beat division thereafter is weaker, and subdivisions are weaker still. **Syncopation** takes place when a musical passage's accentuation conflicts with the underlying meter's expected pattern of stress. It can occur at any level of metrical structure—that of the beat, the division, or the subdivision. Syncopation involves making typically strong beats (or parts of beats) feel weak, or, more commonly, making typically weak beats (or parts of beats) feel strong.

   Strong beats (or parts of beats) can be made to feel weak by tying into them from previous rhythms, or by placing rests on them when the listener would expect an attached note, for example. One instance of such a phenomenon comes from "The Black Pearl," a different piece from the film score to *Pirates of the Caribbean: The Curse of the Black Pearl* that is recreated in Figure 2.11. The syncopation is created when the second eighth note in the fourth bar is tied across the beat into the subsequent half note, weakening or obscuring the anticipated stress on beat 2. Notice how the use of a tied eighth and half note during the syncopation (as opposed to a combination of a tied quarter and dotted quarter, for example) results in a clear understanding of the location of the second beat within the measure.

Always remember that the overall goal of rhythmic notation is to efficiently notate rhythms while clearly showing the meter in every bar, so avoid using beams, dots, note values, or rests in a way that obscures the position of beats within the measure.

Weak beats (or parts of beats) can be made to feel strong via relatively loud dynamics and certain performance articulations, which are discussed later in this chapter. One such articulation is the **accent mark** (<), which is prevalent in the previous example. The accent mark tells the performer to emphasize a note with a sudden increase in

Fig. 2.11   Badelt, "The Black Pearl" theme

volume. When these marks are placed in weak metrical positions, such as **offbeats** (the unaccented divisions and subdivisions within beats), syncopation results.

In certain styles of popular music (particularly those of African-American origin), syncopation is assumed and, ironically, its absence is surprising. This is the case in jazz, for example, where the traditionally weak metrical positions of the offbeat and even numbered beat (in quadruple meter) are consistently accented to form the rhythmic basis of the genre. The "backbeat" often associated with rock music—with its heavy emphasis on beats 2 and 4 in quadruple meter—is another related phenomenon that is technically a syncopation relative to traditional metrical structure, but it is so stylistically normative as to be assumed in all related genres.

Another special type of syncopation is the **hemiola**, which takes place when the accentual or rhythmic pattern of a piece of music in two groups of three (e.g., two bars of triple meter) temporarily becomes regrouped into three groups of two or vice versa, typically at the end of a section leading into a point of conclusion. This device was used very often in Baroque music (1600–1750), in particular. One famous example of a hemiola comes from the *minuet* movement of Mozart's G Minor Symphony, which is provided in Figure 2.12. The overall meter of the movement is simple triple (notated in ¾), but the main theme begins with three two-beat groupings, resulting in a note that is tied over the bar line.

TRIPLETS, TUPLETS, AND BORROWED DIVISIONS

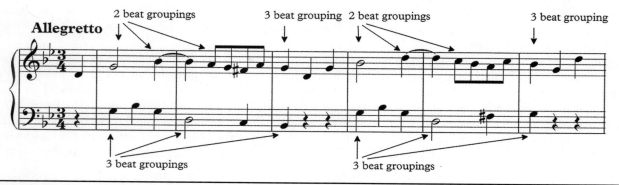

Fig. 2.12   Mozart, Symphony No. 40 mvt. iii, mm. 1–6

Another common rhythmic unit that involves deviating from the normative metrical scheme is the triplet. A **triplet** is a note value that is used to divide into three parts that which is normally divided into two. For example, a quarter note beat, which is usually divided evenly into two eighth note beat divisions, can be divided into three equal triplet values, thus conflicting with the expected duple pattern. Since divisions of three do not naturally occur in simple meter, you will typically see a bracketed "3" above or below triplets in notation, as is the case in Figure 2.13, which features the main theme from John Williams's *Star Wars* score.

Triplets are members of a larger family of **tuplets** (or grouplets) that evenly divide rhythms in ways that conflict with established metrical patterns. They are additionally referred to as an example of "borrowed divisions," as one

Fig. 2.13   Williams, *Star Wars (Main Theme)*, mm. 1–4

can think of a triple division of a beat in simple meter as being borrowed from a compound meter. Similarly, duplets and quadruplets (duple and quadruple divisions of beats in compound meter) can be thought of as being borrowed from a simple meter. Other grouplets that are not considered to be "borrowed divisions" include quintuplets, sextuplets, septuplets, and so on.

The "swing" associated with jazz is a particularly complex rhythmic idea that is related to the concept of triplets: eighth notes are notated in their traditional duple groupings, but are performed similarly to a triplet figure, with the first note occupying the space of the first two triplets (though it may sound as a shorter value), and the second note lasting the length of a third triplet while being accented and possessing a high degree of forward motion into the subsequent beat. Indeed, most jazz musicians consider the second eighth note in a pair of swung eighths to "belong" to the subsequent beat that has yet to arrive.

RHYTHM IN COMPOUND METER

As mentioned previously, compound meters feature beats that are divided evenly into three parts. These beat divisions are usually notated as eighth notes, though other values are sometimes used, such as quarter notes or sixteenth notes. Regardless of the specific value representing the division, compound meters' beats are always notated with dotted values. This can be confusing for beginning performers and composers, as they are usually more familiar with simple meter notation and are made to assume that dotted values terminate on offbeats. However, dotted beat values in compound meters line up cleanly with the metric grid. These dotted beats are not directly reflected in meter signatures, though, in order to prevent confusing images like $\frac{2}{4+8}$ which would indicate that each measure has two beats of a quarter note and eighth note combined (i.e., a dotted quarter note). Instead, compound meter signatures emphasize beat divisions, showing the beat division unit and the total number of beat divisions per bar. Unlike the situation with simple meter signatures, then, one must calculate the number of beats per bar by dividing the top number of the time signature by three. Moreover, the beat unit is ascertained by multiplying the value implied by the bottom number by three.

Figure 2.14 contains an instrumental hook from Dream Theater's 2005 song "Sacrificed Sons." The time signature used is $\frac{6}{8}$, the most common time signature used for compound duple meters. There are two beats per bar here

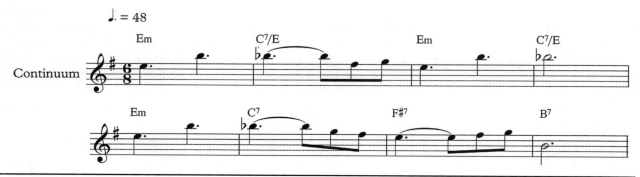

Fig. 2.14 Dream Theater, "Sacrificed Sons" hook

(the top number, 6, divided by 3 yields 2), and the beat unit is the dotted quarter note (3 × 1/8, or three eighth notes combined into a single value). You may have noticed that eighth notes in this compound meter look similar to eighth note triplets in simple meter. In compound meter, though, the beat is naturally divided into three, so each beamed group of three eighth notes here clearly reflects a standard beat and its divisions as opposed to a tuplet. Thus, one does not add the bracket or the "3" above or below a group of three eighth notes in this meter.

One commonality between compound and simple meters, though, is that each division note is itself divided into two subdivisions. Since each beat in compound meter contains three divisions, it therefore contains six subdivisions; these are typically notated as sixteenth notes. Figure 2.15 includes a summary of common rhythmic values and rests in compound meters in the context of the $\frac{6}{8}$ time signature used in "Sacrificed Sons."

Notice that beat divisions are counted differently in compound meters than they are in simple meters. Since there are three eighth note divisions per beat here instead of two, the counting scheme cannot be "One and Two

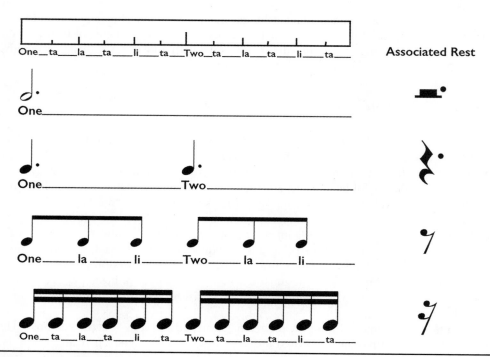

Fig. 2.15 Common rhythmic values and rest values in compound meter

and." Instead, the division level is often counted "One la li Two la li." With this common counting method, the spoken numbers ("One" and "Two" in this meter) line up with the corresponding beats. The subdivision level is counted "One ta la ta li ta Two ta la ta li ta."

Figure 2.16 includes several common beat-length rhythmic units that include combinations of quarter notes, eighth notes, and sixteenth notes. Observe the beaming of the rhythms that include eighth and/or sixteenth notes, which clearly reflect the overall one-beat length of each group. Just as in simple-meter time signatures, notes should only be beamed together if they fall within the same beat—never across beats. This makes it much easier to determine the positions of the beats within the measure.

These beat-length rhythms are commonly used in all compound meters that feature dotted quarter note beats, not just ⁶₈. The most common time signature used for compound triple meter is ⁹₈, which appears in Richard

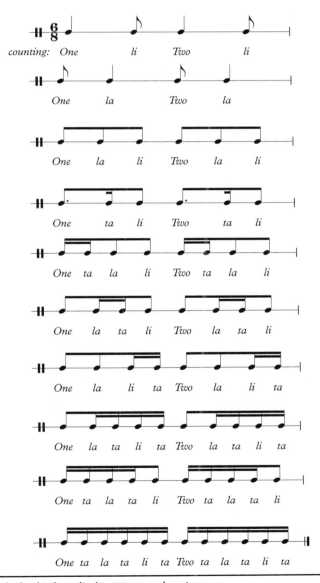

Fig. 2.16 Common beat-length rhythmic units in compound meters

Wagner's famous "Ride of the Valkyries" theme (see Figure 2.17). Again, you can calculate the number of beats here by dividing the top number of the time signature by three (9/3 = 3). Other, less common time signatures for compound triple meter are $\frac{9}{4}$ and $\frac{9}{16}$.

The compound meter equivalent of common time is compound quadruple meter, which is usually notated with the time signature $\frac{12}{8}$. This time signature is very often used for the notation of "shuffle" or "shuffle blues"

Fig. 2.17   Wagner, "Ride of the Valkyries" theme

pieces, which include a characteristic drum groove that is reproduced in Figure 2.18. Note the use of the rhythm clef here, as well as common percussion notation symbols: the "x" notehead is used for various cymbal parts, the notehead placed on the bottom space represents the bass drum's rhythm, and the notes on the third space are to be played by the snare drum. It is common to use upward-facing stems for the rhythms of the cymbals while stemming the drum parts in the opposite direction for clarity. In fact, any time two or more instruments or parts share a single staff, stem directions tend to be modified to clarify the individual lines by consistently using a single stem direction for each part.

Fig. 2.18   A common shuffle blues drum beat in $\frac{12}{8}$

Figure 2.19 summarizes compound duple, triple, and quadruple meters. Note that an entire bar's duration in $\frac{12}{8}$ meter can be notated with a single dotted whole note. The less common $\frac{12}{4}$ time signature requires a dotted *breve* for the same purpose.

Meter Type	Meter Signature	Number of Beats per Measure	Beat Value	Division Value	Full Measure Value
Compound Duple	6/8	2			
Compound Duple	6/4	2			
Compound Duple	6/16	2			
Compound Triple	9/8	3			
Compound Triple	9/4	3			
Compound Triple	9/16	3			
Compound Quadruple	12/8	4			
Compound Quadruple	12/4	4			
Compound Quadruple	12/16	4			

Fig. 2.19 Chart of compound meters and their related time signatures

SYNCOPATION IN COMPOUND METERS

Syncopation exists just as readily in compound meters as it does in simple meters. All that is required is that metrically weak pulses are made to sound strong or vice versa. The metrically weak pulses in compound meter simply take place in different locations than in simple meter (e.g., offbeat divisions take place every third of a beat instead of every half of a beat). Earlier, in Figure 2.16, you were exposed to common beat-length units in compound meters, and a few of these rhythms include mild syncopations, especially the quarter note and eighth note combination counted as "One la." Other common syncopated rhythms used in compound meters are reproduced in Figure 2.20; notice how each of these are beamed as a unit (as they fall within one beat), as well as the way that they emphasize the offbeat subdivisions, which are counted as "ta." Duplets and quadruplets are also included, which, as noted earlier, divide the beat into two and four equal units respectively, acting as "borrowed divisions" from simple meter.

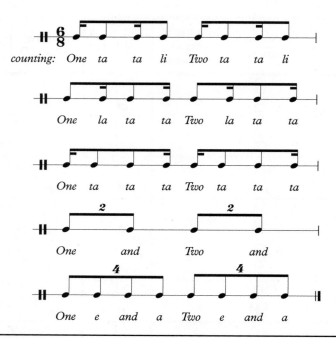

Fig. 2.20　Common beat-length syncopations in compound meters

ARTICULATIONS

A common component of music notation is the use of symbols to indicate the specific manner in which a note or passage is to be interpreted or realized in a performance. These symbols are known as performance articulations (or simply "**articulations**"), and while there are many instrument-specific symbols that every composer needs to understand (e.g., bowing marks for bowed string instruments), this brief introduction will focus on the most commonly used articulations. Each of these articulations is exemplified in Figure 2.22 at the end of this chapter.

ACCENT MARK

As noted earlier, the accent mark tells the performer to perform a note with a sudden increase in volume, resulting in additional emphasis.

STACCATO AND LEGATO

A small dot above or below a notehead (usually on the opposite side of the stem) indicates that the note be performed in a short and detached way. Indeed, *staccato* translates literally to "detached" in English. The opposite articulation of *staccato*, **legato** (translated as either "bound" or "tied together" from Italian), is indicated by a curved arc called a slur that connects two or more different pitches (as opposed to a tie, which connects two or more notes of the same pitch). A slur indicates that a passage be played smoothly, with the least amount of time between notes as possible. A related articulation to *legato* is **tenuto**, which is signified by a horizontal line above or below a notehead that tells the performer to hold the note for its full durational value (if not slightly longer), creating similarly smooth note-to-note connections.

PHRASE MARKS

A slur is often a confusing symbol in music notation, as it can mean a number of different things depending on the situation. Sometimes, slurs are used to visually segment longer musical ideas. These are called phrasing slurs or "phrase marks" and are not necessarily intended to signify a *legato* articulation. Instead, they simply indicate to the performer that a passage is to be considered one musical "thought," which can be helpful for the shaping of a performance. Slurs can also serve as indications to singers that a passage including multiple notes should be sung with one, held syllable. The musical context helps the performer interpret the specific type of slur that is being used.

Returning to the "Trumpet Voluntary" example from earlier (see Figure 2.21), you can see that there are a variety of articulations present, including accent marks, *staccato* marks, and slurs. Phrase marks are also provided to aid the organist in the interpretation of the larger, two and four bar segments. Moreover, there is a **breath mark** (') provided to instruct the trumpet player when to breathe, as well as three instances of "*tr*," a **trill** marking that signifies the need for a rapid alternation of pitches (an aspect that is a defining characteristic of this piece's melody).

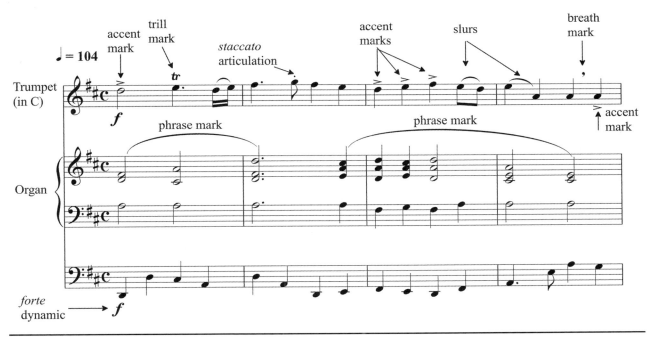

Fig. 2.21 Clarke, "Trumpet Voluntary," mm. 1–8

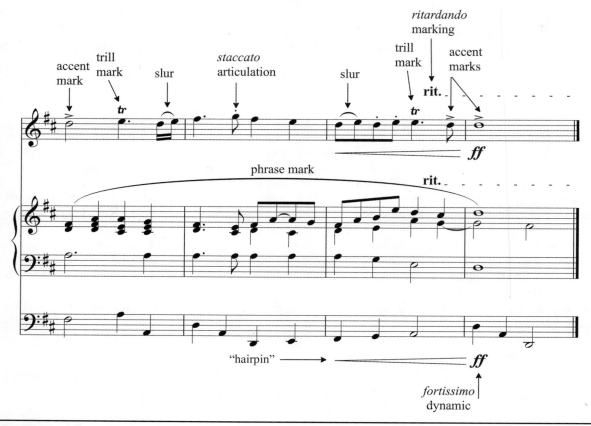

Fig. 2.21   (Continued)

DYNAMICS

The relative volume of a note or phrase is controlled in score notation via dynamic markings, which range from very soft or *pianissimo* (abbreviated *pp*) to very loud or *fortissimo* (abbreviated *ff*). Some composers will indicate extremely loud or soft volumes with *fff* or *ppp* and beyond. However, most utilize only six dynamic markings, which are listed here in order of increasing volume: *pp*, *p* (piano or "soft"), *mp* (*mezzo piano*), *mf* (*mezzo forte*), *f* (*forte* or "strong"), and *ff*. Figure 2.22 includes descriptions of these dynamic markings as well as the common articulations discussed earlier. Note that *mezzo* literally means "half" in Italian, or "half as soft as piano" in the context of *mezzo piano*.

Changes in the volume of a performance can be made suddenly or gradually, and there are specific indicators for each type of change. Sudden dynamic changes are usually made with the word **subito** (often abbreviated *sub.*) before the new dynamic marking, which translates to "suddenly" from Italian. Sudden, forceful accents on specific notes are signified by **sforzando** or *forzato* markings (*sfz* or *fz*). Gradual changes in dynamics are indicated either by the terms **crescendo** (abbreviated *cresc.*, "growing louder") and **diminuendo** (abbreviated *dim.*, "growing softer") or by visual "hairpins" whose lines intersect at the relatively softer volume level. The term *decrescendo* is sometimes used interchangeably with *diminuendo*, though it is less common. In the previous example, the hairpin is used to tell performers to move from the initial *forte* dynamic (ironically the relatively soft dynamic level in this case) to *fortissimo*, which combines with the slowing of pace indicated by the *ritardando* to yield a particularly grand musical statement.

Articulation	Symbol	Description
Accent Mark	>	Perform a note with a sudden increase in volume
Staccato	•	Perform a note in a short and detached way
Tenuto	—	Hold a note for its full durational value
Legato	⌢	Perform all notes within a passage in a smooth and connected way

Dynamic Marking	Symbol	Description
Pianissimo	**pp**	Perform very softly
Piano	**p**	Perform softly
Mezzo Piano	**mp**	Perform half as softly as *piano*
Mezzo Forte	**mf**	Perform half as loudly as *forte*
Forte	**f**	Perform loudly
Fortissimo	**ff**	Perform very loudly
Sforzando	**sfz**	Perform a sudden, forceful accent
Diminuendo	▷	Gradually perform more softly
Crescendo	◁	Gradually perform more loudly

Fig. 2.22 Common articulations and dynamic markings

SUMMARY OF TERMS FROM CHAPTER 2

rhythm
meter
beat
texture
beat division
simple meter
compound meter
beat subdivision
duple meter
triple meter
quadruple meter
downbeat
upbeat
tempo
measure
bar
bar line
meter signature
whole note/rest
half note/rest

quarter note/rest
eighth note/rest
sixteenth note/rest
notehead
stem
beam
rest
flag
rhythm clef
anacrusis
dot
tie
slur
syncopation
accent mark
offbeat
hemiola
triplet
tuplet
articulation

breath mark
trill
dynamics
ritardando
accelerando
staccato
legato
tenuto
pianissimo
piano
mezzo piano
mezzo forte
forte
fortissimo
subito
sforzando
crescendo
diminuendo

CHAPTER 2—EXERCISES

1. Complete the following chart by adding in the correct meter signatures, numbers, and rhythmic units as necessary. Each row must be entirely filled with accurate information for each meter and time signature.

Meter Type	Meter Signature	Number of Beats per Measure	Beat Value	Division Value	Full Measure Value
Simple Duple			𝅗𝅥		
Compound Duple					𝅝·
		2	𝅘𝅥·		
Compound Triple	**9/8**				
Simple Triple				𝅘𝅥𝅮	
		3			𝅝·
Simple Quadruple					𝅝
Compound Quadruple				𝅘𝅥𝅮	
		4			‖𝅝‖

2a. Insert bar lines to accurately reflect the meter indicated by the given time signature.

f.

3a. Fill in the blank spaces within the bars with one or more rhythms to accurately reflect the meter in all measures.

b.

c. Fill in the blank spaces within the bars with one or more rests to accurately reflect the meter in all measures.

d.

e. Fill in the blank spaces within the bars with one or more syncopated rhythms and/or tuplets to accurately reflect the meter in all measures.

f.

4a. Re-notate each short rhythmic excerpt in the provided staff, beaming individually stemmed notes as appropriate.

b.

5a. Re-notate each rhythmic excerpt in the provided staff, using beams and ties to correct and/or clarify rhythms that obscure beat boundaries while consolidating unnecessarily tied values into easier-to-read rhythms.

b.

6a. **Analysis.** On the score provided below, circle and label at least one instance of each of the following musical items: accent mark, *forte* marking, *piano* marking, slur, *staccato* marking, quarter rest, half rest, tempo marking, quarter note, eighth note, time signature.

Muzio Clementi, Sonatina, Op. 36 no. 1, mvt. i, mm. 1–15

Allegro

b. On the score provided below, circle and label at least one instance of each of the following musical items: slur, *pianissimo* marking, metronome marking, half note, dotted quarter note, dotted eighth note, anacrusis, time signature, quarter rest, eighth rest, triplet.

Franz Schubert, "Der Lindenbaum," from Winterreise, *mm. 59–76*

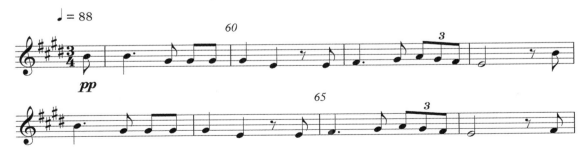

7a. **Composition.** Using notation software or a separate sheet of manuscript paper, compose an 8-measure rhythmic composition using the rhythm clef in simple meter that features at least one of each of the following items: eighth note, sixteenth note, dotted note, tied note, syncopation, triplet, accent mark, *staccato* articulation, gradual change in dynamics.

  b. Using notation software or a separate sheet of manuscript paper, compose an 8-measure rhythmic composition using the rhythm clef in compound meter that features at least one of each of the following items: anacrusis, eighth note, sixteenth note, quarter note, tied note, hemiola, duplet or quadruplet, accent mark, *staccato* articulation, sudden change in dynamics.

8. Visit the companion website for *The Craft of Contemporary Commercial Music* and match each of the numbered audio examples to the appropriate rhythmic device below. Enter the number (1–10) that best corresponds to each device. Each audio example represents only one device.

_____ simple triple meter

_____ triplets

_____ compound triple meter

_____ duplets

_____ simple quadruple meter

_____ hemiola

_____ offbeats

_____ anacrusis

_____ compound quadruple meter

_____ quadruplets

Chapter 3
Introduction to Harmony

A hallmark of Western music is its focus on **harmony**, which results when multiple pitches sound together. Though there are many types of harmonies (or "chords," though these terms are not always used interchangeably), the most common in Western music are tertian harmonies—that is, harmonies that are based on the interval of a third. Third intervals are slightly larger than half and whole steps, as they span three letters of the musical alphabet instead of two. For example, a common harmony that you have probably heard of is called a C major chord, which is spelled C—E—G. This chord is considered a tertian harmony, as it is a stack of third intervals above C: E is a third above C, as three letters are spanned (E—(D)—C), while G is similarly a third above E (G—(F)—E).

Tertian harmonies like these are commonly thought of as being derived from particular scales. **Scales** are ordered series of notes arranged in specific patterns of intervals that encompass an octave. There are many types of scales used in music throughout the world, including the **chromatic scale**, an ordered series of half step intervals, and the **whole tone scale**, an ordered series of whole step intervals (see Figure 3.1).

The most common scales that are used to generate harmonies in Western music, though, are two modes of the diatonic collection known as the major scale and minor scale. The **diatonic collection** is a subset of the chromatic scale that is most readily viewed using the white keys of the piano: it is a collection of seven different notes (plus a repeated note, creating an octave interval above the first) arranged in such a way that five of the adjacent notes are separated by whole steps while two are separated by half steps; these half step intervals are additionally spread apart from one another as evenly as possible within the collection. Figure 3.2 demonstrates one way of viewing the intervallic structure of the diatonic collection.

The major and minor scales represent two possible "rotations" of the diatonic collection that are considered to be the basis of traditional tonal harmony. Traditional tonal harmony is a Western style of combining pitches that was prevalent in the so-called common practice period from the early seventeenth century through the beginning of the twentieth century, and it is still used (or at least referenced) in the majority of Western musical genres today. Traditional tonal harmony is tertian, and it is characterized by its emphasis on major and minor keys that feature a single focal note called "**tonic.**" Tonic, and the tonic chord created by stacking intervals of a third above this focal pitch, provides a gravitational center for a piece of music. All other melodic tones and chords tend to move

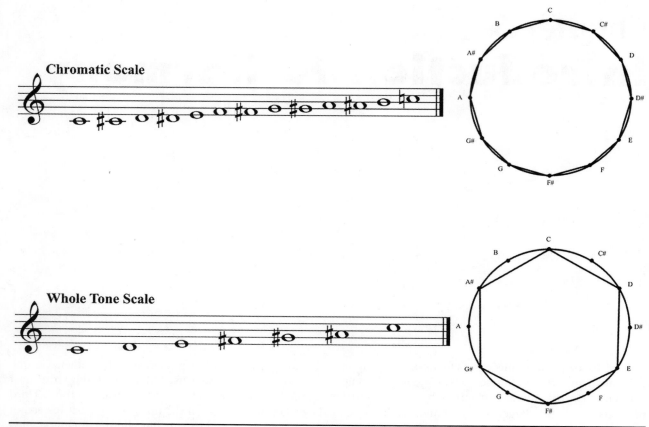

Fig. 3.1 Comparison of chromatic and whole tone scales

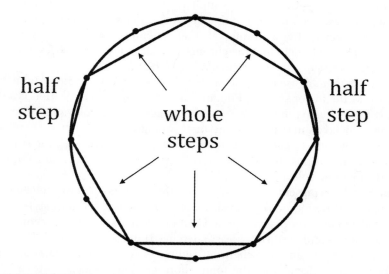

Fig. 3.2 The intervallic structure of the diatonic collection

inexorably toward tonic, and they additionally possess unique identities and associated behaviors or functions that are generated in relation to tonic. While the intricacies of this traditional system of "functional harmony" will be explored in more depth in Chapter 9, its fundamental components—major and minor scales along with the tertian harmonies that are generated from them—are this chapter's focus.

MAJOR KEYS

Music that is described as being in a "major key" typically possesses a bright, happy sound and features the notes of a particular major scale as its principal melodic tones. Its harmonies tend to be derived from these tones as well, through the process of stacking thirds to create tertian chords. Thus, the major scale is the generative seed from which the outgrowths of both melody and harmony in major keys develop.

MAJOR SCALES

The most direct way to visualize a major scale is by looking at the white keys on a keyboard, starting and ending on C, which creates the C major scale (see Figure 3.3). As you can see, this particular rotation of the diatonic collection features an uneven pattern of whole steps (W) and half steps (H): W-W-H-W-W-W-H.

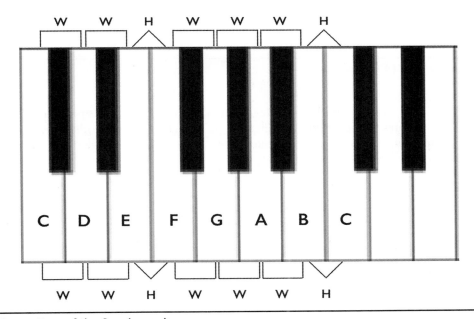

Fig. 3.3   The step pattern of the C major scale

All major scales follow this essential pattern, regardless of the specific tonic or initial pitch class on which the scale is built. Major scales follow the musical alphabet such that each of the seven note letters is always represented in each scale. This means that one or more accidentals are needed to preserve the necessary whole step/half step configuration for any major scale other than C major. For example, the E major scale incorporates four sharp signs, creating the notes F#, C#, G#, and D# (see Figure 3.4); if these accidentals were omitted, the scale would not exhibit the proper intervallic structure and would not sound like a major scale.

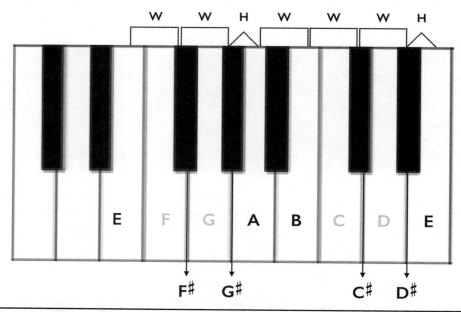

Fig. 3.4   The step pattern of the E major scale

Each member of a scale can be assigned a **scale degree** number that represents its position relative to tonic with an Arabic numeral that features a caret on top (see Figure 3.5). Notice that the major scale includes seven distinct scale degrees with the top note returning to tonic (scale degree 1̂) in a different octave.

Fig. 3.5   Scale degrees of the major scale

Each scale degree has a unique relationship to tonic as well as the other scale degrees, due to the uneven intervallic structure of the diatonic collection. As such, each degree possesses a particular name, shown in Figure 3.6: tonic (scale degree 1̂), supertonic (2̂, so named because it is a step "above" tonic), mediant (3̂, halfway between the two most stable degrees, 1̂ and 5̂), subdominant (4̂, a fifth "below" tonic), dominant (5̂, the very stable degree located a fifth above tonic), submediant (6̂, halfway between tonic and the subdominant, or a mediant "below" tonic), and leading tone (7̂, so named because it usually leads or moves upward to tonic in traditional tonal music).

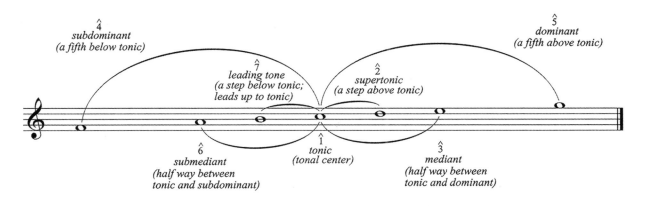

Fig. 3.6 Explanation of scale degree names

Indeed, each degree can be thought of as a separate "character" with individual motivations, abilities, and behavioral tendencies, forming a complex network of "personal" relationships (see Figure 3.7). The leading tone, for example, is one of two so-called "tendency tones" in a major scale, along with the subdominant. Each tendency tone in a key tends to be attracted to a more stable, adjacent degree in both melodic and harmonic contexts: the leading tone tends to resolve upward to tonic, while the subdominant tends to resolve downward to the mediant (though it does so with slightly less urgency than the leading tone). The most stable sounding degrees are those that are associated with the tertian harmony created above tonic (called the tonic triad)—scale degrees $\hat{1}$, $\hat{3}$, and $\hat{5}$. The supertonic and submediant also exhibit a similar, though weaker, tendency to gravitate toward adjacent positions of stability.

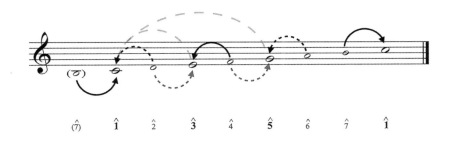

Fig. 3.7 Scale degree tendencies in major keys

Figure 3.8 features an excerpt from the famous song "A Whole New World" from the score to the film *Aladdin* that is analyzed according to its melodic scale degree movements. Note that the tendencies of the various scale degrees are typically heeded, though in certain cases—such as the leading tone that is "activated" in bar 5—resolutions do not take place immediately, creating an artful interplay of tension and release that is characteristic of memorable music.

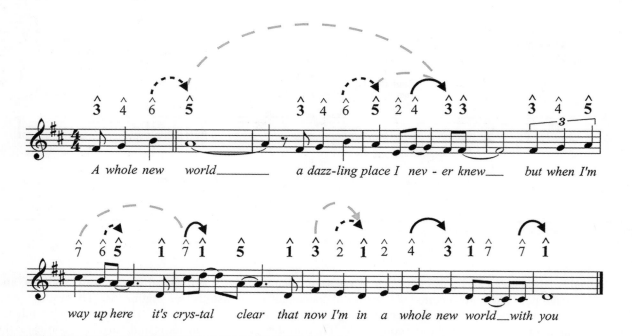

Fig. 3.8 "A Whole New World" theme

INTERVALS AND MAJOR SCALES

In Chapter 1, you were introduced to the concept of intervals, which are defined as distances between pitches. In particular, you learned about half and whole steps, as well as octaves and the general differences between steps, small leaps, and large leaps. In this section, you will gain a more precise understanding of the various intervals that commonly exist in music, focusing on the intervals formed above tonic in any major scale. As a composer, it is crucial to have a clear comprehension of all intervals, as they play a large role in both melody and harmony.

Melodic and Harmonic Intervals

Accordingly, there are two types of intervals: melodic intervals and harmonic intervals. The pitches in a melodic interval sound separately (i.e., one after the other, as in the intervals of adjacent pitches in the melody recreated in Figure 3.8), whereas the notes of a harmonic interval sound together at the same time.

Interval Size

Measuring intervals is a two-part process, as we discuss intervals in terms of two parameters: **interval size** and interval quality. An interval's size is expressed as a number reflecting the sheer number of letters within the musical alphabet A—G that are involved in the span from the first note to the second note. A whole step interval from middle C to D4, for example, is also referred to as a second; this is because the interval spans two letters of the musical alphabet, C and D. The interval from middle C to E4, then, is a third, as it contains three letters (C, D, and E are spanned); from middle C to F4 is a fourth, and so on. Figure 3.9 demonstrates the interval sizes that are created above middle C up to the octave at C5, using the pitches from the C major scale.

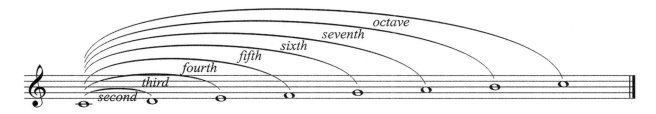

Fig. 3.9   Interval sizes created above middle C in the C major scale

Interval Quality

The second parameter used to describe intervals is quality. **Interval quality** is expressed with terms—though individual letters are used as a shorthand—that further specify each distance by relating to the number of half steps that can be found between two notes. There are five common qualifiers that are used to describe the exact distance between two notes: major (M), minor (m), perfect (P), diminished (d) and augmented (A). Generally speaking, diminished intervals are the smallest for each interval size, while augmented intervals are the largest. However, each interval size is not described according to all five of these qualities. Seconds, thirds, sixths, and sevenths can be diminished, minor, major, and augmented, but never perfect. Unisons, fourths, fifths, and octaves can be diminished, perfect, and augmented, but never major or minor. Figure 3.10 shows the qualities associated with each interval size, arranged left to right from smallest to largest in half step increments. Thus, a diminished fourth is a half step smaller than a perfect fourth, which in turn is a half step smaller than an augmented fourth. Similarly, a diminished third is a half step smaller than a minor third, two half steps smaller than a major third, and three half steps smaller than an augmented third.

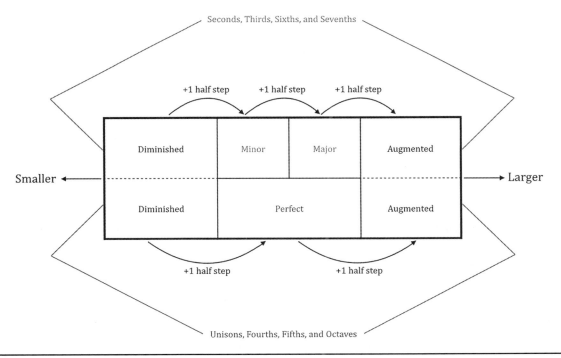

Fig. 3.10   Interval qualities and associated interval sizes

Figure 3.11 lists the intervals from a perfect unison to a perfect octave grouped by size, with the number of half steps contained within each interval indicated in the center column. You will notice that some intervals share the same half step quantity despite possessing different sizes. These intervals, which are indicated in the figure with dotted arrows, are called **enharmonically equivalent intervals**, which are similar to enharmonically related pitches in that they sound the same in isolation but are spelled differently and thus behave differently in traditional tonal music. The enharmonically related major sixth and diminished seventh intervals, for example, each contain nine half steps yet have opposing musical meanings.

Interval Size	Interval Quality	Number of Half Steps	Interval Quality	Interval Size
Unison	P	0	d	Second
	A	1	m	
Third	d	2	M	
	m	3	A	
	M	4	d	Fourth
	A	5	P	
Fifth	d	6	A	
	P	7	d	Sixth
	A	8	m	
Seventh	d	9	M	
	m	10	A	
	M	11	d	Octave
	A	12	P	

Fig. 3.11 Interval qualities and their corresponding half step quantities, arranged by interval size

Intervals of the Major Scale

Figure 3.11 may seem overwhelming, as it includes all possible intervals within an octave (excluding the exceedingly rare cases of doubly augmented and doubly diminished intervals). However, many of the intervals listed in the figure are seldom encountered, such as augmented sevenths, diminished octaves, diminished sixths, etc. Indeed, as most tonal music is derived from major and minor scales, the melodic and harmonic intervals used in this music tend to be limited to those found between the various scale degrees. Thus, music in major keys tends to feature the following intervals: major and minor seconds, thirds, sixths, and sevenths, as well as perfect fourths, fifths, and octaves. The **tritone** interval that spans six half steps—splitting the octave exactly in half—is also a crucial interval in traditional tonal music, serving as a primary source of harmonic tension; it can be spelled as an augmented fourth above the subdominant or a diminished fifth above the leading tone. If you focus exclusively on the intervals found above tonic in a major scale, though, you will only be concerned with major and perfect interval qualities. As you can see in Figure 3.12, the interval sizes above tonic that can possibly be major are all major (the second, third, sixth, and seventh), while those that can be perfect are all perfect (the fourth, fifth, and octave).

All intervals ascending from tonic (or descending to tonic)
are either major or perfect in quality

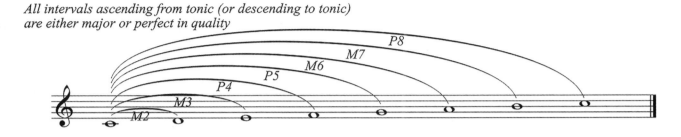

Fig. 3.12   Intervals above tonic in major keys

Interval Inversion

On the other hand, if you observe the intervals formed *below* tonic in a major scale, you will notice that they are all minor or perfect (see Figure 3.13).

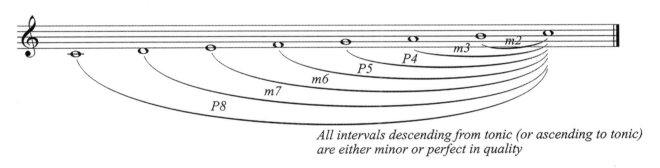

All intervals descending from tonic (or ascending to tonic)
are either minor or perfect in quality

Fig. 3.13   Intervals below tonic in major keys

This is due to a regular pattern of change involving **interval inversion** (i.e., when the lower note of an interval becomes the higher note by being placed in a higher octave or vice versa). Major intervals invert to minor intervals (and vice versa) and diminished intervals invert to augmented intervals (and vice versa), while perfect intervals do not change quality when inverted. There is also a recurring scheme involving interval size with inversion: seconds become sevenths (and vice versa), thirds become sixths (and vice versa), and fourths become fifths (and vice versa). Referring back to the previous examples, you can see that Figure 3.13 represents an inversion of the intervals included in Figure 3.12. For example, in the first figure, the initial interval that is measured is a major second (from C4 up to D4); in the second figure, the C-and-D interval is inverted such that D4 is now measured *up* to the next highest C, C5, creating a minor seventh. Figure 3.14 summarizes the process of interval inversion involving the commonly used simple intervals—that is, intervals that are an octave or smaller—that are generated by combinations of major scale degrees.

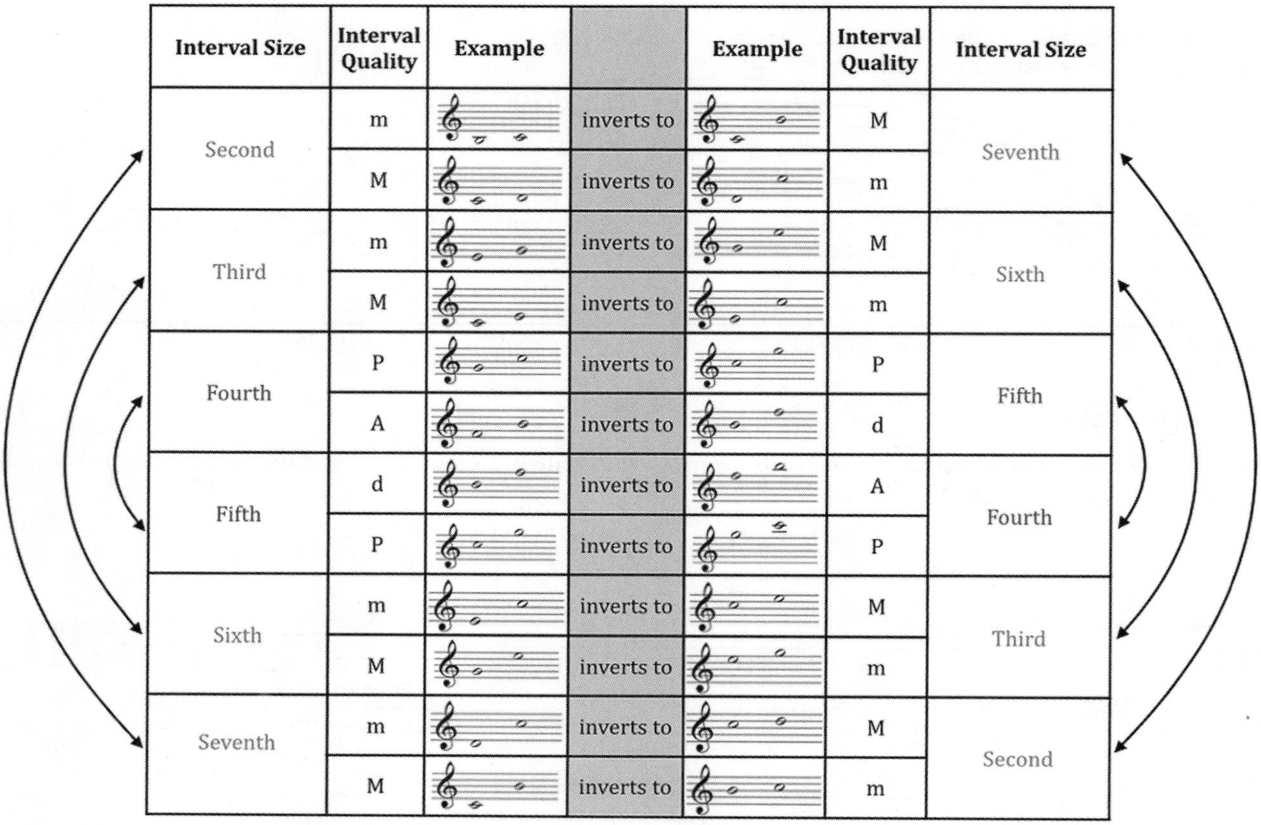

Interval Size	Interval Quality	Example		Example	Interval Quality	Interval Size
Second	m		inverts to		M	Seventh
	M		inverts to		m	
Third	m		inverts to		M	Sixth
	M		inverts to		m	
Fourth	P		inverts to		P	Fifth
	A		inverts to		d	
Fifth	d		inverts to		A	Fourth
	P		inverts to		P	
Sixth	m		inverts to		M	Third
	M		inverts to		m	
Seventh	m		inverts to		M	Second
	M		inverts to		m	

Fig. 3.14   Simple intervals related by inversion

Compound Intervals

Intervals larger than an octave are known as **compound intervals**. They are given interval size labels in the same manner as simple intervals, according to the total number of note letters involved in the span. Just as the interval between C4 and D4 is a second (as the letters C and D are involved in the span), the interval between C4 and D5 is a ninth (as the letters C, D, E, F, G, A, B, C(again), and D(again) are involved with the span). These two intervals are an octave apart, and though they do sound distinct from one another, they are very similar, as they involve the same pitch classes, C and D, in the same order of ascending pitch (see Figure 3.15). For this reason, musicians will often talk about these two intervals simply as seconds, without regarding the octave difference.

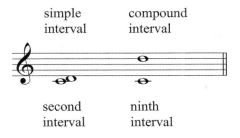

simple interval   compound interval

second interval   ninth interval

Fig. 3.15 An interval of a second and its related compound interval of a ninth

However, in certain contexts, specificity is very important in describing intervals. For example, if you have ever encountered a lead sheet, you've probably come across chord symbols like C^9 or Am^{11} or $E\flat 7^{\flat 13}$. The superscript numbers to the right of each chord symbol refer to **chord extensions**, which are chord members that create compound intervals above the root. Many popular music genres frequently feature chords with extensions; thus, it is crucial for composers and performers to understand compound intervals clearly. Extended chords are discussed with more detail in Chapter 10.

Figure 3.16 is a chart of common compound intervals and their simple interval equivalents. Note that interval qualities are maintained between related simple and compound intervals; the only part of the interval label that differs between these types of intervals is the interval size. Since it would be very cumbersome to count all of the note letters involved in the span of a compound interval, it can be helpful to consider an octave above the lower note as "eight" (as in oct-ave) and simply continue counting from there until you reach the higher note when determining its interval number. A third plus an octave is thus a tenth, for example; a fourth plus an octave is an eleventh, a fifth plus an octave a twelfth, and so on.

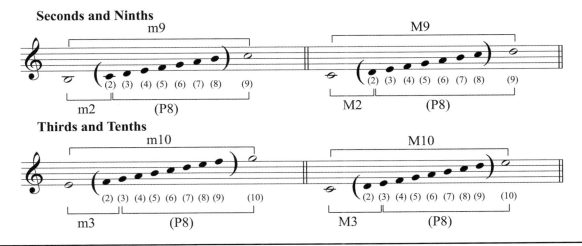

Fig. 3.16 Common compound intervals and their related simple intervals

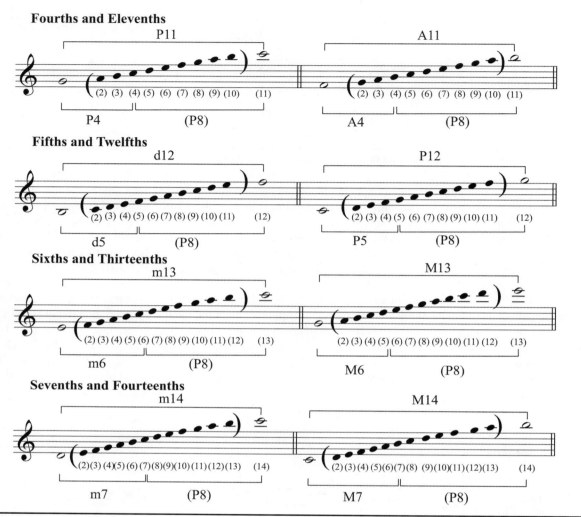

Fig. 3.16 (Continued)

Consonance and Dissonance

Tonal music is characterized by moments of tension and resolution, and certain intervals provide listeners with feelings of tension that suggest a need to resolve to more stable-sounding intervals. Intervals that engender the perception of tension are called **dissonances**, whereas intervals that produce sensations of stability are called **consonances**. Pythagoras and other theorists have historically pointed to scientific, acoustical reasons for considering certain intervals as dissonances and others as consonances. One well-known theory prioritizes simple frequency ratios of sounding tones. When two pitches form a harmonic interval, the ratio of their vibrations is either simple (e.g., the 2:1 ratio of a perfect octave, the 3:2 ratio of a perfect fifth, the 5:4 ratio of a major third, etc.), or complex (e.g., the 15:8 ratio of a major seventh, the 16:15 ratio of a minor second, etc.). Intervals featuring simple ratios are classically considered to be stable and consonant, while intervals with complex ratios are said to exhibit tension and dissonance. However, notions of consonance and dissonance are truly subjective and relate to compositional norms, rather than adhering strictly to mathematical facts—particularly as tuning systems have evolved throughout centuries of musical practice. For example, the dissonant tritone interval was once considered so striking that theorists from the late ninth century through the end of the Renaissance labeled it the "*diabolus in musica*," which means "the devil in music." Today, however, it is used rather freely in most styles of music. Nonetheless, musicians today generally organize intervals into three categories: perfect consonances (P1, P8, P4, P5, and their related compound intervals), imperfect consonances (M3, M6, m3, m6, and their related compound intervals), and dissonances (all diminished and augmented intervals, M2, M7, m2, m7, and their related compound intervals). Note that intervals related by inversion, such as thirds and sixths or seconds and sevenths, are members of the same category, as they sound similar to one another. Figure 3.17 provides a Venn diagram categorizing intervals as consonant or dissonant. Perfect consonances are colored dark grey, imperfect consonances are medium grey, and dissonances are light grey. The perfect fourth interval is a special case, as it is considered to be a consonant melodic interval and a dissonant harmonic interval when it involves the bass (i.e., the lowest-sounding pitch in a musical context) and any other voice. You will learn more about the compositional treatment of melodic and harmonic dissonances in Chapter 4.

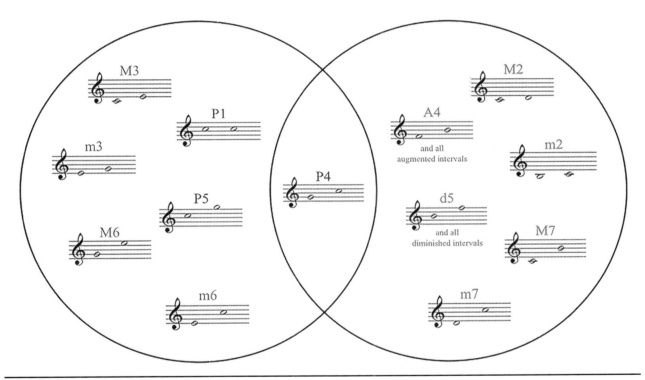

Fig. 3.17 Consonant and dissonant intervals

MAJOR KEY SIGNATURES

When composers write music in major keys, they predominantly use the pitch classes included in the related major scales. Rather than notate every single accidental in every single octave for an entire piece of music, though, they collect these accidentals and notate them in key signatures. A **key signature** is a patterned arrangement of accidentals that signifies the key of a given section or piece of music by including the related scale's accidentals; these accidentals affect all octaves of the indicated notes throughout the entirety of the following music. Key signatures are typically notated at the beginning of compositions, just to the right of the clef.

For example, in B♭ major, B♭ and E♭ are used to preserve the diatonic pattern of half and whole steps (see Figure 3.18, which recreates a melodic excerpt from John Williams's film score for *Jurassic Park*). Rather than write a flat sign next to each B and E in a piece of music in this key, the B♭ major key signature is written at the beginning of the composition, signifying that all octaves of the notes written as Bs and Es will be performed as B♭s and E♭s, respectively, unless otherwise indicated with additional accidentals within the measure.

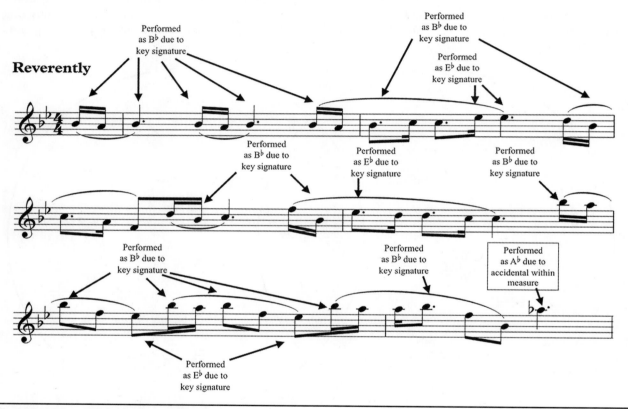

Fig. 3.18　John Williams, theme from *Jurassic Park*

The specific order in which flat signs are notated in key signatures is consistent: B♭ is notated first, then E♭, A♭, D♭, G♭, C♭, and finally F♭. Musicians have come up with certain mnemonic devices to aid in the memorization of this order, including "BEAD+Greatest Common Factor," as the first four pitch class letters spell the word "bead" and the last three, GCF, are learned by elementary math students as an acronym for "greatest common factor." Key signatures featuring sharp signs also feature a consistent ordering of accidentals, which is the retrograde—or reverse—of the order of flat signs: F♯ is notated first, then C♯, G♯, D♯, A♯, E♯, and B♯. A common mnemonic used to remember this order is "Fat Cows Get Down And Eat Barley." Importantly, the placement of the accidentals in all key signatures in both treble and bass clef is such that the first accidental is positioned on a line on the staff. From there, the rest of the key signature's accidentals follow a general pattern: in the "sharp keys," they tend to proceed in a "down, up, down, up" pattern, while in "flat keys," they proceed in an "up, down, up, down" pattern. However, the scheme is eventually broken in certain sharp keys to ensure that no key signature's accidentals are ever notated on ledger lines. Figure 3.19 recreates the geometrical representation of key relationships known as the circle of fifths, which includes the key signatures for all major keys. Here, C major—a key featuring no sharp or flat signs—is positioned at the 12 o'clock position, and the other keys are arranged such that each subsequent clock position in the clockwise direction, representing a tonic ascent by a P5, adds a sharp sign to the key signature (or takes away a flat sign) and vice versa.

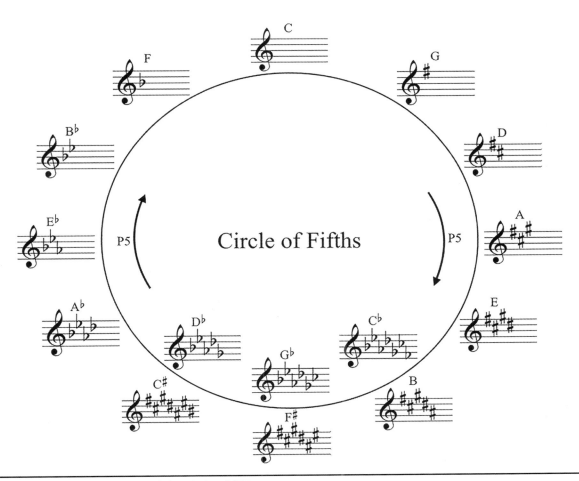

Fig. 3.19 Major key signatures and the circle of fifths

MINOR KEYS

MINOR KEY SIGNATURES

The term "major key signature" is actually somewhat of a misnomer, as a key signature more accurately provides the pitch classes associated with a particular diatonic collection, of which a major scale is but one mode or "rotation." As mentioned previously, Western music focuses on not one but two modes of the diatonic collection: the major scale and the minor scale. As the major scale represents one rotation of a diatonic collection, and the minor scale represents another, major scales and minor scales can be considered rotations of one another, assuming they are members of the same collection (i.e., they share the same pitch classes). Each key signature, then, is shared by a major key and a minor key that possesses a different tonic.

Relative Minor

Keys that share the same key signature but possess different tonics are considered "relatives" of one another. A **relative minor** key shares a key signature with a major key whose tonic is a minor third above its own tonic; conversely, a **relative major** key shares a key signature with a minor key whose tonic is a minor third below (or a major sixth above) its tonic. This is the case with A minor and C major, represented by the white keys on the keyboard. As you can see in Figure 3.20, these scales feature the same pitch classes—the "natural notes" A, B, C, D, E, F, and G—while beginning on different tonics. You can think of A minor as being roughly equivalent to a C major scale that is simply rotated backward to begin and end on A; you can also think of C major as being an A minor scale rotated forward to begin on C.

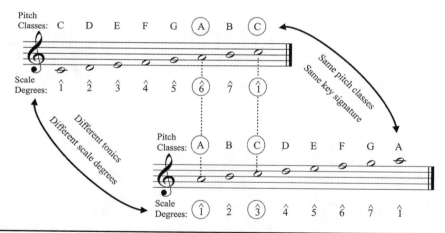

Fig. 3.20   C major and its relative minor, A minor

Though relative keys such as C major and A minor are indeed different, with distinct characters and scale degree tendencies, they are very closely related. Figure 3.21 recreates the circle of fifths diagram with relative minor keys added to each key signature, reflecting the fact that each key signature is shared.

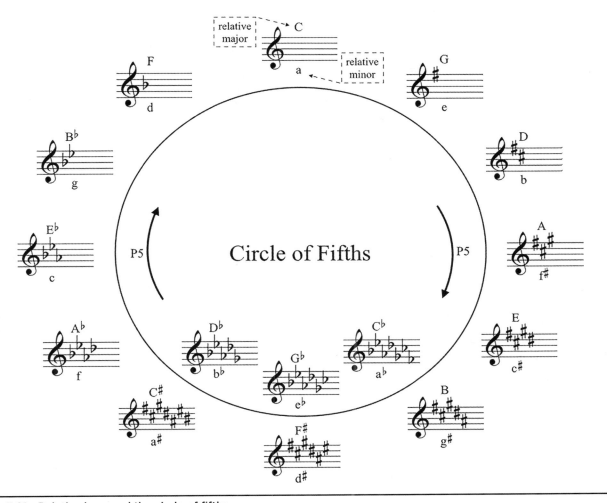

Fig. 3.21 Relative keys and the circle of fifths

In this diagram, relative keys share the same clock positions around the circle, as they share the same key signatures. We consider closely related keys to be those whose key signatures are the same or differ by one accidental. For example, the closely related keys to C major are those occupying the 11 o'clock, 12 o'clock, and 1 o'clock positions in the circle of fifths: A minor, G major, E minor, F major, and D minor. In later chapters, you will learn a variety of ways that composers incorporate closely related—as well as distantly related—keys in their compositions. One key relationship that is quite strong despite not technically being described as "close" is called the parallel relationship. **Parallel keys** share the same tonic but possess different key signatures, such as C major and C minor. The key signatures of parallel keys always differ by three accidentals (e.g., C major has zero sharp signs or flat signs in its key signature, while C minor's key signature has three flat signs).

MINOR SCALES

You can easily understand the structure of a minor scale by comparing it to its parallel major scale—the major scale sharing the same tonic. Figure 3.22 demonstrates the intervallic structure of both the C major scale and the C minor scale using the keyboard and music notation. Music that is described as being in a "minor key" usually possesses a dark or even sad sound that can be attributed to the minor third, sixth, and seventh intervals found above tonic in these keys. Its harmonies, which are generally created via the process of stacking thirds above each scale degree (as before with the major keys), are, as a result, similarly dark sounding.

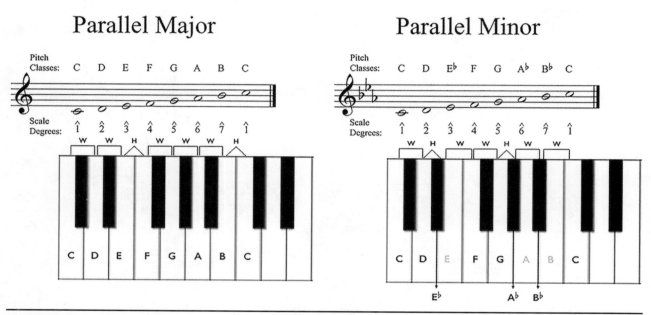

Fig. 3.22 Comparison of parallel keys on the keyboard and staff notation

Note that while the minor scale's whole step/half step pattern is distinct from that of the major scale, resulting in intervallic differences above tonic for the third, sixth, and seventh tones, the scale degrees are numbered and named in nearly the same way: scale degree $\hat{1}$ is tonic, followed by the supertonic ($\hat{2}$), mediant ($\hat{3}$), subdominant ($\hat{4}$), dominant ($\hat{5}$), and submediant ($\hat{6}$), just as in the major scale. The main difference is that in this so-called **natural minor** scale, there is no leading tone located a half step below tonic. Instead, the seventh degree is called the **subtonic**, as it is positioned a whole step below tonic (as opposed to the supertonic, which is positioned a whole step above tonic). The subtonic lacks the strong tendency to resolve to tonic that is so characteristic of the leading tone; instead, it tends downward, often passing through the submediant to arrive at the dominant in traditional tonal music written in minor keys. Figure 3.23 elucidates the similarities and differences regarding scale degree tendencies between parallel keys.

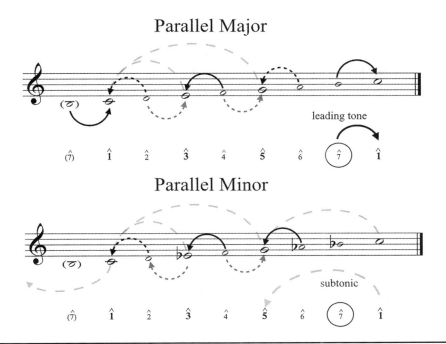

Fig. 3.23 Comparison of scale degree tendencies in parallel keys

Much of the time, the gravitational pull toward tonic that is exhibited by the leading tone—which creates an aesthetically pleasing tension that becomes balanced by resolution—is desired, even in minor key music. Thus, in practice, we speak of three available "forms" of the minor mode that feature variable sixth and seventh scale degrees. In traditional tonal music, the leading tone is very often employed in lieu of the subtonic via an added accidental that raises the seventh degree by a half step; this creates an overall scale collection known as the **harmonic minor**. The harmonic minor is aptly named, as the leading tone is a central component of harmonies used in traditional tonality for the creation of musical tension. The other form of minor, the **melodic minor**, additionally includes a raised sixth degree that is used to help craft melodies that smoothly lead up to tonic in a stepwise fashion while avoiding potential clashes with supporting harmonies that would result from the dissonant augmented second (A2) interval between the harmonic minor's submediant and leading tone. This interval was historically avoided in melodies, as it is difficult to sing and produces a dissonant, non-Western, "exotic" sound that is uncharacteristic of traditional tonal music. The melodic minor scale is typically discussed as having two forms: the ascending melodic minor, which includes the alterations to scale degrees $\hat{6}$ and $\hat{7}$ that are used when melodies ascend up to tonic, and the descending melodic minor, which is the same as the natural minor and is used when melodies descend from tonic. Though beginning students often learn the three forms of minor—natural, harmonic, and melodic—as separate scales, they are more accurately three available forms of a single minor mode whose sixth and seventh members are variable. It is likewise important to note that the melodic and harmonic forms of minor are not separate keys with separate key signatures; rather, they are tools that are typically used to teach beginning musicians about the ways in which melodies and harmonies were organized during the common practice period. Figure 3.24 compares the three ascending forms of minor sharing C as tonic.

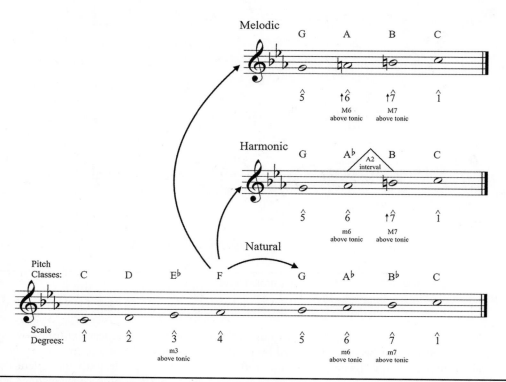

Fig. 3.24   The ascending forms of minor

INTERVALS AND MINOR SCALES

Earlier in this chapter, you learned that the intervals above tonic in major keys are all major or perfect in quality. It would seem logical, then, to assume that all intervals above tonic in minor keys are minor or perfect. In fact, this is nearly the case: the third, sixth, and seventh degrees are, as mentioned previously, a m3, m6, and m7 above tonic in minor keys (respectively), while the fourth, fifth, and octave intervals remain perfect. The one exception, then, is the second interval between tonic and the supertonic. This interval remains major in quality in minor keys, as both the major and minor step patterns begin with a whole step (see Figure 3.25).

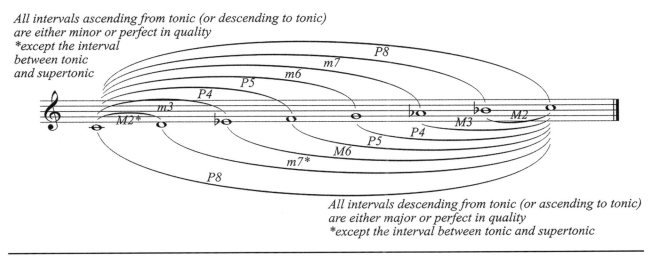

All intervals ascending from tonic (or descending to tonic)
are either minor or perfect in quality
*except the interval
between tonic
and supertonic

All intervals descending from tonic (or ascending to tonic)
are either major or perfect in quality
*except the interval between tonic and supertonic

Fig. 3.25   Intervals of the natural minor scale above and below tonic

Knowing the intervallic structures of the major and natural minor scales makes spelling intervals quite manageable. For example, if you are asked the interval between A and F, you can think of the lower note, A, as tonic, and compare the top note, F, to the major scale built on A. F does not exist in the A major scale, but it is a half step below the submediant in this key, F#. As the interval between tonic and the submediant above is an M6, and minor intervals are a half step smaller than major intervals, you can infer that the interval from A to F is an m6. Alternatively, you can think of the lower note, A, as tonic, and compare the top note, F, to the minor scale built on A (which has F as its sixth degree). Using this method, combined with the knowledge that the submediant in minor keys is positioned an m6 above tonic, you can arrive at the correct answer even faster.

TRIADS

We now move from a consideration of intervals and scales to the tertian harmonies that are generated from stacking thirds above scale degrees in both major and minor keys. Though there are many different types of chords, as chords are very generally harmonic combinations of three or more notes, the most commonly used chords in Western tonal music are **triads** (tertian harmonies composed of three pitch classes) and **seventh chords** (tertian harmonies composed of four pitch classes). We'll start by discussing triads, which include just three chord tones—the root, the third, and the fifth—that can be stacked line-line-line or space-space-space on the staff within an octave. Figure 3.26 shows the C major triad noted at the outset of this chapter, which is spelled with pitch classes C, E, and G. The position or **voicing** of the C major triad on the left is called **close position**, as the chord tones are as close as possible to one another. The voicing in the center is called **open position**, as the chord tones are more spread apart, creating an overall pitch range that is larger than an octave. Note that some of the chord tones in the open position chord are doubled, which is quite common. Though there are technically five pitches in this voicing, there are only three pitch classes, and thus the chord reflects the same triad as the initial close voicing. The example on the right in Figure 3.26 comes from the beginning of Mozart's famous Piano Sonata in C Major, K. 545. The chord is once again a C major triad, but it is placed in a more musical context, with the chord split into rhythmically independent layers called **contrapuntal voices** (or simply "voices"). Though there are two layers and a variety of rhythms present, the sound of the example is still unequivocally a C major triad, as the same three pitch classes are projected throughout the measure: C, E, and G. The lowest part, called the **bass**, features an **arpeggiation** of the chord that involves leaping between chord tones in succession; this particular style of bass arpeggiation, characterized by a pitch contour sequence of low-high-medium-high, is called an **Alberti bass** pattern, named after the early eighteenth-century Italian vocalist and composer Domenico Alberti.

C MAJOR TRIAD

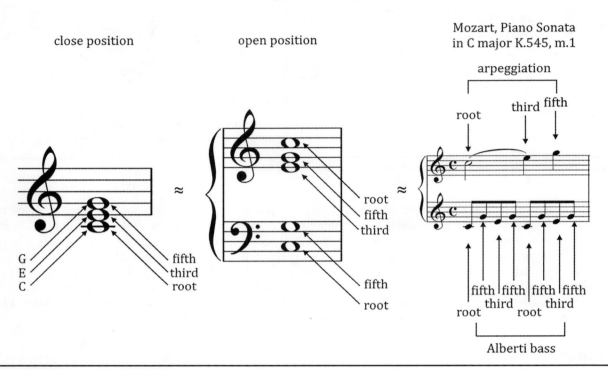

Fig. 3.26 The C major triad in three musical contexts

TRIAD QUALITIES

The triad in Figure 3.26 is described as having a major quality, which is related to the intervallic structure inherent in the chord. While all triads feature the intervals of a third and a fifth above the root in close position (hence the chord tone names "third" and "fifth," respectively), major triads specifically include a M3 and P5 above the root. For example, the C major triad in the previous example has C as its root, followed by E (a M3 above C) and G (a P5 above C). In all, there are four triad qualities: major, minor, diminished, and augmented. Each triad quality is composed of a specific interval pattern. Minor triads, which feature a m3 and P5 above the root, are similar to major triads but have a chordal third that is a half step lower in pitch. Diminished triads also have a m3 above the root, but feature a d5 instead of a P5 (hence the triad's name). Similarly, augmented triads are named after the quality of the chordal fifth, as they feature a M3 and A5 above the root. Figure 3.27 compares the four triad qualities, with each triad built on middle C. Note that raising the fifth of a major triad creates an augmented triad; lowering the third of a major triad creates, again, a minor triad; and lowering the fifth of a minor triad creates a diminished triad.

TRIAD QUALITIES

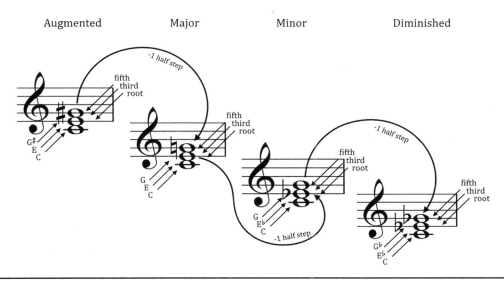

Fig. 3.27   **The four triad qualities**

TRIADS IN MAJOR KEYS

The most commonly used harmonic palette in major keys is generated when two diatonic thirds are stacked above each scale degree of a major scale. The resultant tertian harmonies are known collectively as diatonic triads, and they demonstrate a consistent pattern of chord qualities from the tonic triad through the leading tone triad—major, minor, minor, major, major, minor, diminished—regardless of the specific key in question. Figure 3.28 presents the diatonic triads in C major as well as those of E♭ major, with each chord labeled in a variety of different ways. Above the staff are the scale degrees involved in each triad, as well as chord symbols that identify the root of the chord with an uppercase letter (and any necessary accidentals) followed by an indication of chord quality. In a chord symbol analysis, major triads are represented solely via pitch class letters, minor triads add a lowercase "m" after the root, diminished triads add a superscript degree sign (°) or "dim" after the root, and augmented triads— which do not exist in the diatonic collection—add a superscript plus sign (⁺) or "aug" after the root. Below the staff are indications of each chord's quality as well as **Roman numerals**, which identify the scale degree on which each chord is based with the specific numeral, as well as the quality of each chord with capitalization and additional symbols. In a Roman numeral analysis, major triads are represented with uppercase Roman numerals, minor tri- ads with lowercase numerals, augmented triads with uppercase numerals followed by superscript plus signs (⁺), and diminished triads with lowercase numerals followed by superscript degree signs (°). Though chord symbols are useful in clearly articulating the root and quality of a chord, they change from key to key as pitch classes (and thus chord roots) change. Roman numerals, however, do not change from key to key, as they are based instead on scale degrees within keys. As you will learn in Chapter 9, Roman numeral analysis serves not only in identifying chord roots and qualities, but also in indicating the functions or behavioral tendencies of chords. IV chords, for example, tend to be preceded only by certain chords, and tend to move only to certain chords within a traditional tonal context, regardless of key.

Fig. 3.28   The diatonic triads of C major and E♭ major

TRIADS IN MINOR KEYS

While the process of stacking triads above each scale degree is quite similar in minor keys, it is slightly more complex because of the three available forms of minor, which have the potential to open up a significantly larger harmonic palette. However, the most commonly used sonorities in traditional minor-key tonal music are predominantly diatonic—that is, generated by the natural minor scale—with only two chords being derived from the harmonic minor. Figure 3.29 shows the triads of the natural minor that are formed by stacking diatonic thirds above each scale degree

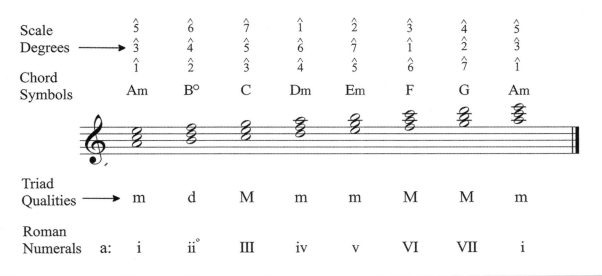

Fig. 3.29 The diatonic triads in A natural minor

in A minor. As expected, these triads represent a rotation of the pattern of chord qualities associated with major keys: the tonic triad is minor in quality, followed by diminished (supertonic), major (mediant), minor (subdominant), minor (dominant), major (submediant), and finally major (subtonic). As with major keys, the chords' scale degrees, qualities, and associated Roman numerals remain the same regardless of key.

These triads directly result from the harmonization of the natural minor scale, and they are used as the harmonic basis for minor key music in a variety of contemporary genres. However, they do not represent the traditionally used chords in minor-key tonal music. In the common practice period, composers tended to raise the seventh scale degree by a half step to become the leading tone in two cases, the dominant triad and the subtonic triad, thereby invoking the harmonic minor. This was done to create the same type of harmonic and melodic tension inherent in the diatonic chords of the major scale that are built on the fifth and seventh degrees. While this practice originated in traditional tonal music, it can still be heard today in many musical contexts—particularly those that are overtly influenced by "classical" music, such as certain heavy metal subgenres and film-scoring scenarios. Figure 3.30 recreates the previous example with the common leading tone additions introduced in the fifth and seventh harmonies in the sequence. These chords are compared to the purely diatonic triads from major keys, which are provided in the second system. Notice how the altered harmonies related to the harmonic minor scale—whose chord symbols and Roman numerals are likewise altered to reflect the chords' qualities—share the same qualities as their counterparts in the major mode. Additionally, the raised leading tone, G♯ in this key, does not substitute for the subtonic in the minor key's III chord, as this would create an augmented triad that is not commonly heard in tonal music.

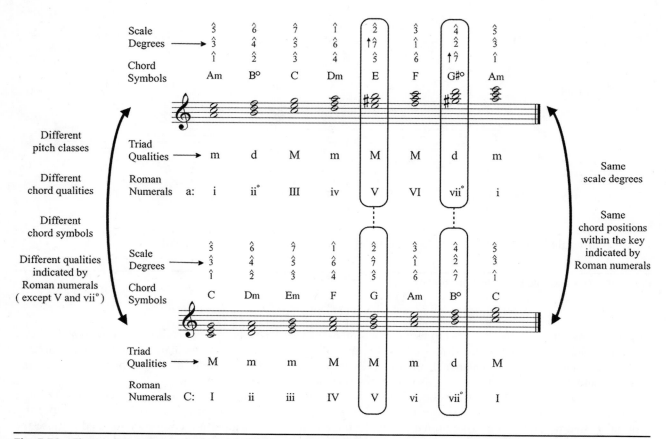

Fig. 3.30 The traditionally used minor key triads compared with the diatonic triads of the relative major

INVERTED TRIADS

The triads you have observed thus far have all been presented with the root of the chord as the lowest-sounding chord tone. This chord position is called **root position**, and it is the most common presentation of a chord. However, triads are not always written in root position; sometimes they appear with the chordal third in the bass (called **first inversion**) or with the chordal fifth in the bass (called **second inversion**). Musicians often employ inverted chords when writing progressions to create smooth, stepwise bass lines, or simply to create a weaker sound when one is desired (as inverted chords don't sound as strong or stable as those that are in root position). Using inverted chords can also help composers avoid certain melodic problems that tend to be created when root position chords follow one another in succession, such as parallel fifths and octaves, which are described in Chapter 4. Figure 3.31 shows a D major triad in each of its three possible chord positions.

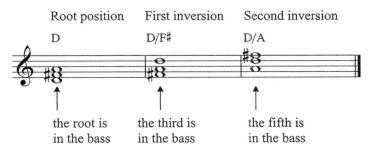

Fig. 3.31 Root position, first inversion, and second inversion D major triads

As you can see, inverted chords are represented in chord symbol notation with "slash chord" symbols above the staff, which place the main chord symbol before the slash and the pitch class in the bass after the slash. Roman numerals are also typically altered to reflect inversion; this topic is considered in detail in Chapter 9. Figure 3.33 revisits Jeremiah Clarke's "Trumpet Voluntary" from the previous chapter, and includes D major triads as well as other diatonic chords from the key of D major that are in either root position or inversion. Notice how the use of inverted chords allows for a very smooth bass line melody at the end of bar 2 into the beginning of bar 3, while successive root position chords—like those at the end of bar 1 and the beginning of bar 2—tend to result in disjunct bass motion.

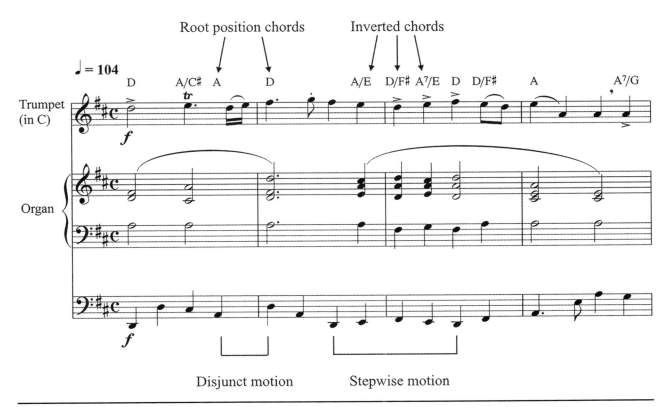

Fig. 3.32 Arrangement of Clarke, "Trumpet Voluntary" mm. 1–4

SEVENTH CHORDS

In the previous example, there are two instances of a seventh chord, A^7, which is spelled A—C#—E—G. Seventh chords like A^7 are tertian harmonies that consist of four distinct pitch classes or chord tones. You have learned that triads are tertian harmonies involving a "stack" of two thirds on top of one another; yet another third is stacked on top of a triad to create a seventh chord. This generates a fourth chord tone that is a dissonant seventh interval above the root of the chord in close position—hence the term seventh chord. Though this chordal dissonance is essential to the intervallic makeup of the chord, it is related to the tonal tradition of avoiding seventh chords in points of rest or arrival in music, which typically featured more consonant and stable triads. However, in genres featuring a freer use of dissonance, like jazz, seventh chords predominate and can be equally used to signify periods of tension and points of arrival.

SEVENTH CHORD QUALITIES

There are many types of seventh chords that are possible, and many of these will be covered in some detail in Chapter 10. For now, examining the seventh chord qualities or types that are generated by stacking thirds in major and minor keys will suffice, as these are the most common. These include major seventh, minor seventh, dominant seventh, half-diminished seventh, and fully-diminished seventh qualities. Figure 3.33 provides an example of each seventh chord type built on C, with an indication of the triad type that forms the base of the harmony as well as the quality of seventh that is formed with the root. Chord symbols are given for each chord as well; note that "maj7" is added after the capitalized root for major seventh chords, "m7" is added for minor seventh chords, a sole "7" is added for dominant seventh chords, "ø7" is added for half-diminished seventh chords, and "°7" is added for fully-diminished seventh chords.

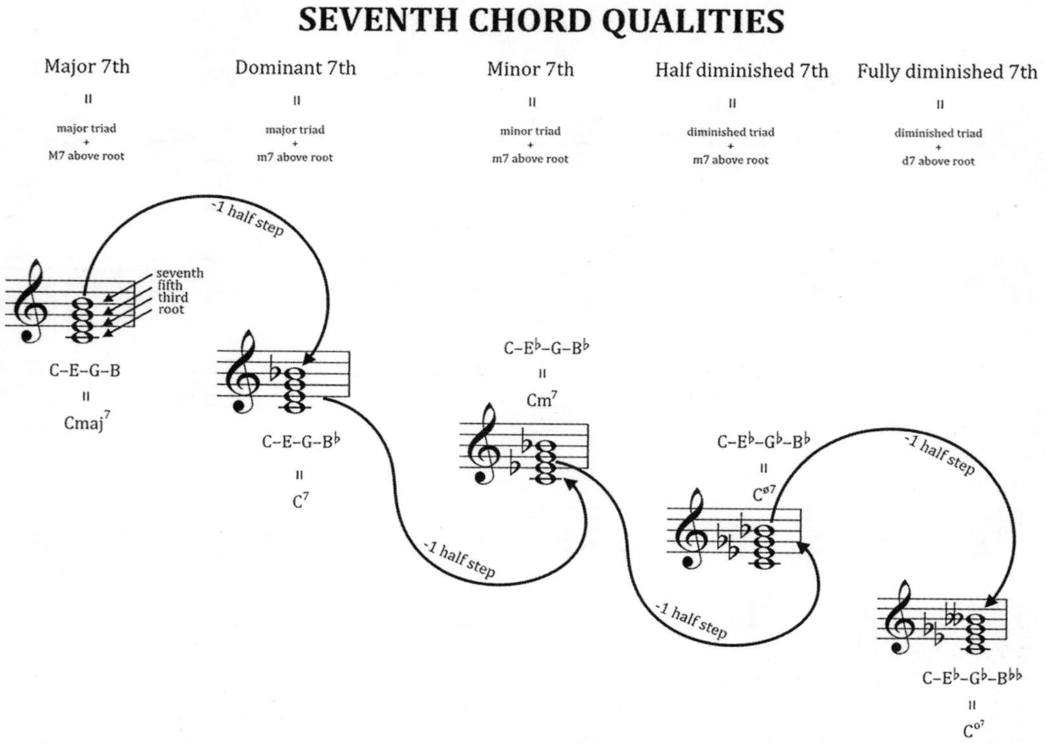

Fig. 3.33   Five common seventh chord qualities

SEVENTH CHORDS IN MAJOR KEYS

Building diatonic seventh chords on each of the scale degrees of a major scale in a manner similar to the generation of diatonic triads in major keys results in four of the five common seventh chord qualities: I^{M7} and IV^{M7} are major seventh chords; ii^7, iii^7, and vi^7 are minor seventh chords; V^7 is a dominant seventh chord; and the diatonic seventh chord built on the leading tone is half-diminished (which is represented by the symbol ⌀, after the Roman numeral vii). This pattern of seventh chord qualities is consistent in every major key (see Figure 3.34). The dominant seventh chord merits special mention, as it is a frequently encountered seventh chord that is a foundational element of traditional tonality. The dominant seventh chord quality is also known as a "major minor seventh" quality, as it can be thought of as being composed of a major triad with an additional minor seventh added above the chord's root. In the context of a key, dominant seventh chords are created by scale degrees $\hat{5}$, $\hat{7}$, $\hat{2}$, and $\hat{4}$, with the seventh degree always being a leading tone in both major and minor keys. While dominant triads—or V chords—represent a kind of harmonic tension that demands resolution or closure, dominant seventh chords heighten this sense of tension by including a tritone interval between their chordal third and seventh, which tends to resolve in a specific way in order to clarify the overall key. You will learn more about voice-leading traditions involving seventh chords in Chapter 9.

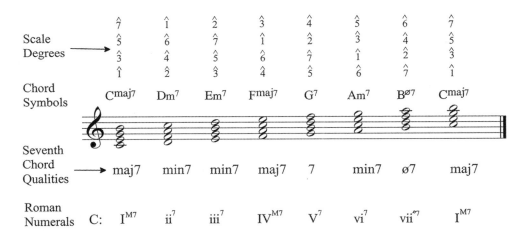

Fig. 3.34 Diatonic seventh chords in C major

SEVENTH CHORDS IN MINOR KEYS

The commonly used minor-key seventh chords that are associated with the tonal tradition can be generated in a similar manner as the seventh chords in major keys, but with one additional step. First, create purely diatonic triads using the natural minor scale exclusively; next, add diatonic sevenths to the chords; and finally, alter the fifth and seventh chords by raising the leading tone and invoking the harmonic minor, as before with the minor key triads associated with the common practice period. As you are already aware, the tonic triad in a minor key is minor. If a diatonic seventh is added above the root (a m7 in this case), the result is a minor seventh chord, i^7. If a diatonic seventh is added above the root of the diminished triad built on the supertonic, the result is a half-diminished seventh chord—a diminished triad plus a minor seventh that is represented by $ii^{\varnothing 7}$. Continuing in this manner yields the following pattern of diatonic seventh chords: III^{M7} is a major seventh chord, iv^7 is minor, v^7 is minor, VI^{M7} is major, and VII^7 is a dominant seventh chord. The important final step in creating the traditionally used seventh chords in minor keys is to raise the seventh scale degree by a half step to form the leading tone for chords built on scale degrees

$\hat{5}$ and $\hat{7}$. Again, using these chromatically altered sonorities creates dominant and leading tone chords that create more tension for the listener, closely simulating the related harmonies in major keys that provide a strong sense of magnetism toward the tonal center. Figure 3.35 provides a comparison between the purely diatonic seventh chords and the traditionally used seventh chords in A minor that involve the raised leading tone.

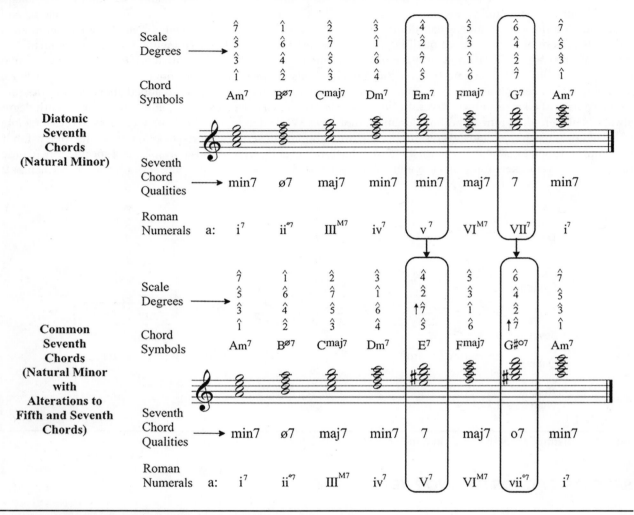

Fig. 3.35 A comparison of seventh chords in A minor

INVERTED SEVENTH CHORDS

As with triads, seventh chords often appear in inversion in order to create relatively weak sounds, provide fluid, stepwise bass lines, or solve melodic problems that may exist when using root position chords exclusively. The key difference between triads and seventh chords is that seventh chords possess one additional chord tone, the chordal seventh. This results in an additional inversion that is possible when using seventh chords, the **third inversion**, which features the dissonant chordal seventh in the bass. Figure 3.36 places a dominant quality A[7] chord in each of its four possible positions: root position, first inversion, second inversion, and third inversion.

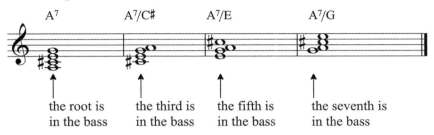

Fig. 3.36 An A⁷ chord in root position and all inversions

Third inversion chords are extremely unstable, as they possess both a dissonant fourth interval and a dissonant second interval above the bass, which need to resolve. In traditional tonality, third inversion chords almost always move to first inversion triads that are major or minor in quality, as is the case with the resolution of the A⁷/G chord in Clarke's "Trumpet Voluntary" that was presented earlier, which moves to a first inversion D major triad at the beginning of measure 5 (see Figure 3.37).

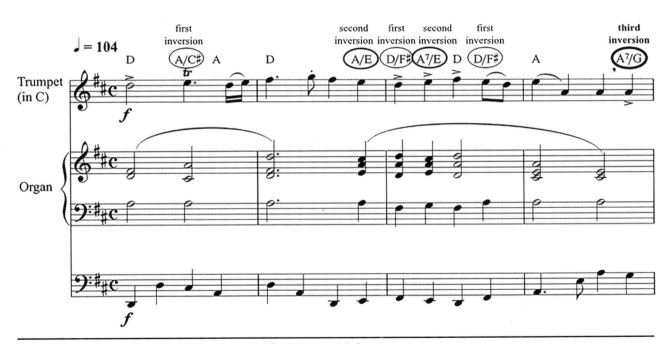

Fig. 3.37 Arrangement of Clarke, "Trumpet Voluntary," mm. 1-8

Fig. 3.37 (Continued)

Much of this chapter has focused on the harmonic procedures of common-practice tonality, and Chapter 9 continues in the same vein. Although we are historically well beyond the common practice period, producers of commercial music still borrow a variety of techniques from the tonal tradition. This is because much of modern music has directly or indirectly evolved out of older practices. Indeed, contemporary styles tend to exhibit a range of harmonic traditionalism, with certain genres being quite tonal, some being loosely tonal, and others being barely tonal or even atonal. Having a command of traditional tonality allows you to gain a comprehensive understanding of modern genres and recognize the degree to which they exhibit the harmonic attributes of common practice music, which in turn can inform your compositional decision-making and allow you to craft authentic-sounding musical projects. Moreover, while most music today does not strictly adhere to the compositional norms of past eras, an understanding of the ways in which earlier composers approached harmony expands your artistic palette as a modern composer by affording you a wide range of harmonic possibilities with which to create great music.

SUMMARY OF TERMS FROM CHAPTER 3

harmony	chord extensions	voicing
scale	dissonance	close position
chromatic scale	consonance	open position
whole tone scale	key signature	contrapuntal voices
diatonic collection	relative keys	bass
tonic	parallel keys	arpeggiation
scale degree	natural minor	Alberti bass
interval size/quality	subtonic	Roman numerals
enharmonically equivalent intervals	harmonic minor	root position
tritone	melodic minor	first inversion
internal inversion	triad	second inversion
compound intervals	seventh chord	third inversion

CHAPTER 3—EXERCISES

1. Using stemless noteheads, notate the following major and minor scales—in their ascending forms only—on the staves provided, without using key signatures.

    a. A major

    b. F natural minor

    c. B harmonic minor

    d. E melodic minor

    e. C harmonic minor

2. Fill in the blank with the pitch class name representing the indicated scale degree within the given key.

    A♭: dominant _____

    g: leading tone _____

    A: mediant _____

    B♭: subtonic _____

    F: submediant _____

3. Notate two pitches to create the following intervals on the provided staves.

    a. P5 above B

    b. P4 below D

    c. M3 above B♭

    d. m7 below D♭

    e. A4 below A♯

4. Provide the interval label for the *inversion* of each notated interval in the spaces provided below the notation.

_____   _____   _____   _____   _____

5. Identify each compound interval and indicate its related simple interval in the spaces provided below the notation.

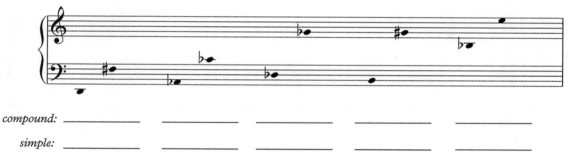

compound: _____   _____   _____   _____   _____

simple: _____   _____   _____   _____   _____

6. In the space to the right of the notation, indicate the two relative keys that share each key signature.

a.    d.

b.    e.

c.

7. Using stemless noteheads, notate the following triads and seventh chords in close position without using key signatures.

    a. Fm   b. E♭+

c. B°

d. A

e. D♭⁷

f. C♯m⁷

g. Eø⁷

h. F♯maj⁷

i. Bm⁷

j. E♭maj⁷

8. Using chord symbols to fill in the blanks, identify each of the triads and seventh chords notated below.

a.

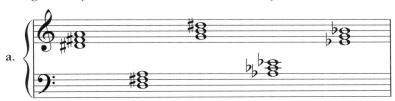

_____   _____   _____

b.

_____   _____   _____

c.

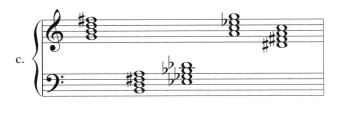

_____   _____   _____   _____

d.

9. Using stemless noteheads on the provided staves, notate the following inverted triads and seventh chords in close position. Provide a slash chord symbol above the staff for each chord.

a. A, first inversion

b. Cm, first inversion

c. B, second inversion

d. G°, first inversion

e. F#°7, first inversion

f. E♭7, third inversion

g. Dmaj7, first inversion

h. C#7, second inversion

10. **Analysis.** Listen to the provided recording and answer the questions below, based on the score to John Williams's famous theme to the film *Schindler's List*.

   a. Which scale is exemplified by the melody? Indicate the focal pitch as well as the type of scale.

   b. This melody features a characteristic pattern of repeated large interval leaps during beats 1 and 2 of every odd-numbered measure. Indicating both interval size and interval quality, and taking into account the key signature, what are these intervals?

     m. 1 and m. 3, beats 1 and 2 _____

     m. 5 and m. 7, beats 1 and 2 _____

     m. 9, beats 1 and 2   _____

   c. What are the two consecutive large intervals performed melodically by the violin across the bar line into m. 2 and immediately afterward into the second half of the first beat of the second measure? Indicate both the size and quality of each interval, taking into account the key signature.

     m. 1, beat 4b into m. 2, beat 1a   _____

     m. 2, beat 1a into m. 2, beat 1b   _____

   d. What is the compound interval formed between the left hand of the piano (written in bass clef on the grand staff) and the violin melody on the downbeat of m. 7?

   e. Taking into account both the left and right hand parts of the piano, as well as the violin melody, provide a harmonic analysis of the triads present at the following locations using chord symbols.

     m. 1, beats 1 and 2   _____

     m. 2, beat 3   _____

     m. 8, beats 1 and 2   _____

   f. Taking into account both the left and right hand parts of the piano, as well as the violin melody, provide a harmonic analysis of the seventh chords present at the following locations using chord symbols.

     m. 4, beats 1 and 2   _____

     m. 5, beats 1 and 2 _____

     m. 5, beats 3 and 4 _____

   g. Measure 9 begins with an inverted seventh chord. In the space below, analyze this chord using a slash chord symbol.

   h. This piece moves briefly to a major key, F major, that is the mediant (III) of the overall key. What is the term used to describe such major keys, which share the same key signature with related minor keys?

11. **Composition.** Compose an 8-measure piece in a minor key whose melody incorporates all three forms of minor and one leap that is larger than a diatonic fourth. The melody shall be used appropriately in combination with underlying harmonies, such that each melodic pitch on a downbeat is either the root, third, fifth, or seventh of the chord sounding during that measure. The harmonies should change every measure and should be labeled with chord symbols above the staff. The piece should begin with a tonic triad, and the first four bars should terminate on the dominant triad. The second four bars should conclude with a dominant seventh chord followed by a tonic triad in the chosen key. Beyond tonic and dominant harmonies, at least four other diatonic chords should be used, including at least one non-dominant seventh chord.

Chapter 4
Melody and Counterpoint

Melody is a defining characteristic of music, along with rhythm, harmony, and form. However, it is not entirely distinct from these other domains; in fact, it relates directly to each of them. Although harmony is often thought of as the "vertical" aspect of music (wherein pitches combine as simultaneities) and melody is considered to be the "horizontal" aspect (wherein pitches unfold in a linear fashion through time), the idea of harmonic progression historically came to be discussed as a separate musical parameter only after composers were combining individual melodies for hundreds of years. Thus, melodies created our notion of harmony by being combined together. Melody, too, is related to rhythm; a melody can be defined as a combination of pitches and rhythms that is perceivable as a single musical unit. **Form** is in turn related to all three other domains; it is the overall shape of a composition that is described in terms of individual sections that are based on the ideas of melodic or thematic design (which is in turn related to rhythm) and harmonic structure. Put differently, composers manipulate pitch and rhythm to craft melodies that combine to yield and reinforce harmonies, and the resultant melodic and harmonic structures in turn yield a piece's overall form.

Producers who are able to create artful, memorable melodies are prized in all genres of music. Those who can skillfully compose melodies are also able to more logically connect chords in progressions using a technique called **voice leading**, which creates coherent and successful harmonic schemes. In this chapter, you will learn how to craft and combine melodies by following a modified treatment of a centuries-old compositional method called **species counterpoint** that remains the standard for composers of all types of music.

MELODIC PRINCIPLES

Counterpoint, a main focus of this chapter, involves the combination of melodies that could stand on their own as independent, beautiful musical entities. This section delves into the structural characteristics that make melodies beautiful and worthy of such independence. Four main areas are commonly discussed when describing melodies: motion, shape, long-range planning, and harmonic considerations.

MELODIC MOTION

One of the most crucial aspects of a successful melody is that it is able to be performed or sung without excessive strain or difficulty. Though certain instruments can render the performances of melodies with wide ranges and/or leaps with ease, it is often best to consider how a melody would sound when sung while composing, regardless of the instrumentation that will be used. If you cannot sing the melody you are writing, it is probable that the melody requires revision. To ensure that your melodies are singable, make them primarily move in **conjunct** motion—that is, motion by step. **Disjunct** motion—melodic progression by leap—is expressive and useful when writing melodies, but should be used sparingly. A general guideline regarding melodic motion is to strive for around 70%–90% step-wise motion, saving leaps for poignant or climactic moments. Both the steps and leaps used in your melodies should form consonant melodic intervals almost exclusively, which additionally supports the goal of performability. Finally, avoid leaping consecutively, unless the leaps arpeggiate a chord that is easy to sing, such as the tonic triad. Figure 4.1 isolates the primary melodic line from the first movement of Rachmaninoff's famous Piano Concerto no. 3 (1909), which is considered to be one of the staples of the piano literature and was featured in the award-winning 1996 film *Shine*. This melody is quite chromatic at times (i.e., it uses pitch classes from outside the piece's overall key of D minor), but nearly all of its leaps are small and consonant, with the exception being the second of the expressive chro-matic leaps that enclose scale degrees $\hat{4}$ and $\hat{5}$ during the ascent to the climactic B♭ in m. 19. In all, the melody exhibits around 90% stepwise motion, making it simple to both hear and sing—particularly for a twentieth-century work.

Fig. 4.1 Rachmaninoff, Piano Concerto No. 3, mvt. i, mm. 3–27

MELODIC SHAPE

In addition to its primarily stepwise character, Rachmaninoff's melody is made approachable by possessing a range that is only slightly over an octave—a M9 from the lowest pitch, B♭4, to the highest pitch, C6. Most melodies simi-larly span less than a tenth between registral extremes. Beyond its performability, the melody exhibits a classic shape. Overall, it begins on tonic in m. 3, smoothly undulates and eventually ascends to a climax in m. 19, and systematically descends afterward through each scale step to close on tonic in m. 27. This melodic arch is a very appealing, common shape: melodies tend to ascend, reach a climax around two-thirds or three-fourths of the way through, and descend toward the final **cadence** (a point of rest that signals the completion of the musical idea). The arch shape mimics the typical dramatic plot structure described in 1863 by Gustav Freytag's pyramid, which is commonly taught in literature classes: exposition is followed by rising action, climax, falling action, and finally denouement. Figure 4.2 recreates Freytag's pyramid, and Figure 4.3 includes both an analysis of Rachmaninoff's melody using Freytag's dramatic concepts and an analysis of a reduction of the melody that focuses on its most structurally important scale degrees.

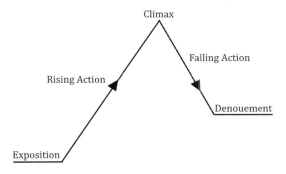

Fig. 4.2 Freytag's pyramid

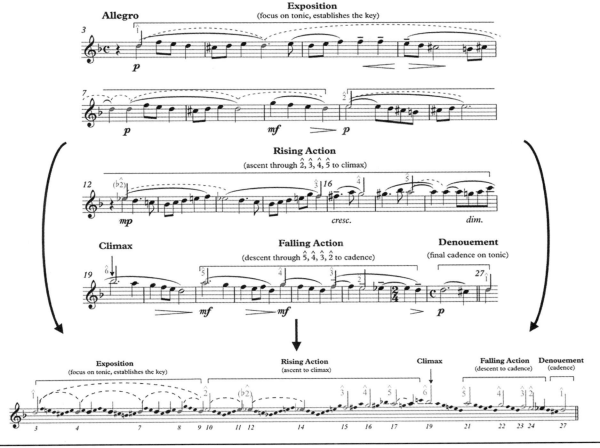

Fig. 4.3 Analysis of Rachmaninoff melody and melody reduction using Freytag's dramatic terms

LONG-RANGE PLANNING AND STEP PROGRESSIONS

The melodic reduction at the bottom of Figure 4.3 elucidates the very logical overall structure of Rachmaninoff's melody: it begins on $\hat{1}$ and proceeds in a more or less straightforward fashion through $\hat{2}$ (and the chromatically altered $\flat\hat{2}$), $\hat{3}$, $\hat{4}$, and $\hat{5}$ to a climax on $\hat{6}$ before falling back through $\hat{5}$, $\hat{4}$, $\hat{3}$, and $\hat{2}$ to an eventual close on $\hat{1}$. These large-scale melodic motions between structural scale degrees are called **step progressions**, and they demonstrate the propensity of composers to create melodies that exhibit both long-range planning and short-range melodic goal tones. The structurally significant scale steps highlighted in Figure 4.3 should not be understood as the only important pitches in Rachmaninoff's melody, however. Indeed, while a skeletal sketch of logically ordered step progressions can serve as a useful blueprint during the beginning stages of composition, it does not ensure a great—or even good—piece of music. Rather, artfully crafted "surface" pitches and rhythms are necessary to create a memorable piece's unique character and identity, while its structurally significant, foundational goal tones engender the valued characteristics of order, coherence, and progress.

HARMONIC CONSIDERATIONS

Melodies tend to follow certain scale degree patterns that are key dependent and that relate to supporting harmonies that may be stated or implied. For example, melodies almost always heed the typical resolutions of the key's tendency tones, which are the leading tone (which resolves up by half step to tonic) and subdominant (which resolves down by step to the mediant). In Rachmaninoff's melody, for instance, the key is D minor and thus the leading tone is C♯ while the subdominant is G. Note how each C♯ moves up to D (either immediately or after an embellishment) and each G moves down to F. As you will learn in Chapter 9, these motions mimic the common resolution of the V^7 chord's tritone in a progression to tonic, which helps to reinforce the listener's perception of the overall key.

In minor key melodies like the previous example, the altered sixth degree is only used when progressing through the leading tone to tonic. This invocation of the ascending melodic minor form is again related to the dominant harmony, as progressing to the leading tone from the diatonic submediant clashes harshly with the root of the dominant chord while also creating a melodic A2 interval that is difficult to sing. Observe the two raised sixth degrees (B naturals) in the Rachmaninoff melody, which move through C♯s (as the harmony focuses on the dominant) and eventually land on tonic. Though these are chromatic alterations and may seem to make the melody more "difficult," they actually lend a smoother sound to the music.

Now that you have explored a variety of strategies for composing successful melodies, the next step is to investigate effective methods for uniting them together to form thicker and more complex musical textures.

COUNTERPOINT

Counterpoint is a technique that involves combining two or more melodies—or contrapuntal "voices," though the melodic lines may not necessarily be written for voice—in a way that creates both unity and variety. Unity is generated "vertically" in notation via harmony, as the intervals between the voices are generally consonant. Though multiple melodies are featured, they work together in a coherent way to form a single, pleasant sound. Variety is attained "horizontally" through time, as the individual melodies retain their own unique identities. Variety is related to the melodies' individual pitches, contours, and, at times, rhythms. Though the lines work together and create motion toward the shared goal of a cadence on tonic, they remain distinct.

Species counterpoint is a graduated, step-by-step method of teaching the technique that has remained in favor since the writings of Johann Joseph Fux in the late seventeenth and early eighteenth centuries. At first, many important musical parameters (e.g., rhythm, embellishment, development, dynamics, articulations, instrumentation, form) are eliminated in the context of short melodic exercises for two voices that force the student to focus exclusively on—and learn to control—a small number of characteristics. Gradually, many of the initially absent parameters are added to the exercises until the study culminates in free counterpoint, which is equivalent to real music. It is important to clarify that counterpoint exercises are not intended to be real pieces of music; rather, they are abstract training modules that promote the writing of real music that exhibits control, complexity, unity, and variety. Nonetheless, it is crucial to be physically involved with the exercises by playing and singing them, which can aid in a clearer understanding of how counterpoint feels and sounds (as opposed to simply how it looks on a notated page).

FIRST SPECIES

The species counterpoint method begins with 1:1 counterpoint, in which the two voices possess the same rhythm; this is called first species counterpoint. First species is the most restrictive species (or stage) in the system, and it allows you to focus on harmonic relationships between the given voice (called the *cantus firmus*, which means "fixed song") and the added counterpoint without being concerned with rhythm. The *cantus firmus* can be provided in either the bass (the lower part) or the soprano (the higher part), which requires you to be able to write the counterpoint in either voice. This can help you learn to consider the voices as equal melodies, which can be difficult at first, as bass lines often take a supportive role in modern music. Traditionally, the *cantus firmus* and counterpoint were notated using movable C clefs in the same or similar registers, and they were not to exceed a distance of a tenth from one another. In your exercises, though, you will be notating the bass in bass clef and the soprano in treble clef, which will create larger distances between the parts. Importantly, most of the guidelines associated with writing first species counterpoint apply to all later stages, so it is crucial to become very familiar with them.

Contrapuntal Motion in First Species

Figure 4.4 is an example of first species counterpoint in D minor that uses a loose reduction of the *Schindler's List* theme encountered in the previous chapter as its soprano line. This melodic skeleton is the product of the same analytical technique used in the Rachmaninoff theme earlier, which is based on the writings of the noted twentieth-century theorist Heinrich Schenker.

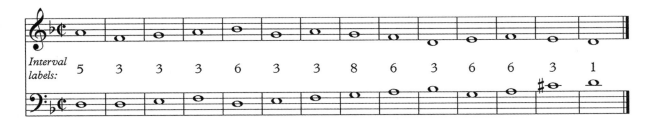

Fig. 4.4   First species counterpoint example using a melodic reduction of the *Schindler's List* theme

When melodies are combined together in this way, we can speak not only of the types of motion observable in each voice, but also of the types of motion created when the voices move together from measure to measure. In all, there are five types of **contrapuntal motion** that are possible when writing for two voices: static, oblique, parallel, similar, and contrary motion.

Static motion is not shown in this example, and for good reason. **Static motion** takes place when neither voice changes pitch, and this does not result in good counterpoint (or counterpoint at all). Related to static motion is **oblique motion**, which occurs when one voice moves and the other repeats the same note. Oblique motion is not traditionally used in first species counterpoint, but you may use one instance of it in your exercises, as has been done in mm. 1–2 in the example (with D3 being repeated in the bass while the soprano descends by a third). **Parallel motion** exists when the two voices move in the same direction in the same way, such as when the voices both ascend by step (e.g., mm. 2–4). The result of parallel motion is that the same interval size is maintained (e.g., the interval of a third persists between the voices in mm. 2–4); for this reason, it is to be used only for a short period of time with imperfect consonances, as longer stretches of parallel motion do not create the desired effect of melodic independence in counterpoint. Therefore, when composing your counterpoint exercises, you should avoid repeating the same interval in more than three consecutive measures using parallel or any other kind of motion. **Similar motion** takes place when the two voices move in the same direction, but in different ways (i.e., one voice moves by step and the other moves by leap in the same direction). Similar motion is not used in Figure 4.4, but it is often used in first species counterpoint, with a few limitations that will be described shortly. **Contrary motion** (where the voices move in opposite directions) is used most often, though, as it usually results in the best counterpoint by most clearly engendering melodic variety. If you are composing a counterpoint exercise and are unsure of how to navigate a problematic section, using contrary motion is often the best solution. In the previous example, contrary motion is used well over half of the time—this is not at all uncommon. Figure 4.5 reproduces the previous example with an analysis of the types of contrapuntal motion that are employed.

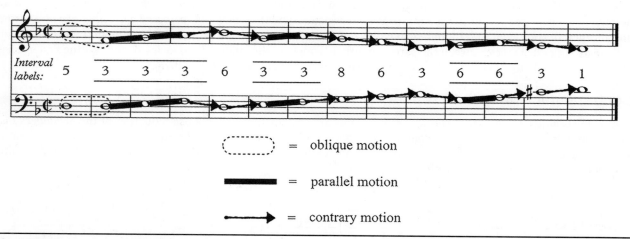

Fig. 4.5 Contrapuntal motion in first species counterpoint

Harmonic Considerations

In the previous example, you may have observed that some intervals were labeled as "5," "3," or "6" despite actually being twelfths, tenths, and thirteenths, respectively. It is typically preferred in this context to use simple interval equivalents when labeling compound intervals, which makes analyzing the exercises slightly easier. You may also have recognized that the only intervals used in the counterpoint were perfect unisons, fifths, and octaves, as well as diatonic thirds and sixths. This will always be the case, as consonant intervals are exclusively used in first species. No dissonances are allowed at all, including perfect fourths, which are considered dissonant when they involve the bass (and intervals always involve the bass in two-voice writing).

Consonant intervals are not used interchangeably in first species, however. Instead, there is a consistent "sandwich" scheme that pervades 1:1 counterpoint, in which perfect intervals are used at the beginning and end of an exercise, while imperfect consonances predominate in the center. Unisons and octaves are used exclusively in the last measure, representing the final cadence created by the two parts as they converge on tonic, and, traditionally,

P1s, P8s, or P5s are used in the first measure. Since the goal of the first bar in a counterpoint exercise is to firmly establish the overall key (which may be accomplished using any member of the tonic triad in the soprano above tonic), though, you may use a unison, third, fifth, or octave in this measure, provided that $\hat{1}$ is used in the bass.

The center of the "sandwich" needs to be composed primarily of thirds and sixths, with no more than three of the same type of interval in a row. Occasionally, P5s and P8s are used in the center of the counterpoint, as is the case in m. 8 of the previous example. However, perfect intervals used in this manner need to be handled with great care, as they detract from the desired perception of melodic individuality and forward motion. If you use a perfect interval in the middle of an exercise, you should be sure that it is approached and left by step in the soprano in contrary motion with the bass. Additionally, ensure that the perfect interval is flanked on either side by imperfect consonances—in other words, avoid using consecutive perfect intervals. The P8 in m. 8 of Figure 4.5 follows each of these guidelines, and additionally represents the common function of mid-exercise P8s in first species as the center of a 3-bar **voice exchange** scheme in which the melodies swap pitch classes via contrary stepwise motion. In bar 7, F is in the bass while A is in the soprano; by passing through the P8 on G in both parts, the result in bar 9 is that the F is exchanged to the soprano while A takes its place in the bass. Voice exchanges like this are quite useful when composing contrapuntal textures, as they can create the perception of forward motion while prolonging a single harmonic idea.

Two other considerations involving perfect intervals merit special mention. One common pitfall is the use of "objectionable parallels"—specifically, **parallel fifths** or **parallel octaves**—which involve consecutive perfect intervals of the same type being connected by parallel motion. Parallel fifths and octaves are not unpleasant to the ear, but they possess a hollow, static sound that is not typical in traditional counterpoint. Parallel octaves, in particular, create the impression of a single melody, as opposed to independent voices. Another problem related to perfect intervals takes place when the soprano line features a leap into a P5 or P8 above the bass that is created via similar motion. This calls attention to the fact that the composer is using a perfect interval, heightening the perception of stasis or hollowness associated with these intervals. As well, theorists traditionally posited that one could easily imply the notes spanned by the leaping voice, and that the mind would connect the "hidden" notes in stepwise motion to the goal pitch of the leap, which would silently create objectionable parallels with the bass. Thus, such leaps into P5s and P8s in the soprano via similar motion are called **hidden** or **direct fifths** and **octaves** and should be avoided.

A final harmonic consideration in species counterpoint involves the chromatically altered sixth and seventh scale degrees in minor keys, which are typically used when dominant chords are implied or stated in a musical phrase. Care must be taken when using these altered tones to avoid strange-sounding **cross relations**, which take place when different pitch classes sharing the same note letter (e.g., C and C♯) are used in adjacent measures in different voices. While it is not typical in first species to follow a scale degree with an inflected version of the same degree in the same voice (such as a C in the soprano being followed by a C♯ in the soprano in the next measure), it is even less typical to follow a scale degree in one voice with an inflected version of the degree in a different voice (such as a C in the soprano being followed by a C♯ in the bass).

Melodic Considerations

Adhering to the guidelines provided in this chapter's earlier section on melodic principles will ensure that you are successful when composing your counterpoint in a first species exercise. Remember that stepwise motion should be used the strict majority of the time, and consecutive leaps are to be avoided (as are leaps larger than a P5). Traditionally, leaps larger than a P4 were prohibited, but you may use a P5 leap provided that it is easy to sing (such as the P5 from tonic up to the dominant, which exists in the tonic triad). Importantly, though, you should always follow any leap larger than a third with a step in the opposite direction of the leap, filling in the gap created by the large leap. The larger the leap used, the stronger the tendency to move in the opposite direction immediately afterward by step. Figure 4.6 demonstrates this tendency with a counterpoint (in the bass) added to a melodic reduction of the theme from "The Black Pearl" (in the soprano), a piece that was first encountered in Chapter 2. Note that the final leap of a third in the soprano is followed by a step in the same direction as the leap; this is not problematic in general, and in fact it is advisable in this particular context, as the final descending step to tonic is needed to create a strong cadence to finish the exercise.

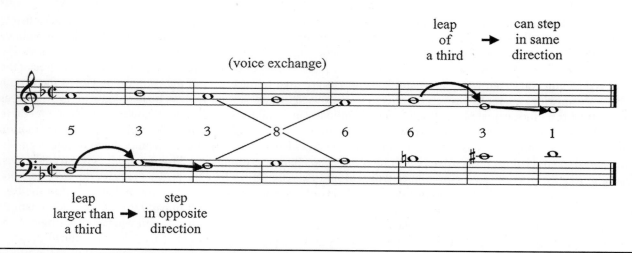

Fig. 4.6 The "gap fill" tendency with large leaps

While the counterpoint in this example terminates on a perfect unison with the soprano (which is common), it never ventures further into its registral territory. This is because **voice crossing** (in which the bass is written in a higher register than the soprano or vice versa) is prohibited in species counterpoint, as is **voice overlap** (wherein the soprano leaps lower than the previously used note in the bass or vice versa, despite the voices not technically crossing). Both voice crossing and voice overlap make it difficult for the listener to aurally trace the path of each line, which weakens the perception of melodic independence that is so prized in counterpoint.

Strategies for Success

It is important to understand that counterpoint exercises promote your ability with musical problem-solving and may take some time to complete. While their musical purpose is to serve as a set of instructional tools for learning how to successfully craft and combine melodies, they also teach you how to both fail and persevere as a composer, which are important lessons. For instance, writing a fantastic melody in one segment of an exercise may actually make it impossible to finish the rest of the counterpoint without creating significant problems; this is known as "writing yourself into a corner." The solution may be as simple as incorporating more contrary motion into the added voice overall, but it may also be the case that the entire counterpoint needs to be rewritten from scratch. This is common, and you should take solace in the fact that every student of species counterpoint has been in a similar situation. The main strategy for success that you should employ is to avoid purely chronological writing—that is, don't try to write the counterpoint starting in the first measure and proceed in turn to bar 2, then bar 3, then bar 4, and so on. Instead, start at the final cadence (where the voices usually resolve in contrary stepwise motion to tonic, making your decisions rather easy) and work backward, connecting the pitches in stepwise motion when possible until you are unsure of how to continue. At this point, move to the beginning and compose forward. Finally, address any problems that exist in the middle of the counterpoint while working to fuse the melodic strands you've created. When you think you are satisfied with the overall result, analyze the melody and resultant intervals with the *cantus firmus* once more while being sure to assess the counterpoint's overall shape, which should be smooth and, ideally, arch-like, as discussed earlier.

SECOND SPECIES

Second species counterpoint is quite similar to first species counterpoint, with the main difference residing in the domain of rhythm. Whereas first species involves a 1:1 relationship between the rhythm of the *cantus firmus* and that of counterpoint, second species features a 2:1 relationship—there are typically two notes in the counterpoint for every note in the *cantus firmus*. A clear duple meter therefore emerges, with pitches sounding on both the downbeat and the upbeat within the added voice.

Another crucial addition in second species is harmonic dissonance, which is allowed in a very limited fashion. While consonances are required on all downbeats, dissonances can be used when writing the second note in each bar within the added voice, provided that they are **passing tones** (though some instructors may also allow neighbor tones, which are described in the subsequent section on third species in this chapter). A passing tone is an **embellishment** that is approached by step and left by step in the same direction, filling in the melodic interval of a third. Crucially, passing tones and most other dissonances used in later species follow a three-step preparation-dissonance-resolution scheme. This means that there are no consecutive dissonances: the isolated dissonant interval is flanked on either side with consonant intervals. Figure 4.7 provides an example of a 2:1 counterpoint added to the previously encountered melodic reduction of the theme from "The Black Pearl."

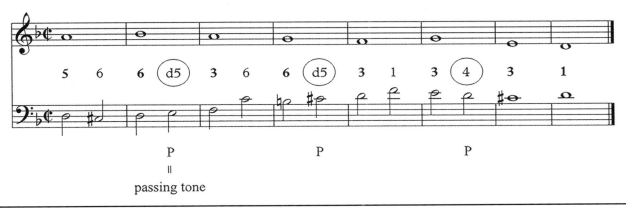

Fig. 4.7 Second species counterpoint example using a melodic reduction of the theme from "The Black Pearl"

Melody in Second Species

As you can see in this example, the rhythm of the added melody is twice as "fast" as the rhythm of the *cantus firmus*: whole notes are typically used in the *cantus firmus*, while half notes are typically used in the counterpoint. There are two exceptions to this practice, however. First, the initial bar often features a whole note in the *cantus firmus* and a lone half note in the added voice that is positioned on the upbeat, which adds to the perception of melodic independence as the voices enter the texture separately. (This is not always the case, however; both voices can enter simultaneously on the downbeat, as in the previous example.) Second, the penultimate bar traditionally features whole notes in both voices, similar to a first species exercise. This rhythmic deceleration initiates the closing cadence and enhances its sense of finality.

In second species, the overall texture is a bit freer, with the counterpoint typically possessing a greater range than in first species (though both melodies still need to be singable). For example, the second species setting of the theme from "The Black Pearl" includes a counterpoint whose range exceeds a tenth (see Figure 4.8). Melodically, most of the tenets of first species still hold true: stepwise motion should be used the strict majority of the time, adjacent notes should differ in pitch, and consecutive, simultaneous, and extremely large leaps should all be avoided. Additionally, leaping may only take place from consonance to consonance within a measure. However, some restrictions are lifted with regard to leaps—you may use a leap of a perfect fifth, a diatonic sixth, or even a perfect octave within a measure in this species. Remember, though, that these larger leaps should be followed immediately by stepwise motion in the opposite direction, as discussed earlier. Stepwise motion should also be used across every bar line.

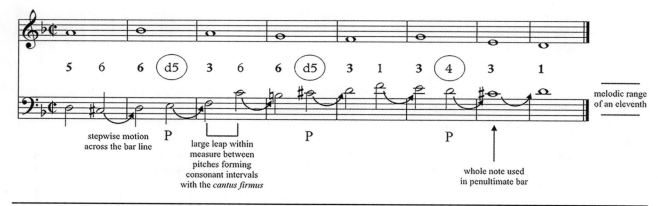

Fig. 4.8   Analysis of melodic motion and range in second species

Harmony in Second Species

The primary harmonic difference between first and second species is the availability of the dissonant passing tone, which should be employed as often as possible in this setting. However, it is rarely possible to successfully include a passing tone in every measure in the interior of a second species exercise, as there are so many requirements related to their use. When writing a passing tone is not possible within a measure, use two consonances instead; this will probably involve a melodic leap from downbeat to upbeat, and it is not problematic to leap into or out of a perfect interval in these cases.

Perfect intervals can cause issues in other ways in second species, however. One pitfall is parallel fifths and octaves, which are to be avoided in both adjacent and next-to-adjacent positions. In other words, be sure that you do not compose consecutive perfect intervals (as before in first species), and additionally avoid positioning perfect intervals of the same type on consecutive downbeats or upbeats (even if you use a different interval between them).

Contrapuntal Motion in Second Species

While first species counterpoint rarely involves oblique motion, it predominates in second species (and all later species), as the *cantus firmus* retains the same pitch throughout the measure while the counterpoint changes tones. From downbeat to downbeat, however, the movement should be primarily in contrary motion, with instances of parallel and similar motion taking place occasionally. Focusing on the motion between downbeats in this way can be quite valuable, as it uncovers the underlying first species "skeleton" that drives the entire texture.

Strategies for Success

An efficient method for composing a second species counterpoint begins, in fact, with the composition of the "skeleton" pitches taking place solely on downbeats. These pitches should create consonant intervals with the *cantus firmus* exclusively, as in first species, and should follow the "sandwich" scheme detailed earlier in this chapter. However, composing a first species skeleton for use in a second species counterpoint is not exactly the same as composing a true first species counterpoint. Indeed, you should preemptively plan for the insertion of passing tones by intentionally crafting a predominantly leapwise melody that moves by melodic third as much as possible (save for the final two bars, which should involve a smooth "wedge" into tonic from a step above and below). Dissonant melodic leaps do not necessarily need to be avoided in a first species skeleton, either, as consonant mid-measure leaps that are followed by stepwise motion can smooth out such potentially jarring sounds. Figure 4.9 compares the previous second species solution to its reduced form, noting the unique features of the first species skeleton relative to a typical 1:1 counterpoint.

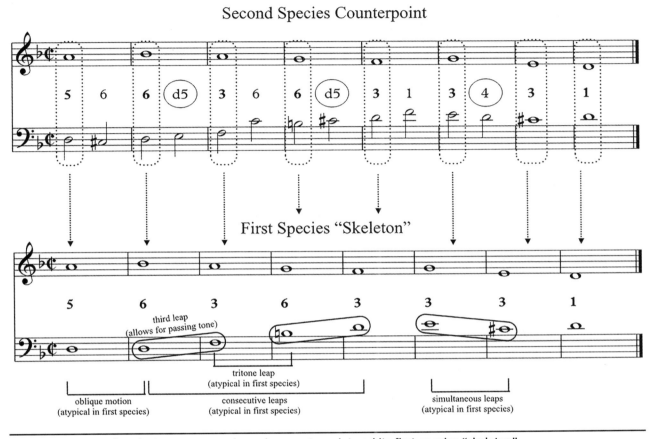

Fig. 4.9 A comparison between a second species counterpoint and its first species "skeleton"

THIRD SPECIES

Third species, or 4:1 counterpoint, introduces quarter note rhythms in the added voice while the *cantus firmus* continues to employ whole notes exclusively. Metrically, this creates a situation where there are two weak pulses in each bar (the second and fourth pulses), a strong downbeat, and a semi-strong third pulse that serves as the upbeat in the duple meter. Though this third pulse is weak relative to the downbeat, it is stronger than the offbeats that serve as the second and fourth pulses in each bar. Though the downbeats in third species all feature consonant intervals (as in the previous species), passing tones and a few other types of dissonance are used in the other metrical locations within the measure. One new type of dissonance that is used in this species is the **neighbor tone**, which is approached by step and left by step in the opposite direction, returning to the original note that preceded it. Neighbor tones and passing tones routinely take place on the second, third, and fourth quarter notes in each bar, embellishing and/ or connecting the skeletal consonances that form the foundation of the counterpoint. Larger embellishment figures featuring otherwise atypical leaps out of dissonances are also used in this species. One such figure is called the **double neighbor**, where a note in the counterpoint that forms a consonance with the *cantus firmus* sounds in the first and fourth metric positions, while the second and third positions feature dissonant tones that are a step above and below the consonance (or vice versa), separated by a leap of a third. This double neighbor pattern is the sole pattern that is allowable in this species that features consecutive dissonances. Another figure including a third leap out of a dissonance is called a *nota cambiata* (or "changing tone") figure. Here, a consonance sounds on the downbeat, followed by a dissonance that is a step above or below that consonance. Afterward, there is a leap of a third out of the dissonance in the same direction as the previous step, followed by two steps in the opposite direction into pitches that also form consonant intervals. The result when using a *nota cambiata* is that the tones on the adjacent downbeats are separated by a single step. Figure 4.10 features an example of third species counterpoint, again using the melodic reduction of the theme from "The Black Pearl" as a *cantus firmus* in the soprano. Each of the dissonance types used in this species is highlighted: passing tone, neighbor tone, double neighbor, and *nota cambiata*.

Fig. 4.10   Third species counterpoint example using a melodic reduction of the theme from "The Black Pearl"

Melody in Third Species

Despite the preponderance of pitches per measure relative to earlier species, the melody in this example is very smooth overall. You should strive to create a very singable, smooth melodic shape when crafting your counterpoint, and stepwise motion should always be used across bar lines. It is important, though, to try to begin planning your counterpoint according to larger, measure-length patterns that bridge melodic gaps between downbeats, rather than compose in a note-to-note fashion. Certain dissonance figures work well in connecting downbeat pitches that are separated by step, while others are typically used when downbeat pitches are farther apart. The chart in Figure 4.11 provides a few melodic patterns that are typically successful in bridging specific melodic gaps between downbeats. Each metric position is labeled as being consonant (C) or dissonant (D); thus, these melodic shapes cannot simply be deployed in an exercise without considering the intervals that are created between the *cantus firmus* and the counterpoint. As well, producing music according to measure-length contour segments is not a very nuanced compositional method; you should expect to revise your work after choosing certain measure-length patterns to ensure a smooth overall shape with an appropriate climax.

Interval between downbeats	Description of pattern	Melodic motion	Example Label	Example	Example Label	Example
Unison	Two passing tones	Step, step, step, step	A1	 C D C D C	A2	 C D C D C
Second	Passing tone + leap to consonance	Step, step, leap, step	B1	 C D C C	B2	 C D C C
	Leap to consonance + passing tone	Leap, step, step, step	C1	 C C D C C	C2	 C C D C C
	Double neighbor	Step, leap, step, step	D1	 C D D C C	D2	 C D D C C
	Nota cambiata	Step, leap, step, step	E1	 C D C C C	E2	 C D C C C
Third	Neighbor tone + passing tone	Step, step, step, step	F1	 C D C D C	F2	 C D C D C
	Passing tone + neighbor tone	Step, step, step, step	G1	 C D C D C	G2	 C D C D C
Fourth	Neighbor tone + leap to consonance	Step, step, leap, step	H1	 C D C C C	H2	 C D C C C
Fifth	Two passing tones	Step, step, step, step	I1	 C D C D C	I2	 C D C D C
Sixth	Leap to consonance + passing tone	Leap, step, step, step	J1	 C C D C C	J2	 C C D C C

Fig. 4.11 Common measure-length melodic patterns used in third species counterpoint

Harmony in Third Species

One of the common pitfalls in third species writing is the tendency to use lots of consonant, chordal skips within a measure to unequivocally state a specific harmony. This creates pleasing harmonic sounds, but leads to a jagged, difficult-to-sing contour that can sound more like an instrumental accompaniment figure than a true melody. You should expect to use one or two dissonant harmonic intervals in every measure in third species; as these dissonances are typically approached and/or left by step melodically, a disjunct arpeggiation pattern should never result from their use. Also, as in second species, avoid parallel fifths and parallel octaves in third species—between consecutive pitches as well as pitches on adjacent downbeats within the first species "skeleton" that underlies the counterpoint.

Strategies for Success

As in second species, the best method for composing a third species counterpoint begins with the creation of a first species "skeleton," focusing only on the pitches taking place on downbeats. These pitches should again follow the "sandwich" scheme detailed earlier in this chapter. Ideally, most of the melodic motion between tones in the added voice within the skeleton will be by step or by third, though unisons and fifths between consecutive downbeats are also quite easy to navigate in this species. This is because most of the smooth melodic contour options featuring neighbor tones and passing tones are available in these cases. Referring back to Figure 4.11, for example, you can see that there are no completely stepwise options that connect melodic intervals of fourths, while there are multiple stepwise options involving downbeat tones separated by thirds. Figure 4.12 compares the previous third species solution to its 1:1 skeleton (which is the first species solution from Figure 4.6), noting the melodic intervals between the counterpoint's downbeats and the specific pattern from Figure 4.11 used to connect downbeat pitches. Asterisks indicate patterns used to connect downbeat pitches that differ slightly from those shown in Figure 4.11, such as those in the third and sixth measures.

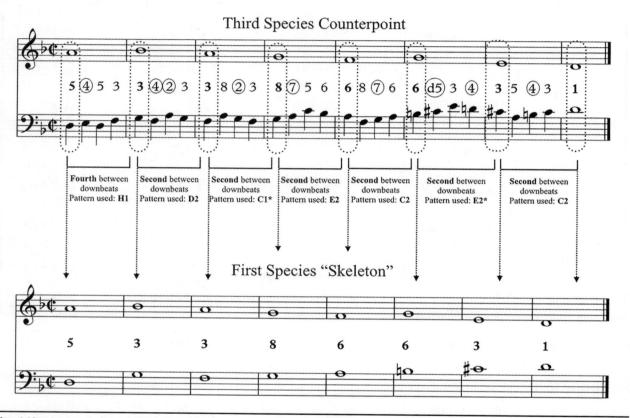

Fig. 4.12   A comparison between a third species counterpoint and its first species "skeleton"

FOURTH SPECIES

Fourth species counterpoint is quite similar to first species, with the main difference being that the newly added voice is rhythmically offset from the *cantus firmus*. Typically, the given voice consists of whole notes while the counterpoint begins a half note later on beat 2 and features groups of tied half notes, resulting in a mild syncopation before a final cadence on whole notes (on tonic) in both voices. This syncopation yields several dissonant **suspensions** on the downbeats of the measures, which are approached or "prepared" by consonant common tones and resolve down by step into consonances afterward. Put differently, each dissonant suspension in fourth species is preceded by the same (tied) pitch in the previous bar's weak beat, where it forms a consonant interval with the *cantus firmus*; after the dissonance sounds on the subsequent downbeat, the suspension resolves by step down into an imperfect consonance. Overall, fourth species can be characterized as possessing "chains" of consecutive suspensions, where the resolution tone of one suspension also functions as the preparation tone of a subsequent suspension. Suspension chains create a nice emotional effect and as a result are still used frequently in today's music. An example of fourth species counterpoint is given in Figure 4.13, where the *cantus firmus* is in the bass and the rhythmically offset added voice closely resembles the melodic reduction of the theme from "The Black Pearl." Note that the interval labels with lines in between them signify suspensions in the figure; this allows the reader to easily understand that a suspension is taking place and resolving to the structural interval of a third or sixth within each bar. Additionally, the interval label of each resolution tone is in bold (as well as the labels of all downbeat consonances), which makes it possible to focus on the underlying first species skeleton.

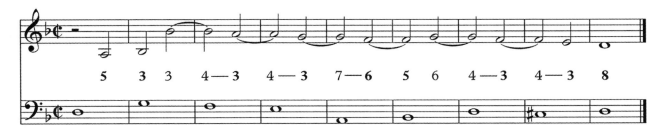

Fig. 4.13 Fourth species example using an altered melodic reduction of the theme from "The Black Pearl" as the counterpoint

The strict majority of the tied rhythms in this species involve suspensions, as is the case in this example. However, you may hold a pitch over the bar line in the counterpoint that does not form a suspension if it creates a consonant interval with the *cantus firmus* in both measures while the *cantus firmus* changes pitch from bar to bar. In m. 6, for example, F is held across the bar line in the counterpoint as the bass changes from A to B♭; this creates both a consonant m6 on the second beat of the fifth bar and a consonant P5 on the downbeat of the sixth bar.

Melody in Fourth Species

As suspensions—which predominate the texture in fourth species—resolve by descending step, melodies in this species feature descending stepwise motion the majority of the time. However, you may "break the species" and resort to second species counterpoint (two un-tied half notes in a bar) for a brief time in order to avoid a constantly descending melodic line or a line that falls too low in register. This often involves an ascending leap, which should be followed immediately by stepwise motion in the opposite direction. The result is that the usual contour of a fourth species counterpoint features longer periods of descending scalar motion that are interrupted by infrequent, disjunct, ascending leaps; this creates an overall shape that is similar to a saw blade or series of dorsal fins. Observe the broken species in the previous example, which takes place immediately in the second bar and includes an octave leap that sets up a long chain of suspensions. (Though it is not possible with the *cantus firmus* in Figure 4.13 while preserving the melodic makeup of "The Black Pearl," the second measure typically includes a suspension, with the species being broken only after a few suspensions in order to establish the species.) The second to last bar always involves a suspension before the final cadence on whole notes, as well; traditionally, a 7–6 suspension is used above scale degree $\hat{2}$ in the bass when the counterpoint is in the soprano, and a 2–3 suspension is used below $\hat{2}$ in the soprano when the counterpoint is in the bass. Such is the case in Figure 4.14, where the altered melodic reduction from the theme from "The Black Pearl" is presented as the *cantus firmus* in the soprano and the counterpoint is added below. Note that in this example, the species is broken on the downbeat of m. 5 before an octave leap that sets up a second chain of 2–3 suspensions. Also, the counterpoint does not begin on a rest; this is simply done to establish tonic harmony in the initial measure while setting up a suspension in bar 2.

Fig. 4.14 Fourth species example using an altered melodic reduction of the theme from "The Black Pearl" as the *cantus firmus*

Harmony in Fourth Species

While third species allowed for multiple types of dissonance to be used, the suspension is the only legal dissonance in fourth species, and it should be used as much as possible without causing other voice-leading errors. When the counterpoint is added in the bass, as in the previous example, the only suspension that should be used is the 2–3 suspension, which embellishes the structural third interval of a measure. When the counterpoint is added in the soprano, as in the initial example within this section, two suspension types are possible: the 4–3 suspension (which decorates a structural third interval) and the 7–6 suspension (which decorates a structural sixth). There are other types of suspensions that appear in music, such as the 9–8 suspension (which is used in textures with more than two voices) and the 6–5 consonant suspension, but these are not used in fourth species. Moreover, ensure that no more than three identical suspension types appear consecutively in this species (following the tradition of avoiding more than three consecutive intervals of the same type in first species).

Contrapuntal Motion in Fourth Species

Oblique motion predominates within each measure in fourth species, involving the static *cantus firmus* and the descending stepwise motion of the added voice whenever a suspension takes place. The underlying first species skeleton, however—which exists between the *cantus firmus* and the resolution tones in the added voice—tends to feature mostly parallel and contrary motion.

Strategies for Success

While the main essence of fourth species counterpoint resides in the misaligned, syncopated rhythms among the two parts, in reality, the two voices possess the same rhythm (whole notes) the majority of the time—the added voice simply begins later in the first bar, which results in tied half notes across the bar lines. Thus, creating the first species skeleton represents the majority of the compositional work associated with this species. Once that is done, the added voice can just be "shifted backward" a beat to create suspensions (though additional editing is then needed to polish the counterpoint). When planning your first species skeleton, you should avoid using too many P5s and P8s outside of the first and last bars, as 2–3, 4–3, and 7–6 suspensions require imperfect consonances as resolution tones. Instead, start with a very sixth- and third-heavy skeleton that emphasizes descending stepwise melodic motion. Once you are satisfied with your first species skeleton, rewrite the counterpoint with rhythmic displacement against the *cantus firmus*, but break the species whenever you run into problems. When breaking the species, try to use ascending leaps between consonances within the measure, especially when the skeleton is about to have a series of descending steps, which will set up a chain of suspensions. Simply choose your suspension type and leap into the common tone preparation that effectively sets up the chain.

FIFTH SPECIES AND FREE COUNTERPOINT

The final step in the species method prior to writing "free counterpoint" is fifth species, which is closest to true music composition, as all of the parts within a texture are rhythmically varied. Here, the *cantus firmus* once again features whole notes, while the added voice freely mixes rhythms and dissonance types from the previous species. Figure 4.15 provides an example of fifth species that uses the same *cantus firmus* as the previous fourth species example.

Fig. 4.15 Fifth species example using an altered melodic reduction of the theme from "The Black Pearl" as the *cantus firmus*

Fifth species solutions tend to resemble those of fourth species at the beginning and end, as they typically begin on the second beat of the first bar and end with a suspension leading to a final tonic. Suspensions are also used in the center of the counterpoint, though they are very often elaborated with new rhythmic patterns that support a general rhythmic acceleration throughout the melody prior to the cadence, such as the ones found in the fourth and fifth measures of the previous example. In m. 4, for example, the resolution to the structural tone E4 that forms a third interval with the *cantus firmus* is decorated by an eighth note neighbor tone figure on beat 2. This type of eighth note pattern is quite common in fifth species in the context of an embellished resolution of a suspension. Bar 5 includes another common pattern that is used for the same purpose; here, there is a leap out of the dissonant suspension into a consonant quarter note on beat 2, followed immediately by a leap back to the resolution tone of the suspension that is a step below the downbeat dissonance.

When writing a fifth species solution, feel free to use tied half notes (for suspensions, as in fourth species), half notes within the same bar (as in second species), quarter notes (as in third species), and occasionally eighth notes (to embellish suspensions), but try to build tension by gradually increasing rhythmic activity as the melody progresses. This can add impact to a melodic climax, creating a very impactful counterpoint. As well, try to include as many different types of embellishment as possible within your added voice, following the guidelines for each specific dissonance that were introduced throughout the earlier species. Figure 4.16 summarizes all of the embellishment types used in species counterpoint. Note, however, that several other categories of dissonance exist; these are covered in Chapter 9.

Consonant Preparation	Dissonant Embellishment Type	Consonant Resolution
Step	**Passing Tone**	Step in same direction as previous step
Step	**Neighbor Tone**	Step in opposite direction
Step	**Double Neighbor**	Step in same direction as initial step (but opposite direction of leap between consecutive dissonances separated by third)
Step	*Nota Cambiata*	Consecutive steps in opposite direction of initial step as well as leap out of dissonance
Common tone	**Suspension**	Descending step

Fig. 4.16 List of the melodic embellishments featured in species counterpoint

INTRODUCTION TO MOTIVIC DEVELOPMENT

Counterpoint exercises, such as those exemplified earlier, are usually quite short, lasting on average between 8 and 12 measures. Thus, it is not typical to create, repeat, and develop musical motives in these contexts. A **motive** (or motif, or "cell") is a salient, identifiable combination of pitch and rhythm that is shorter than a true theme yet still represents a musical idea. **Motivic development** describes the process of repeating and altering an initial motive throughout a phrase or piece of music, which simultaneously engenders the desired aesthetic attributes of unity and variety that were referenced earlier in this chapter. Though motivic development is not featured in species counterpoint exercises, it is prized in free contrapuntal music—indeed, it is valued in nearly all music—and will be treated thoroughly in Chapter 11. A brief example of motivic development from Beethoven's Piano Sonata No. 1 is provided in Figure 4.17.

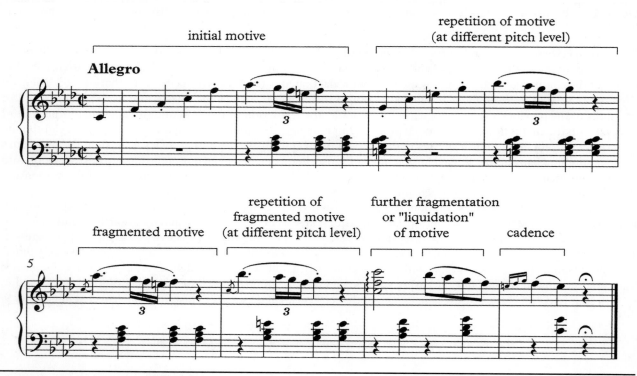

Fig. 4.17   Beethoven, Piano Sonata No. 1, Op. 2 no. 1, mm. 1–8

In this example, an initial 2-bar motive is stated that features a disjunct arpeggiation of the F minor tonic triad in quarter notes, followed by melodic movement by descending third that is embellished with a noteworthy sixteenth note triplet figure. This is followed by a **melodic sequence**, wherein the melody is repeated at a different pitch level. This particular melodic sequence is known as a "tonal sequence," as the melodic intervals between each note in the repeated motive are adjusted to fit the key signature and/or underlying harmony (e.g., the first full bar of the initial motive proceeds by m3, then M3, then P4, while the sequence begins with a P4 followed by a M3 and a m3 afterward). (Had the exact intervallic pattern of the initial motive been heeded during the transposed repetition in mm. 3–4, the result would be a "real sequence" or "mirror sequence," though the sound would be quite jarring, as the tonality of the piece would be destabilized. For this reason, tonal sequences are far more common than real sequences in traditional tonal music.) In bars 5 and 6 of the example, the initial motive is further developed, transposed, and abbreviated, such that the focus becomes the dotted quarter/sixteenth note triplet combination that occupied the motive's second half. This leads to what is known as a "liquidation" of the motive, where its characteristic elements are all but eliminated via a more substantial fragmentation that aids in the transition to the final cadence.

Overall, the entire phrase is dedicated to the initial motive, though it is developed in such a way that the phrase sounds as if it is progressing both harmonically and melodically to a climax while avoiding incessant repetition. In fact, the melodic development of the melody follows a common guideline that is used to teach composition students, which is known as the **Rule of Threes**. The Rule of Threes states that while the repetition of a motive is important for the formation of an audible pattern that establishes it as a primary point of musical interest, literally repeating a motive three or more times is often perceived as uninspired and monotonous, and should be avoided. Thus, one should deviate from the original motive upon its third iteration, using development techniques (such as fragmentation, which is used in this example). Importantly, the accompaniment figure in Beethoven's sonata is developed along with the right hand melody; though it is not as striking and memorable as the melody, its systematic fragmentation aids in the perception of motion and climax in the piece. In today's popular genres, which arguably feature more literal repetition than the contrapuntal style composed by Beethoven and his contemporaries, motivic development remains crucial, and its use tends to separate great producers from their peers. Your ability to craft and combine beautiful, memorable melodies while ensuring unity, variety, and coherence with developmental procedures will likewise set you apart from other contemporary composers. To this end, the *Composition Essentials* section later in this book continues to foster your melodic writing skills, while additionally providing harmony, form, and orchestration topics to help you become a professional, well-rounded composer of great music. First, however, we turn to the fundamentals of audio engineering and sequencing, which will allow your compositional ideas to come to fruition through the use of industry-standard music technologies.

SUMMARY OF TERMS FROM CHAPTER 4

melody	oblique motion	embellishment
form	parallel motion	neighbor tone
voice leading	similar motion	double neighbor
species counterpoint	contrary motion	*nota cambiata*
conjunct	voice exchange	suspension
disjunct	parallel fifths/octaves	motive
cadence	direct fifths/octaves	motivic development
step progression	cross relation	melodic sequence
counterpoint	voice crossing	Rule of Threes
contrapuntal motion	voice overlap	
static motion	passing tone	

CHAPTER 4—EXERCISES

1. **Melody Analysis.** The following melodies suffer from various compositional problems. In the spaces provided after each example, briefly describe the undesirable aspect(s) of each melody.

a.

b.

2. **Melody Composition.** Using the notation provided, compose an 8-bar melody in the given key that features an arch shape while exemplifying long-range planning, step progressions, and the dramatic structure summarized in Freytag's pyramid. Be sure to employ a variety of rhythms, and attempt to introduce and develop a motive via a melodic sequence. You may choose the meter of the melody, but remember to add the appropriate meter signature along with the necessary key signature at the beginning of the notated passage.

   a. Key: B♭ major

   b. Key: F minor

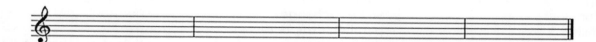

3. **Counterpoint analysis.** The following counterpoint examples suffer from various compositional problems. In the spaces provided after each example, briefly describe the aspects of each counterpoint that are undesirable, according to the tenets of that particular species.

   a. First Species

b. Second Species

c. Third Species

d. Fourth Species

4. **Counterpoint Composition: First Species.** Using the notation provided, compose a solution to the counterpoint exercise by completing the added melody above the *cantus firmus*. Your counterpoint must form consonant harmonic intervals with the *cantus firmus* exclusively, and it must end on a perfect octave on tonic in the key of A♭ major. Be sure to label the intervals created between the parts, reducing any compound intervals to simple intervals for this purpose.

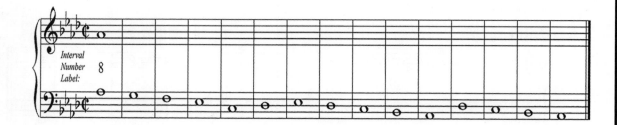

5. **Counterpoint Composition: Second Species.** Using the notation provided, compose a solution to the counterpoint exercise by completing the added melody above the *cantus firmus*. Your counterpoint must form consonant harmonic intervals with the *cantus firmus* on downbeats while making use of weak beat passing tones as often as possible, and it must end on a perfect octave on tonic in E minor. Be sure to label the intervals created between the parts, reducing any compound intervals to simple intervals for this purpose.

6. **Counterpoint Composition: Third Species.** Using the notation provided, compose a solution to the counterpoint exercise by completing the added melody below the *cantus firmus*. Your counterpoint must form consonant harmonic intervals with the *cantus firmus* on downbeats while making use of weak beat embellishment patterns that feature passing tones, neighbor tones, double neighbors, and *nota cambiata* figures. The counterpoint must end on a perfect octave on tonic in E major. Be sure to label the intervals created between the parts, reducing any compound intervals to simple intervals for this purpose.

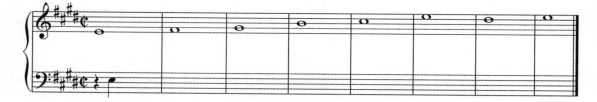

7. **Counterpoint Composition: Fourth Species.** Using the notation provided, compose a solution to the counterpoint exercise by completing the added melody above the *cantus firmus*. Your counterpoint must create appropriately prepared, dissonant suspensions as often as possible, and it must end on a perfect octave on tonic in B minor. Be sure to label the intervals created between the parts, reducing any compound intervals to simple intervals for this purpose.

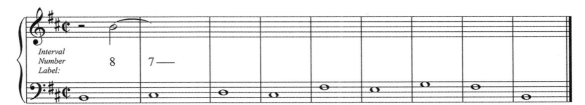

Interval
Number   8   7 ——
Label:

PART IB
FUNDAMENTALS OF AUDIO ENGINEERING AND SEQUENCING

Chapter 5
Introduction to Audio and MIDI

As mentioned in the Introduction section of this book, today's commercial composer needs to be fluent in both music and music technology. In Part Ia, you learned about the fundamentals of music. In Part Ib, you'll begin to investigate music as sound from an acoustic standpoint, which will in turn allow you to understand the various ways it is captured, translated, and manipulated from an engineering perspective.

SOUND

Without the presence of an elastic medium such as air, sound could not exist. At the start of any sound source, air molecules are pushed outward in straight lines in the form of pressure waves. As these waves travel through the ear, three tiny bones in the eardrum vibrate and transmit this data to the inner ear, where it is collected by hair cells and sent through the cochlear nerve, helping us perceive this information as sound.

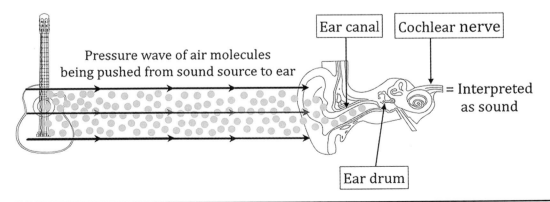

Fig. 5.1   The perception of sound

FREQUENCY

Air molecules involved in a pressure wave vibrate back and forth a certain amount of times per second, based on how quickly the source is vibrating. This is **frequency**, and it allows us to perceive a sound's highness or lowness.

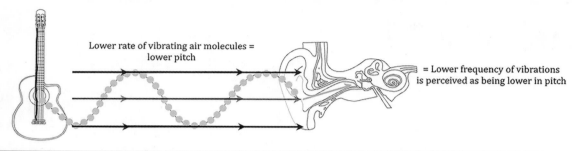

Fig. 5.2   The perception of low frequencies

If the molecules vibrate at a faster rate, the sound will be recognized as being higher in pitch.

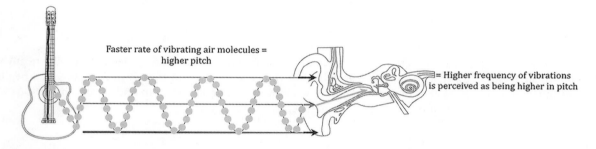

Fig. 5.3   The perception of high frequencies

The frequency of vibrations is typically expressed in **Hertz**, with one Hz equaling one vibration per second. If the fifth string of a guitar is played, for example, you will hear the note A2, which equals 110Hz. This simply means that the string is vibrating 110 times per second.

Vibrating 5th string of a guitar sounds like A2

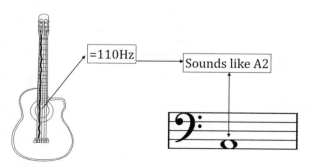

Fig. 5.4   Relationship between frequency and pitch

When an ensemble tunes before a performance, all of the instruments tune to 440Hz, which equates to A4. Modern digital instrument tuners are set to 440Hz, so that all members of an ensemble can tune to the same pitch.

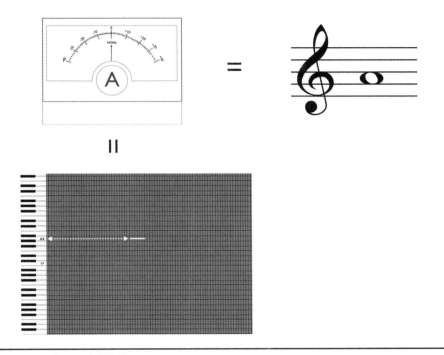

Fig. 5.5 **Various representations of 440Hz**

AMPLITUDE

Amplitude refers to the intensity of energy in a given pressure wave, which is perceived by the human ear as loudness. Amplitude is expressed in dB or **decibels**, with 0dB being generally considered as the lower threshold for human hearing. If you consider this as a basis with which to compare the loudness of other sounds, a soft conversation would have an amplitude of around 40dB, power tools would be assigned 110dB, and an active airport runway would be about 120dB.

To sum up the important properties of a pressure wave from a musical standpoint: *frequency* is analogous to *pitch*, and *amplitude* is analogous to *loudness*.

Frequency ≈ Pitch   Amplitude ≈ Loudness

Fig. 5.6 **Analogous properties of sound and music**

DECIBELS IN THE STUDIO ENVIRONMENT

In the audio production world, a different, *relative* decibel scale is used, in which 0dB is equal to 100% of the volume threshold of the audio output device used or audio file created (e.g., MP3, etc.). Anything over 0dB will create an overload distortion known as **clipping**. Virtual mixing boards make it possible to monitor a sound's decibel level.

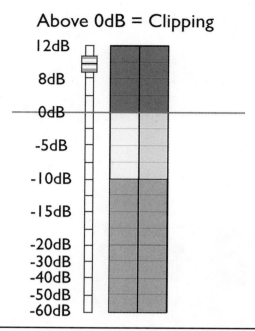

Fig. 5.7　Visualization of the decibel scale in a virtual mixing board

ANALOG SIGNAL CAPTURING

Now that you understand a bit about how audio works acoustically, you can examine how it is recorded into a computer. An analog recording device captures a pressure wave by varying the voltage of a signal so that it is analogous to the amplitude of the incoming sound, following the changing levels of intensity of a given pressure wave. Essentially, the recording device is functioning like a human ear by capturing and translating the information contained in the pressure wave. In the case of a tape machine, this information is imprinted directly onto tape. This fragile representation of the original sound is easily corrupted by the slightest electronic anomaly. Analog recording devices such as tape machines will always have some degree of random noise, which is an unavoidable consequence of dealing with electronic tools. Despite such practical issues, some composers and producers still opt for analog recordings, as they produce a sound and feel that is often described as "warm." Analog warmth is not easily duplicated in a digital recording environment. There are many theories behind exactly which parts of an analog setup cause this phenomenon, but the discussion is beyond the scope of this book. Despite the warm qualities of analog recording, digital recording offers many advantages and is becoming increasingly popular in contemporary studios, both large and small. As such, this book concentrates on digital recording only.

ANALOG-TO-DIGITAL CONVERSION

An analog-to-digital convertor is a device used to capture an analog signal and convert it into a language that is understandable by computers. To complete this process, an analog-to-digital convertor takes samples (digital snapshots) of an analog signal at a specified rate. The more samples taken per second, the higher the **sample rate** that is yielded, resulting in a closer depiction of the incoming sound.

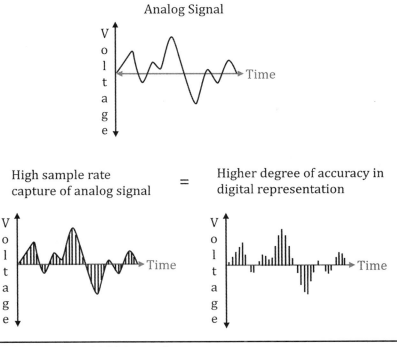

Fig. 5.8 Analog to digital conversion with high sample rate

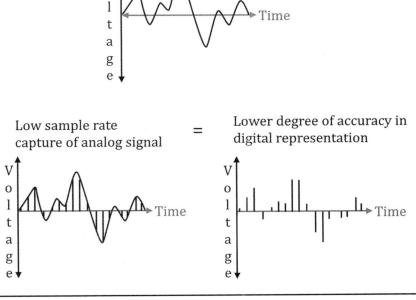

Fig. 5.9 Analog to digital conversion with low sample rate

SAMPLE RATE AND THE NYQUIST THEOREM

A higher sample rate requires more of a computer's hard drive storage but will create a more accurate representation of an analog signal. This creates a dilemma with an easy solution known as the **Nyquist theorem**. Simply put, the theorem states that a sample rate should be set to at least two times the value of the highest frequency one wants to capture. The approximate range of audible frequencies for humans is between 20Hz and 20,000Hz; therefore, to capture the full spectrum of human hearing, a sample rate should be set to at least 40,000Hz. It is common to employ a sample rate of 44,100Hz (44.1kHz), which is used in compact disc recordings, although higher sample rates are commonly used to avoid sonic distortions caused when a frequency is recorded that exists beyond the range of a given sample rate. This is known as **foldover** or **aliasing**. Cymbals are an example of an instrument that will sound clearest when recorded at a higher sample rate because they generate such high frequencies.

BIT DEPTH

The amount of bits used for each sample of an analog signal is known as **bit depth**. Bit depth relates directly to sample resolution: the more bits assigned to each sample, the more accurately the digital signal will recreate the analog signal.

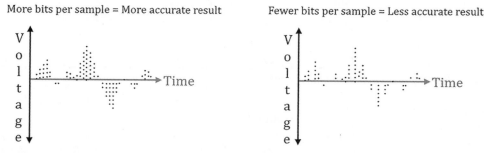

Fig. 5.10   Visualization of various bit depths

Once an analog signal is captured, each sample is assigned a binary digit—0 or 1—and the information is ready to be passed along to a computer and into a digital audio workstation. The new, digital representation of sound can be viewed in a waveform or sample editor. Amplitude is expressed in the vertical height of the waveform. Figure 5.11 demonstrates a sound visualization option within Apple's Logic Pro X software, using a window referred to as the File Editor.

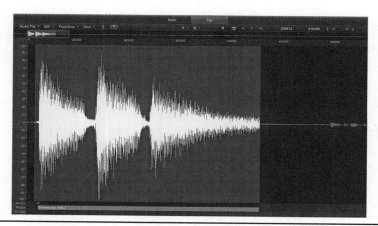

Fig. 5.11   Waveforms in the File Editor window of Logic Pro X

As shown in the Introduction of this book, **DAWs** (digital audio workstations) such as Logic Pro X afford the producer many tools designed to streamline the creative process; the File Editor shown in Figure 5.11 is but one of the many valuable functions found in a DAW. You will explore these capabilities in greater detail as you work your way through this book, but it is first necessary to briefly examine MIDI—one of the most important communication protocols used in music technology.

MUSICAL INSTRUMENT DIGITAL INTERFACE (MIDI)

MIDI is simply a method that allows two devices to communicate. It is important to note that MIDI itself is not audio; it is a communication protocol. Via MIDI, one device tells another *what* to do, *when* to do it, and for *how long*. Essentially, music notation serves the same purpose. A performer is informed *what* notes to play, *when* to play them, and for *how long*.

MIDI ON/OFF MESSAGES: MOMENTARY AND TOGGLE CONFIGURATIONS

MIDI data is a complex series of message packets that are transferred from one device to another. Each packet sends information when in the *on* position and stops sending information when in the *off* position. A MIDI controller (e.g., a keyboard, a drum pad, etc.) that is set to **momentary configuration** will send an *on* message when a certain apparatus is depressed and an *off* message when the apparatus is released. As noted in Chapter 1, the most prevalent way of sending MIDI information is with a keyboard controller, which is typically set to momentary messages. If, however, a controller is set to **toggle configuration**, an *on* message is sent when a mechanism is depressed and it will remain in the *on* position until it is pressed down again, like a button. This is a more common setup for control pads that are often used for triggering looped samples.

CONTINUOUS CONTROLLER (CC) MESSAGES

The musical information that is sent via MIDI is composed of what are known as **continuous controller messages** or CC messages. All CC messages fall into one of two main categories: channel messages and system messages. Channel messages have to do with an instrument's patch (sound), timbre (tone color), and velocity (intensity), whereas system messages have to do with information and synchronization between multiple devices. There are 128 different types of CC messages, numbered 0 through 127. This affords the composer a wonderful amount of control over a variety of musical details, and as such MIDI can be used to create extremely nuanced, realistic music within the DAW environment. It is not surprising that the protocol, first unveiled in January of 1983, persists as a prominent compositional tool today. A full list of all CC messages can be found in the Appendix.

MIDI SETUPS: MIDI COMMUNICATION FROM KEYBOARD/SYNTHESIZER TO DAW AND FROM DAW TO KEYBOARD/SYNTHESIZER

Many modern MIDI connections are made without MIDI cables at all (USB cables are often used instead, for example), but it is important to examine how MIDI communication originated in order to understand how it works in more typical, contemporary environments.

There are a variety of setup possibilities involving MIDI that producers commonly use in their home studios. One such setup involves two simultaneous methods of communication.

- A keyboard controller sends MIDI data out of its MIDI OUT port

- Into a MIDI interface's MIDI IN port

- Then, the data is sent out of the MIDI interface's MIDI OUT port

- Into a computer.

Essentially, the keyboard in this first step tells the computer what note(s) to play and for how long. This information that is transmitted to the computer is translated and arranged in a DAW. The next step in this setup is as follows:

- Information is sent back out of the computer

- Into the MIDI interface's MIDI IN port

- Then, the data is sent out of the MIDI interface's MIDI OUT port

- Into the keyboard's MIDI IN port

The computer, in this second step, is now telling the keyboard what patch to use to create the specified pitch(es).

Fig. 5.12　MIDI bidirectional communication

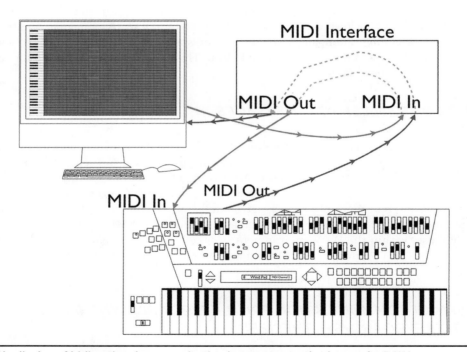

Fig. 5.13　Graphic display of bidirectional communication between a synthesizer and a DAW

As mentioned previously, MIDI information travels through MIDI or USB cables between MIDI-capable devices. The MIDI information within these pathways is organized into MIDI channels. You can think of these channels as being similar to channels on a television. When a TV is set to receive data from one channel, it ignores the other incoming signals set for other channels. MIDI works in the same fashion. Digital audio workstation software in a computer can tell a MIDI device what to do by sending the MIDI information through one of its MIDI channels, and as long as the MIDI device is set to receive that information on the correct channel, the desired result will be achieved. Put differently, MIDI information can be sent to and from a computer and MIDI device by assigning both pieces of equipment to send or receive on the same MIDI channel.

MULTITIMBRAL MIDI CONFIGURATION

All modern digital audio workstations are capable of transmitting MIDI data across multiple channels. Most modern MIDI devices (e.g., sound modules, samplers, synthesizers) possess the same functionality. The reason for this is that these devices are **multitimbral**. Most of these machines are 16- or 32-part multitimbral, meaning that they are able to create sounds using up to 16 or 32 different instruments within each device simultaneously. You will learn how to take advantage of multitimbral configurations within the DAW environment in conjunction with software instruments later in this book.

MIDI SETUPS: DAISY CHAIN SETUPS

Many MIDI instruments also have a MIDI THRU feature, which allows multiple MIDI devices to be "daisy chained" together. In a daisy chain setup, one of the available MIDI channels in a MIDI device can be set up to ignore all information received, and instead pass the data through the MIDI THRU port of the device into the MIDI IN port of the next MIDI device in the chain. This setup is shown in Figure 5.14.

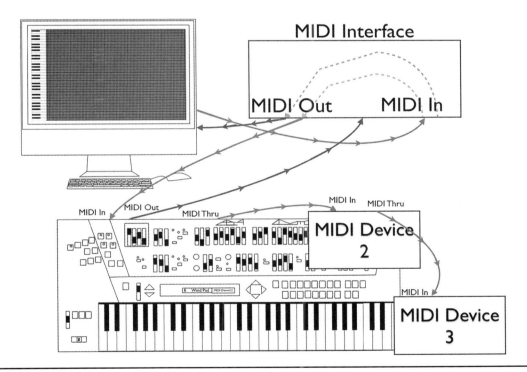

Fig. 5.14 A sample daisy chain setup

Daisy chaining devices together in a MIDI setup is great for connecting different pieces of gear at the same time, but you will experience latency (slow responses) farther down the chain of connections, and you'll also need to sacrifice

MIDI channels in order to make the chain possible. Daisy chaining external gear is also becoming obsolete as virtual instruments (software instruments) and effects plugins (software effects) continue to become increasingly powerful.

POLYPHONY

When discussing MIDI, **polyphony** simply refers to the number of notes or sounds a MIDI device is capable of producing simultaneously. You have learned that MIDI information is passed through MIDI channels from one device to another and that multitimbral pieces of equipment are capable of outputting up to 16 or 32 different instruments from within a single device. Polyphony relates to the maximum amount of shared notes used among all multitimbral channels of a single piece of MIDI equipment. A 32-note polyphonic keyboard, for example, has the potential to produce 32 notes at the same time. If 33 notes were depressed on this keyboard simultaneously, one of them would not sound. Now, if a composer had 16 different instrument channels of MIDI data coming from a single sound module with the same limitations, this would severely constrain the number of notes the composer could use at a given time. Luckily, most modern MIDI devices are capable of up to 128-voice polyphony and some are even capable of 256-voice polyphony.

MIDI TODAY

Contemporary composers take advantage of the creative power of MIDI every day. Though computers have become faster and hard drive storage has become increasingly affordable, producers continue to rely on the efficient communication that MIDI offers. MIDI is easy to set up, easy to edit, and easy to use, yet it offers many complex possibilities for advanced users. Working composers in today's industry are expected to understand how MIDI works and have a firm command of MIDI sequencing techniques. You'll continue to develop in these areas as you work through this book, discovering the power and speed of MIDI editing and exploring the ways it is implemented in the modern composer's array of creative workflows.

SUMMARY OF TERMS FROM CHAPTER 5

frequency	Nyquist theorem	momentary configuration
Hertz	foldover	toggle configuration
amplitude	aliasing	CC messages
decibels (dB)	bit depth	multitimbral device
clipping	DAW	MIDI polyphony
sample rate	MIDI	

CHAPTER 5—EXERCISES

Important: Some of these questions involve information that may be found in the Introduction of this book.

True or False. Circle "true" for each statement below that is true. Circle "false" for each false statement.

1. MIDI is audio.

   True　　　False

2. Volume depends on frequency.

   True　　　False

3. Amplitude determines pitch.

   True   False

4. The Nyquist theorem states that you should always choose a low sample rate to save hard drive space.

   True   False

5. Polyphony refers to the number of possible MIDI channels in a MIDI controller.

   True   False

Matching. Fill in each space with a letter corresponding to an accurate description of each term below.

6. DAW _____   a. Digital distortion

7. bit depth _____   b. Used to manipulate audio and MIDI

8. clipping _____   c. Visual representation of pitch and time

9. sample rate _____   d. Examples include MP3, AIFF, WAV

10. piano roll editor _____   e. Commonly set to 44.1 kHz

    f. Refers to how deep bits move in MIDI

    g. Corresponds to sample resolution

Multiple Choice. Circle the letter corresponding to the best choice for each question below.

11. Bit depth refers to:

    a. The amount of MIDI information found within a given bit

    b. The amount of bits used for each sample of an analog signal

    c. The amount of voltage used in a given bit to capture a sound

    d. A communication protocol used by MIDI-capable instruments

12. A keyboard controller is most commonly set to:

    a. Toggle mode

    b. Momentary mode

    c. Polyphony

    d. MIDI event list

13. All CC messages fall into one of two main categories: channel messages and system messages. Channel messages have to do with an instrument's patch (sound), timbre (tone color), and velocity (intensity), whereas system messages have to do with:

    a. Information and synchronization between multiple devices

    b. Audio outputs shared between multiple devices

    c.   The amount of samples taken per second

    d.   Amplitude

14. Frequency is best described as:

    a.   How loud a sound is

    b.   How often a sound can be heard

    c.   The rate at which air molecules in a pressure wave vibrate, which is based on how quickly the sound source is vibrating

    d.   Air molecules in a pressure wave vibrating 100dB or more

15. MIDI (Musical Instrument Digital Interface) is a communication protocol designed to send which type of information?

    a.   Bit depth rate

    b.   Sample rate information

    c.   Audio information

    d.   Continuous controller messages

16. Draw lines with arrowheads, showing the flow of information from the computer to the third MIDI device in a daisy chain configuration. Be sure to include all pieces of equipment in the daisy chain.

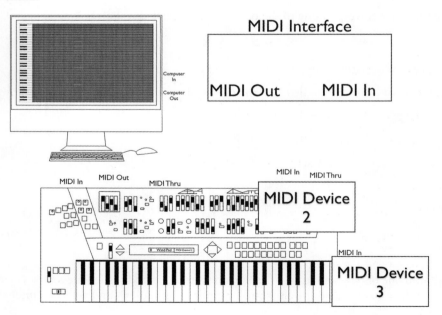

17. Circle and list any errors you find below and describe how to correct them in the available space below the figure.

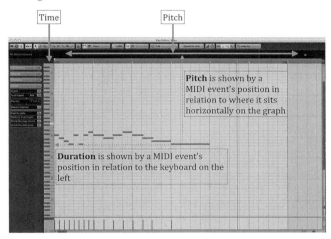

Pitch is shown by a MIDI event's position in relation to where it sits horizontally on the graph

Duration is shown by a MIDI event's position in relation to the keyboard on the left

18. In the following figure of Logic X's Event List window, circle the column that indicates when a MIDI event is taking place.

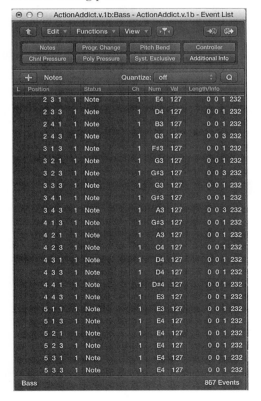

19. Circle the following three areas found within the Logic Pro X Main View figure below. Use the space provided for each item to describe each area.

    a.   Control Bar

    b.   Tracks view

    c.   Mixer View

20. In the following figure of Digital Performer 9's tracks view, fill in the missing information describing each highlighted area in the spaces provided.

_____ are listed vertically on the left

_____ is displayed horizontally

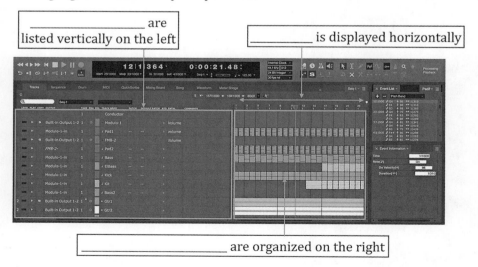

_____ are organized on the right

21. In the following Pro Tools Mix window figure, circle the track that is clipping. Then, describe clipping in the space next to the figure.

22. In the space provided, briefly describe what "DAW" stands for, the two main parameters that DAWs manipulate, and why DAWs generally incorporate visual design features of analog equipment.

23. In the space provided, briefly describe the path that MIDI information would take in a bidirectional communication setup between a synthesizer and a DAW.

24. In the space provided, briefly describe the compositional limitations presented by a sound module with 32-voice polyphony.

25. In the space provided, briefly describe why MIDI continues to be widely used by composers and producers in the industry.

Chapter 6
Manipulating Rhythm in the DAW Environment

This chapter introduces you to the ways in which music and MIDI are represented and manipulated in a DAW with a specific emphasis on rhythm. In Chapter 2, you were first familiarized with a passage from "The Black Pearl." Here, we return to that score to demonstrate how a musical idea can be manifested in a DAW environment, while also exploring common functions found in all DAWs. It is important to note that inputting notes from an already completed score is only one way to create music in a DAW. In fact, for many composers, it is more typical to begin composing ideas directly into a DAW, bypassing notation software or pencil and paper altogether. Regardless of the phase within the compositional process in which a DAW is engaged, it needs to be set up properly in order to appropriately serve the specific requirements of the music.

SESSION SETUP: RHYTHM, METER, AND TEMPO IN A DAW

Most DAWs include a view or toolbar—often called the **transport control window**—that allows you to view and adjust parameters specifically related to rhythm such as tempo, time signature, and the visualization of rhythmic values on the grid (which will be further explained shortly). Figure 6.1, for example, shows the Custom Control Bar, which is the main transport control window within Logic Pro X. Although each item needs to be set at the beginning of each project to allow the visual aspect of the DAW to most accurately reflect the temporal nature of the music, they may be adjusted at any point.

Fig. 6.1 Custom Control Bar from Logic Pro X

Figure 6.2 demonstrates how Logic Pro X should be set up to handle the first bar of Klaus Badelt's "The Black Pearl." You can see that the piece is in $\frac{3}{4}$ and that there is a tempo marking of *Allegro* (between 120 and 145bpm); these parameters are reflected in the corresponding areas of the Custom Control Bar.

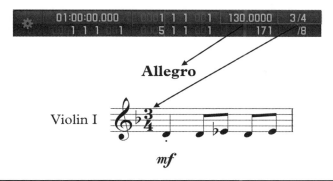

Fig. 6.2   Logic Pro X Custom Control Bar—tempo and meter change

SETTING UP THE GRID

Editing MIDI and audio events in a DAW can be very efficient; this is due in part to the way in which time is presented. Running across the top of most editing windows within a workstation is a unique type of adjustable ruler used to show the division of time. The resolution of this ruler (i.e., the specificity with which it delineates duration) is determined by the rhythmic value the producer has chosen, and it can be changed at any time based on specific editing needs of a particular musical passage. In Logic Pro X's Custom Control Bar, you'll see a fraction without a numerator directly under the meter display. The isolated denominator relates to a rhythmic value used to evenly partition the visual space dedicated to each measure within the **grid** (e.g., "/16" results in a visual division of measures into sixteenth note "slices" or columns, "/8" divides bars into eighth note slices, "/4" divides them into quarter note slices, and so on). Typically, producers will set this parameter to reflect the smallest rhythmic value found in the composition. For the excerpt from "The Black Pearl" in Figure 6.3, a resolution displaying eighth notes would be suitable. Note that the MIDI event for the first quarter note isn't a full quarter note in length. This is to accommodate the *staccato* articulation in the score.

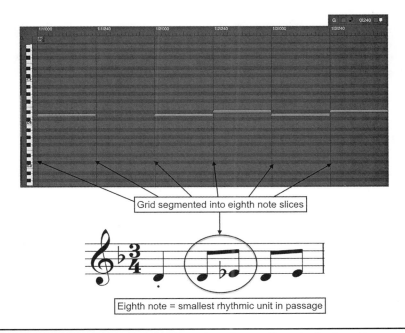

Fig. 6.3   Digital Performer 9—rhythm resolution change based on the smallest rhythmic unit

REGIONS AND EVENTS

Within Figure 6.4, you can see a shaded area with lighter-colored horizontal lines that appear intermittently. The larger shaded area is called a **region** and the lighter colored lines inside it are individual MIDI **events**. Note that specific colors will vary depending on the DAW being used and may be modified at any time. A region is a unit that contains either audio or MIDI information. Regions can be moved, duplicated, or copied and pasted wherever a producer desires, making editing and composing a very efficient experience. The information housed within a region is referred to collectively as a series of events. Audio and MIDI events contained inside a region may be viewed using a variety of editing windows. In some DAWs, though, only the events within a selected region will be viewable in any of the editing windows. This is especially important when dealing with a score that doesn't begin in bar 1, since the start of a passage may take place before the initial boundary of a region.

ANACRUSIS IN A DAW

The music from the "Black Pearl" excerpt begins on the downbeat of the first bar. If, however, a score calls for an anacrusis, like the music in Richard Wagner's "Ride of the Valkryies" theme (shown in Figure 6.4 within Logic Pro X), you'll need to add a "measure zero" before the start of the first full bar within the workstation. The left border of the region must be aligned exactly with the anacrusis in order for the score editor to reflect the appropriate amount of time before the downbeat. Most DAWs allow you to drag the edge of a region's border to the left or right giving you control over where the start of a region takes place. However, every workstation handles the creation of an anacrusis in a slightly different manner, so the manual for your DAW will help illuminate any software-specific procedures.

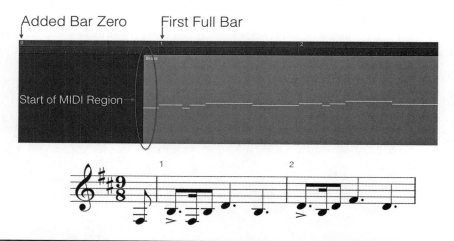

Fig. 6.4   Wagner's "Ride of the Valkryies" theme: added "bar zero" for an anacrusis in Logic Pro X

RHYTHM AND MIDI SEQUENCING

Now that you've learned how to set up a session, it is time to turn to MIDI sequencing and editing techniques as they pertain to musical rhythms. Again, MIDI and audio are different entities; while you'll work with both as a composer to create rhythms in a DAW, the workflows related to MIDI differ from those related to audio. As such, rhythm-based audio editing techniques appear at the end of this chapter.

MIDI AND THE REPRESENTATION OF RHYTHM

MIDI is represented in a DAW in a variety of ways. As mentioned in the Introduction, three types of available representation methods typically predominate: the notation editor, the piano roll editor, and the MIDI event list.

Notation Editor

Every DAW includes a notation editor, though it can be accessed in a number of different ways depending on the specific program being used. Notation editors provide the ability to directly edit any MIDI event in a project by altering the corresponding note within a notated score. A notation editor may display anything from a single instrument's part to a full orchestral score, and the view can be customized and adjusted at any time. Alterations to an event in a notation editor will manifest simultaneously in all other MIDI editing windows, allowing for real-time editing capabilities. Figure 6.5 includes the MIDI events from Figure 6.4 displayed in Logic Pro X's Score Editor.

Fig. 6.5   Richard Wagner's "Ride of the Valkryies" theme excerpt in Logic Pro X's Score Editor

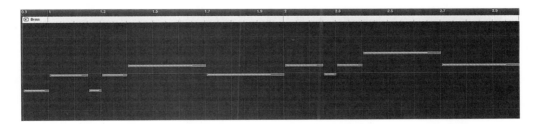

Fig. 6.6   Richard Wagner's "Ride of the Valkryies" excerpt in Logic Pro X's piano roll editor

Piano Roll Editor

Figure 6.6 recreates the same phrase from Wagner's "Ride of the Valkryies" theme in Logic X's piano roll editor. Although the appearance of the MIDI data differs between a notation editor and a piano roll editor, the information shared by the editors is the same. In a piano roll editor, one can identify the rhythmic value of any MIDI event based on its horizontal length, which is in turn measured by the ruler running across the top of the window. Figure 6.7 compares the two views of the initial "Ride of the Valkryies" passage and clarifies how MIDI event blocks express time in conjunction with the grid in a piano roll editor.

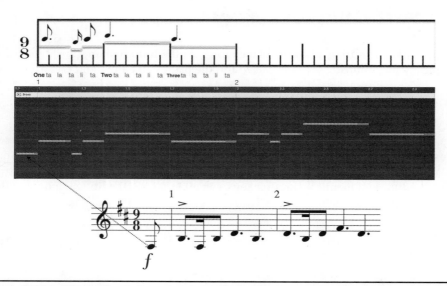

Fig. 6.7 Wagner's "Ride of the Valkryies" excerpt in Logic Pro X's Score Editor and Piano Roll Editor

Figure 6.8 below recreates the simple quadruple meter rhythm tree from Chapter 2 to further elucidate the relationship between notated rhythms and MIDI events on the grid.

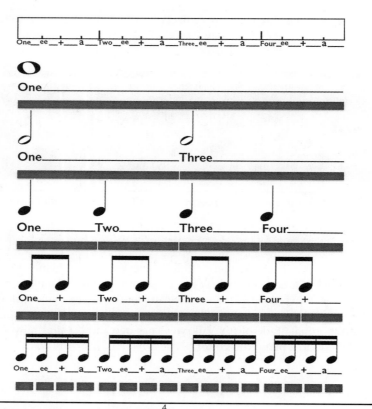

Fig. 6.8 Common note values and MIDI event blocks in $\frac{4}{4}$ time

MIDI Event List

Another common way of displaying MIDI information is in an event list. In this editing window, time flows vertically from top to bottom, with the rhythmic position of each event indicated in the far left column and the rhythmic value of each event specified in the far right column. The way in which rhythmic specificity is displayed and handled in DAWs is based on a system that divides the span of each quarter note into a certain amount of partitions or **ticks**. Ticks are measured by how many **pulses per quarter** note (**ppq**) a DAW is capable of identifying. The shortest amount of time recognizable by a DAW between one MIDI event and the next determines its ppq resolution. The default setting in Digital Performer 9 assigns a value of 480ppq, which means there are 480 ticks per quarter note, assuming a time signature of $\frac{4}{4}$ and a tempo of 120bpm. Logic Pro X has a default setting of 960ppq. The amount of ticks that span a quarter note may be customized, offering the producer a wide range of editing capabilities. It is significant to note that tempo plays an important part in determining the actual time between MIDI events as well. A faster tempo will decrease the time between one event and the next, while a slower tempo will do the opposite. The data housed in the center columns of a MIDI event list is dependent on the default settings of the specific DAW being used, but will typically include note on/off messages and velocity settings. The information presented in an event list may be customized, offering an abundance of parameter options. Once the desired information is displayed, editing is performed with a mouse and an alphanumeric keyboard. Again, altering events in one edit window creates simultaneous alterations in all other edit windows; thus, adjusting rhythmic values in an event list creates corresponding rhythmic changes in the Score Editor and piano roll editor. Figure 6.9 compares the MIDI event list and Score Editor for the "Black Pearl" excerpt.

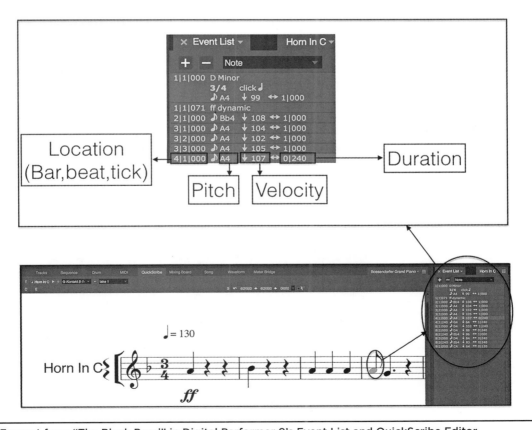

Fig. 6.9 Excerpt from "The Black Pearl" in Digital Performer 9's Event List and QuickScribe Editor

As you have seen, there are many ways to view and edit MIDI. While each editing window displays the exact same information, composers typically utilize multiple windows over the course of a project, depending on the specific parameters requiring modification at a given moment. Some edits are simply made more efficiently when viewed one way instead of another. For instance, while the piano roll editor may initially seem more abstract or confusing than a notation editor for trained musicians, it is more efficient to cut, copy, and paste data in this window than it is in a notation editor. Moreover, the piano roll editor affords the composer many complex MIDI transformation capabilities not included in the notation editor. However, if a producer needs to quickly analyze the pitch content of a specific phrase, the notation editor may seem more fitting. Regardless of the specific window used to edit or create MIDI data, the musical outcome is of singular importance.

SEQUENCING

Now that you have been exposed to the primary ways in which MIDI is viewed in the main editing windows, the process of entering and editing information in a DAW—called **sequencing**—can be more easily understood. A sequence is an arrangement of MIDI and audio events laid out over a series of one or more tracks. **Tracks** are editable lanes of information that are displayed horizontally and stacked on top of one another in a workstation. A track can be thought of as one instrument within a score, although there are other types of tracks that you will learn about shortly. As is the case with a score, a sequence may contain as many different instruments or tracks as a composer desires. Nonetheless, a project containing a single track would still be considered a sequence because of the succession of events taking place within it.

Track Types

There are three main types of tracks in a DAW: MIDI tracks, audio tracks, and auxiliary tracks or "aux tracks," which are addressed in Chapter 13. Many programs also include virtual instrument tracks, which are discussed in Chapter 8. Other common track types that are used to assist producers' workflows include tempo tracks, meter tracks, key signature tracks, and movie tracks. Figure 6.10 is a screenshot from a Digital Performer 9 session displaying a variety of track types within the arrange window. Many DAWs additionally include track options related to proprietary workflow designs. Digital Performer 9, for example, houses an assortment of track features within a larger structure called the Conductor Track. Although composers at times take advantage of the benefits of a particular track option from among the several available types, audio and MIDI tracks are employed most frequently when composing a piece of music.

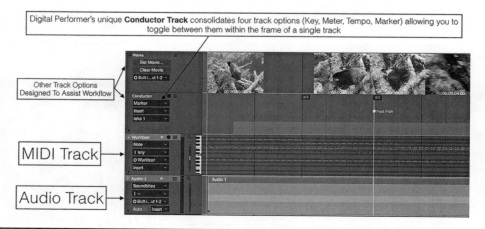

Fig. 6.10 Multiple track options in Digital Performer 9

Performance-Based Sequencing

There are several ways to enter MIDI information into a sequence. The most common method is to perform or "play in" the data with a MIDI keyboard controller. Prior to the start of any performance, the metronome and count in settings need to be adjusted properly. Transport control windows usually allow these functions to be turned on and off quickly with a single click of the mouse (see Figure 6.11), but performing specific adjustments to the count in duration or metronome "click" sound, for example, can be slightly different depending on the program being used.

Fig. 6.11 Logic Pro X Track Metronome and Count In On/Off

The process of playing in MIDI data closely resembles the way audio information is produced on an instrument and recorded to tape. As mentioned in the Introduction of this book, the record buttons in a transport control window look similar to those found in an analog tape machine. DAWs and analog tape recorders are designed to capture distinct types of information, however. In the case of a tape machine, pressing the record button will capture sound by imprinting the shape of an incoming pressure wave onto a piece of tape. When you press the record button on a MIDI track within a DAW, the program will capture a succession of MIDI data that is performed, not an actual audio signal. Once the information is captured, the details of each MIDI event may be edited in any of the editing windows. Figure 6.12 outlines the process of recording a performance into a DAW using MIDI equipment.

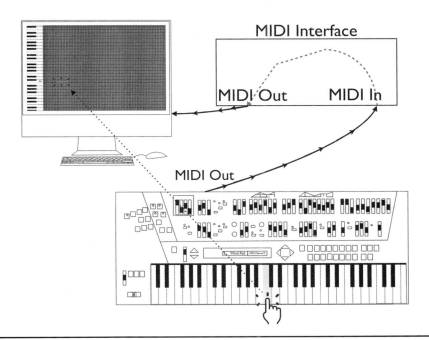

Fig. 6.12 Performance-based sequencing

Step Sequencing

"Playing in" data is very efficient, but it requires a modicum of keyboard proficiency. Those without keyboard skills often utilize an alternative to real-time MIDI recording called **step sequencing** or step entry. This technique offers the producer the option to enter any note or rest value asynchronously. This is particularly useful for crafting passages that are impossible to perform, and it also aids in the intentional creation of mechanical-sounding parts, which may be desirable in certain electronic dance music (EDM) contexts, for example. Step entry tools allow the composer to select a desired rhythmic value and, without needing to perform at any particular moment, play the desired pitch on a MIDI keyboard controller. The pitch is then combined with the designated rhythmic value to form an event that appears within the selected track, and the step entry tool advances to the next *step* in time, which is based on the previous rhythmic value. Figure 6.13 demonstrates how the first quarter note A4 from "The Black Pearl" theme would be "stepped in" using Digital Performer 9's Step Record function. Once the first quarter note is entered, the step editor would advance to the second beat of the first bar, at which point the producer would leave the quarter note rhythmic value selected and press the *step* button two times to create two quarter rests.

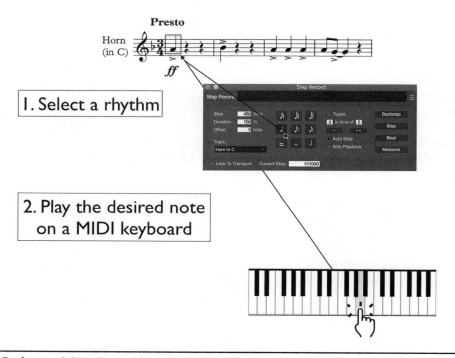

Fig. 6.13   Digital Performer 9 Step Record function for the "Black Pearl" theme's first bar

Velocity and Dynamics

Logic Pro X additionally offers dynamic control over each note entry within the step editor. In a DAW, dynamics are achieved by adjusting the **velocity** levels of MIDI events. For example, since *mf* roughly translates to "half loud" or "medium loud," Logic sets the velocity level to 80 within the continuous controller range from 0 to 127 that was addressed at the beginning of this book. (In the Introduction, you were familiarized with continuous controller messages, which are numbered 0 through 127. MIDI interaction is based on a scale of 128 possible degrees, allowing for a wide range of variable control. This data can be manipulated in a number of ways, which will be further explored in Chapter 8.) In most DAW step editors, velocity is recorded based on the speed at which a MIDI controller's keys are depressed.

Sequencing with a Pencil Tool

If a MIDI controller isn't available, or if a producer prefers to compose with a mouse, a **pencil tool** is another useful alternative that is one of a series of editing devices included in every DAW. Among the pencil tool's many features is the ability to add MIDI events to a region. Once a region has been created, a composer can click directly into the piano roll editor while the pencil tool is selected and the desired note will appear, based on the location of the cursor in relation to both the rhythmic grid and the rotated keyboard on the left hand side of the window. "Penciling in" music is desirable for producers who may be less efficient keyboard players or for those who opt for a slower-paced composition process (which often affords a more detailed experience). The pencil tool is also very useful during the editing phase, when a producer may decide to add notes (such as embellishments) to an already recorded, stepped-in, or penciled-in series of MIDI events.

Quantization

Whatever entry method is used, a certain degree of editing is almost always required, making **quantization** one of the most valuable functions of a DAW. Quantizing a passage of MIDI events **snaps** (or pulls) the starting points of rhythmically inaccurate notes to the closest rhythmic value selected in the quantization settings. For example, if eighth notes were set as the rhythmic value in the quantization settings, all selected MIDI events would be pulled to begin on the closest eighth note location within the grid. In most musical situations, a sixteenth note setting will suffice, but every circumstance warrants its own rationale. It is common for composers to use a setting based on the shortest rhythmic value of a certain passage, which ensures that every intended rhythm can be recreated via quantization. Setting the quantization value "too short" can lessen the impact of the editing process, as certain incorrect rhythms will remain incorrect. For example, if you performed a note within a passage one thirty-second note behind an intended downbeat and then set the quantization value to a thirty-second note while editing, there would be no change in the incorrect note's position. Conversely, setting the value "too long" can overedit your performance, snapping correctly sequenced rhythms to incorrect nearby grid positions of larger values (see Figure 6.14).

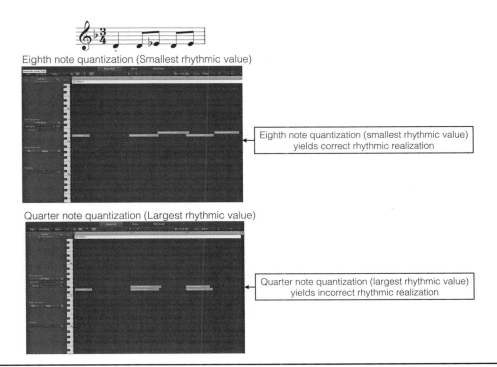

Fig. 6.14 Logic Pro X quantization value comparison

Swing Quantization

Composers often desire a less mechanical rhythmic feel and make use of a special type of quantization to create such an effect. **Swing quantization** works by quantizing every other instance of a selected rhythmic value ahead or behind (typically behind) its position in a standard duple division by a fixed amount, giving a performance a looser quality that can emulate the swing feel discussed in Chapter 2. The amount by which every second rhythm is offset is determined by a swing percent calibration. There are two main ways in which DAWs approach this, but in all cases, a setting of 100% (or "full swing") quantizes each pair of notes to the first and third positions within a triplet. The first method, which uses a 50%–100% scale, is based on the idea that a *straight* (pure duple) division possesses 50% of the duration of the next-largest rhythmic value. To create a swing feel, a percentage greater than 50 is assigned, causing the first of two division notes to last longer while pushing back the second. To streamline the quantization process, some DAWs (e.g., Logic Pro X) offer a series of preset swing options, each at a fixed percentage commonly used by producers. The standard range of swing percent calibration is between 50% and 75%, but it is up to the ear of the composer to decide how high or low any percentage is set. Other DAWs (e.g., Cubase) use a second method that features a 0%–100% scale, with "0% swing" translating to a straight or pure duple division while maintaining the "100% swing" threshold as a pure triple division. While all DAWs offer eighth and sixteenth note swing options, some, like Digital Performer 9, offer swing control at any rhythmic level. It is typical for hip-hop, jazz, and R&B performances, for example, to feature rhythms that fall between pure duple and pure triple divisions. Swing quantization allows for such passages to be edited without removing the distinguishing rhythmic flexibilities that make these styles distinct. For genres like techno, swing quantization may not create the desired sound a composer is looking for.

Quantization Amount

DAWs allow the user to vary the amount or strength of quantization to help maintain a more human quality in an edited piece of music. Most DAWs offer a scale ranging from 0 (un-quantized) to 100 (fully quantized). Figure 6.15 displays a passage from "The Black Pearl" that was "played in" with a MIDI controller. The piano roll window on top displays the original performance, while the other two windows below include varying degrees of quantization strength applied to the same passage.

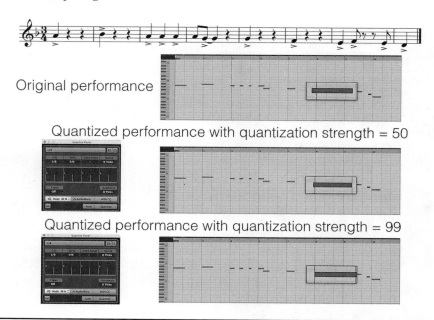

Fig. 6.15 Comparison between unquantized and quantized performances featuring different quantization strengths in Cubase Pro

Although quantization is one of the DAW's most powerful and useful features, it is a batch-editing tool that can omit smaller details and nuances. Selecting the quantization type based on a passage's smallest rhythmic value, the amount of quantization strength, and the swing strength (if needed) allows you to begin the rhythmic editing process in a MIDI context; however, once this is completed, you will typically need to tailor a passage at a more detailed level.

Editing MIDI

Most DAWs feature additional quantization options that allow you to change the event durations within an entire passage to a single value. There are certain situations where this feature is useful; for example, when editing a bass line that needs to consist solely of eighth notes in a driving rock feel. The practicality of such an operation is limited, though, as most musical phrases are rhythmically varied. In many cases, then, producers choose to alter the lengths of individual notes manually within a piano roll editor. There are a number of tools available in workstations that are designed to aid such an editing process. The **pointer tool** is perhaps the most useful, as it affords the composer the ability to move individual MIDI events—or groups of selected events—up or down (changing pitch) as well as left or right (altering their rhythmic positions within the grid). This feature is demonstrated in Figure 6.16.

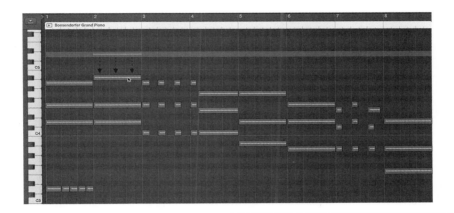

Fig. 6.16 Changing the pitch of a note using the pointer tool in Logic Pro X

The pointer tool additionally allows the composer to change the length of MIDI events. In most DAWs, hovering over the end of a note with the cursor temporarily changes the pointer tool into a note length–changing tool, which allows for adjustments to be made to the rhythmic value of the event by selecting its right border and moving the cursor right (to extend) or left (to truncate). In Digital Performer 9, this note length–changing tool is called the hand tool (see Figure 6.17).

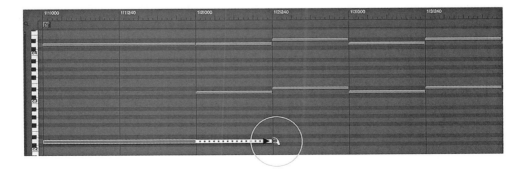

Fig. 6.17 Extending a MIDI event in Digital Performer 9 using the hand tool

Note that if a group of MIDI events is selected, alterations made to one event will affect all others in the group by the same factor. For example, if a quarter note and an eighth note are highlighted, and the user then truncates the quarter note by a sixteenth note value (yielding a dotted eighth note), the eighth note will be similarly shortened to a sixteenth note (see Figure 6.18).

Selecting a group of MIDI events and editing one event

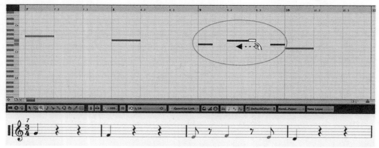

Net effect: entire group of events is edited by same factor

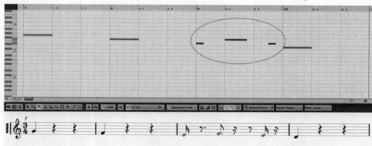

Fig. 6.18   Truncating a group of MIDI events in Cubase Pro

Beyond pitch and duration, there are many other MIDI parameters that can be manipulated within the DAW, including velocity and patch changes. These topics will be explored beginning in Chapter 8.

RHYTHM AND AUDIO

Now that you've explored the basic ways in which rhythm is approached in the form of MIDI, we move to some common DAW features that relate to the manipulation of audio from a rhythmic standpoint. It is important to revisit the fact that MIDI is not audio; rather, it is a protocol involved in the communication of events that are far easier to edit than audio waveforms. As the capabilities of computers continually expand, however, so do the options available within workstations to edit components of audio files.

AUDIO QUANTIZATION

Quantizing audio is a similar process to quantizing MIDI, but it requires a few additional steps, as audio files are not segmented neatly into discrete events that are readily quantized. As mentioned previously, MIDI quantization works by pulling the starting points of selected MIDI events to the closest rhythmic value chosen in the quantization settings.

This is relatively easy to accomplish, as MIDI events are viewed in a variety of DAW windows as separate entities that may be manipulated individually or in groups (as is the case when one selects an entire MIDI region before selecting a specific quantization option). If, for example, you were to record a MIDI snare drum pattern into a DAW, the snare's rhythms would be translated directly to MIDI events, with the left border of each event representing a point of rhythmic initiation whose position could be quickly altered via quantization functions. If, however, you were to record the same musical phrase with an acoustic snare drum, a single, continuous audio stream would result, with rhythmic segmentation visible only via relative spikes in the waveform that correspond to the louder moments of the passage. These spikes are visual representations of the sudden, temporary interruptions in output level that take place at the beginning of waveforms (i.e., transitory events) that are referred to as **transients**. The **attack** or starting point of a sound—such as the initial strike of a snare drum—is therefore directly related to the transient of a waveform. Audio files are filled with transients that correspond to rhythms being performed, making the quantization of audio a possibility—but only after the waveforms are segmented into discrete units in a manner similar to MIDI events.

Transient Analysis

Once an audio file has been recorded or imported into a DAW, an analysis of its transient locations (or **transient analysis**) is needed to inform the computer of the specific moments that are to be adjusted during quantization. Figure 6.19 shows a waveform in Logic Pro X's Audio File Editor before and after the Transient Edit mode—the proprietary utility for analyzing waveforms—has been activated.

Logic Pro X's Audio File Editor **before** the activation of Transient Edit Mode

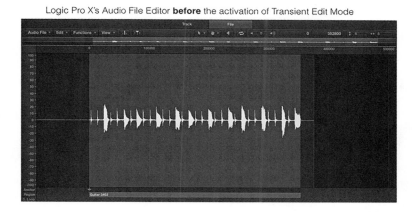

Logic Pro X's Audio File Editor **after** the activation of Transient Edit Mode

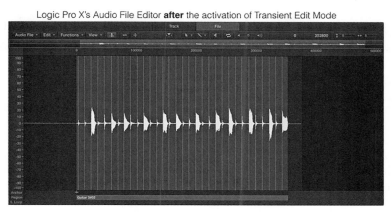

Fig. 6.19 Logic Pro X Audio File Editor before and after the activation of Transient Edit mode

After the transients have been analyzed, modifications or corrections can be made to the newly added transient markers—the lines running vertically through the waveform marking the position of each transient—by clicking on them and moving them left or right. Once you are satisfied that the transient markers are in the correct places, the quantization process may begin. Although it is possible to skip this process in most programs and allow the DAW to automatically quantize before inspecting the transients the program has selected, it is wise to make sure the software has chosen the exact transients you desire to quantize and make adjustments accordingly.

Each DAW has a slightly different approach to audio quantization, but the results are typically the same. Similar to MIDI quantization, the composer selects a rhythmic value, and the DAW "snaps" the selected transients to the closest position reflecting that value within the grid. In Logic Pro X, quantization occurs when **Flex mode** is activated. In Pro Tools 11, **Elastic Audio** must be selected; otherwise, the initial transient of a waveform will be the only attack quantized while its other transients are ignored. In Cubase Pro, the audio quantization is carried out via the **Audio Warp** function. Regardless of the specific brand of software or proprietary function name involved, however, audio quantization accomplishes a singular goal: it allows the producer to program a computer to analyze the transient attacks of inaccurate rhythmic performances and adjust or correct them.

Tempo Matching

Most DAWs also have the ability to alter the tempo of an audio file to match the tempo of a project. This **tempo matching** function is especially useful for hip-hop and EDM producers, who often build tracks around previously recorded parts (which may not be at a desired tempo). In Logic Pro X, a waveform will automatically conform to a change in the project's tempo as long as the **Follow Tempo** box is checked within the Inspector window (see Figure 6.20).

Fig. 6.20   The Follow Tempo feature in Logic Pro X

The ability to record and edit both MIDI events and audio files within a DAW provides composers with an abundance of control over the rhythmic parameters of a project. Producers have the ability to correct and shape rhythmic performances and even change their tempi to correspond with the tempo of a given project. The arsenal of rhythmic editing options continues to expand as home computers become more and more powerful, yet quantization remains at the heart of a DAW's power.

SUMMARY OF TERMS FROM CHAPTER 6

transport control window
grid
regions
events
ticks
pulses per quarter
sequencing
tracks
step sequencing

velocity
pencil tool
quantization
swing quantization
MIDI quantization
audio quantization
snap
pointer tool
transient

attack
transient analysis
Flex mode
Elastic Audio
Audio Warp
tempo matching
Follow Tempo

CHAPTER 6—EXERCISES

Use the image below of Logic Pro X's Custom Control Bar to answer the first three questions. Provide your answers in the available space below each question.

1. What is the tempo of the project currently set to?

2. What time signature is the project currently set to?

3. What rhythmic resolution will the grid be set to in the piano roll editor?

True or False. Circle "true" for each statement below that is true. Circle "false" for each false statement.

4. MIDI regions house audio events.

   True   False

5. The only way to create an anacrusis in a project is to think of bar 1 as measure 0 and mentally offset everything by one measure.

   True   False

6. Altering MIDI events in a piano roll editor will change how they appear in a Score Editor.

   True   False

7. An event list editor allows you to control rhythm and pitch only.

   True   False

8. Logic Pro X has a default setting of 960ppq.

   True   False

9. Velocity is also recorded when entering in MIDI information with a step editor.

   True   False

10. Using a quantization setting larger than a passage's smallest rhythmic value will cause some notes to snap to incorrect positions.

    True   False

11. In the space provided, briefly define a transient using audio terminology.

12. In the space provided, briefly describe why transient analysis is an important step in the process of audio quantization.

13. In the space provided, briefly describe what Flex mode, Elastic Audio, and Audio Warp are.

14. In the space provided, briefly describe why tempo matching features are attractive to some hip-hop and EDM artists.

15. In the space provided, briefly describe why Elastic Audio should be selected before quantizing audio in Pro Tools 11.

Circle the following items found within the Logic Pro X Main View image below. Then, use the spaces provided to describe each item.

16. MIDI region

17. Audio track

Use the notated example of Richard Wagner's "Ride of the Valkryies" theme below to answer the following three questions. Provide your answers in the available space below each question.

18. If the above passage were to be performed into a DAW with a MIDI controller, describe why a quantization setting of an eighth note would be a poor choice.

19. What tempo should be entered into the DAW's transport control window for this passage?

20. How many measures should exist within a MIDI region dedicated to the above passage if a composer wanted to edit it using a notation editor?

Chapter 7
Introduction to Acoustics

The arts of orchestration and equalization may at first appear to be distantly related topics, but an experienced producer will consider the two to be close relatives. This chapter explores the connections between orchestration and equalization forged by the scientific properties of sound. An understanding of acoustics will help you avoid the "muddiness" found in poorer orchestrations that in turn affects the overall effectiveness of a final mix. Additionally, this chapter introduces simple equalization processes that can enhance the clarity of a project.

THE OVERTONE SERIES

In Chapter 5, you were introduced to the idea that vibrating bodies send out pressure waves that we perceive as sound. To take this concept further, when a pitched instrument vibrates, a phenomenon known as the **overtone series** is heard, which is a succession of simultaneously sounding tones stemming from the **fundamental** pitch (lowestsounding tone). On a stringed instrument, the full length of the string vibrating back and forth produces a fundamental tone. The sounding overtones—also called **harmonics**—above the fundamental are separately vibrating fractional divisions of the full length of the string. If the vibrating source produces frequencies that are not multiples of the fundamental, the sound is often perceived as noise. Many non-pitched percussion instruments fall into this category of vibrating sources. Harmonics above pitched instruments are multiples of the fundamental pitch's frequency, which become gradually more difficult to audibly discern the higher in the series you go. The note A1, for example, has a frequency of 55Hz. The first seven multiples (harmonics) of 55Hz (A1) include 110Hz (A2), 165Hz (E3), 220Hz (A3), 275Hz (C#4), 330Hz (E4), 385Hz (G4), and 440Hz (A4). Figure 7.1 illustrates the overtone series above the fundamental pitch C2. The numbers next to each note indicate a specific harmonic above the fundamental.

Fig. 7.1 **The overtone series above C2**

Note that some of the frequencies found within the overtone series don't conform exactly to the Western tuning system. The **well-tempered** tuning system divides each octave into 12 equal parts, which is slightly out of tune with some of the harmonics present in the overtone series. A classification system exists to help illustrate the degree of "sharpness" or "flatness" of harmonics compared to their positions within the well-tempered system of tuning. This method further divides each semitone into 100 equal parts known as **cents**, allowing for a more specific description of a pitch's intonation based on a scale of 100. Figure 7.2 provides the overtone series from the previous diagram and adds the specific degree of sharpness or flatness of each harmonic related to its closest pitch in the well-tempered system.

Harmonic	1 (Fundamental)	2	3	4	5	6	7	8	9	10	11	12	13	14	15	16
Approximate pitch locations on the staff	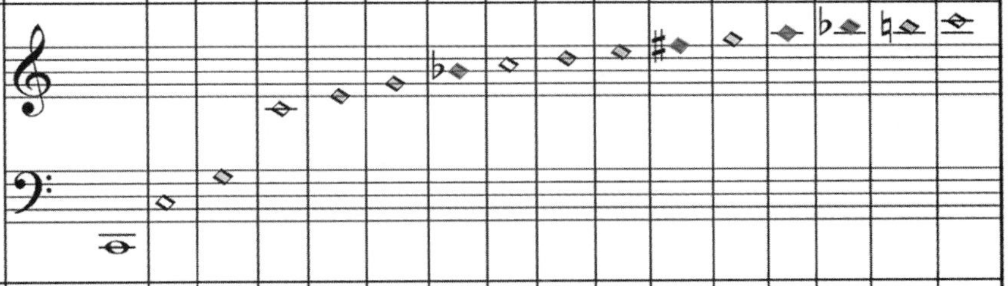															
Degree of sharpness/flatness (in cents)	0	0	+2	0	-14	+2	-31	0	+4	-14	-49	+2	+41	-32	-12	0
Well-Tempered Pitch in Hertz	65.4	130.8	196.00	261.6	329.6	392.00	466.16	523.2	587.33	659.26	739.99	783.99	880	932.33	987.77	1046.5
Actual Frequency in Hertz	65.4	130.8	196.2	261.6	327	392.4	457.8	523.2	588.6	654	719.4	784.8	850.2	915.6	981	1046.4

Fig. 7.2 **Intonation differences between well-tempered pitches and the harmonics of C2**

Although slight discrepancies exist between naturally occurring overtones and the pitches of the well-tempered tuning system, the system has been the standard in Western music for centuries, and it affords each note within an octave equal weight. Regardless of the tuning system used, though, some argue that the basis for Western music may be found within the first few harmonics of the overtone series.

OVERTONES AS THE BASIS OF WESTERN TONALITY

The phenomenon of the overtone series exists above any fundamental pitch. The first six harmonics form a major triad, which some consider to be the basis of the Western tonal system. Although this theory is somewhat controversial and beyond the scope of this book, it is important to recognize that certain harmonic structures do in fact exist within a single pitch. As well, the specific distribution of each harmonic within the overtone series can serve as a natural, acoustic example of how to orchestrate any style of music. Figure 7.3 again references the fundamental C2, and demonstrates that the first six harmonics of any fundamental exist within that fundamental's major scale; furthermore, the fourth, fifth, and sixth harmonics create a major triad whose root is the fundamental.

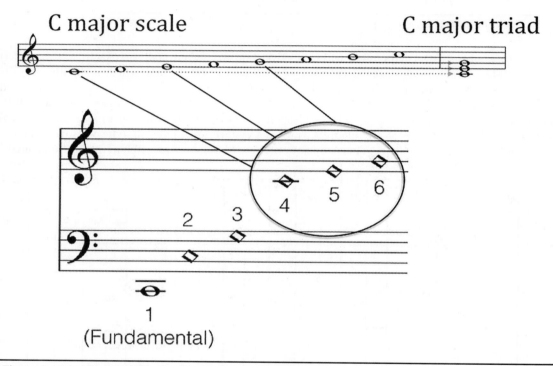

Fig. 7.3 **The major triad found within the first six harmonics of a pitch**

TIMBRE

Timbre, or tone color, is a unique set of characteristics that differentiates the sound one instrument makes from another. The reason you are able to determine when a clarinet is playing versus a marimba, for example, has to do with two main components: the sound's unique amplitude envelope and the distinct array of excited harmonics that are created above each sounding fundamental.

ADSR

An **amplitude envelope** is a way of describing how a sound unfolds over time from its first transient to the point at which it fades out. The attack (A) is the time it takes for a sound to climb to its highest amplitude. After the initial amplitude spike, a varying degree of decay takes place until the sound reaches a period of steadiness or sustain (S), where the amplitude doesn't change very much. Release (R) is the time it takes for a sound to fade out. Figure 7.4 demonstrates the difference in **ADSR** between a recorded electric guitar waveform and a recorded string pad waveform. Note that the electric guitar has a quicker attack than the string pad, but less of a sustained amplitude after the decay period. These are key features that help the ear identify the instrument that is being performed.

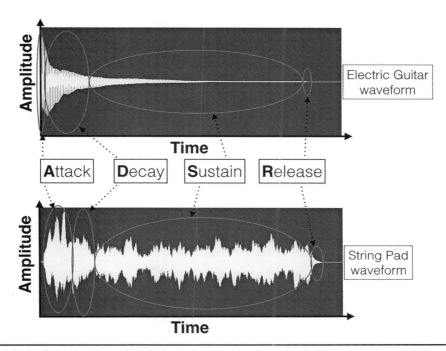

Fig. 7.4 ADSR profiles of an electric guitar and a string pad

The harmonic series additionally provides information that helps listeners distinguish between different instruments. The physical makeup of a particular instrument—as well as the manner in which it is performed—causes certain overtones to be emphasized, helping the ear identify the instrument's timbre. A bowed violin, for example, produces pitch via the friction caused by dragging a bow across a string that in turn creates vibrations that oscillate through a wooden body. This excites different overtones than a piano does when playing the same pitch, as the piano produces sound when a key is depressed and a hammer strikes a steel string that vibrates inside a larger wooden body. Figure 7.5 demonstrates such overtone differences by comparing three different software patches (instruments). Each patch has been programmed to perform at a velocity setting of 80, which equates to a relative dynamic level of *mf*. Each instrument's sonic signature is evaluated by a Waves PAZ frequency **spectrum analyzer**, which is a tool that shows the exact frequencies that are excited during playback along with the decibel levels for each frequency. The graph below the spectrum analyzers provides the following information: each harmonic above the fundamental C4, the associated pitch name, the nearest well-tempered frequency, and the actual frequency that is heard. The shaded decibel levels refer to lower dB levels relative to the other two instruments in the graph. Note that it is the differences in the harmonics' dB levels that create each instrument's unique timbral qualities.

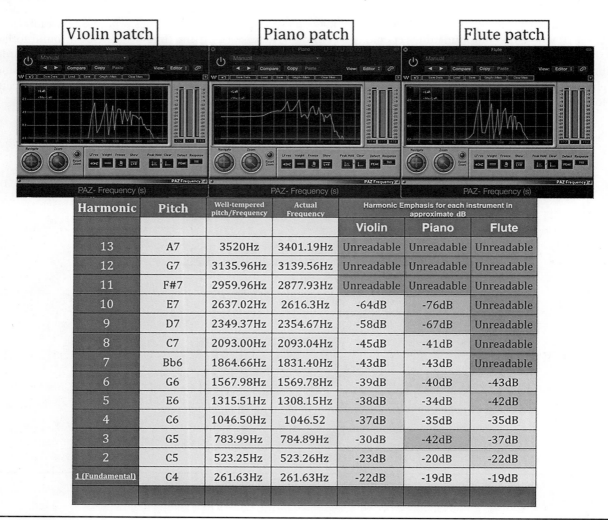

Harmonic	Pitch	Well-tempered pitch/Frequency	Actual Frequency	Harmonic Emphasis for each instrument in approximate dB		
				Violin	Piano	Flute
13	A7	3520Hz	3401.19Hz	Unreadable	Unreadable	Unreadable
12	G7	3135.96Hz	3139.56Hz	Unreadable	Unreadable	Unreadable
11	F#7	2959.96Hz	2877.93Hz	Unreadable	Unreadable	Unreadable
10	E7	2637.02Hz	2616.3Hz	-64dB	-76dB	Unreadable
9	D7	2349.37Hz	2354.67Hz	-58dB	-67dB	Unreadable
8	C7	2093.00Hz	2093.04Hz	-45dB	-41dB	Unreadable
7	Bb6	1864.66Hz	1831.40Hz	-43dB	-43dB	Unreadable
6	G6	1567.98Hz	1569.78Hz	-39dB	-40dB	-43dB
5	E6	1315.51Hz	1308.15Hz	-38dB	-34dB	-42dB
4	C6	1046.50Hz	1046.52	-37dB	-35dB	-35dB
3	G5	783.99Hz	784.89Hz	-30dB	-42dB	-37dB
2	C5	523.25Hz	523.26Hz	-23dB	-20dB	-22dB
1 (Fundamental)	C4	261.63Hz	261.63Hz	-22dB	-19dB	-19dB

Fig. 7.5   Timbre analysis

Since the timbre of any instrument is determined by its unique array of frequencies that are excited above performed fundamentals, many distinctive colors may be achieved by simultaneously performing the same pitch on two or more different instruments. By doubling (or layering) wind and string instruments on the same pitch, for example, a rounder, smoother sound is created. With an understanding of the overtone series, a composer can achieve an even richer, fuller sound in this example simply by raising the winds up an octave from the strings, allowing the overtone series of each instrument to vibrate without the clutter that results from too many instruments sharing a common fundamental. While you will explore orchestration in more depth in Chapter 12, an understanding of the overtone series will arm you with a sufficient, common-sense approach to building a musical project from the ground up that can help you avoid problematic frequency clashes.

LOW INTERVAL LIMIT

Some of the most common frequency clashes occur when composers use smaller harmonic intervals in the lower registers. If a performer played a melodic interval of a minor second using the notes C2 and C#2, for example, the frequencies 65.41Hz (C2) and 69.30Hz (C#2) would sound one after the other. The difference in frequency between both pitches is only 3.89 cycles—or vibrations—per second. When played harmonically, the human ear has difficulty identifying the notes separately and the consequence is a "muddy" texture. Compare that with the frequencies of the harmonic minor second between the notes C4 (261.63) and C#4 (277.18). The frequency difference in this case is 15.55 cycles per second, which creates a much clearer quality. Thus, greater distances of frequencies between simultaneously sounding pitches in low registers result in clearer sonorities. Since every sounding fundamental produces an overtone series above itself, care must be taken to ensure that enough space is provided between fundamentals of lower frequency to avoid clashes not only among fundamental frequencies cycling at similar speeds, but among all of the harmonics above them. Put differently, smaller harmonic intervals should be reserved for the middle and high registers to avoid murky textures. Figure 7.6 indicates the lowest useful register for each simple harmonic interval (the **low interval limit**); placing each interval in a lower frequency range than the interval limit provided in the figure tends to result in clashing tones or textural "muddiness." Notice that the P5 can be placed in the lowest register of all of the intervals indicated. Since it is the second interval heard in the overtone series, the P5 supplies composers with a reinforced foundation above which to build vibrant, rich-sounding harmonic structures. It is important to note that there are many examples of great compositions that deviate from the guidelines given in Figure 7.6; these guidelines do, however, offer a general strategy that is useful for beginning composers to consider.

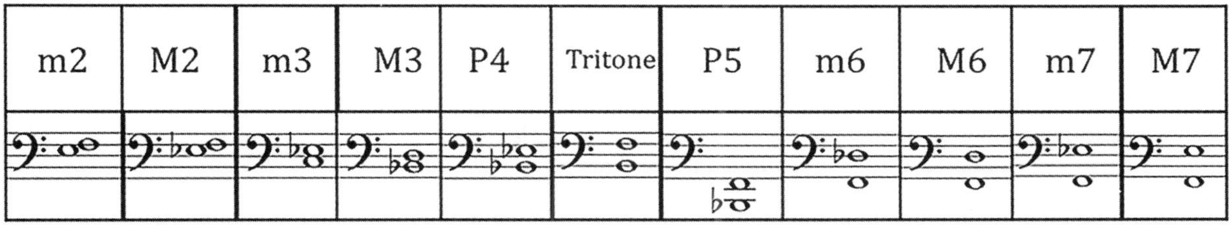

Fig. 7.6   Low interval limit chart

The best solution when orchestrating music is to mimic the natural intervallic distribution found within the overtone series as closely as possible. Recall that there are no intervals smaller than a minor third between successive overtones until the seventh and eighth harmonics are reached; thus, harmonic m3s tend to appear higher in chord voicings, rather far from the fundamental of the bass. Additionally, the first interval found between a fundamental and its second harmonic is a perfect octave. When orchestrating, it is therefore common for composers to create an interval of an octave between the lowest and second-lowest pitch, reinforcing the second harmonic above the fundamental. Figure 7.7 demonstrates this stock orchestration technique with a bar from Gustov Holst's "Mars" movement from his famous suite for orchestra, *The Planets*. To the left is a bar of the full score as it sounds, followed by a piano reduction of all of the parts in the center. To the right of the reduction, the first six harmonics above the fundamental G1 are provided.

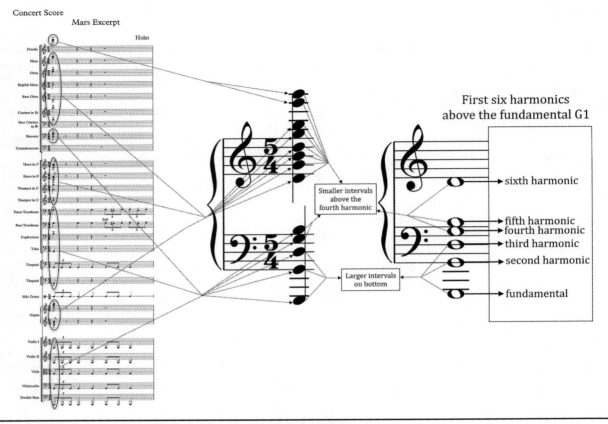

Fig. 7.7　**Score reduction from Holst's "Mars" movement from *The Planets***

Many things can be learned from studying scores for full orchestra such as the one provided in this example. Not only will you gain insight into what has proven successful for other composers in the orchestral medium, you can also take note of the parts of compositions composers choose to layer and identify the effects produced by such layering choices. Studying scores from a variety of genres can additionally help you identify style-specific orchestration techniques. Most techno tracks, for example, layer basses, melodic lines, and other components of a piece to create thick, dense textures. Layering can create rich, intense qualities, but the biggest benefit is that of tone color. As noted earlier, a single instrument will provide its own amplitude envelope and excite a specific array of harmonics above every performed fundamental. When layering, you must consider this as well as the envelope and the excited harmonics of all instruments being considered for doubling. An understanding of the overtone series will also help you appropriately place harmonic intervals where they sound the most balanced and clear. Though your ear should always guide your final decisions as a producer, regardless of any theoretical concepts or guidelines, a solid comprehension of acoustics provides a foundation upon which to build clear ideas. There are, however, inevitable situations wherein you will be forced to further shape an arrangement after it has been orchestrated, performed, and recorded. One of the primary ways in which producers accomplish such shaping is with equalization.

EQUALIZATION

There are three main areas into which the sonic spectrum is categorized: low (20Hz to 500Hz), mid (500Hz to 5kHz), and high (5kHz to 20kHz). Further subcategories will be explored later in this chapter. An equalizer (or EQ) is a tool that **boosts** or **attenuates** (cuts) certain frequencies of an audio signal, affording the producer important control over each of these parameters. **Equalization** is thus the act of shaping a signal by attenuating and/or boosting frequencies, which is typically done to help the signal sit comfortably within a mix.

FIXED EQ

Most car and home stereo systems have at least a fixed equalizer, which is the most basic equalizer. You'll also often see some form of a fixed EQ on certain pieces of music equipment such as amplifiers and mixing boards. Typically, a **fixed EQ** has three knobs that modify high, mid, and low frequencies; these are generally used for broad changes in sound rather than fine-tuning. Each knob is assigned a certain frequency range, allowing the producer control over the boosting or attenuation of that specific sonic spectrum. The **bandwidth** or range of frequencies controlled by each knob is normally quite large in EQs of this type, which is why the effects created by adjustments within fixed EQs are more widespread and less nuanced. The low and high knobs work like "shelving EQs." A low knob is a **high pass shelf** EQ that does not affect any frequencies above a designated cutoff point (instead boosting/cutting frequencies below the cutoff point), whereas a high knob works like a **low pass shelf** EQ, leaving frequencies below a designated cutoff point unaffected. Using high and low pass equalization is an excellent way for producers to attenuate undesirable noise; this will be explored further in Chapters 13 and 14. The center knob in a fixed EQ works like a **peak or bell curve EQ**, which targets frequencies falling within a specific range. Since the bandwidth of a fixed EQ is so large, the mid knob often alters some frequencies that fall within the ranges that are also manipulated by the low and high knobs. Common target frequency ranges for each knob of a fixed EQ are 80Hz, 2.5kHz, and 12kHz. Figure 7.8 demonstrates an audio signal that has been run through a fixed equalizer with the low knob attenuating all frequencies under 80Hz, the mid knob boosting all frequencies around 2.5kHz, and the high knob boosting all frequencies above 12kHz. Take note of how the mid-frequency boost is also affecting areas of both high and low frequencies due to the high bandwidth of the EQ.

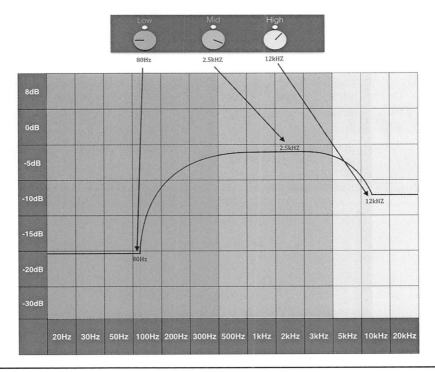

Fig. 7.8   A fixed EQ attenuating lows while boosting mids and highs

GRAPHIC EQ

Graphic equalizers are often found in higher-end car and home stereo systems, as they offer more control over a larger number of frequencies. In the studio environment, this is the simplest form of equalization, which works by displaying multiple sliders that control the boosting or attenuation of specific frequencies. As in fixed equalizers, the bandwidth affected by each adjustment cannot be altered. As a result, many graphic EQs offer a large number of sliders, affording command over a greater amount of frequency "bands." Figure 7.9 shows Apple's AUGraphicEQ plugin, which offers both 10-band and 31-band equalization settings. Compare Figure 7.8 with Figure 7.9, which involve boosting and attenuating the same frequencies. Notice how the graphic EQ allows the producer to boost 2.5kHz without altering the surrounding frequencies to the same extent as the fixed EQ, which has a larger bandwidth fixed to each control mechanism.

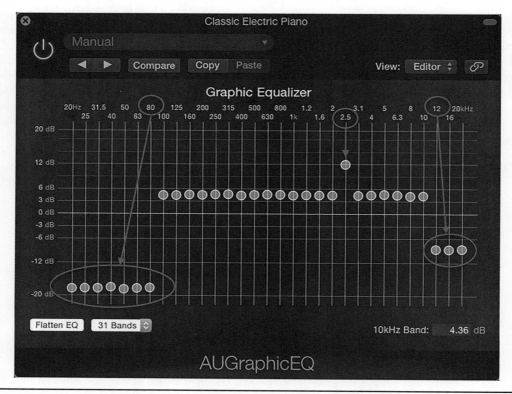

Fig. 7.9   Apple's AUGraphicEQ attenuating lows while boosting mids and highs

PARAMETRIC EQ

Arguably the most powerful equalizers available are **parametric EQs**, as they offer the most control over the greatest number of parameters. As mentioned previously, the bandwidth of each control mechanism in a fixed or graphic equalizer is set to alter a fixed spectrum of frequencies. Parametric equalizers additionally give the producer control over the bandwidth by altering the **Q factor**, or quality factor. The Q factor is the ratio of the core frequency—the frequency in focus—to bandwidth. By lowering the Q, a producer expands the bandwidth of affected frequencies.

Raising the Q does the opposite. Thus, lower Q settings relate to broader adjustments of various frequencies, while higher Q settings relate to smaller, more precise alterations. Figure 7.10 demonstrates both high and low Q settings in the Waves REQ6 parametric equalizer.

 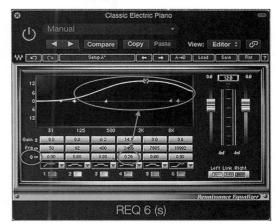

Higher Q setting = narrower
bandwidth

Lower Q setting = wider
bandwidth

Fig. 7.10 Waves REQ6 High and Low Q Factor

Since most parametric EQs come with multiple bands, the center frequencies are normally altered using peak or bell curves, while the low frequency (far left) and high frequency (far right) bands are adjusted with shelving curves. Figure 7.11 shows the Waves REQ6 again, this time calibrated to attenuate and boost the same frequencies as before with the fixed EQ from Figure 7.8 and the graphic EQ from Figure 7.9.

Fig. 7.11 Waves REQ4 parametric EQ

To summarize, the fixed EQ allows for quick, broad changes. Since there isn't any control over the Q factor, the center (mid) knob will alter frequencies outside of what may be desired. The graphic EQ affords a greater degree of control by giving the producer the ability to adjust multiple sliders, with each fixed to a certain frequency; however, this still does not offer any control over the bandwidth that each fader controls. The parametric equalizer provides the same multiband functionality as the graphic EQ while adding the ability to widen or narrow the bandwidth of targeted frequencies. Parametric equalizers are therefore the most common EQs used by most producers. The ability to high- and low-pass filter as well as boost or attenuate certain frequencies gives the composer a great deal of flexibility.

THE OVERTONE SERIES AND EQUALIZATION

Since every sounding fundamental also creates a series of overtones above it, care must be taken during the equalization process. The bass guitar provides a good example of how to use the overtone series in tandem with equalization, as it commonly plays the lowest-sounding pitched fundamental. Although five-string basses and altered tuning can produce lower pitches (and many performers play much higher notes), most bass guitar fundamental tones exist between 43.65Hz (E1) and 130.81Hz (C3). By applying a high-pass filter at around 40Hz to 60Hz, the bass often begins to sound clearer, as the low-end "rumble" around the fundamental is attenuated. The overtones of a bass guitar's signal are so complex that even an attenuated fundamental will still be recognized by the human mind. Sometimes, producers will boost the frequencies between 500Hz and 1kHz, since this is where many of the first few harmonics are located. If a bass is perceived as "dull" within a mix, this generally helps to enliven its sound. It is important to note that there are no automatic settings that will work on every mix, however; the ear of the producer will always need to guide the final decision. Figure 7.12 represents a filtered bass signal. The image on the top of the diagram is a bass signal run through the Waves PAZ frequency spectrum analyzer. Take note of the shape that the bass signal creates before any processing occurs. Directly below the "clean" signal analysis, the Waves REQ4 equalizer is shown, which has been adjusted to process the signal by applying a high-pass filter that attenuates everything below 53Hz as well as a bell curve boost to the 500Hz range with a wide Q setting. The bottom image is another frequency spectrum analyzer showing the post-processing changes that the equalizer has made to the original bass signal.

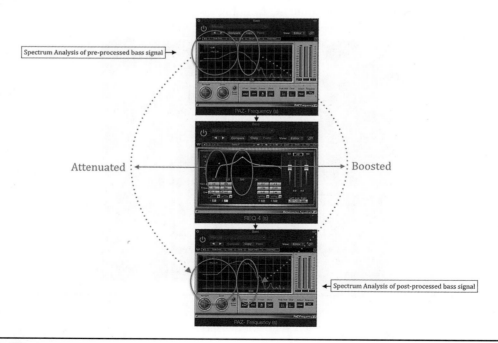

Fig. 7.12   Bass filtering

An understanding of the overtone series allows you to recognize how equalization can enhance the unique tone qualities of instruments. It can also help you organize the audio signals of multiple instruments by ensuring that they are not clashing with one another in certain frequency ranges. A kick drum and bass guitar share many common frequency ranges, for example, and often create "muddy" mixes if not dealt with properly. The full audio spectrum will be explored more in Chapter 15, but a general description is provided in Figure 7.13 that can aid in the visualization of its various frequency ranges and their associated instruments, pitch ranges, and staff regions. Importantly, most of the adjacent ranges in Figure 7.13 overlap slightly; furthermore, an instrument that is organized inside a particular register within the graph typically can produce pitches outside of that region.

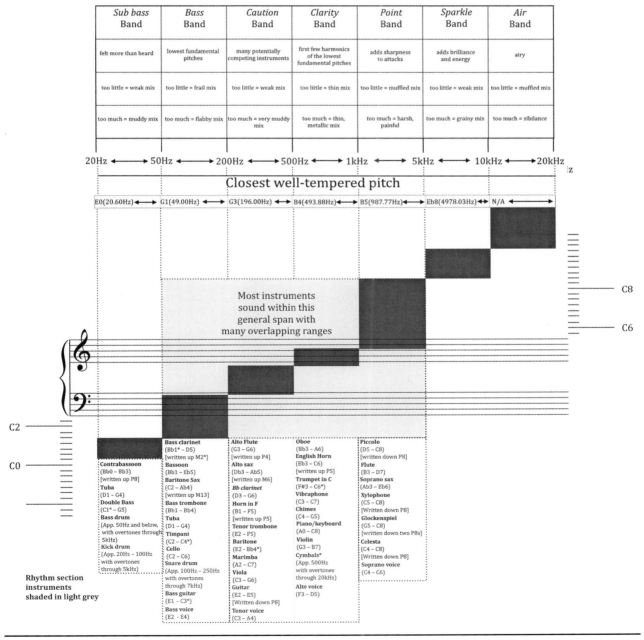

Fig. 7.13 General audio spectrum with instrument ranges

An understanding of the overtone series provides producers with a solid foundation for building clear, vibrant-sounding voicings and orchestrations as well as balanced and effective mixes. By following the natural intervallic structure of the harmonic series as closely as possible, composers can be confident that they have taken important steps to ensure that each member of a chord is in a position to sound its strongest. Assigning larger intervals to lower registers and smaller intervals to the mid and high registers additionally helps to avoid unclear, muddy-sounding sonorities. Sometimes, though, certain frequency clashes are unavoidable and equalization can be used in these instances to ensure a high-quality project. The arts of orchestration and equalization are therefore intertwined, and you should consider both processes during every step of the creative process.

SUMMARY OF TERMS FROM CHAPTER 7

overtone series	ADSR	bandwidth
fundamental	spectrum analyzer	high-pass shelf
harmonics	low interval limit	low-pass shelf
well-tempered (tuning)	boost	bell curve EQ
cents	attenuate	graphic EQ
timbre	equalization	parametric EQ
amplitude envelope	fixed EQ	Q factor

CHAPTER 7—EXERCISES

True or False. Circle "true" for each statement below that is true. Circle "false" for each false statement.

1. Overtones occur above any pitched fundamental.

    True   False

2. A major triad exists within the first three harmonics of the overtone series.

    True   False

3. Timbre is only determined by how loud an instrument is played.

    True   False

4. ADSR stands for attack, decay, sustain, and resonance.

    True   False

5. Every instrument will naturally emphasize the same frequencies above a shared fundamental.

    True   False

Multiple Choice. Circle the letter corresponding to the best choice for each question below.

6. Of the choices below, which is the lowest recommended note above which to form a harmonic minor second, in order to avoid the low interval limit?

   a. C2

   b. F2

   c. E2

   d. C1

7. Of the choices below, which is the lowest recommended note above which to form a harmonic major third, in order to avoid the low interval limit?

   a. B1

   b. B♭2

   c. A2

   d. G2

8. Of the choices below, which is the lowest recommended note above which to form a harmonic perfect fifth, in order to avoid the low interval limit?

   a. A1

   b. B♭1

   c. C1

   d. E♭1

9. The perfect octave and the perfect fifth are the two most commonly used harmonic intervals in the lower registers because:

   a. The left hand is generally reserved for supportive textures in piano music

   b. Perfect intervals work well in all registers

   c. Large intervals should be avoided in the higher registers

   d. They are the first two intervals found in the overtone series, occurring above any pitched fundamental

10. Layering can create rich, intense qualities, but the biggest benefit is that of:

    a. Tone color

    b. Volume

    c. Separation of parts

    d. Melodic integrity

11. An understanding of the overtone series will help you appropriately place harmonic intervals where they sound:

    a. The loudest

    b. The most balanced and clear

    c. Most dynamic in range

    d. Rhythmically appropriate

12. Using whole notes, stack the overtone series up to the twelfth harmonic above the given fundamentals in the grand staves below.

a. F2

c. D2

b. E♭3

13. Using whole notes, voice the following chords above the given notes in a way that best takes advantage of how the overtone series appears above each given fundamental.

a. Amin

b. B♭

14. Use the image below of the Waves REQ4 to answer the next three questions. Provide your answers in the available space below each question.

a. Is the circled area's Q factor setting high or low? How could the shape of the equalization curve give you this information?

b. Would a higher Q factor setting for the circled area affect the 500Hz range?

c. To alter the 8k range, would you raise or lower the Q setting for the circled area?

15. Use the image below of the audio spectrum with instrument ranges to answer the following two questions. Provide your answers in the available space below each question.

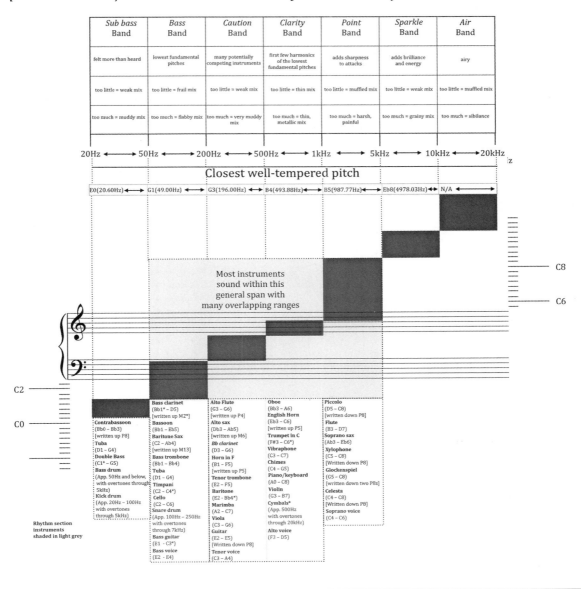

a.   Do a bass guitar and kick drum potentially share the same frequency range?

b.   A mix with too much energy in the 300Hz range would result in what kind of sound?

Chapter 8
Melodic Sequencing

Sequencing music involves capturing and managing of all the parts that combine to form the performance of a piece of music. The producer is therefore responsible for every detail of each part involved. Quantization and rhythmic manipulation were covered in Chapter 6 and represent the first step toward creating realistic performances. This chapter introduces virtual instruments as well as ways to control both volume and dynamics, which will prepare you to create a truer representation of a musical performance within a DAW.

VIRTUAL INSTRUMENTS

A **virtual instrument** is a piece of software that emulates the sound of an instrument and can be accessed as a plugin within a DAW. Virtual instruments work the same way as synthesizers, but are accessed via plugins rather than peripheral hardware. A plugin format (or software connector) is needed to transmit audio and MIDI data between a plugin and a host DAW, and there are a number of common formats. A **DSP** (Digital Signal Processor) plugin requires the use of a separate outboard interface for processing, whereas a **native plugin** uses the processor within a host computer. An example of a DSP plugin is Pro Tools's **TDM** (Time Division Multiplexing), which requires a separate, dedicated processor. The native version of TDM is called **RTAS** (Real Time Audio Suite), which pulls its power from a producer's computer. More recent versions of Pro Tools require a newer plugin format called **AAX** (Avid Audio eXtension), which is available in DSP and native plugin formats. Since modern computers are capable of handling far more processing than was the case in the past, native plugins have become more regularly used. Some popular native plugin formats include Apple's **AU** (Audio Units) and Steinberg's **VST** (Virtual Studio Technology), which work in all commonly used DAWs. Some plugins are designed to create effects like reverb, delay, etc., which will be explored more in Chapter 15. This chapter instead focuses on using virtual instrument plugins to create realistic-sounding melodic phrases.

Some virtual instruments are recreations of classic synthesizers, while others are **samplers** that play back recordings of actual sounds. Most virtual instruments are programmable on some level, yet the biggest benefit is that they allow one computer to access millions of sounds without having to connect to a single piece of hardware.

SYNTHESIZERS

An analog **synthesizer** is a piece of hardware that generates one of four types of sound waves: sine waves, square waves, sawtooth waves, and triangle waves. Each wave type is named by the shape that is created when run through an **oscilloscope**, which is a device used to graphically represent the frequency of an electronic signal over time. Figure 8.1 shows the four types of sound waves a synthesizer is capable of producing.

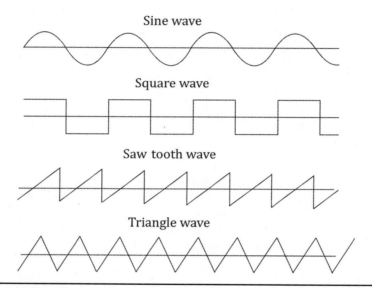

Sine wave

Square wave

Saw tooth wave

Triangle wave

Fig. 8.1   Four types of sound waves that synthesizers can generate

Each sound wave generator within a synthesizer is called an **oscillator**; there are typically multiple oscillators in a single synthesizer, allowing for combinations of different sound waves to sound simultaneously. The envelope (ADSR) of a wave can also be adjusted to allow for further sonic potential. In the early days of synthesizers, multiple oscillators could be connected via quarter-inch patch cables to create new sounds or **patches**. When referring to sounds within a synthesizer or sampler, the term "patch" is still used today. This type of synthesis is called **modular synthesis**, because multiple sound modules (oscillators) are connected to create patches. A digital synthesizer is a computer—typically with a keyboard attached to it—that generates and manipulates sound like an analog synthesizer, but with digital processing (binary representations of signal) used instead of analog circuitry. There are many different approaches to modern synthesis, and many are beyond the scope of this book; however, a general understanding of synthesizers as they pertain to basic production is valuable. Figure 8.2 provides an image of Logic Pro X's Retro Synth. The features here are common in all synthesizers, and thus need to be understood by any professional producer.

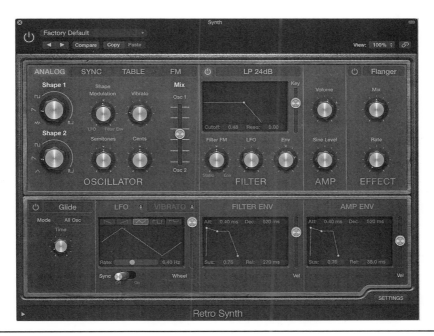

Fig. 8.2 Logic Pro X's Retro Synth

The top left portion of this synthesizer is dedicated to the oscillator, which is explored further in Figure 8.3. In this area of the synth, a composer can choose different sound wave options, tuning specifications, modulation shapes, and *vibrato* amounts, as well as adjust the mixture of the sound waves as they are combined together. An **LFO** is a low frequency oscillator, which is used to rhythmically modify the sound to create *tremolo* or *vibrato* effects. A **filter envelope** allows for some frequencies to be attenuated and others to pass through unaffected.

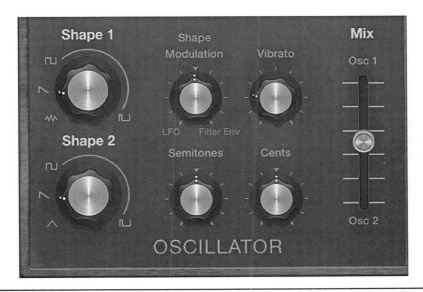

Fig. 8.3 The oscillator section of Logic Pro X's Retro Synth

The top right portion of the Retro Synth (illustrated in Figure 8.4) allows for further filtering adjustments, volume increases or decreases, sine wave additions, and effects. The selected filter in this example is set as a low-pass filter at 24dB, which may be adjusted to taste. The filtering options in this section of the synth alter the combined signal of both oscillators, shapes 1 and 2 examined in Figure 8.3. The amp area is dedicated to adjusting the output volume of the synth while allowing the producer to mix in a sine wave at the frequency of the first oscillator. The effects region applies certain effects such as chorus or flanger at a programmable rate and mix.

Fig. 8.4   **The filter, amp, and effects sections of Logic Pro X's Retro Synth**

The bottom section of the Retro Synth is devoted to glide, LFO, and other filtering and envelope modifications. **Glide** is *glissando*, which is a smooth, gliding way of moving between different pitches. A *glissando* on an instrument is a sliding effect that passes through all notes between the starting and ending pitches. The rate at which the *glissando* occurs is typically very rapid, but in the case of synthesis, the producer has the option to glide quickly or slowly. The LFO allows for further *vibrato* effects to be added to the combined signal of both oscillators. The filter envelope and amp envelope subsections allow the composer to alter the ADSR of the outgoing signal. Figure 8.5 focuses on the bottom section of the Retro Synth.

Fig. 8.5   **The bottom section of Logic Pro X's Retro Synth**

The parameters covered in the context of the Retro Synth are common among most synthesizers, though many synths allow for even more control over the generation and combination of oscillators' signals. The features discussed above are also present in most modern samplers.

SAMPLERS

Although many manipulative controls are shared by synthesizers and modern samplers, the main difference between a synthesizer and a sampler is that a synthesizer generates an initial sound and a sampler does not. Instead, a sampler records a sound and maps it across the keys of a MIDI keyboard controller. Figure 8.6 displays the Nanosampler from Digital Performer 9. Some samplers, like this one, show an image of the recorded waveform in the display window. Notice the similarities in function between this sampler and the Retro Synth discussed previously. Both virtual instruments, for example, offer control over filtering and amplitude parameters.

Fig. 8.6   Digital Performer 9's Nanosampler

For instruments that are capable of sustaining pitch for long periods of time, a sample needs to loop at some point. Thus, in the Nanosampler, there is a section dedicated to manipulating the waveform's loop start and end points. Figure 8.7 focuses on the looping parameters of the Nanosampler.

Sample loop point adjustment capabilities

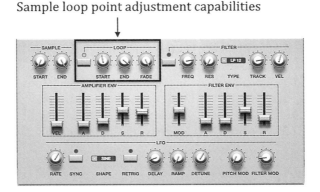

Fig. 8.7   The loop capabilities of Digital Performer 9's Nanosampler

Older samplers could only sample one sound at a time and relied on pitch-shifting original recordings so that one recorded sample could be played using any key of the keyboard. For example, if a flute was sampled while playing the note C5, the sample could be pitch-shifted and spread out over all of the keys of a keyboard, giving the composer the sound of the original recording, as well as several artificial adjustments to that recording that allow for the creation of any note. Unfortunately, the farther away a producer would play on the keyboard from the original recorded pitch, the less authentic the sample became. In contrast, modern sampling typically involves recording every note within the entire range of an instrument, and assigning each key of a MIDI keyboard its own sample, rendering the pitch-shifting approach obsolete. Moreover, most modern samplers trigger different samples recorded on the same pitch depending on the velocity expressed in a DAW or played on a MIDI keyboard. This means that C4 performed at a dynamic level of pp, for example, will trigger an entirely different sample than C4 performed at a louder dynamic level. This more detailed approach to sampling creates a great deal of realism and makes the sampler an important tool for the composer.

MULTITIMBRAL VIRTUAL INSTRUMENTS

A multitimbral instrument is one that offers the ability to produce up to 16 sounds simultaneously while accessing each sound on a separate MIDI channel. Hardware synths and samplers that are multitimbral are essentially sixteen synths or samplers combined into one unit. Multitimbral virtual synths and samplers work the same way, but are software-based plugins instead of hardware. The benefit of using a multitimbral setup is that it requires less of a computer system's resources. If a composer loads 16 separate instances of the same virtual instrument plugin, for example, valuable CPU power will be drained, as most virtual instrument plugins require a high number of system resources to run smoothly. As modern computers become more powerful, this is becoming less of an issue; however, the ability to save CPU power with efficient workflows remains important, particularly for larger sessions—and certainly for beginning producers who may not own a tremendously powerful computer.

Multitimbral Configurations within a DAW

The basic routing of a multitimbral configuration is ostensibly the same across all DAWs, though the specific procedure for setting one up will vary from DAW to DAW. To create a multitimbral setup, the synthesizer/sampler needs to be set in multi-mode, assigning a specific MIDI channel to each added instrument. Likewise, the host DAW needs to be prepared to connect each MIDI track with the corresponding MIDI channel for each instrument. At this point, the synthesizer/sampler instance housing each instrument of the multitimbral configuration will be supplying only one audio signal for all instruments, rendering the advanced mixing capabilities of the host DAW useless. Put differently, each instrument will be routed through a single audio output coming from the multitimbral synth, rather than being routed to individual audio channels in the DAW. Each instrument will be capable of MIDI manipulation, and the DAW will display a separate track for each instrument, but the audio output will only produce one combined signal of all instruments under the umbrella of the host synthesizer/sampler. Figure 8.8 demonstrates a multitimbral setup of 10 instruments coming from one synthesizer.

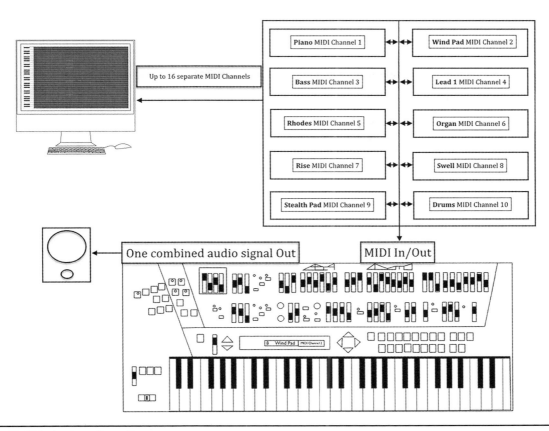

Fig. 8.8 Multitimbral configuration

At this point in the setup, the composer is able to mix each individual instrument within the synthesizer, but not separately in the DAW, which is where the professional-grade mixing features are found. The main method of addressing these limitations involves multi-outputs, which create separate audio outputs for each instrument within a virtual instrument's multitimbral configuration. Each DAW and virtual instrument approaches multi-outputs differently, however.

Multitimbral setups provide access to several instruments within a single instance of a virtual synthesizer or sampler while saving valuable processing power. However, setting up a multitimbral configuration requires advanced routing that is not standardized among the commonly used DAWs and virtual instruments, causing some level of confusion. Since most modern computers have strong CPUs, the need to rely on multitimbral setups is arguably becoming obsolete; nonetheless, a producer may still find it useful to consider using a multitimbral configuration, depending on the size of a project and the CPU of the particular computer being used. Regardless of whether a multitimbral setup has been used, though, most synthesizer and sampler tracks require a good deal of MIDI editing once they have been recorded or stepped into a sequence to make a passage sound realistic. This is especially the case for sampled orchestral instruments, which are capable of producing different articulations for each note within the range of the instrument.

CREATING REALISM WITH VIRTUAL INSTRUMENTS

Some samples are recorded with only one articulation or rhythmic value (e.g., short, sustained), requiring the producer to set up a new patch for every articulation change within a project. If a passage called for a *legato* trumpet line for two bars and a *staccato* trumpet line for the next two bars, for example, the composer would need to load a *legato* trumpet patch on one track and a *staccato* trumpet patch on another. This workflow can be very cumbersome, especially since a single trumpet player would be able to easily switch between multiple articulations and record an entire part on a single track. To accommodate this, many modern patches provide multiple layers of sampled articulations within a single instrument. A violin patch, for example, might have *arco* (bowed), *pizzicato* (plucked), *tremolo*, and *staccato* samples all loaded within a single instrument. Switching between each articulation is typically accomplished via MIDI commands in this context. The two most common methods for switching between articulations are key switching and velocity switching.

KEY SWITCHING

In the passage below from the "Raiders March" theme from the film *Raiders of the Lost Ark*, you can see that the trumpet part changes between short and long rhythms. Figure 8.9 illustrates some of the challenges that a producer faces when sequencing this passage.

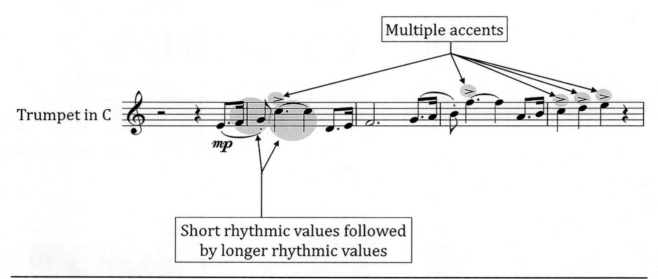

Fig. 8.9 Challenging rhythms and articulations in a passage from the "Raiders March" from the movie *Raiders of the Lost Ark*

If a producer recreated this score, a separate track and patch for each type of rhythm would need to be created (with the short rhythmic values sequenced on one track and the long rhythmic values sequenced on another), unless the virtual instrument being used had multiple articulations and rhythmic value samples built into the patch (which would allow the entire passage to be recorded on one track). In the Kontakt library, for example, many samples take advantage of **key switching**, which allows the producer to trigger articulation changes by pressing certain keys of a MIDI keyboard. In a DAW, key switching can be achieved by placing MIDI events on designated key switching pitches. Notes that are allocated to key switching are generally found outside of the range of a specific instrument; for example, low-pitched instruments like bass would likely use the upper portions of the keyboard for key switching. Designated key switching pitches also tend to be indicated visually with different-colored keys in the piano roll editor, though samplers vary with regard to this practice. Figure 8.10 demonstrates key switching in Digital Performer 9 with Native Instruments' Kontakt Solo Violin patch. Here, the sustained, bowed (*arco*) articulation sample is triggered by the note C0, and the key switch to the note D#0 activates a change to a *staccato* articulation sample. Note that articulation will remain unchanged until a new key switch is programmed. Thus, any notes performed after the MIDI event on C0 in Figure 8.10 will have a sustained articulation until the MIDI event on D#0 occurs, which changes the articulation to *staccato*. All violin pitches after that point will remain *staccato* until otherwise altered.

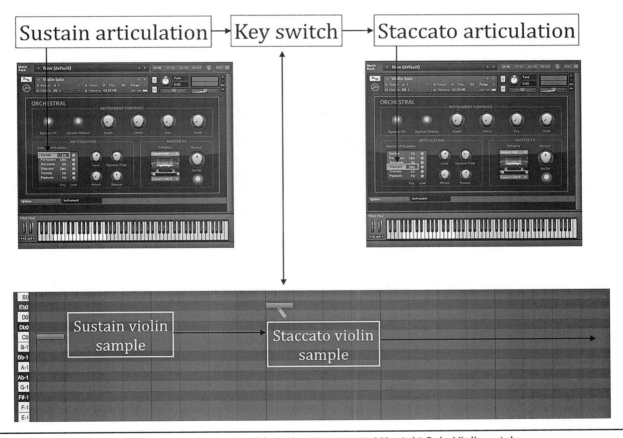

Fig. 8.10   **Key switching in Digital Performer 9 with Native Instruments' Kontakt Solo Violin patch**

VELOCITY SWITCHING

Another common method of changing between articulations involves **velocity switching**. Some sound libraries are beginning to use velocity as the parameter used to switch between different layers of samples within a single instrument instead of pitch (which is used in key switching). Most of the time, velocity is reserved for dynamic control, but since MIDI is simply a communication protocol, programmers are free to experiment with assigning non-standard messages to various parameters. Figure 8.11 demonstrates velocity switching in Logic Pro X with the Twelve Horn Ensemble Articulations patch from the Cinesamples library Cinebrass Pro. In this example, any MIDI event with a velocity value greater than 70 will trigger a sustained articulation, and any velocity setting under 70 will activate a *staccato* articulation.

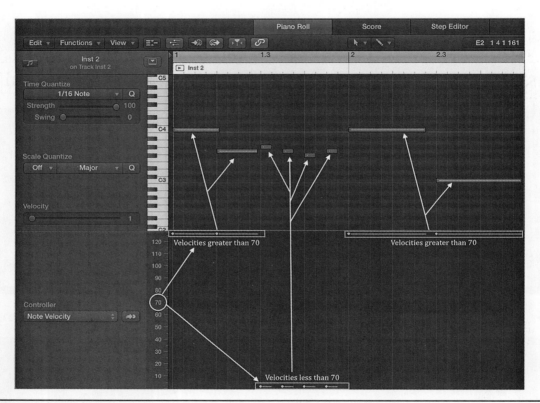

Fig. 8.11   Velocity switching in Logic Pro X with Cinesamples's Twelve Horn Ensemble Articulations patch

Returning to the passage from the "Raiders March," Figure 8.12 demonstrates the solutions to the challenges—changing articulations and accented notes—that were illustrated in Figure 8.9. Notice the unique way Digital Performer 9 overlays MIDI events and velocity levels within the Sequence Editor view. The accented velocity levels have been highlighted for clarity.

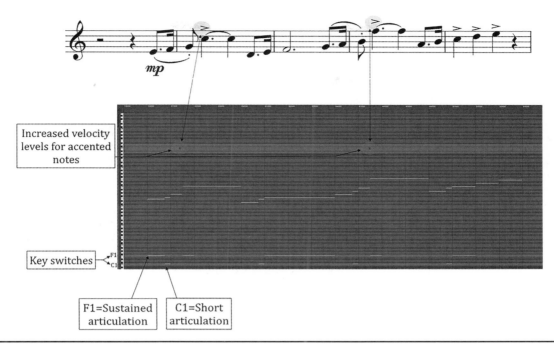

Fig. 8.12 Sequenced passage from the "Raiders March" theme from the film *Raiders of the Lost Ark* in Digital Performer 9

There are many ways in which composers can create and maintain interest within a musical phrase. Tasteful use of articulation and rhythmic variation are certainly important aspects of a good composition, but there are several other areas to consider as well. A DAW allows a producer to control a variety of sonic properties—from basic volume control to complex synthesis elements—as well as adjust how these properties manifest over time throughout a project. Since music is a time-based art, it is important to have the ability to manipulate musical domains over time.

AUTOMATION

Automation is a way of recording modifications to a parameter over time by means of fader/knob movements that are generated from a mouse or control surface, either during live playback or via asynchronous manipulations of a graphic display. A **control surface** is a piece of hardware that connects to a computer—usually by MIDI or USB cable—to control various functions of software. The faders and knobs of a control surface can be programmed to control almost any parameter within a DAW, and can even manipulate many virtual instrument and plugin effect properties. It is important to note that a control surface is not an audio mixer, even though its main utility lies in controlling the virtual mixing board within a DAW. When a fader or knob is moved on a control surface, a MIDI message is sent to a computer, telling the software to adjust certain parameters, such as raising or lowering the faders within a virtual mixer. Though a mouse can be used to execute anything that a control surface can accomplish, the benefit of using a control surface is the ability to physically touch faders and knobs instead of clicking and dragging, which provides a more efficient workflow and a more traditional, hands-on approach to modern recording and automation. However, it is not necessary to own a control surface to produce great-sounding music—many professionals do not own one.

REAL-TIME AUTOMATION

When a producer is ready to record the adjustments of a parameter in real time with a mouse or control surface, a DAW needs to be set up to receive them. There are four modes for recording and playing back automation in a DAW.

When a track is in **write mode**, adjustments will be recorded in real time. If a composer leaves write mode on, any additional adjustments made to that track during playback will override any previously recorded automation data. Care must therefore be taken when using write mode; many producers deliberately avoid it because of its potentially destructive power. **Read mode** simply follows any previously recorded automation during playback. If it is turned off, automation will not be heeded during playback. **Latch mode** overrides automation in the areas that are changed during playback. However, once the producer lets go of a fader during playback, the adjusted parameter will "latch on" to the most recent value and remain at that level for the rest of the passage. **Touch mode** is very similar to latch mode, except that the parameter will jump back to its originally recorded value(s) after the fader is released. Figure 8.13 shows a fader within Pro Tools 11's virtual mixer being assigned to write mode.

Fig. 8.13 Write mode in Pro Tools 11

GRAPHIC DISPLAY AUTOMATION

After automation data has been recorded, it can be edited with a mouse for more precise adjustments or re-recorded in real time. Automation can also be accomplished with a mouse by clicking and dragging across the lanes of a track in the shape a producer wants a certain parameter to follow.

Once any adjustments have been recorded, the automation can be viewed graphically in lanes running across (or under) the tracks that are being automated. Figure 8.14 displays how recorded automation appears in Cubase Pro.

Fig. 8.14 Recorded automation in Cubase Pro

VOLUME AUTOMATION

Volume is the most common parameter that producers automate. The volume of any audio file can be automated, as can the output of a virtual instrument. When working with MIDI, there are two additional areas of volume automation to consider: **volume controller** (MIDI CC7) and **expression controller** (MIDI CC11). Expression controller is normally reserved for the creation of a *crescendo* or *decrescendo*, whereas volume controller controls the overall volume of a track that may or may not include any expression control. Put differently, CC7 (volume controller) sets the fluctuating maximum volume for a MIDI track, and CC11 (expression controller) works as a sub-volume, allowing for volume adjustments to be made within the boundaries set by CC7 at any given moment. When an external multitimbral sound source is used (e.g., a keyboard or tone generator), CC7 is the only way to control the volume of each individual instrument. As demonstrated in Figure 8.8, all instruments are filtered through one audio output in a standard multitimbral setup, forcing the producer to mix each instrument within that sound source via MIDI message CC7. Expression and volume control can both be adjusted within a piano roll editor or other MIDI editing window in the context of a virtual instrument, but it is wise to consider separating the tasks to avoid confusion. As previously mentioned, the output of a virtual instrument can also be automated, giving the producer two options for achieving the same goal—CC7 and normal channel automation. If a composer automates the output volume of a virtual instrument *and* creates a series of CC7 messages, the messages may conflict. However, since it is now possible to create multi-output configurations for most multitimbral virtual instruments, automating volume via MIDI message CC7 is becoming obsolete; composers generally rely on automating the virtual instrument's output(s) instead. A more organized approach places expression automation in the piano roll editor and volume automation in a DAW's tracks view window, which is where audio and MIDI automation may be viewed simultaneously as channel volume. Figure 8.15 demonstrates how both channel volume and expression controllers work in tandem. Here, they are organized such that channel volume is shown in the tracks view window, while expression (CC11) is shown in the piano roll editor in Logic Pro X.

VOLUME

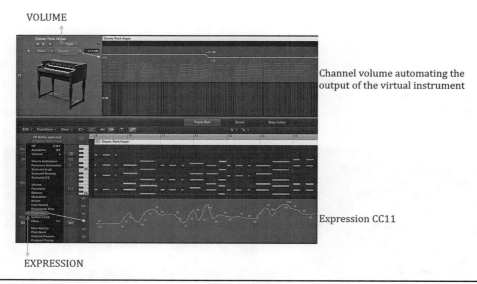

Channel volume automating the
output of the virtual instrument

Expression CC11

EXPRESSION

Fig. 8.15 Output volume and expression automation in Logic Pro X

Notice that CC11 changes are occurring regardless of the level at which the channel volume automation is set. This allows each part to individually express the dynamics of a musical phrase, providing realism and energy to a passage of music regardless of the overall volume level of that part in relation to the levels of other instruments. While volume is the most commonly automated parameter, other musical features may be modified as well. Most virtual instruments allow a great deal of control over domains such as filter cutoff, LFO rate, and envelope (ADSR). Figure 8.16 demonstrates the available parameters for automation within Logic Pro X's Retro Synth.

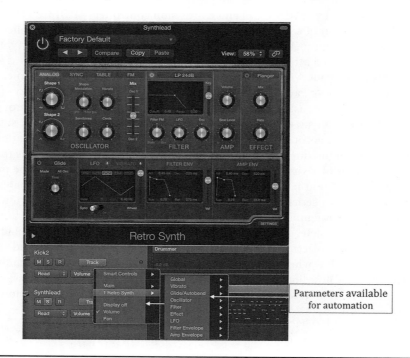

Parameters available
for automation

Fig. 8.16 Automatable parameters in Logic Pro X's Retro Synth

Automating a variety of a virtual instrument's parameters can help create energy and movement in a track that might otherwise seem static. Many electronic pieces, for instance, automate the opening and closing of a filter to help drive a section of music forward or bridge one section of music with another, which functions much like a drum fill. Understanding virtual instruments, especially in tandem with automation, ensures your control over the sequencing of a performance and brings you closer to a professional-quality creation.

SUMMARY OF TERMS FROM CHAPTER 8

virtual instrument	synthesizer	velocity switching
DSP	oscilloscope	automation
native plugin	oscillator	control surface
TDM	patch	write mode
RTAS	modular synthesis	read mode
AAX	LFO	latch mode
AU	filter envelope	touch mode
VST	glide	volume controller (MIDI CC7)
sampler	key switching	expression controller (MIDI CC11)

CHAPTER 8—EXERCISES

True or False. Circle "true" for each statement below that is true. Circle "false" for each false statement.

1. DSP plugins use a host computer's CPU to operate.

    True   False

2. VST plugins are examples of native plugins.

    True   False

3. Sine waves, square waves, sawtooth waves, and triangle waves are the four types of waves that samplers use to produce sound.

    True   False

4. Connecting multiple oscillators to create patches is known as modular synthesis.

    True   False

5. LFO and filter envelopes work the same way.

    True   False

    Multiple Choice. Circle the letter corresponding to the best choice for each question below.

6. The benefit of using a multitimbral setup is that it
    a. allows for seamless collaboration between producers.
    b. takes less time to set up than creating a new instance for each sound.

   c.   requires less of a computer system's resources.

   d.   is easier to route than multiple instances of synths and samplers.

7. Key switching allows a composer to change articulations by

   a.   changing the tonality of a certain passage.

   b.   pressing or triggering certain keys of a MIDI keyboard.

   c.   programming an oscillator in a virtual synthesizer.

   d.   assigning certain values of velocity to specific samples.

8. A control surface is

   a.   a piece of hardware designed to sample live instruments.

   b.   a piece of hardware designed to control software.

   c.   an absolutely essential piece of hardware for a professional producer.

   d.   a piece of hardware designed to record audio.

9. What is the difference between touch mode and latch mode?

   a.   Touch mode begins recording automation as soon as a fader is touched, but latch mode does not.

   b.   Latch mode assigns LFO and filter envelope automation only.

   c.   Latch mode will override automation data and leave any values where they are last positioned after the producer stops touching a fader. Touch mode will override automation data, but all values will return to their previously recorded levels once the producer lets go of a fader.

   d.   Touch mode will override automation data and leave any values where they are last positioned after the producer stops touching a fader. Latch mode will override automation data, but all values will return to their previously recorded levels once the producer lets go of a fader.

10. What is the difference between CC7 and CC11?

   a.   A CC7 message can create a *crescendo* or *decrescendo*, whereas CC11 controls the volume of the overall track.

   b.   A CC11 message can create a *crescendo* or *decrescendo*, whereas CC11 controls the volume of the overall track.

   c.   CC7 is always louder than CC11.

   d.   CC11 is always louder than CC7.

11. In any DAW, sequence the melody provided below, which is from the "Raiders March" theme from the film *Raiders of the Lost Ark*. Be sure to raise the velocity levels for the accented notes and use key or velocity switching for any changes in articulation. In bar 7, program the *crescendo* with expression control (CC11).

12. In any DAW, sequence the concert score provided below, which is from "The Realm of Gondor" from *The Lord of the Rings* trilogy. Create one track for each of the four horns and program all instances of dynamic expression with expression control (CC11). Be sure to use key or velocity switching for any changes in articulation.

PART II
MUSIC PRODUCTION ESSENTIALS

PART IIA
COMPOSITION ESSENTIALS

Chapter 9
Functional Diatonic Harmony

In Chapter 3, you learned that harmonies in Western music tend to be tertian chords that are derived by stacking diatonic thirds above each scale degree in major and minor keys. These chords can be analyzed with chord symbols as well as Roman numerals, which elucidate both the qualities of the chords and the individual scale degrees that represent the chords' roots. This rather formulaic method of labeling harmonies may at first give the impression that each chord within a key is equal in importance. However, this is not the case; each diatonic harmony plays a specific set of roles or functions within the key. Each chord—indeed, each inversion of each chord—can be thought of as a separate character (as in a play or musical), with individual motivations, abilities, and behavioral tendencies, forming a complex network of "interpersonal" relationships among chords. To continue the analogy, some chords are best thought of as lead characters, while others are merely bit players with lesser roles. Some chords can even be considered to be understudies that occasionally substitute for lead roles. Moreover, some of these chord "characters" are very attracted to one another, while others seemingly despise each other and are rarely seen together. This chapter explores the full cast of characters in traditional tonality and reveals the common ways in which harmonic drama unfolds in pieces of common practice music. While most genres of contemporary commercial music deviate from traditional tonal schemes, the degree to which they do so varies; learning the basics of classical harmonic practice serves as an excellent frame of reference and allows you to understand and authentically recreate a variety of styles as you develop your own compositional voice.

FUNCTIONAL HARMONY AND FUNCTIONAL AREAS

Beyond indicating the scale step of the root and providing chord quality information, a Roman numeral serves to allow the reader to quickly identify the role or function of a chord within a key. Most chords fulfill one of three basic functions: tonic function, dominant function, or predominant function. Accordingly, musical ideas are often described as being composed of three different harmonic areas: the tonic area, the dominant area, and the predominant area. Chords with **tonic** function establish the key and tonic area, giving the listener a sense of stability. They are typically found at the beginning and end of a musical idea, serving as points of departure and arrival. As the name implies, tonic function is typically fulfilled by tonic chords (I in major keys and i in minor keys). Chords with **dominant** function lend an opposing force to those with tonic function and represent the fundamental source of harmonic tension or instability within a piece of tonal music. While some musical phrases end on dominant function chords, this creates a feeling of inconclusiveness; generally, the activation of dominant function chords signals to the listener that the phrase has reached the dominant area and a strong point of arrival on tonic is about to take place. This is related to the fact that dominant function chords contain the leading tone, which is a tendency tone with a strong desire to resolve up by step to tonic. In traditional tonal music, the dominant triad (V) and seventh chord (V^7) are the most common dominant function chords, though triads and seventh chords built on the leading tone can at times fulfill the same role. **Predominant** function is usually best served by chords built on scale degrees $\hat{2}$ and $\hat{4}$, such as ii and IV chords in major keys and ii° and iv chords in minor keys. Importantly, these chords differ by only one scale degree—ii involves $\hat{2}$, $\hat{4}$, and $\hat{6}$, while IV involves $\hat{4}$, $\hat{6}$, and $\hat{1}$—and thus are viewed as essentially the same harmony, with a particular sonority being chosen in order to serve specific melodic goals. The submediant chord, vi or VI, can be used as a predominant harmony; however, it functions in a weaker fashion. Predominant chords are so named because they tend to be followed by dominant function chords. They signal a move away from the tonic area and into the dominant area, initiating the building of tension that ultimately resolves at the end of an idea or piece.

PART WRITING BASICS

Before delving into more specific ways in which the three functional harmonic areas tend to be created, prolonged, embellished, and arranged in common-practice tonality, it is first necessary to explore a very common manner of working with harmonies on the staff known as **part writing**. Part writing traditionally involves composing individual parts for each member of a choir—soprano, alto, tenor, and bass, in a typical "SATB" arrangement—that combine on a single grand staff to create chordal textures in the manner of a chorale. In the context of compositional training, however, students work on part writing not to create choir pieces, but rather to more abstractly practice and visualize four-voice counterpoint, with smooth voice leading used to connect chords. Part-written chord progressions can in turn be used as templates for a variety of orchestrations, including but not limited to vocal ensembles.

Figure 9.1 provides an analysis of a C major triad in both close position and open positions in an SATB context. Each different chordal manifestation of the C major triad in this example is referred to as a different **voicing**; thus, there are four unique voicings present. Notice the atypical stemming associated with SATB notation: the soprano's stems always point upward while the alto's stems point downward on the treble clef staff; the tenor's stems point upward and the bass's point downward on the bass clef staff. This is done to allow the reader to quickly identify which voice is associated with each pitch on the grand staff.

The group of four voices in an SATB arrangement can be further segmented into a few subgroups: the outer voices (bass and soprano), inner voices (tenor and alto), and upper voices (tenor, alto, and soprano). Each subgroup is used to discuss various part-writing guidelines and spacing considerations. For example, each adjacent pair of upper voices is traditionally required to be separated by an interval that is no larger than an octave, while the bass may be positioned more than an octave apart from the tenor (e.g., a tenth is common between the bass and tenor in certain keys). The larger intervals that are common between the bass and tenor are related to the

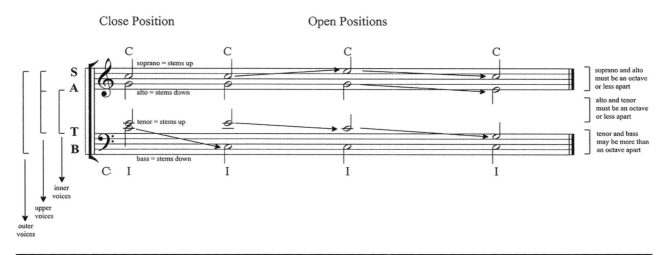

Fig. 9.1   C major triad in close and open positions

low interval limit discussed in Chapter 7; voicing these parts close together tends to result in a lack of harmonic clarity. The upper voices tend to be even closer to one another in keyboard-style voicings, which differ from SATB chorale voicings in that all three upper voices are placed in the right hand (RH) of the keyboard while the bass is placed in the left hand (LH) by itself in the bass clef staff. The three upper voices on the treble clef staff in keyboard voicings may be notated using a single stem, though the soprano is often stemmed separately. A common method of creating a keyboard voicing from a chorale voicing is to simply move the tenor up an octave (and vice versa), as shown in Figure 9.2.

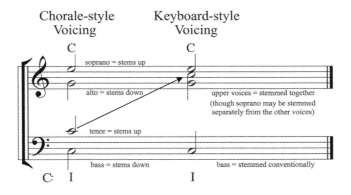

Fig. 9.2   Chorale and keyboard voicings of a C major triad

In both Figure 9.1 and Figure 9.2, you may have noticed that the root of the C major triad was doubled. Since both chorale-style and keyboard-style voicings involve four parts, all triads require a chord tone to be doubled. (At times, seventh chords involve doubling as well, when a chord tone is omitted for effect or to avoid certain voice-leading problems.) Generally speaking, root position triads have doubled roots, as in the previous examples. First inversion triad voicings tend to double the root, as well, though doubling the bass (the third of the chord) is often necessary to avoid parallels. Second inversion triad voicings almost always feature a doubled bass (the fifth of the chord). Figure 9.3 shows a C major triad in each of its possible inversions in SATB style, with common doublings highlighted for each inversion.

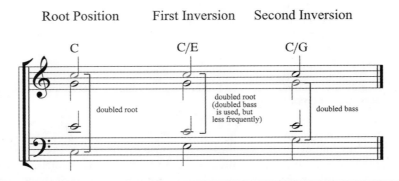

Fig. 9.3 Chord tone doubling by inversion

VOICE LEADING IN FOUR-PART HARMONY

Crucially, these voicing guidelines are not hard and fast rules; rather, they are tendencies that have been observed that relate to writing good counterpoint. It is more important to consider the voice leading when connecting chords than to mechanically double chord tones based solely on inversion. Generally, the principles of melody writing and first species counterpoint drive the voice-leading traditions associated with part writing. For example, parallel fifths and octaves are to be avoided entirely—something that becomes a bit more difficult to identify in a four-voice context, given that there are six possible pairs of voices that could potentially create these errors (bass/soprano, bass/alto, bass/tenor, tenor/soprano, tenor/alto, and alto/soprano). However, there are a few differences and additional considerations that merit mention in this denser textural context. One consideration involves the perfect fourth interval. In two-voice writing, the bass is involved in every harmonic interval, and, since the P4 is a harmonic dissonance above the bass, the result is that P4s are always considered dissonant. However, in four-voice writing, dissonant harmonic P4s are more difficult to identify, as they only exist above the bass voice. As a result, P4 intervals are considered consonances more frequently in SATB voicings.

When writing music in four parts, pay particular attention to avoiding counterpoint problems with the outer voices, as they are the easiest to hear. The inner voices, which are more difficult to hear, do not have to feature elaborate or inspiring melodies; rather, they tend to function in filling out the harmonies without being distracting. Accordingly, inner-voice melodic motion should not be very disjunct. In fact, inner-voice motion tends to be extremely smooth, with stepwise motion being used frequently, as well as motion by **common tone** that creates oblique motion with outer-voice parts. While species counterpoint principles generally forbid repeated notes in a single voice, they are more common in four-voice writing, particularly when placed in one of the inner voices. Figure 9.4 analyzes the chord voicings and voice leading in a short, three-chord passage in the key of B♭ major that opens a progression used in the exercises at the end of this chapter.

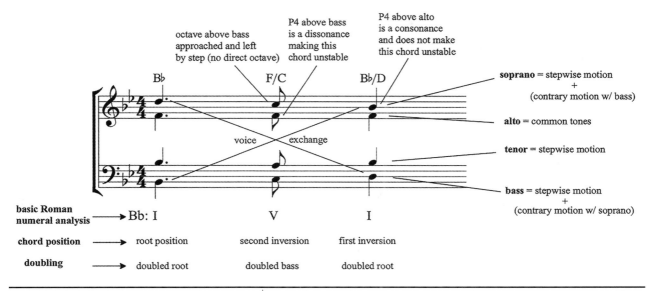

Fig. 9.4 Chord voicings and voice leading in B♭ major

TENDENCY TONES AND RESOLVING DOMINANTS

Just as with the individual diatonic chords, scale degrees and chord tones are not created equal. Tendency tones, for instance, must be identified and handled with care. As you've learned previously, the leading tone is a strong tendency tone that needs to resolve upward to tonic in most cases. For instance, in the previous example, the leading tone in the key of B♭, A, resolves up to tonic in the tenor when the second inversion V chord moves to a first inversion I chord. This scale degree is very salient for listeners, and should not be doubled, as doing so would create an unbalanced sound in a chord voicing. Additionally, doubling a leading tone and resolving it in both voices creates parallel octaves, while doubling the leading tone and only resolving it in one voice leaves the other leading tone "frustrated" without resolution—there is simply no satisfactory way to resolve a voicing with a doubled leading tone. Similarly, it is impossible to create quality voice leading when doubling the seventh of any seventh chord in a four-voice texture, as chordal sevenths are tendency tones that tend to resolve down by step and create issues of the same nature (not to mention the fact that doubling chord tones in seventh chords is usually unnecessary in SATB settings). The most common chordal seventh is scale degree $\hat{4}$, which serves as the seventh of the V⁷ chord in major and minor keys (the most common seventh chord in traditional tonality). For this reason and others, the subdominant is also considered a strong tendency tone that needs to resolve down by step to the mediant. Figure 9.5 features an altered version of the previous example, with the second inversion dominant triad substituted with a second inversion dominant seventh chord.

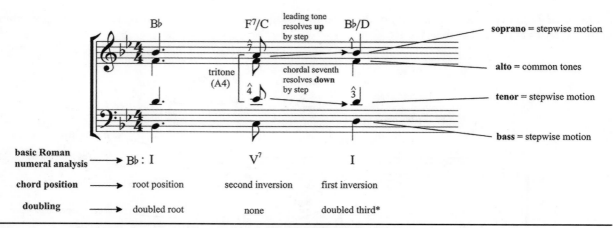

Fig. 9.5   The resolution of tendency tones in a dominant seventh chord

In Chapter 3, you learned that a dissonant tritone interval is formed between the chordal third ($\hat{7}$) and seventh ($\hat{4}$) of a V[7] chord. This tritone is the main source of harmonic tension in a piece of traditional tonal music, and it has the tendency to resolve in a specific way. In Figure 9.5, the leading tone resolves upward by half step into the root of the subsequent tonic triad, as mentioned previously, while the chordal seventh of the dominant seventh chord—$\hat{4}$, which is E♭ in this key—resolves downward by step into the third of the tonic triad, D. These two voice-leading traditions—the upward resolution of the leading tone by half step and the downward resolution of chordal sevenths—provide smooth motion into tonic triads, helping to establish a stronger sense of tonality in the ears of the listener. Note that the need for the resolutions of these tendency tones is so strong that other part-writing guidelines, such as doublings based on inversion, are not always heeded. For example, the first inversion tonic triad at the end of the previous example features a doubled chordal third, which is less common than a doubled root. Figure 9.6 provides another example in C major in which the resolution of the tritone in a V[7] chord causes a part-writing anomaly, as the root position harmonies combine with the upper voice resolutions to result in a final tonic triad that lacks a chordal fifth entirely. While you should typically strive to create complete chords when part writing, this is a classic exception.

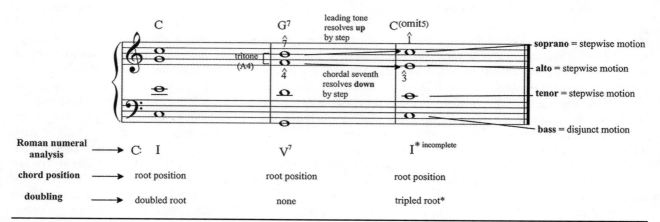

Fig. 9.6   An incomplete tonic triad resulting from the proper resolution of tendency tones

There are only two common cases in traditional tonal music wherein a tendency tone does not resolve properly. The first is known as the "leading tone drop," which takes place when a leading tone in an inner voice of a dominant chord voicing does not resolve up by step, but instead leaps down to $\hat{5}$ to create a complete tonic triad. The other takes place during an idiomatic progression involving a second inversion dominant seventh chord, when parallel tenths between the outer voices override the chordal seventh's tendency to descend by step, instead moving upward with a $\hat{1}$—$\hat{2}$—$\hat{3}$ bass line and a $\hat{3}$—$\hat{4}$—$\hat{5}$ soprano.

THE BASIC PHRASE MODEL IN TRADITIONAL TONALITY

TONIC—(PREDOMINANT—)DOMINANT—TONIC

The general progression exemplified in Figure 9.6, I—V$^{(7)}$—I, is one of the simplest and most important chord progressions in tonal music. This progression serves as a skeletal harmonic scheme that underlies most every piece of common practice music, doing so on multiple structural levels. Put differently, individual phrases tend to be governed by a move from tonic eventually to V$^{(7)}$ and back to tonic, as do larger formal sections of a piece, as does the piece's overall multi-section form. This basic phrase model begins with a tonic harmony that establishes the key, followed by several chords that expand, prolong, and reinforce the listener's sense of tonic harmony to create a larger tonic area of the phrase. Eventually, near the end of the basic phrase, the dominant harmony enters, providing contrast and a sense of tension in need of resolution. Finally, the concluding tonic harmony releases the dominant's tension and provides the desired resolution as the music returns to a state of rest. You have probably heard someone claim that "music is all about tension and resolution"; this basic phrase model is a chief contributor to that idea, as it underlies every structural level of nearly every piece of common practice music. Figure 9.7 reproduces a phrase from one such piece of common practice music, the third movement of Mozart's Symphony in A Major, K. 114. Note that embellishments such as passing tones and neighbor tones are slightly grayed out to allow focus to be placed on the more structurally significant chord tones in the excerpt. While there are several tonic and dominant harmonies within this short passage, pay particular attention to those in root position, as they have the strongest identities and most clearly exemplify the different harmonic areas of the phrase.

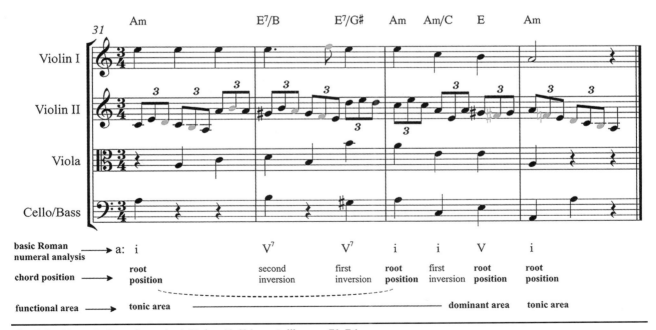

Fig. 9.7 Mozart, Symphony in A Major, K. 114, mvt. iii, mm. 31–34

The basic phrase model is usually expanded or embellished by the addition of one or more chords possessing predominant function, thereby creating the predominant area of a phrase. Expanding a harmonic progression in this way prolongs the building of tension and ultimately heightens the effect of the final resolution to the tonic at the end of the phrase. Traditionally, the most common predominant harmony is the first inversion supertonic chord, which features $\hat{4}$ in the bass like a IV or iv chord, yet does not suffer from the voice-leading problems—parallel fifths and octaves in particular—that tend to be created when moving between chords whose roots are a step apart, as in IV—V or iv—V. Nonetheless, the subdominant chord is very commonly used, and it is the true archetype for predominant function; in fact, many textbooks use the term "subdominant function" in lieu of "predominant function" to more clearly attribute the phrase area to the IV/iv chord. Figure 9.8 revisits and reduces John Williams's famous "Raiders Theme" from the score to *Raiders of the Lost Ark*, which exemplifies the embellished basic phrase model that includes the IV chord as the predominant harmony.

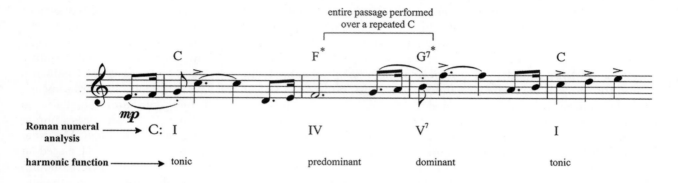

Fig. 9.8   John Williams, "Raiders Theme"

Importantly, this entire progression actually takes place over a repeated tonic in the score, making the basic phrase model serve as a very superficial "progression" that more accurately serves to reinforce tonic in the key of C. This idea of progressions that aren't actually progressions is crucial to the understanding of traditional tonal music. While musicians colloquially refer to a "chord progression" as any sequence of chords, a true chord progression in traditional tonality is specifically a sequence of chords that follows the basic phrase model either in whole or in part, moving from the tonic area through the predominant area to the dominant area and ultimately back to tonic. Chord sequences that do not conform to the basic phrase model, such as the blues turnaround of V—IV—I, are traditionally regarded as retrogressions. Retrogressions do not necessarily sound weak (in fact, the blues turnaround is a very strong chord sequence in many popular styles); rather, they were simply uncommon during the common practice period.

CADENCES

A **phrase** can be defined as a complete musical idea that terminates with a cadence. A **cadence** is a point of rest or repose at the end of a phrase that can be thought of as a compositional "punctuation mark" that signifies the completion of a musical thought. Phrases may end inconclusively (as in a clause that forms the beginning of a larger idea) or conclusively (as in the final sentence of a paragraph). The most important elements for creating such feelings for the listener are metrical position, harmony, and melody. As cadence points of all types tend to appear on downbeats or other strong beats, though, theorists have devised labels that are used to identify specific types of cadences based solely on the harmonies and melodic lines involved.

The most conclusive type of cadence is called an authentic cadence. Authentic cadences are metaphorically similar to periods and exclamation points in the written word, as they signal the true completion of musical thoughts. All authentic cadences involve harmonic motion from the dominant to the tonic of a key, as in the final V$^{(7)}$—I in the basic phrase model. The strongest type of authentic cadence, called the **perfect authentic cadence** (PAC), features root position dominant and tonic chords, specifically, and additionally requires that the soprano (or main melody) comes to rest on tonic via stepwise motion. Another type of authentic cadence that is not quite as conclusive as the PAC is the **imperfect authentic cadence** (IAC). The IAC still possesses harmonic motion from the dominant to the tonic, but it may feature one or both of the harmonies in inversion, or, more commonly, may have scale degree $\hat{3}$ or $\hat{5}$ in the soprano upon the arrival to the final tonic. Figure 9.9 provides two very similar progressions, with one ending on a PAC and another ending on a less conclusive IAC. These examples demonstrate the tendency for there to be a decrease in **harmonic rhythm** (or rate of harmonic change per unit of musical time) at the end of phrases in traditional tonality, adding to the perception of decreased energy associated with cadences. Harmonic rhythm frequently increases immediately before the entrance into the cadential area, as well, which can add to the decelerating effect of the cadence.

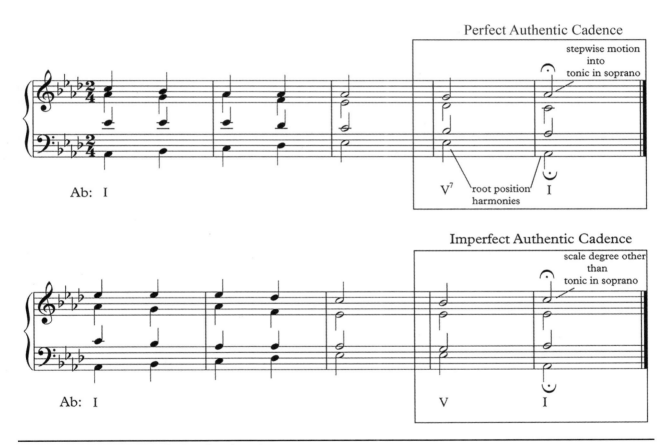

Fig. 9.9 Perfect and imperfect authentic cadences

The most common type of inconclusive cadence is called the **half cadence**, which involves resting on the dominant triad at the end of a phrase. A half cadence is metaphorically similar to a comma or semicolon in writing, as it punctuates a smaller idea or clause yet still leaves room for the completion of the larger idea or sentence (see Figure 9.10).

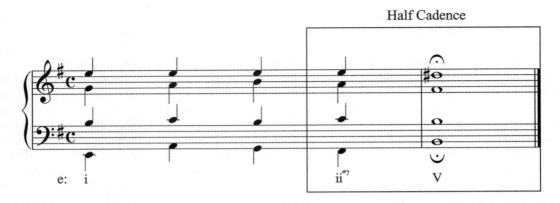

Fig. 9.10   Half cadence

While this example certainly sounds as a complete unit of musical thought, the hanging leading tone begs for resolution at some later time to complete the larger idea. Thus, a half cadence may also be thought of as being similar to a question mark, with a phrase ending on a half cadence representing a yet-unanswered question. In fact, composers at times play with listeners by ending a piece on a half cadence, which is similar to punctuating a narrative with the phrase "to be continued . . ." One special type of half cadence that is common only in minor keys is the **Phrygian half cadence** or Phrygian cadence, which features descending half step motion—akin to the half step motion from $\flat\hat{2}$ to $\hat{1}$ in the Phrygian mode (see Chapter 10)—from $\flat\hat{6}$ to $\hat{5}$ in the bass and harmonic progression from a first inversion iv chord to a root position V triad. Figure 9.11 demonstrates the typical voice leading associated with the Phrygian cadence: tonic, the chordal fifth of the iv chord, is doubled, and the soprano features an ascending step to $\hat{5}$ to create an octave interval with the bass that is approached by contrary motion.

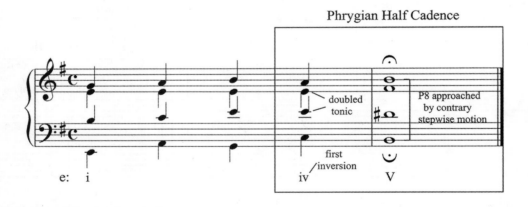

Fig. 9.11   Phrygian half cadence

Another type of inconclusive cadence that can be quite surprising is the **deceptive cadence**, which involves a harmonic move from V to vi (or VI in minor keys) wherein the submediant chord serves as a tonic substitute. The deception of a deceptive cadence stems from the fact that the upper voices move in the exact manner of an authentic cadence, with the only difference being that the bass moves up by step to the submediant instead of leaping to tonic; this tricks the listener into expecting the tonic triad at the end of the phrase (see Figure 9.12, which uses the same progression as Figure 9.9 but ends on vi).

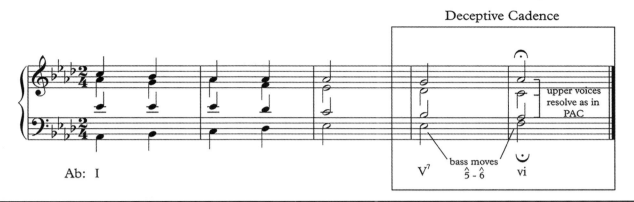

Fig. 9.12 Deceptive cadence

While a true deceptive cadence—one that literally takes place at the end of a phrase, which is rare—may bring to mind the punctuation combination of a question mark and exclamation point used to portray shock and dismay (?!), the more common, mid-phrase **deceptive resolution** traditionally functioned like a comma in an extended sentence; composers tended to rectify the deception by immediately writing a stronger authentic cadence afterward to more satisfactorily conclude the phrase. One contemporary example that features multiple deceptive resolutions comes from Williams's theme to *Schindler's List* that was referred to in previous chapters (see Figure 9.13). Note that there are several moves from predominant to dominant that signal the impending tonic, but deceptive resolutions—including a less common deceptive resolution that moves not to VI but rather to an inverted iv chord with $\hat{6}$ in the bass—continuously change the course of the phrase; only after the third activation of the dominant area does the harmony finally arrive home at tonic.

Another type of harmonic motion involved in phrase extensions is called plagal motion, which involves a IV—I or iv—i retrogression. The **plagal cadence**—colloquially referred to as "the Amen cadence"—traditionally appeared tacked on to the end of hymns and included harmonic motion from the tonic to the subdominant and

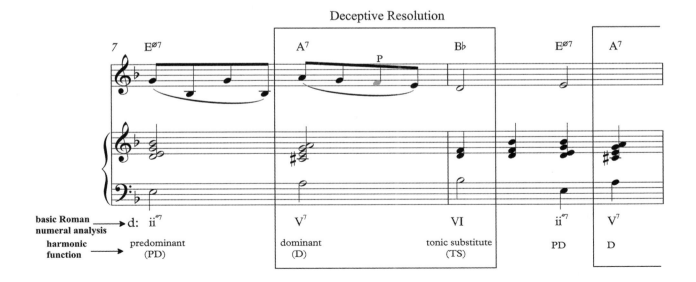

Fig. 9.13 Williams, theme from *Schindler's List*, mm. 7–10

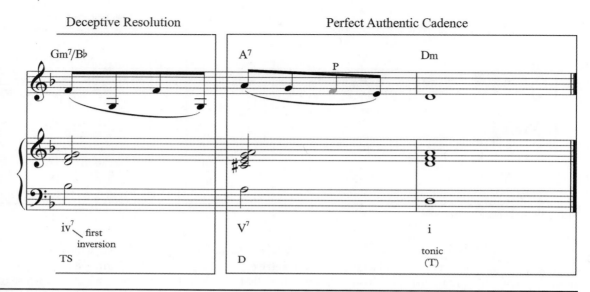

Fig. 9.13 Continued

back (I—IV—I, as in Figure 9.14). Historically, the plagal cadence sounded after an emphatic, piece-ending authentic cadence, and thus sounded less like a true cadence and more like a decoration of tonic harmony that reinforced or commented on previous ideas. In this way, plagal cadences were metaphorically similar to parentheses. However, in today's music, plagal cadences are exceedingly common (as are many so-called retrogressions that have become normative), and are considered to possess a similar strength of harmonic closure to authentic cadences.

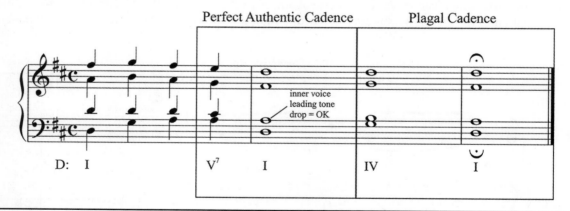

Fig. 9.14 Plagal motion after an authentic cadence

EXPANDING THE TONIC AREA

In a manner similar to the strategies outlined for creating solutions to counterpoint exercises in Chapter 4, you have focused first on the ends of phrases with the previous discussion of cadences. Now we move—perhaps counterintuitively—to the beginnings of phrases, which tend to serve in prolonging and expanding the tonic area. Harmonically speaking, the tonic area is by far the largest region of a phrase, and it is characterized by repeated, intermittent statements of tonic harmony (either in root position or first inversion, though root position I/i chords do the best job of reinforcing the identity of the key and area). These tonic chords are not typically repeated one after another, but instead are linked by a variety of other, relatively weak diatonic harmonies that add interest and harmonic motion without lending a strong sense of progression outside of the tonic area. The perceived "weakness" of these chords is due to a variety of factors: some are inverted, others do not follow their typical functional tendencies, and still others are best understood as the result of voice-leading patterns rather than as true harmonic entities. In all, these relatively weak chords serve as "bit players" in the unfolding harmonic drama and can additionally be thought of as embellishing the background tonic harmony in a somewhat superficial way. Thus, it is beneficial to first review the various types of melodic embellishing tones common in traditional tonal music before delving into the related embellishing harmonies that serve to expand the tonic area.

Embellishing Tones

In Chapter 4, you encountered some of the most common embellishing tones through an exploration of the various species of counterpoint. Second species introduced passing tones, third species added neighbor tones (as well as the larger embellishing patterns of the double neighbor and *nota cambiata*), and fourth species focused on suspensions. While these represent the most frequently encountered embellishments in traditional tonal music, there are quite a few others that merit mention. One such melodic ornament is the **accented passing tone**, which is quite similar to the standard passing tone in second species writing in that it is approached and left by step in the same direction; the only difference is that it takes place in an accented metrical position, such as a strong beat or strong part of a beat (e.g., the first eighth or sixteenth note within a quarter note beat in $\frac{4}{4}$ time).

Another, more general type of embellishment that is related to the neighbor tone of third species is the **incomplete neighbor**, so named because it only features stepwise motion on one side of the dissonance (whereas a true neighbor tone features stepwise motion into and out of the dissonance). There are two subtypes of incomplete neighbor: the *appoggiatura* and the escape tone. An *appoggiatura* is a very expressive dissonance that is preceded by leap—typically an ascending leap—and followed by step in the opposite direction; conversely, an **escape tone** is preceded by step and left by leap in the opposite direction into a chord tone.

Just as these incomplete neighbor tones bring to mind the more standard neighbor tones of third species, the melodic ornament known as a retardation brings to mind the more standard suspension of fourth species. A **retardation** is essentially an inverted suspension, in that it a) is prepared by the same pitch (often featuring a tie), b) becomes a dissonance on a strong beat or strong part of a beat, and c) resolves up by step instead of down by step. While common suspensions above the bass feature 7–6 and 4–3 interval patterns, common retardations feature 7–8 and 9–10 (or 2–3) interval patterns. Importantly, retardations are far less common than suspensions in most music, though the 9–10 retardation above tonic harmony at the end of a song is a classic idiom in country music that is often played by the lap steel guitar.

Two other types of embellishment that feature repeated pitches are the anticipation and the pedal point. Whereas suspensions and retardations are dissonances that are preceded by the same pitch, the **anticipation** is preceded by stepwise motion, with the repeated pitch taking place after the dissonance. The anticipation is aptly named, as the ornament anticipates a subsequent chord tone, arriving slightly early to transition into an upcoming harmony. The **pedal point** takes things a step further, as there is no change in pitch whatsoever—the dissonance is preceded by the same pitch and left into the same pitch. Pedal points take place in the bass the strict majority of the time; it can appear as though the harmony changes in the upper voices, but the bass simply refuses to oblige. The term pedal point hearkens back to traditional organ playing, in which long, sustained tones might be performed using a foot pedal while more intricate passages could be played on the manuals that temporarily conflicted with the pedal tone before resolving. A pedal point is thus fundamentally different than the other types of embellishment; most ornaments involve the melodic voice reaching a state of dissonance and then moving (typically via step) to create its own resolution. A pedal point, on the other hand, can be thought of as a dissonance that only resolves when the other parts within the texture move. Figure 9.15 includes two versions of a short phrase in SATB style; the first version is presented in an unornamented fashion, while the second version includes several melodic embellishments, including a neighbor tone, a pedal point, an *appoggiatura*, an accented passing tone, an anticipation, and two suspensions. Figure 9.16 summarizes all of the melodic embellishment types discussed thus far.

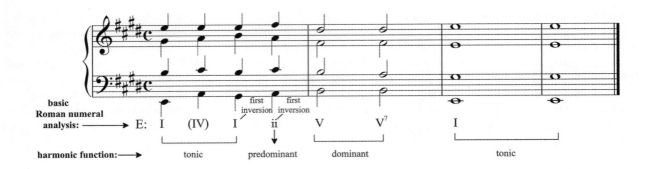

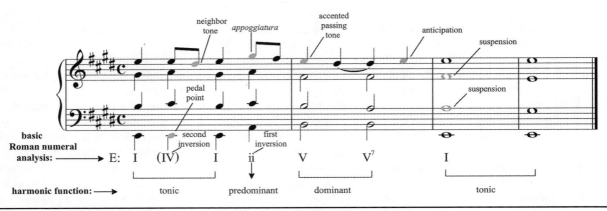

Fig. 9.15   A short SATB phrase decorated with various melodic embellishments

Consonant Preparation	Dissonant Embellishment Type	Consonant Resolution
Step	**Passing Tone**	Step in same direction as previous step
Step	**Accented Passing Tone** (takes place in strong metrical position)	Step in same direction as previous step
Step	**Neighbor Tone**	Step in opposite direction
Leap (usually up)	*Appoggiatura*	Step in opposite direction (usually down)
Step	**Escape Tone**	Leap in opposite direction
Step	**Double Neighbor**	Step in same direction as initial step (but opposite direction of leap between consecutive dissonances separated by third)
Step	*Nota Cambiata*	Consecutive steps in opposite direction of initial step as well as leap out of dissonance
Common tone	**Suspension**	Descending step
Common tone	**Retardation**	Ascending step
Step	**Anticipation**	Common tone
Common tone	**Pedal Point**	Common tone

Fig. 9.16   List of melodic embellishment types

Inverted Chords

One of the most common ways to embellish a harmonic region such as the tonic area is to use inverted chords—chords whose bass, or lowest note, is not the root. These chords can often be understood as fully harmonized passing tones, neighbor tones, or pedal points that take place in a particular voice (usually the bass). Inverted chords do not sound as strong or stable as those that are in root position, and they often aid in creating smooth bass lines; thus, they serve as excellent choices to ornament root position tonic triads while creating a sense of melodic and harmonic motion. Using inverted chords in combination with root position harmonies can also help you avoid writing parallel fifths and octaves, which is an added benefit. Figure 9.17 revisits an arrangement of Jeremiah Clarke's "Trumpet Voluntary" in the context of inverted chords.

Fig. 9.17   Clarke, "Trumpet Voluntary," mm. 1–8

One of the salient inverted triads in this example takes place on the downbeat of the third bar. Since the bass pitch, F$\sharp$, is the third of this tonic triad (D—F$\sharp$—A), and chords whose thirds are in the bass are first inversion chords, this chord is a D major triad in first inversion; it serves to create the apex of a nice, flowing melodic arc in the bass while prolonging the listener's sense of the tonic area without incessantly repeating a root position triad.

This chord can be represented in a basic chord symbol analysis with a "slash chord" symbol above the staff: a capital letter D (signifying a D major triad) is placed before the slash, and the note that is in the bass is placed after the slash. As D major is the tonic triad in this key, a Roman numeral I should be used in an analysis. However, this would not indicate that the chord is in inversion, as the slash chord symbol does in the chord symbol analysis. To indicate inverted chords with a Roman numeral analysis, superscript Arabic numerals are traditionally added after the Roman numeral that relate to the specific pattern of intervals above the bass that is created by each particular inversion. This practice follows the Baroque tradition called "figured bass" or "thoroughbass," in which accompanists would be given a notated bass line instead of a full score, with groups of numbers or figures below the staff added that related to the intervals that needed to be created above each bass note in order to form chords. Accompanists such as keyboard players used these **figured bass symbols** in the same way that pop and jazz musicians use lead sheets today, as a shorthand form of notation that provides rhythmic and harmonic guidelines as opposed to extremely specific details. While figured bass notation is not used in the same way anymore, vestiges of the practice remain when analyzing chords with Roman numerals. For example, first inversion triads like the D/F$\sharp$ chord in bar 3 will always have the intervals of a sixth and a third above the bass in some octave. In this case, the sixth above the bass, F$\sharp$, is D, while the third above the bass is A. For this reason, the set of figures $^6_3$ can be added after the Roman numeral for this chord as well as those for all other first inversion triads (including the first inversion V chord in the first bar, which serves to harmonize the metrically accented neighbor motion, D—C$\sharp$—D, in the bass line). To make figured bass symbols as quick and easy to read as possible, the 3 below the 6 is typically omitted, as it is traditionally understood that the lone 6 is itself a shorthand for $^6_3$.

Another example of figured bass symbols being omitted for the sake of ease is with root position triads. Technically, the intervals above the bass for any root position triad are a fifth and a third, forming the chordal fifth and third, respectively. Thus, one could place a 5 and a 3 after the Roman numeral for every root position triad in an analysis, but that would typically be a waste of time if the chord were not stated previously in a different inversion, as it is generally understood that Roman numerals without figured bass symbols indicate root position triads. Second inversion triads like the A/E chord in m. 2 will always have the intervals of a sixth and a fourth above the bass; in this case, the sixth above the bass, E, is C$\sharp$, while the fourth above the bass is A. The figures 6 and 4 are thus placed after the Roman numeral for this chord, as well as those for all other second inversion triads.

The analysis of seventh chords involves the same processes as the analysis of triads, though a key difference that needs to be accounted for is the fact that there are more intervals above the bass in each chord, as there is one extra chord tone (the chordal seventh). These intervals above the bass in turn yield different figured bass symbols that are commonly used to express each inversion in a Roman numeral analysis. For example, first inversion seventh chords feature the interval pattern above the bass of $^6_3$, which is typically abbreviated to $^6_5$ in an analysis. The pattern of intervals above the bass in the case of second inversion seventh chords—like the A^7/E chord at the end of bar 6 of the previous example—is $^6_4$, which is usually expressed more simply as $^4_3$ in an analysis. Third inversion seventh chords, which have the chordal seventh in the bass, involve a $^6_4$ pattern of intervals above the bass that is shortened to $^4_2$ after a Roman numeral. $^4_2$ chords tend to resolve to first inversion chords (as the temporary A^7/G chord does at the end of the first phrase in the previous example), following the tendency of the chordal seventh to resolve down by step. Figure 9.18 summarizes the typical practices related to analyzing root position and inverted chords with Roman numerals and figured bass symbols.

Chord example	*(musical staff)*	*(musical staff)*	*(musical staff)*	*(musical staff)*	*(musical staff)*	*(musical staff)*	*(musical staff)*
Chord type	Triad	Triad	Triad	Seventh chord	Seventh chord	Seventh chord	Seventh chord
Chord tone in the bass	Root	Third	Fifth	Root	Third	Fifth	Seventh
Chord position	Root position	First inversion	Second inversion	Root position	First inversion	Second inversion	Third inversion
Chord symbol example	A	A/C$\sharp$	A/E	A^7	A^7/C$\sharp$	A^7/E	A^7/G
Intervals above the bass	5 3	6 3	6 4	7 5 3	6 5 3	6 4 3	6 4 2
Figured bass shorthand	(add nothing)	6	6 4	7	6 5	4 3	4 2
Roman numeral analysis example (in the key of D)	V	V^6	V$^6_4$	V^7	V$^6_5$	V$^4_3$	V$^4_2$

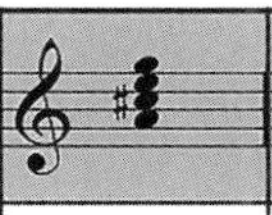

Fig. 9.18 Roman numeral analysis of inverted triads and seventh chords with figured bass symbols

As you may recall, harmonic fourth intervals above the bass are considered dissonant, and for this reason, second inversion chords (as well as third inversion chords, which additionally possess harmonic second intervals above the bass) are very unstable and tend to resolve to stronger-sounding chords. Second inversion chords also tend to appear only in a few specific situations, and theorists have thus devised labels for each second inversion chord that is used for a particular context. For example, the **passing** $^6_4$ (or passing $^4_3$ in the context of a second inversion seventh chord) is a second inversion triad (usually a V triad) that harmonizes a passing tone in the bass between more structurally significant chords. The previously mentioned A/E chord in bar 2 of the "Trumpet Voluntary" arrangement in Figure 9.17 is an example of a passing $^6_4$, while the subsequent A^7/E chord in bar 3 is an example of a passing $^4_3$; they both prolong tonic harmony by bridging the gap between the metrically accented I and I^6 chords's bass pitches of D and F$\sharp$. Passing $^6_4$ and passing $^4_3$ chords can be analyzed in a few different ways; they can be indicated in typical fashion using a Roman numeral followed by $^6_4$ or $^4_3$, or they can be analyzed with a capital "P" (for "passing") followed by $^6_4$ or $^4_3$. Another special type of $^6_4$ chord is the **arpeggiating** $^6_4$ (or Arp$^6_4$), which is an apparent second inversion triad formed when the bass line of a piece simply arpeggiates up or down between chord tones (e.g., root—third—fifth—root, root—fifth—third—root, or simply root—fifth—root) to embellish a root position harmony. These sonorities are rarely analyzed with a Roman numeral at all, but if they happen to be analyzed for the sake of clarity, Arp$^6_4$ may be used. Arpeggiating $^6_4$s appear frequently in the arrangement of the "Trumpet Voluntary," taking place during the second beat (or second half of the second beat, as the case may be) of bars 2, 4, 6, and 8. Figure 9.19 provides a complete Roman numeral analysis of the "Trumpet Voluntary" arrangement, including appropriate figured bass symbols that are added to Roman numerals to help signify inverted chords along with special symbols for certain

$^6_4$ chords. Observe that Roman numerals do not need to be provided in a repeated fashion when a chord is simply restated in a different inversion; adding lone figured bass symbols is sufficient for indicating inversion changes for a static harmony. Also note that some instructors may refer to figured bass symbols in these contexts simply as "bass position symbols" in order to more clearly indicate their contemporary usage in reflecting chord inversions, which is indebted to—yet distinct from—true figured bass practice.

Fig. 9.19   Complete Roman numeral analysis of Clarke's "Trumpet Voluntary," mm. 1–8

The other two common $^6_4$ chord types are the neighboring or pedal $^6_4$ and the cadential $^6_4$. The **neighboring** (or pedal) $^6_4$ is an apparent second inversion triad that is created when a harmony is expanded with a $^5_3$—$^6_4$—$^5_3$ interval pattern taking place over a static bass. The most common neighboring $^6_4$ expands tonic, with scale degree $\hat{1}$ being held or repeated in the bass while $\hat{3}$—$\hat{4}$—$\hat{3}$ and $\hat{5}$—$\hat{6}$—$\hat{5}$ melodic figures embellish the triad's chordal third and fifth, respectively, with upper neighbor tones. As the neighboring $^6_4$ consists entirely of linear voice-leading strands that happen to temporarily spell a second inversion triad, the Roman numeral analysis used for this chord clearly indicates the primacy of the harmony being expanded. In the case of the neighboring $^6_4$ that opens each phrase in Figure 9.20, the Roman numeral reflects tonic: I^5_3—$^6_4$—$^5_3$. Some analysts may prefer to use N$^6_4$ to indicate a neighboring $^6_4$, however.

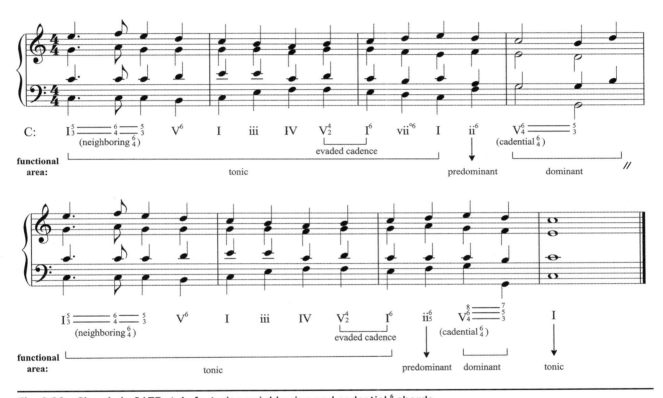

Fig. 9.20 Chorale in SATB style featuring neighboring and cadential $^6_4$ chords

The previous example features two instances of a cadential $^6_4$ as well: the first takes place on the downbeat of bar 4, while the second is heard on beat 3 of bar 7. The **cadential** $^6_4$ is an apparent I$^6_4$ sonority that embellishes the dominant at or near a cadence, with an upper voice tonic that resolves down to the leading tone of the dominant and an upper voice mediant that resolves down to the supertonic of the dominant. While some analysts label the cadential $^6_4$ with a bracketed [I$^6_4$] before a V$^{(7)}$ with a second level V below both labels to indicate that it belongs to the dominant area, this text (and others) more clearly indicates the embellishing function of the sonority and its attendant voice-leading resolutions to the focal dominant harmony by labeling the entire dominant area with V$^{8—7}_{6—5}$$_{4—3}$. The cadential $^6_4$, unlike most $^6_4$ chords, tends to take place on strong beats (although it often lands on beat 2 in triple meters), and it truly signals a dominant arrival to the listener despite being spelled as a tonic triad in second inversion. It is also effective in helping composers avoid parallels when moving to V chords—particularly when the phrase's predominant chord is IV.

Other Diatonic Harmonies and Voice-Leading Chords

At the outset of this chapter, you learned that most diatonic harmonies fall into one of the three functional categories—tonic (I in major keys), predominant (IV or ii, and vi more weakly), or dominant (V). You may have noticed, though, that the mediant triad (iii) and leading tone triad (vii°) were more or less left out of the discussion. This is because they tend to serve as "understudies" that substitute for more common functional harmonies in order to fulfill a specific melodic purpose (or to avoid a voice-leading issue related to the use of the more common harmony). In major keys, for instance, the iii chord often substitutes for I⁶—the chord employed the strict majority of the time when $\hat{3}$ is in the bass—when $\hat{7}$ is in the melody as part of a larger $\hat{1}$—$\hat{7}$—$\hat{6}$ idiom in which the leading tone does not move up to tonic (refer back to m. 2 and m. 6 of Figure 9.20 for such an example). The mediant triad can also serve as a very weak predominant in major keys, but typically it will either function as a tonic substitute or as part of a harmonic sequence, which is discussed later in this chapter. The leading tone triad, on the other hand, is almost never heard in root position in traditional tonal music, as this position of the chord includes a dissonant tritone above the bass. Instead, it tends to appear in first inversion, serving as a common understudy for a passing dominant, V^4_3 or P^4_3 (for example, see m. 3 of Figure 9.20). This is because the chord tones of any vii° triad are equal to the third, fifth, and seventh of any V⁷ chord; thus, the vii° triad can be thought of as a V^6_5 chord without a root. While the vii°⁷ chord in major keys is not common, as the half-diminished sound is rather out of place within major tonality, the vii°⁷ is heard frequently in minor keys, functioning as a worthy substitute for V^6_5.

While most diatonic harmonies possess the same function in minor keys as they do in major keys (e.g., I and i both function as tonic; IV and iv both function as predominants, etc.), the III chord in minor keys has a different character than the iii chord in major keys. This is because it serves as the tonic triad of the relative major key. As many minor-key pieces tend to employ the relative major (either as a simple sonority used to add brightness to the otherwise dark harmonic landscape, or as a new key center used in a modulation), the III chord often serves a tonic function—tonic of the relative key. However, III can also be used in a manner similar to iii when involved in the harmonization of a melody that descends from tonic to $\hat{7}$. One such idiom also features another lesser-used diatonic harmony in minor keys, VII, which tends to function as the dominant of the relative major—the V of III. The VII chord can be found in root position when a tonal piece actually moves away from the home key to the relative key; however, when there is no key change, VII is usually found in first inversion, connecting I and III as part of a brief nod to the relative key before moving on to a predominant chord (see Figure 9.21). In contemporary music, though, the VII chord is far more common (especially in root position), and tends to possess the same function as a dominant harmony (see Chapter 10).

Fig. 9.21 A common usage of the VII, III, and v chords in minor keys

One noteworthy aspect of this example is that it employs the minor dominant, v, from the natural form of minor. While the v chord can be found far more frequently in contemporary minor-key music, it was infrequently heard in traditional tonal music, as the major V functioned as the true dominant harmony. However, while root position v chords were rare, v^6 chords were employed as passing sonorities that helped accomplish a descending $\hat{1}$—$\hat{7}$—$\hat{6}$ bass line, as in Figure 9.21, where it is used to set up a Phrygian half cadence.

Each of the chords discussed thus far in this section are specific diatonic harmonies, and though they do not have strong functional roles themselves (as they substitute for others' roles or simply accomplish a linear, melodic goal), they would be indicated with scale step–specific Roman numerals in an analysis. There are, however, other sonorities that would not be analyzed with Roman numerals at all, as their scale-step identities are substantially mitigated or even eliminated by their lack of function; instead, these sonorities are best understood simply as the result of contrapuntal voice leading. Though they may spell certain diatonic triads or seventh chords, they do not truly sound as salient harmonies. One example of a voice-leading chord is the apparent "vi^6" sonority, which is better understood as 5–6 intervallic motion that embellishes a tonic triad before a real harmonic change (see Figure 9.22). Such 5–6 motion, which prevents parallel fifths when moving between chords whose roots are separated by step (as in I-ii), can truly elaborate most any chord, though it tended to involve tonic most often in the music of the common practice period. Another voice-leading chord is known as the "passing $\frac{4}{2}$" chord, which involves a move from a root position triad to an apparent third inversion seventh chord sharing the same root before a change of harmony. The purpose of the passing $\frac{4}{2}$ is to harmonize descending passing motion in the bass from the initial chord's root to a third below, as in Figure 9.22.

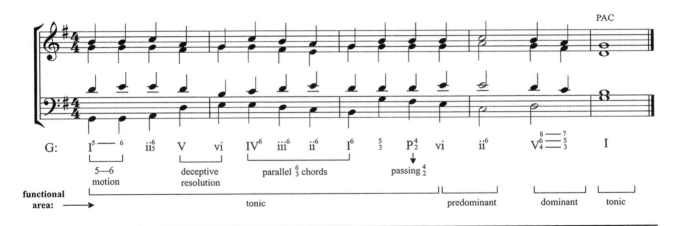

Fig. 9.22 Voice-leading chords

Another tonal idiom found in Figure 9.22 is the use of "parallel $\frac{6}{3}$" chords, which are voice-leading chords that are often used to harmonize linear intervallic patterns of parallel thirds or sixths between outer voices. Traditionally, strings of chords separated by step are not found in tonal music (e.g., I—ii—iii—IV), as this would either result in parallel fifths, parallel octaves, or extremely disjunct melodic motion used to avoid parallels. When placed in first inversion, however, issues related to parallels are all but eliminated. The byproduct of placing consecutive chords in inversion in this manner, though, is that their functional roles are likewise diminished, to the point that they are not worthy of Roman numerals in an analysis. In Figure 9.22, for example, the apparent subdominant triad (IV^6) does not signal a move to the predominant area, but rather serves as part of a larger idiom used to expand tonic.

Non-functional Chords and Progressions

First inversion IV chords, in fact, tend to lack predominant function in major keys in a variety of circumstances (as opposed to first inversion iv chords in minor keys, which are usually found participating in Phrygian half cadences).

One common use of the IV⁶ is to expand tonic as part of a I—IV⁶—I⁶ idiom that was often used at the very beginning of phrases, as in Figure 9.23.

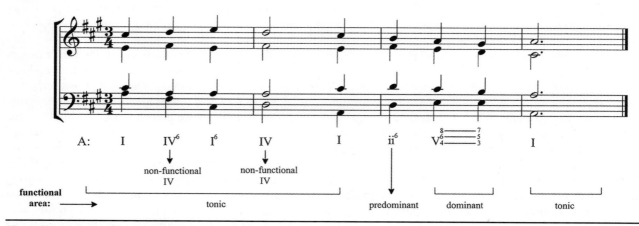

Fig. 9.23   Non-functional diatonic harmonies

This progression also features another IV chord that does not adhere to its typical functional role of bringing a progression to the dominant area. The most baffling aspect of this IV chord is that it is in root position, which typically correlates to a higher degree of functional strength and identity. In fact, IV chords were at times used to prolong tonic in the common practice, due to the smooth voice leading that accompanies plagal motion (with $\hat{6}$ and $\hat{4}$ serving as neighbor tones to $\hat{5}$ and $\hat{3}$ of the tonic triad, as discussed earlier in the context of the neighboring $\overset{6}{4}$). A tonic-expanding IV chord is simply known as a **non-functional IV chord**, as it does not behave in a functional manner. Figure 9.24 provides a chorale arrangement of a contemporary example featuring a non-functional iv chord, Klaus Badelt's "Underwater March" theme from the score to *Pirates of the Caribbean: The Curse of the Black Pearl* (transposed from the original key of D♯ minor to E minor for ease of reading). Aside from the frequent use of suspensions and other voice-leading embellishments, this example is noteworthy for incorporating a melodic reduction of the theme from another movement, "The Black Pearl," into a completely different key, tempo, and texture. As was the case in a previous example in this chapter, this excerpt from the "Underwater March" movement actually takes place over a consistent tonic pedal; however, the progression is far more audible than the pedal and thus the various functional areas in Figure 9.24 are perceived readily.

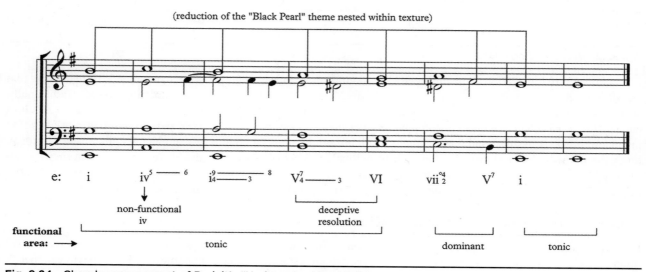

Fig. 9.24   Chorale arrangement of Badelt's "Underwater March" theme

While non-functional IV chords are relatively common, other chords may sound in a phrase that do not fulfill their expected obligations within the key, including root position dominants that sound "too soon" in a phrase and lead to I or i in a prolongation of tonic harmony. Even more confusing are **harmonic sequences**, which feature multiple non-functional chords that are bonded together by consistent voice-leading patterns. Harmonic sequences often possess transitional function, connecting phrases rather than serving as progressions within them; however, sequences can be instantiated within phrases in a brief manner to bridge harmonic areas. The most common harmonic sequence is the falling fifths sequence, so named because it features root motion by falling fifths that can be either consistently perfect (allowing for modulations to different keys) or diatonic (allowing the music to stay in key). The diatonic falling fifths sequence, which moves from tonic to tonic in its complete form (I—IV—vii°—iii—vi—ii—V—I in major keys), involves one of the only common bass line successions by tritone—the diatonic diminished fifth between the roots of the IV and vii° chords. As the latter portion of the falling fifths sequence (vi—ii—V—I) is both functional and common in a variety of styles of music (especially jazz), analysts do not typically describe such a progression as a harmonic sequence. Instead, the label tends to be applied only when the very atypical and non-functional I—IV—vii°—iii succession takes place. The falling fifth sequence may be elaborated in a variety of ways, such as including seventh chords instead of triads, or using alternating root position and first inversion triads and seventh chords.

Another common sequence is known as the descending thirds sequence, which features a two-chord pattern that consistently descends by diatonic third (I—V⁶, vi—iii⁶, IV—I⁶ in major keys). This scheme is alternatively known as a descending 5–6 sequence, as the two-chord groupings involve 5–6 intervallic motion created by a descending stepwise bass line. For example, the initial I—V⁶ move is characterized by a bass line, $\hat{1}$—$\hat{7}$, that creates 5–6 motion with a static $\hat{5}$ in an upper voice, as shown in Figure 9.25. While the descending thirds sequence typically utilizes alternating root position and first inversion chords, Johann Pachelbel famously employed the sequence with root position chords exclusively in his *Canon in D* (est. 1694), which is provided in reduced form within Figure 9.26. A variety of other harmonic sequences exist, as well, including the ascending version of the 5–6 sequence (e.g., I—vi⁶, ii—vii°⁶, iii—I⁶ in major keys) and the ascending fifths sequence (e.g., I—V—ii—vi—iii in major keys), though these are far less common.

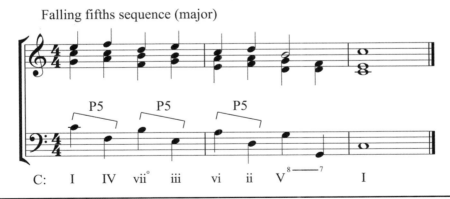

Fig. 9.25   Common diatonic sequences in major and minor keys

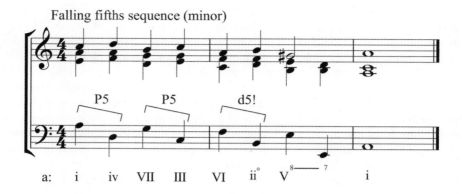

Falling fifths sequence (minor)

a: i   iv   VII   III   VI   ii°   V$^{8——7}$ i

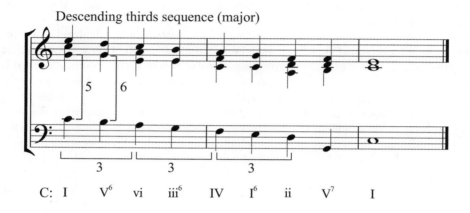

Descending thirds sequence (major)

C: I   V^6 vi   iii^6 IV   I^6 ii   V^7 I

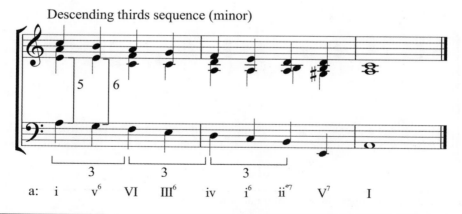

Descending thirds sequence (minor)

a: i   v^6 VI   III^6 iv   i^6 ii^{ø7} V^7 I

Fig. 9.25   (Continued)

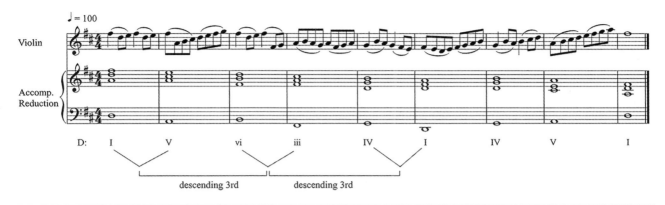

Fig. 9.26 Descending thirds sequence in Pachelbel's *Canon in D*

When analyzing a piece of music, remember that the finality associated with the cadential area of a phrase is in truth related to a confluence of factors that are harmonic, melodic, rhythmic, and metric in nature. At times, you may come across non-functional chords within a phrase, sequences within phrases (or between phrases), and even entire "progressions" that seem to move from tonic through the predominant to the dominant and back, all in the span of a few measures. Chord successions like these do take place, and while they usually serve to prolong tonic, they can be very confusing to a beginning student. The key to unlocking issues like these in an analysis is to listen repeatedly to the music you are exploring; a Roman numeral analysis ultimately serves to provide insight into how a piece sounds, after all. If you find yourself mechanically labeling vertical sonorities in a piece solely according to how they are spelled, you are definitely making a mistake.

EXPANDING THE DOMINANT AND PREDOMINANT AREAS

Much of this chapter to this point has focused on the plethora of ways composers traditionally expanded the tonic area of phrases. This is because the tonic area is by far the largest region in a phrase and thus there is a relatively wide variety of strategies for such expansion; the (optional) predominant area and dominant area tend to come immediately before a cadence, and do not require as much space within a phrase. Nonetheless, there are common methods for briefly expanding the predominant and dominant areas that warrant explanation. Expanding the dominant area usually involves one of two strategies. The first strategy involves moving between inversions of the V chord, which may be accomplished by literally changing inversions in immediate succession (e.g., V^6—V) or by doing so with the added embellishment of passing chords (e.g., V^6—P^6_4—V). The second strategy invokes the cadential $^6_4$ discussed earlier, which may be further elaborated via repetition and the addition of the chordal seventh (e.g., $V^{6-5-6-7}_{4-3-4-3}$). Expanding the predominant area can also involve moving between inversions of the same harmony using passing chords (e.g., IV^6—P^6_4—IV), though the greater number of possible predominant chords allows composers to enliven such progressions by changing harmonies (e.g., IV^6—P^6_4—ii^6, which features the same bass motion as before). Generally speaking, expansions of the predominant area tend to involves moves from weaker predominants to stronger ones, with the strongest predominant being ii (as it proceeds to V with the very strong root motion of a falling fifth that echoes the falling fifth motion from V to I). Figure 9.27 is a progression featuring expanded dominant and predominant areas, with the predominant expansion connecting the relatively weak predominant of vi to the relatively strong predominant ii^6 by way of a passing $^6_4$.

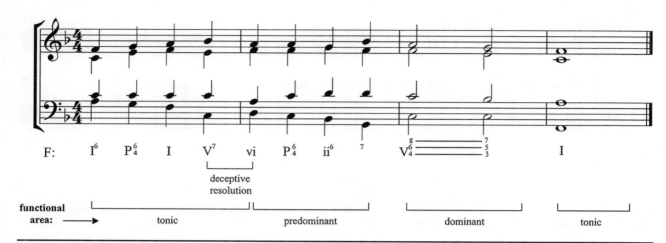

Fig. 9.27 Prolongations of the dominant and predominant areas

MELODY HARMONIZATION STRATEGIES

Now that you have explored harmonic structure in some depth within the context of common-practice tonality, you are able to harmonize a melody in a coherent manner that adheres to traditional norms. Doing so can be quite similar to completing a species counterpoint exercise, except that you are, in a way, reverse engineering the exercise by composing the slower and/or less intricate *cantus firmus* to the provided counterpoint line. One of the main differences between harmonizing a melody and crafting a species counterpoint solution, though, is that the focus tends to be on fitting the melodic tones into a progression that follows the basic phrase model when harmonizing a melody. A good *cantus firmus* should steer the counterpoint into a functional scheme, as well, but the composer is freer to attend to interval and line more exclusively in a species exercise. When presented with a melody that needs to be harmonized, the following strategies can be helpful in guiding your choices. First, decide on the most appropriate harmonic rhythm for the progression. It might be enticing to harmonize homorhythmically (that is, to have the rhythms of all of the parts be the same), but this may not always yield good results—especially if the provided melody features a lot of quicker rhythms, such as eighth notes in common time. Instead, try audiating the melody (i.e., singing it silently in your head) with a few different rates of harmonic change; it is common to change chords once per bar in faster tempos, with faster harmonic rhythms predominating in slower tempos. Traditionally, a cadence would take place in the last measure of a phrase, with the harmonic rhythm increasing immediately beforehand. Second, as in a species exercise, it can be helpful to work backward from the final bar instead of writing chronologically starting in the first measure. If the final bar features a cadence on tonic (or, in the case of an IAC, $\hat{3}$), expect to precede a final tonic harmony with one or more dominant function chords, with the predominant area optionally taking place slightly earlier. The beginning of the phrase, on the other hand, has the function of establishing the key center, so expect to use tonic harmony followed by quite a few chords that prolong tonic. Third, do not be afraid to cast certain melodic pitches as embellishments, such as passing tones, neighbor tones, etc. As noted previously, not every melodic pitch needs to be harmonized with a chord change. Typically, you will want to focus on the metrically accented melodic pitches—i.e., those that take place on strong beats, especially the downbeat—and ensure that these pitches represent chord tones from the chosen supporting harmony. However, feel free to make use of (rhythmically normative) accented passing tones, suspensions, and, less commonly, retardations if the result is a convincing, coherent chord progression. Finally, consider employing inverted harmonies in appropriate phrase locations to allow the bass line to create a nice counterpoint with the provided melody. It may be helpful to list the possible chords that cast each accented melodic pitch as a chord tone at first, reducing the process to a multiple-choice scenario. In time, you will develop such harmonic facility that this decision-making process will become second nature, and listing out each possible chord will be unnecessarily time-consuming. Figure 9.28 provides a melody as well as a few possible harmonizations that produce varying results. The first harmonization does not cast many of the melodic pitches as chord tones, resulting in a very atypical sound. The second harmonization uses homorhythm unnecessarily, creating chord tones with every single melodic pitch. Finally, a more successful solution featuring an appropriate harmonic rhythm is provided in the final system. This solution includes passing tones and an incomplete neighbor (specifically, an escape tone), as well as an accented passing tone that creates a delayed resolution to the dominant triad in the fourth bar. This accented passing tone is indicated with the label "APT" as well as an asterisk to denote that it is the sole accented pitch that does not represent a chord tone of the supporting harmony.

Fig. 9.28 Possible harmonizations of a given melody

DIATONIC HARMONY IN COMMERCIAL MUSIC

Importantly, the three functional areas of common-practice tonality that are focused upon in this chapter should not be regarded as representing rules that always need to be followed, especially in the twenty-first century, since modern music is free to be influenced by these traditions or reject them entirely. Generally speaking, though, tonic pitches and chords do remain in use as a means of establishing a sense of key, even in popular styles; as well, the submediant is often used as a tonic substitute. Moreover, dominant chords often maintain their dominant function, though a few other chords are often employed for this purpose (see Chapter 10). Predominant chords, on the other hand, are used more freely, and may appear at any point within a progression. Cadential structure in contemporary commercial music also tends to differ substantially from that of common practice music. Traditionally, a cadence would take place in the fourth bar of a 4-bar phrase (or the eighth bar of an 8-bar phrase), such that the phrase terminated in a prolonged state of rest. In modern popular styles, however, cadences tend to take place later, coinciding with the downbeat of the subsequent phrase to maintain an elevated perception of harmonic and rhythmic energy. In this scheme, the end of one phrase takes place simultaneously with the beginning of another, resulting in what is known as a **phrase elision** or phrase overlap. In the music of the Classical period, phrase elisions were noteworthy, surprising occurrences that deviated from standard phrase structures; however, they are entirely normative in pop styles, as they were in the music of the earlier Baroque period. Yet another distinction between traditional tonality and contemporary harmonic practice is that voice-leading restrictions—particularly regarding parallel and direct fifths and octaves—tend to be loosened dramatically. While smooth voice leading and tendency tone resolution remain largely in practice, modern music is characterized by a much freer use of dissonance and chromaticism.

Overall, however, you should avoid considering the harmonic language of contemporary commercial music to be at odds with that of so-called classical music, as in a black-or-white dichotomy. Instead, recognize that today's popular genres have evolved out of the common practice period in combination with several other musical traditions; as a result, there exists a spectrum of harmonic traditionalism within a variety of styles. Some popular songs may adhere strictly to the conventions of tonal practice, following the basic phrase model exactly from the tonic area through the predominant area to the dominant area and ultimately back to tonic. One such example is the tonal I—vi—ii—V progression from The Penguins's famous hit "Earth Angel" that is highly characteristic of the doo-wop style of the 1950s. This song was highly influential to other artists and has been featured in numerous films, including *Back to the Future*. Figure 9.29 provides an excerpt from this song in a special format known as a **lead sheet**, which is a concise, score-based overview of a song that includes a basic representation of the melody on the staff along with chord symbols above the staff that indicate the progression.

In many other cases, progressions are used in commercial music that subvert tonal norms despite being entirely diatonic. One extremely common harmonic device that is used in pop styles begins in a manner similar to

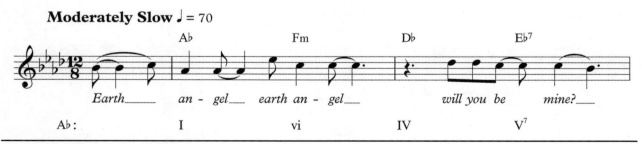

Fig. 9.29   Lead sheet excerpt of The Penguins' hit "Earth Angel"

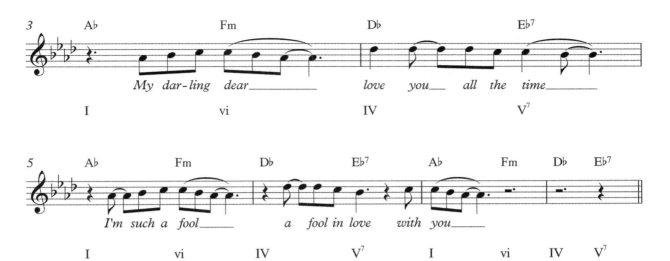

Fig. 9.29 (Continued)

a descending thirds sequence (I—V—vi) before moving to IV in a major key, ultimately moving back to tonic via plagal motion to repeat the scheme: I—V—vi—IV. A famous use of this progression—which would be considered a "retrogression" in the eighteenth century—can be heard in U2's 1987 hit "With or Without You" (see Figure 9.30). Note that the V chord is specifically an example of what is known as a "sus" chord, with a suspended P4 above the bass that does not resolve. This is a common sonority in popular styles that is related to the freer voice-leading practices of contemporary music. Sus chords are covered in more detail in Chapter 10.

Fig. 9.30 Lead sheet excerpt of U2's hit "With or Without You"

Another major-key chord progression that is heard quite frequently in a variety of popular styles is vi—IV—I—V, which again does not adhere to the basic phrase model (though its elided deceptive resolution V—vi at the beginning of every phrase is highly reminiscent of tonal practice). This progression is in fact a simple rotation of the sequence of chords shown in Figure 9.30: I—V—vi—IV rotated two positions in either direction creates vi—IV—I—V. Together, these two rotationally related progressions can be heard in hundreds of pop hits throughout recent history, and yet they only feature four different chords in a major tonality. Indeed, with regard to crafting chord progressions in major and minor keys, the possibilities are seemingly endless—especially given that the basic phrase model needn't be followed literally. Nevertheless, there are far more harmonic idioms that have yet to be explored, including chromatic harmony, modal harmony, and several other contemporary strategies.

SUMMARY OF TERMS FROM CHAPTER 9

tonic	half cadence	pedal point
dominant	Phrygian half cadence	figured bass symbols
predominant	deceptive cadence	passing 6/4
part writing	deceptive resolution	arpeggiating 6/4
voicing	plagal cadence/motion	neighboring 6/4
common tone	accented passing tone	cadential 6/4
phrase	incomplete neighbor	non-functional IV/iv
cadence	*appoggiatura*	harmonic sequence
PAC	escape tone	phrase elision
IAC	retardation	lead sheet
harmonic rhythm	anticipation	

CHAPTER 9—EXERCISES

1. **Chord Realization.** Using the notation provided, voice each chord indicated by the Roman numeral analysis in SATB style following traditional part-writing guidelines. Add a chord symbol above the staff as well, using slash chord symbols when appropriate.

a.

F: ii

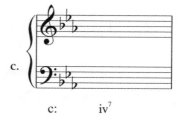

c.

c: iv⁷

b.

D: I⁶

d.

f#:   V⁶₅

2. **Error Detection.** The following examples feature attempted SATB-style cadences in various keys. Using the space provided below each notated example, explain why each cadence is improperly written, and indicate how each error should be addressed upon revision.

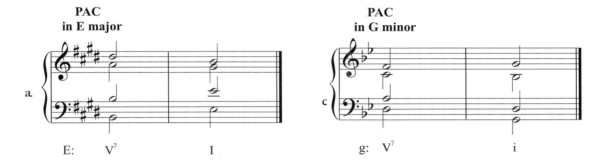

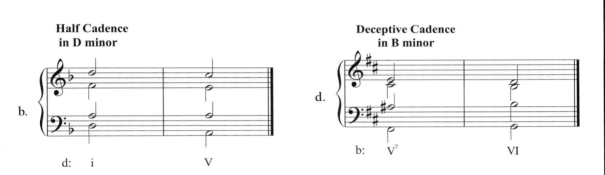

3. **Part Writing in Four Voices.** Using the notation provided, complete the realization of the indicated progression in SATB style using appropriate voice leading. The provided soprano voice may not be altered, and the remaining voices should use the same rhythms as the soprano. The first few chords have been voiced for you.

(Perfect Authentic Cadence)

I　　P$^6_4$　I^6　I　　ii^6　P$^6_4$　ii　V^7　　vi　ii^6　V$^{8\,-\,7}_{6\,-\,5}_{4\,-\,3}$　　I

4. **Melody Harmonization.** Using the notation provided, harmonize the given melodies using both root position and inverted chords as appropriate in four-part keyboard style (with downward-facing stems for the inner voices, which should both be notated in the treble clef staff). Ensure that the resulting progression follows the basic phrase model. Provide a Roman numeral analysis of the progression below the staff (complete with figured bass symbols as necessary) as well as a chord symbol analysis above the staff (complete with slash chord symbols as necessary).

    a. *Arranged reduction of Badelt, "The Black Pearl"*

    F:

    b. *Arranged reduction of Williams, theme from* Schindler's List

    B:

5. **Score Analysis.** Analyze the following score excerpt from Beethoven's Piano Sonata Op. 2 no. 1 using Roman numerals and figured bass symbols as appropriate. After providing the Roman numeral analysis, use labeled brackets to identify the tonic area, predominant area, and dominant area of the phrase. Additionally, circle all embellishing tones and identify the cadence that terminates the phrase.

f: _____   _____

cadence type: _____

_____   _____   _____

6. **Composition I.** Using the grand staff provided, compose a functional progression in SATB style that includes the following melodic and harmonic items: tonic prolongation via an inverted chord, tonic prolongation via a non-functional iv chord, an inverted predominant chord, a cadential $^6_4$, a deceptive cadence, and at least four melodic embellishments (chosen from passing tone, neighbor tone, anticipation, suspension, retardation, and incomplete neighbor). Be sure to include a Roman numeral analysis below the staff as well as a chord symbol analysis above the staff. After you have finished notating and analyzing your composition, recreate it in a DAW of your choice. Use one virtual instrument track for the piece, and choose a keyboard patch that best supports the mood of the composition. Once you are satisfied with the result, export the track as an uncompressed audio file (e.g., WAV or AIFF) and be prepared to deliver the session file to your instructor.

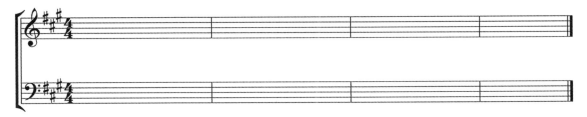

A:

7. **Composition II.** Using the notation provided below, create a lead sheet featuring an original melody that is supported by an indicated diatonic progression that features at least one inverted chord. The progression may be traditionally functional or may deviate from common-practice norms, but it must include at least four different diatonic harmonies. The progression may not repeat the first four bars exactly and must come to a cadence in the ninth bar. While the progression will not be realized in four voices, it must be indicated using both Roman numerals and chord symbols. Lyrics are not required. After you have finished notating your lead sheet, realize the composition in a DAW of your choice. Use a virtual instrument track for the melody, as well as any number of virtual instrument and/or audio tracks for supporting instrumentation, choosing patches that best support the mood of the composition. Once you are satisfied with the result, export the track as an uncompressed audio file (e.g., WAV or AIFF) and be prepared to deliver the session file to your instructor.

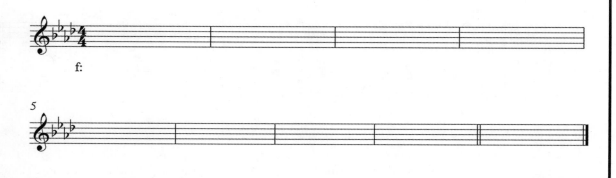

Chapter 10
Expanding Your Harmonic Vocabulary

In the previous chapter, you began to explore harmony from a traditional, functional perspective and learned some ways that modern music incorporates (or abandons) common-practice schemes. However, Chapter 9 focused entirely on diatonic harmonies—those that are more or less generated from major and minor scales and can be created using key signatures without additional accidentals. Though melodies and chord progressions in a variety of genres both old and new tend to use diatonic pitches the majority of the time, most music additionally incorporates chromatic sounds that involve notes from outside the key signature. This chapter focuses on chromatic harmonies, beginning with sonorities that tend to be associated with the common practice and moving chronologically into more modern harmonic trends from jazz and pop/rock music. Importantly, most of the scales and chord types discussed in this chapter are used in all three genres (concert music, jazz, and pop/rock styles), as well as many others; thus, the organization of harmonic topics should not be taken literally as an indication that certain styles incorporate specific sonorities exclusively.

CHROMATIC COMPOSITION: THE COMMON PRACTICE AND BEYOND

While chromatic composition was centuries old by the time of J. S. Bach, music from his time along with that of later composers in the common practice serves as an excellent introduction into the technique, as it adhered rather strictly to functional norms. Chromatic harmony from this era can thus be viewed as a set of colorful elaborations of the basic phrase model discussed in the previous chapter.

HARMONIC WRITING IN THE COMMON PRACTICE AND BEYOND

Chromaticism in the common practice period tended to be positioned in the middle of phrases, rather than at the beginning (the establishment of the tonic area) or the end (the cadential area). Most chromatic chords are therefore considered to possess predominant function and are often labeled as "chromatic predominants." This section will discuss several chromatic predominants that were used throughout traditional tonality, including secondary dominants and leading tone chords, borrowed chords from the parallel key, Neapolitan sixth and augmented sixth chords, and more. Though each of these chromatic harmonies was indeed used to instantiate **modulations** or changes of keys within compositions, they were more often used to embellish the arrival to dominant function chords—and other chords—in a colorful way without disrupting the listener's overall sense of tonic.

Secondary Dominants and Leading Tone Chords

One very common method of introducing chromaticism into a phrase is to accentuate an arrival on an important harmony (such as V) by preceding it with its own dominant function sonority, called a **secondary dominant** (or **secondary leading tone chord**, if the chord used is built on the note that is a half step below the target chord). Composing such an idiomatic progression—which is known as a **tonicization**, as it allows the target harmony to be heard fleetingly as a new tonic—involves thinking in the key of the target harmony temporarily, as opposed to the home key. This unique type of "forward thinking" is due to the fact that the chromatic chord relates to and applies to the upcoming harmony, not the preceding ones. The forward-relating nature of secondary dominants and secondary leading tone chords is reflected in Roman numeral analyses, as slashes are used to indicate that these chromatic harmonies function locally in tonicizing a target chord. For example, "V/V" in a Roman numeral analysis indicates that the labeled harmony is the V chord taken from the key of the phrase's dominant—thus, it functions secondarily as the "dominant *of the* dominant" and creates a stronger arrival to the primary V chord in the overall key. Similarly, "vii°7/V" indicates that the labeled harmony is the vii°7 chord taken from the key of the phrase's dominant, and that it is a secondary leading tone chord that ornaments the upcoming V chord within the overall tonal context. Figure 10.1 is an excerpt from Schubert's art song "An die Musik" (1817) that includes a vii°7/V chord that acts in concert with a cadential $^6_4$ to both tonicize and emphasize the arrival on the dominant at the end of the phrase. Importantly, however, this type of chromatic progression was not at all unique or noteworthy in the common practice; it was simply a common way to enliven a predominantly diatonic phrase.

Fig. 10.1 Schubert, "An die Musik," Op. 88 no. 4, mm. 3–6

Another example from the early Romantic era that includes secondary function chords comes from Beethoven's famous second movement to his Piano Sonata No. 8, the *Sonata Pathétique* (see Figure 10.2). The first secondary dominant takes place in second inversion as a V$^4_3$/V leading to the dominant triad, E♭, in bar 4. Note that the seventh of the B♭⁷ chord, A♭, resolves down by step in the accompaniment, while the D natural can be heard to lead in step-wise motion up to E♭ in the melody; the resolution of the tritone in secondary dominant and leading tone chords tends to follow the same pattern as it does in diatonic V and vii° chords—the (secondary) leading tone resolves up by half step, while the chordal seventh resolves down by step. Following these voice-leading tendencies is crucial, as it allows the tonicization to be convincing by recreating the same resolutions that take place in a move from V (or vii°) to I in the overall key.

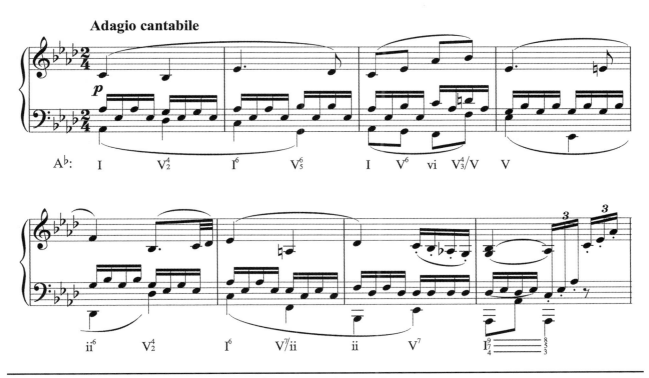

Fig. 10.2 Beethoven, Piano Sonata No. 8 (*Pathétique*), mvt. ii, mm. 1–8

Though the voice leading is much more disjunct (and thus non-traditional), another instance of a toniciza-tion takes place in the previous example in mm. 6–7. Here, however, the supertonic triad (ii, or B♭m in the key of A♭) is tonicized with a secondary dominant instead of the V chord. While the dominant is the most frequently tonicized diatonic harmony, any triad within a key may be tonicized, provided that it is not diminished in quality (as diminished chords cannot represent tonic in any secondary key due to their instability). Common secondary dominants in major keys thus include V$^{(7)}$/V, V$^{(7)}$/IV, V$^{(7)}$/ii, and V$^{(7)}$/vi; V$^{(7)}$/iii is rarely heard, as the median triad itself is an infrequently used harmony, as discussed in Chapter 9. Tonicizations in minor keys are somewhat less common, though V$^{(7)}$/V, V$^{(7)}$/iv, and especially V$^{(7)}$/III chords are used, with the latter being employed to move to the relative major.

Modulation to Closely Related Keys

Secondary function chords tend to be used most often in the relatively brief process of tonicization, where the target "tonic" is not confirmed with a cadence in the new key. They can be used to transition to new keys, too, via the process of chromatic modulation (discussed later in this chapter), but this can sound relatively jarring to the listener, especially if not handled properly. A smoother way of changing keys in a piece of music is via **pivot modulation** or common chord modulation, where a chord that exists diatonically in both the original and target keys creates a seamless transition. Pivot modulation is somewhat limited, however, as suitable pivot chords tend to be shared only by keys that are considered to be closely related—that is, keys whose key signatures are equal or differ by only one accidental. Figure 10.3, taken from the theme of the final movement of Mozart's Piano Sonata No. 6 in D Major, K. 284, demonstrates the common strategy used to modulate to the key of the dominant in a major key piece: using the original key's submediant harmony (vi) as the pivot chord, which becomes retrospectively reinterpreted as the supertonic triad (ii) in the target key. In this example, the pivot chord is in first inversion, allowing it to serve as the strong predominant ii⁶ in the key of the dominant.

Fig. 10.3 Mozart, Piano Sonata No. 6, mvt. iii, mm. 1–8

The smoothest pivot modulations are similar to Mozart's example in that the chosen pivot chord functions as a predominant harmony in both keys. This is because it is difficult for listeners to reinterpret tonic and dominant function harmonies in new keys—they possess such strong sonic identities that the result is a relatively jarring transition. Figure 10.4 provides a chart of pivot modulation strategies involving the closely related keys to C major, with pivot chords indicated for each modulation that serve as predominant harmonies in both the original and target keys.

COMMON PIVOT CHORDS BETWEEN CLOSELY RELATED KEYS			
Initial Key	Target Key	All Common Chords	Common Chords with Predominant Function in Both Keys
C (I)	a (vi)	C (I becomes III) Dm (ii becomes iv) Em (iii becomes v) F (IV becomes VI) G (V becomes VII) Am (vi becomes i) B° (vii° becomes ii°)	Dm (ii becomes iv) F (IV becomes VI)
C (I)	G (V)	C (I becomes IV) Em (iii becomes vi) G (V becomes I) Am (vi becomes ii)	Em (iii becomes vi) Am (vi becomes ii)
C (I)	F (IV)	C (I becomes V) Dm (ii becomes vi) F (IV becomes I) Am (vi becomes iii)	Dm (ii becomes vi) Am (vi becomes iii)
C (I)	d (ii)	C (I becomes VII) Dm (ii becomes i) F (IV becomes III) Am (vi becomes v)	F (IV becomes III)
C (I)	e (iii)	C (I becomes VI) Em (iii becomes i) G (V becomes III) Am (vi becomes iv)	Am (vi becomes iv)

Fig. 10.4   Chart of common pivot chords used to modulate to closely related keys

Mode Mixture

As noted earlier, traditional pivot modulation is rather restricted, as there is a low number of suitable "common chords"—especially predominant function chords that are diatonic in both the original and target keys—among pairs of keys, and as a result the technique tends to be used to move between closely related keys only. However, adding the chromatic harmonies created by the practice of **mode mixture** (alternatively known as "modal mixture," "modal interchange," or "modal borrowing") into the fold allows for a wider variety of key relationships to be manifested in pieces of music, which is discussed with more detail in the section on chromatic modulation later in this chapter. Mode mixture involves using **borrowed chords** from the parallel key, such as using harmonies from C minor in a phrase in C major. Perhaps the most well-known type of mode mixture is the use of the **Picardy third** in a progression, where the chordal third of the final tonic harmony in a minor-key piece is raised by a half step to create a major I chord, lending an uplifting sound to an otherwise dark harmonic landscape (see Figure 10.5). The Picardy third was commonly employed to support religious settings in the Baroque era, where it imbued more dismal musical contexts with a sense of divine hope.

Fig. 10.5   Chord progression involving the Picardy third

Mode mixture allows composers to create poignant, dramatic effects in pieces of music; it is often used in vocal music for the purpose of **text painting**, where the meaning of a word or phrase is reflected by musical parameters such as harmony. While mode mixture does take place in minor-key pieces (with chords such as I and IV being borrowed), it is far more common in major keys, with the borrowed tonic (i), supertonic (ii°), subdominant (iv), and submediant (♭VI) harmonies from the parallel minor employed to reflect negative or dark sentiments. Figure 10.6 is taken from Robert Schumann's art song "Ich Grolle Nicht" in C major from the song cycle *Dichterliebe* (composed in 1840); it features the use of the borrowed ii°6/5 chord from the parallel minor, C minor, during the word "Herz" (heart) to echo the narrator's broken heart in an instance of text painting.

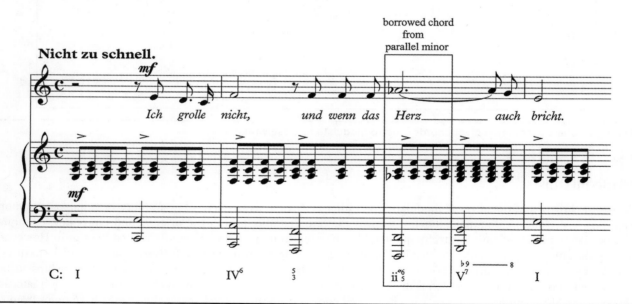

Fig. 10.6   Schumann, "Ich Grolle Nicht," mm. 1–4

Note that the only difference between the borrowed ii°6/5 chord (from C minor) and the diatonic ii6/5 chord in C major is the A♭, or ♭6̂, which is used in place of A (6̂). In fact, while borrowed chords from the parallel minor necessarily employ one or more of the scale degrees ♭3̂, ♭6̂, or ♭7̂ (as these are the scale degrees that differ from those of the major scale in minor scales), they tend to use $\flat\hat{6}$ most frequently. This is because strong predominant function chords employ the sixth scale degree, and mode mixture tends to involve these chords most often.

Neapolitan and Augmented Sixth Chords

Other very common chromatic predominants that utilize $\flat\hat{6}$ include the so-called **Neapolitan sixth** chord—a major triad in first inversion built on the lowered supertonic, $\flat\hat{2}$—and a trio of **augmented sixth chords** that additionally involve $\flat\hat{4}$ (and are so named because the interval from $\flat\hat{6}$ up to $\flat\hat{4}$ is an A6). The Neapolitan sixth (or N[6]) chord tended to appear in minor keys most frequently in traditional tonality, and created a very strong emotional effect before moving to the dominant. The move to the dominant would take place either directly (with a characteristic d3 melodic interval involved in the move from $\flat\hat{2}$ down to the leading tone, often voiced in the soprano to create contrary motion in the outer voices and avoid parallel fifths with the concomitant $\flat\hat{6}$—$\hat{5}$ resolution), or, more commonly, indirectly (via a cadential $\frac{6}{4}$, which avoids the d3). One famous example of an N[6] chord comes from the opening of Beethoven's "Moonlight Sonata," Piano Sonata No. 14 in C♯ Minor (see Figure 10.7). Here, the N[6] moves directly to V[7], with $\flat\hat{2}$, D natural, moving by d3 to B♭.

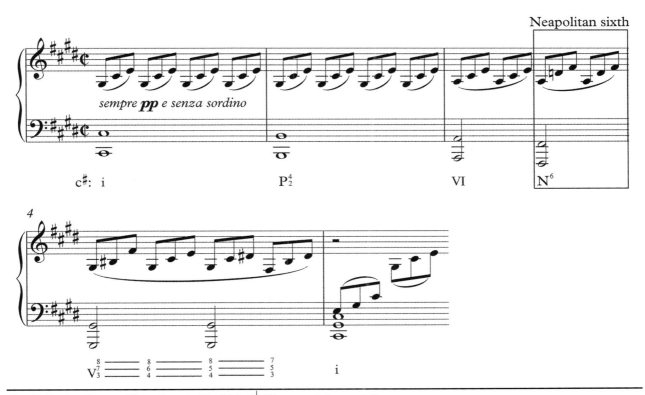

Fig. 10.7   Beethoven, Piano Sonata No. 14 in C♯ Minor, mvt. i, mm. 1–5

A more modern usage of the Neapolitan chord comes from John Williams's theme to the film *Raiders of the Lost Ark* (see Figure 10.8). Here, it takes place in root position (as opposed to first inversion) within a phrase in a major key—both rarities in traditional tonality with regard to this sonority. Nonetheless, the "♭II" chord does move to a repeated cadential $^6_4$—V resolution that hearkens back to the common practice.

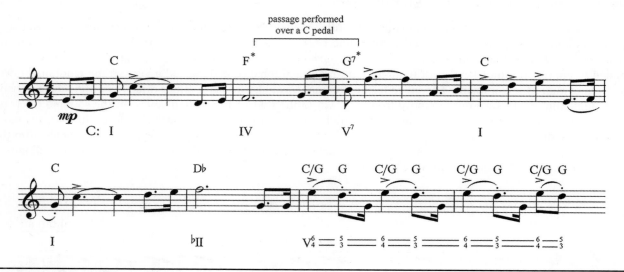

Fig. 10.8 Williams, theme from *Raiders of the Lost Ark*

While the traditional N⁶ chord can be thought of as a chromatic combination of voice-leading moves in a resolution to V ($\hat{4}$—$\hat{5}$, ♭$\hat{6}$—$\hat{5}$, and ♭$\hat{2}$—$\hat{7}$), it neatly stacks into thirds as a major triad built on ♭$\hat{2}$, and thus we can speak of "the Neapolitan" as a harmony that is located a half step above tonic in a key, in a manner similar to speaking of "the supertonic" as a harmony located a whole step above tonic in a key. Augmented sixth chords, however, are truly voice-leading chords with predominant function that are best thought of as combinations of scale degree "lines" resolving to V. There are three types of augmented sixth chords, and each includes a harmonic A6 interval from the bass, ♭$\hat{6}$, to #$\hat{4}$ above it in some voice (often the soprano) that resolves in contrary motion into a P8 on the dominant. The Italian augmented sixth chord (or It⁺⁶) includes these two degrees as well as tonic, which resolves down by half step to the leading tone within the dominant harmony. The French augmented sixth (Fr⁺⁶) adds tonic as well as the supertonic, which moves by common tone to the fifth of the dominant. The German augmented sixth (Ger⁺⁶) features both ♭$\hat{3}$ (moving to $\hat{2}$, usually after a cadential $^6_4$ sonority that is used to prevent parallel fifths with the bass) and $\hat{1}$ (moving to $\hat{7}$) in addition to ♭$\hat{6}$ and ♭$\hat{4}$, creating a sonority that is enharmonically equivalent to a V⁷ chord built on ♭$\hat{6}$—a circumstance that tended to be exploited by composers seeking to modulate to very distantly related keys. Figure 10.9 provides the voice-leading tendencies of each augmented sixth chord type (featuring cadential $^6_4$ chords for consistency, though only the Ger⁺⁶ requires it), while Figure 10.10 includes an excerpt from Beethoven's Bagatelle Op. 33 no. 4 that can be thought of as temporarily referencing all three augmented sixth chords in succession—though it is more appropriately considered to be a single Ger⁺⁶ that is embellished melodically via passing motion in a single voice.

Fig. 10.9 Augmented sixth chord resolutions by type

Fig. 10.10 Beethoven, Bagatelle Op. 33 no. 4, mm. 24–26

Chromatic Mediants

As the Romantic era progressed, composers more frequently exploited distant key relationships in their music—keys whose key signatures differ by more than one accidental. Often, these distantly related keys would represent the **chromatic mediant** relationship, especially a major tonic key (I) moving to the major mediant (III or III♯) or submediant (VI or VI♯). The first movement of Beethoven's famous *Waldstein* sonata, Piano Sonata No. 21 in C Major, for example, moves from the key of C to a second theme in E major, representing a move to the key of the major mediant. Schumann's fourth entry in the *Papillons* ("Butterflies") suite, Op. 2, on the other hand, begins by moving from the tonic key of A major to the major submediant (VI) key of F♯ major. Seamlessly moving from the tonic key to the key of a chromatic mediant often involved special chromatic modulation techniques, which are discussed in the subsequent section.

Chromatic mediant relationships weren't always instantiated by way of key changes, however. Indeed, as time passed, it became more common for composers to write progressions consisting of chords reflecting chromatic mediant relationships, particularly in the twentieth century. In major keys, this would result in moves from I to III, VI, ♭III, ♭VI, or even ♭iii or ♭vi. In traditional tonality, chords spelled like III and VI typically functioned as V/vi and V/ii, respectively, while chords spelled as ♭III and ♭VI were understood to be "borrowed chords" resulting from mode mixture. In each case, the chromatic chords were considered to either ornament or substitute for more common harmonies. In the more consistently dissonant music of the twentieth century, however, such harmonies would be used freely, without any "secondary" function categorization or lesser role within the harmonic drama. One famous example of a series of chromatic mediants comes from John Williams's main theme to *Star Wars* (see Figure 10.11), whose chord progression is D♭—B♭—F♭—D♭ or I—VI—♭III—I above a C pedal. This non-traditional set of harmonic moves can also be viewed as an example of **planing** from a D♭ major triad both down a m3 to B♭ major as well as up a m3 to F♭ major. Planing involves simply transposing a sonority to a different pitch level with all voices moving in parallel motion. Note the parallel fifths that result from planing the root position chords throughout the right hand of the piano reduction, particularly in mm. 6–7 with the quick alternation of major triads on F♭, E♭, F♭, E♭, and finally D♭.

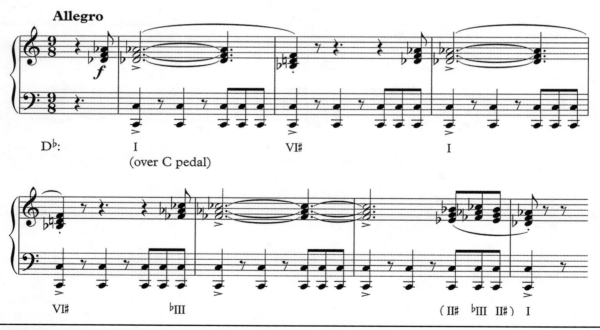

Fig. 10.11   Reduction of Williams, *Star Wars* (main theme)

Chromatic Modulation

As mentioned previously, moving between distantly related keys typically involves special modulatory techniques, as diatonic pivot chords are not shared between the original key and the target key in these instances. For example, C major and E♭ major share no common chords despite their key signatures differing by a modest three accidentals. There are, however, several **chromatic modulation** strategies that can be used to mitigate the potentially jarring effects of directly moving to distantly related keys such as these, including the use of chromatic pivot chords, chromatic sequences, enharmonic reinterpretation, and, simply, smooth voice leading (including voice leading by common tone).

A chromatic pivot chord is a chord used to modulate that is not diatonic in both the original and target keys. Figure 10.12a features a modulation from C major to E♭ major using the chromatic pivot of an Fm chord, which functions as the borrowed iv chord in the original key and the diatonic ii chord in the target key. Another harmonic tool used in chromatic modulations is the chromatic falling fifths sequence, which moves exclusively by descending P5 around the circle of fifths. Importantly, this sequence usually makes use of dominant seventh chords and involves irregular resolutions that create descending chromatic lines (see Figure 10.12b, which again modulates from C major to E♭ major).

A third modulatory method involves enharmonically reinterpreting a chord within the original key to yield a new meaning within the target key. There are two such types of modulation: enharmonic modulation featuring German augmented sixth chords and enharmonic modulation featuring fully-diminished seventh chords. The first type exploits the fact that dominant seventh chords and German augmented sixth chords are enharmonically equivalent (consider C—E—G—B♭, which is V^7 in F major, and its enharmonically equivalent counterpart C—E—G—A♯, which is a Ger^{+6} in E minor), and can be used to modulate to keys whose tonics are a half step apart. Figure 10.12c, for instance, begins in C major and moves to the V^7 chord, G^7, which is then reinterpreted as the Ger^{+6} (G—B—D—E♯) of the target key, B minor. Enharmonic modulation using fully-diminished seventh chords allows for even more possibilities, as fully-diminished seventh chords are symmetrical stacks of minor third intervals that can be respelled in at least four different ways, allowing for seamless moves to at least eight different keys. For example, a C^{o7} chord is enharmonically equivalent to a $B\sharp^{o7}$ chord, a $D\sharp^{o7}$ chord, an $F\sharp^{o7}$ chord, and an A or $G\times^{o7}$ chord, and thus has the potential to resolve as vii^{o7} to tonic in any of the following ten keys: D♭ major, C♯ major, C♯ minor, E major, E minor, G major, G minor, B♭ major, B♭ minor, and A♯ minor. Figure 10.12d features an enharmonic respelling of the borrowed vii$^{o6}_5$ chord in C major, B^{o7}/D, as the vii$^{o4}_2$ chord (F^{o7}/E♭♭) in the very distantly related key of G♭ major.

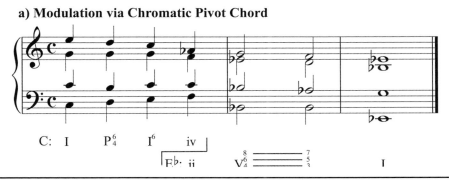

a) Modulation via Chromatic Pivot Chord

C: I   P$^6_4$ I^6 iv

E♭: ii   V$^6_4$ $\frac{8—7}{6—5}$ $\frac{}{3}$ I

Fig. 10.12 Chromatic modulation via chromatic pivot, chromatic sequence, and enharmonic reinterpretation

b) Modulation via Chromatic Sequence

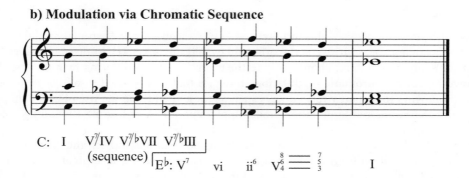

C: I   V⁷/IV V⁷/♭VII V⁷/♭III
(sequence) ⌐E♭: V⁷   vi   ii⁶   V⁶₄ ᵇ ⁸₆ ═══ ⁷₅₃   I

c) Modulation via Enharmonic Reinterpretation w/ Ger+6

C: I⁶   P⁶₄   I   V⁷
    ⌐b: Ger+6   V⁶₄ ⁸₆ ═══ ⁷₅₃   i

d) Modulation via Enharmonic Reinterpretation w/ vii°⁷

C: I⁶   P⁶₄   I   vii°⁶₅
    ⌐G♭:vii°⁴₂   V⁶₄ ⁸₆ ═══ ⁷₅₃   I

Fig. 10.12   (Continued)

While the preceding strategies for modulating to distantly related keys have each utilized chords, it is also possible to create such modulations by way of smooth voice leading. Simply holding or repeating a common dyad (two notes) or even a common tone (one note) as a bridge between a sonority in the original key and one in the target key, for instance, lessens the surprising effect of changing keys without any transition. Figure 10.13 is an excerpt from Schumann's art song "Widmung" from his song cycle *Myrthen*, Op. 25; in this F major edition of the piece, there is a common tone modulation from F major to the key of the lowered submediant, D♭, by way of a repeated F in both the vocal melody and the piano accompaniment.

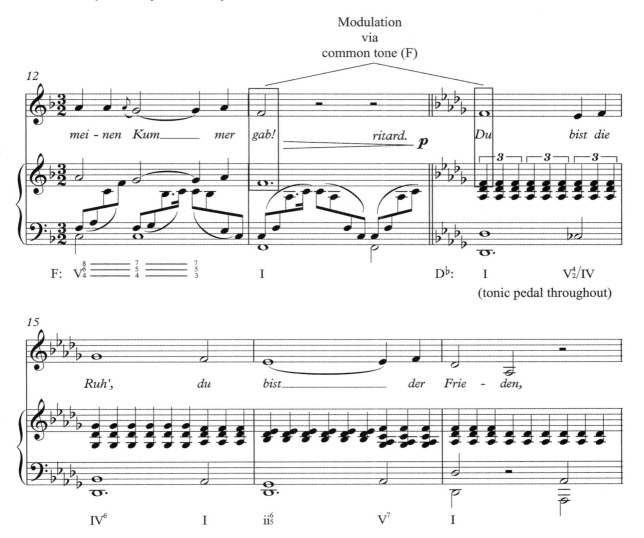

Fig. 10.13 Schumann, "Widmung," mm. 12–17

Common tone modulations, like the one in this example, have become quite common, particularly in film music, as they allow for smooth yet poignant transitions between scenes that portray different emotions or that take place in different settings.

MELODIC WRITING IN THE COMMON PRACTICE AND BEYOND

As music evolved into the late Romantic period, both harmonic and melodic chromaticism increased substantially. However, musicians still considered melodies to be written in major or minor keys using major and minor scales, with various chromatic alterations taking place for dramatic effect and/or to fit complex harmonic progressions that required melodic pitches from outside a given key. Around the beginning of the twentieth century, however, composers began crafting melodies using non-traditional scales more frequently. Two scale types that were prevalent in this period were whole tone and octatonic scales. While these scales are certainly featured in other styles of music (particularly in jazz), their use tends to be attributed to the so-called "art music" composers of the late nineteenth and early twentieth centuries.

Whole Tone Scale

The whole tone scale, as discussed in Chapter 3, is a scale composed exclusively of whole step intervals, dividing the octave symmetrically into a hexatonic or six-note collection of pitch classes. There are two whole tone scales, with one including C (e.g., C—D—E—F♯—A♭—B♭—C) and another including C♯/D♭ (e.g., C♯—D♯—F—G—A—B—C♯). Both versions of the whole tone scale are included in the famous "Prelude to the Afternoon of a Fawn" by Claude Debussy, a piece that has been included in the soundtracks to many films and television shows, including *True Blood* and even *The Ren & Stimpy Show* (see Figure 10.14). The whole tone scale was also a stylistic hallmark of jazz pianist Thelonious Monk, who used the scale throughout his career in both improvised solos and composed melodies.

Fig. 10.14   Debussy, *Prélude à l'après-midi d'un faune*, mm. 33–37 (flute melody)

Octatonic Scales

While the whole tone scales feature six different notes, the **octatonic scales**—as the name suggests—include eight notes in a consistent, symmetrical pattern of alternating half and whole steps. In fact, as this pattern of half and whole steps can be considered to result in two fully-diminished seventh chords that are a half step apart, jazz musicians call octatonic scales "diminished scales" and refer to them as either "half-whole" or "whole-half" diminished scales based on the pattern of steps above a given pitch class. For example, the C♯ half-whole diminished scale could be spelled as C♯—D—E—F—G—A♭—B♭—B—C♯. Other musicians instead consider there to be only three octatonic scales: Collection I that includes C♯ and D (e.g., C♯—D—E—F—G—A♭—B♭—B—C♯), Collection II that includes C and D (e.g., C—D—E♭—F—F♭—G♭—A—B—C), and Collection III that includes C and D♭ (e.g., C—D♭—E♭—E—F♯—G—A—B♭—C). These octatonic collections were used extensively in both melodies and harmonies by twentieth-century composers including Claude Debussy, Igor Stravinsky, Béla Bartók, Maurice Ravel, and others. Figure 10.15 is a piano reduction of the famous "Psalms chord" opening to Stravinsky's *Symphony of Psalms* (1930) that includes a snaking, repetitive sixteenth-note line that combines with the chordal punctuation to nearly complete octatonic Collection I (the E half-whole diminished scale), omitting pitch class C♯/D♭ only.

Octatonic Collection I [(C♯)-D-E-F-G-A♭-B♭-B-(C♯)]

Fig. 10.15 Stravinsky, *Symphony of Psalms* mvt. i, mm. 1–4

CHROMATIC COMPOSITION: JAZZ

HARMONIC WRITING IN JAZZ

Jazz harmony, while often quite complex, has a strong relationship with traditional tonal harmony—particularly that of the Romantic era. While this became less and less the case as jazz developed into the 1960s and '70s, the jazz standards that predominated in the bebop and hard bop periods—which were originally written during the 1920s and '30s as show tunes for Broadway musicals—do exhibit many of the traits of traditional tonality. Figure 10.16 recreates the standard "Have You Met Miss Jones?" (1937) by Rodgers and Hart in a jazz lead-sheet style. Note that the initial A section (mm. 1–8) within this standard, 32-bar AA'BA" form is almost entirely diatonic, featuring functional harmonic motion and a single secondary leading tone chord that tonicizes the supertonic. The B section or "bridge" is quite complex, though it does possess an internal logic: it is structured by tonicizations of keys separated

Fig. 10.16 Lead sheet of Rodgers and Hart, "Have You Met Miss Jones?"

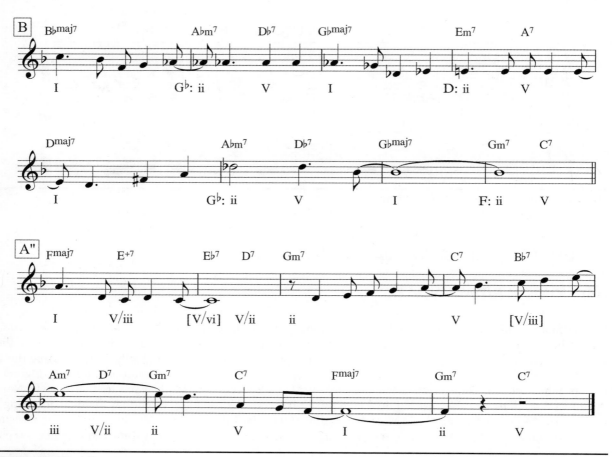

Fig. 10.16 (Continued)

by major thirds, creating chromatic mediant motion (from I to ♭VI to III♯ in the key of B♭) similar to that of pieces by Beethoven and his contemporaries.

Basic Jazz Progressions

While much of the harmonic structure of "Have You Met Miss Jones?" and other jazz pieces (or "charts") can be explained using terms that were originally used to describe common practice music, some of it is unique to the style and is best understood with separate terminology. For example, note that while the progressions do feature root motion by falling fifth or falling third (typical of traditional tonality), they also exhibit root motion by step and tritone in equal measure. Another difference between jazz harmony and common-practice harmony is the preponderance of tonicizations within jazz; they are so common that jazz musicians rarely discuss harmonic progressions of entire 8-bar sections of music as single entities and instead consider these sections to be composed of a series of brief visits to different keys. For example, the chromatic mediant relationships relative to the initial key of B♭ in the bridge of "Have You Met Miss Jones?" would be an unlikely topic of discussion during a rehearsal with jazz musicians; instead, the progression might be discussed simply as beginning on B♭ major, followed by a ii—V—I in G♭, followed by a ii—V—I in D, back to a ii—V—I in G♭, and finally to a ii—V—I in F to start the final A' section. This is because the ii—V(—I) pattern with sequential root motion by falling fifths (more typically ii⁷—V⁷(—Imaj7) in major keys and ii^{ø7}—V^7(—i^7) in minor keys, as seventh chords predominate in jazz harmony) is a hallmark of the style that is considered to be an important harmonic and formal unit in a manner similar to the basic phrase unit of I—IV—V—I from traditional functional harmony.

Another key harmonic progression within jazz is the 12-bar blues scheme. Importantly, jazz blues chord changes differ slightly from the traditional, guitar-based blues progressions that features I, IV, and V chords, as they instead include ii—V(—I) motion to lead into phrase beginnings (see Figure 10.17).

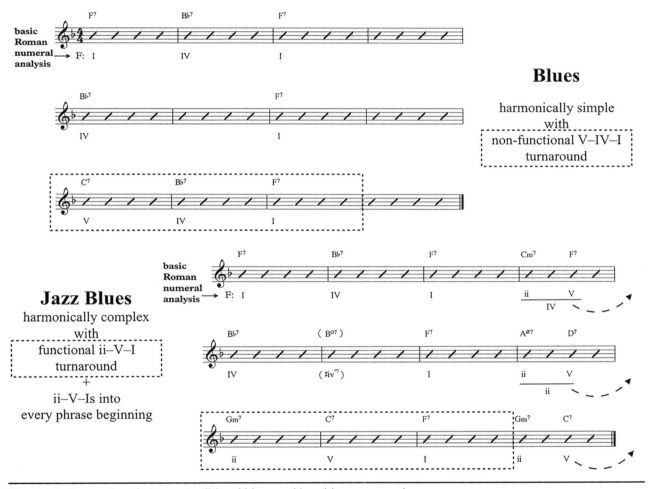

Fig. 10.17 Comparison between traditional blues and jazz blues progressions

Chords with Altered Fifths

Figure 10.18 recreates the final A' section of "Have You Met Miss Jones?" once more, as there are a couple of complex harmonic phenomena included in this section that merit mention. One such phenomenon is the E^{+7} chord within the purported key of F major, which is a dominant seventh chord featuring an altered fifth. The use of these so-called **altered dominants**—which can have either diminished or, more commonly, augmented fifths—can be traced back to the early Romantic era, as Beethoven, Chopin, Schubert, and others used these chords with some regularity in their music. In jazz, chords with altered fifths became quite prevalent and were used freely, with a classic example being the second harmony in Billy Strayhorn's standard "Take the A Train," which is a surprising $D^{\flat 7}_{5}$ chord in the key of C that moves to the more typical, diatonic Dm^7 afterward. In the "Have You Met Miss Jones?" example, the E^{+7} is used to harmonize pitches C (enharmonically equivalent to B♯, the augmented fifth above E) and D (the seventh of the chord), and it aids in the creation of a sequential root motion descent by half step to D^7, which in turn is used to tonicize the subsequent Gm^7 chord (the "ii" within the upcoming ii—V in F major).

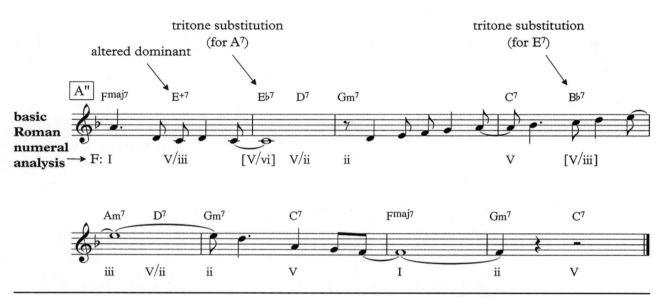

Fig. 10.18 Lead sheet of the final A' section of Rodgers and Hart, "Have You Met Miss Jones?"

Tritone Substitutions

Such sequential root motion descents by half step (as in the previous example) are characteristic of another complex harmonic technique that is idiomatic to the jazz style: the **tritone substitution**. In Figure 10.18, there are two instances of root motion by descending half step; the first is the E^{+7}—$E^{\flat 7}$—D^7 progression mentioned a moment ago, and the second is the $B^{\flat 7}$—Am^7 motion that leads into the final four bars of the form. In each case, the penultimate chord is a dominant seventh chord that can be thought of as substituting for a more normative dominant seventh chord (whose root is located a tritone away) that would create root motion by falling fifth in a manner similar to a ii—V(—I) progression. In the first instance, the $E^{\flat 7}$ chord substitutes for an A^7 that would create typical, circle-of-fifths root motion of E—A—D within the progression. The resulting $E^{\flat 7}$—D^7—Gm^7 progression possesses a somewhat traditional sound despite the tritone substitution, as it is enharmonically equivalent to Ger^{+6}—V^7—i^7 in the key of G minor; indeed, all Ger^{+6} chords are enharmonically equivalent to—and share predominant function with—the tritone substitution for V^7/V in this manner. The later $B^{\flat 7}$ chord in Figure 10.18 substitutes for an E^7, which would function as the dominant in the tonicization of the upcoming Am^7 sonority. Tritone substitutions "work" within progressions because dominant seventh chords located a tritone away from one another share two common tendency tones: the characteristic chordal third and seventh of a normative dominant seventh chord (e.g., C♭ and F within G^7, the V^7 in C major) simply become enharmonically recast as the chordal seventh and third of the harmony representing the tritone substitution (e.g., C♭ and F within $D^{\flat 7}$, the "tritone sub" of ♭II^7 in C major). Generally speaking, harmonies such as these, which share two or more chord tones with one another, can serve as effective chord substitutes; this is discussed with more depth in the later section on reharmonization.

"Add Chords" and Extended Chords

An important characteristic of jazz harmony is the use of chords beyond standard triads and seventh chords, as alluded to earlier in the section on altered dominants. One important category of sonorities featured in both jazz and popular music is that of the **add chord**, in which a note is simply added to a triad that creates an interval of a major sixth or major second above the chord's root in some octave. In practice, chord symbols for added sixth chords may spell out the word "add" after the indication of the triad (e.g., $E\flat^{add6}$ for an $E\flat$ major triad to which a C is added, representing a M6 above the root), or they may simply include a "6" (e.g., $E\flat^6$). Importantly, major sixth intervals are also added to minor triads for such "add chords," despite the M6 not being diatonic in the minor key of the chord's root. For example, a Cm^6 chord would be spelled C—$E\flat$—G—A, despite A not being the diatonic submediant within the key of C minor. Another important clarification regards the difference between Arabic numerals within chord symbols and those used as figured bass symbols: while figured bass symbols are added to Roman numerals below the staff and represent intervals above a given bass pitch (and, indirectly, chord inversions), numerals added to chord symbols above the staff always represent intervals above a chord's root. In a figured bass context, then, Cm^6 would refer to a C minor triad in first inversion with $E\flat$ in the bass; however, in a chord symbol context, Cm^6 refers to a C minor triad with an added major sixth above C.

In addition to "add 6" chords, musicians commonly use "add 2" (or "add 9") chords that include an added interval of a M2 above the root in some octave (as well as "6/9" chords that add both a M6 and a M2 above the root). Thus, a C^{add2} chord would include the note of the C major triad (C—E—G) as well as the note located a major second above C, which is D.

While the chord symbols C^{add6} and C^6 are interchangeable, however, C^{add9} and C^9 are not. C^9 represents yet another type of jazz harmony, an **extended chord** that consists of a seventh chord with one or more additional third intervals added "on top" to create a large tertian sonority of four or more consecutive thirds. Each chord tone creating a compound interval above the root is considered a **chord extension**, and the common, tertian extensions represent the intervals of a ninth, eleventh, and thirteenth above the root. In order to avoid extremely dissonant m9 intervals between the chord tones of the root, third, fifth, and seventh and the added chord extensions, jazz composers tend to use M9, A11, and M13 extensions above major seventh and dominant seventh chords, creating chord symbols such as C^9, $C^{9(\sharp 11)}$, and C^{13}. For the same reason, M9, P11, and M13 extensions are used above minor seventh chords, creating chord symbols such as Cm^9, Cm^{11}, and Cm^{13}. Importantly, these guidelines related to adding chord extensions are not always followed; when crafting a progression that makes use of extended chords, choose the extensions that result in the smoothest voice leading into the harmonies that follow.

A few other pieces of information regarding chord extensions merit mention. First, extensions tend not to be used frequently with half- and fully-diminished seventh chords. Second, chord symbols with a lone superscript [11] or [13] assume the inclusion of the chordal seventh, along with a potential ninth ([11] and [13]) and eleventh ([13]). Moreover, chord symbols without a quality designation such as "maj" or "m" represent a dominant seventh chord quality. Thus, the C^9 chord mentioned earlier would be spelled C—E—G—$B\flat$—D, as opposed to the C^{add9} chord that does not include $B\flat$. Finally, dominant seventh chords—which are relatively dissonant sonorities due to their included tritones—routinely involve altered chord extensions, such as $\flat 9$, $\sharp 9$, and $\flat 13$ in addition to the standard $\sharp 11$. This is especially the case in minor keys, as the $\flat 9$, $\sharp 9$, and $\flat 13$ extensions above a V^7 chord represent diatonic scale degrees from the natural minor that can resolve smoothly into tonic harmonies. Figure 10.19 reproduces a section of Vince Guaraldi's famous jazz chart "Christmas Time Is Here," which was featured in the animated film *A Charlie Brown Christmas* (1965); this tune is notable for its use of chord extensions in the melody, such as the A natural representing the $\sharp 11$ extension of the $E\flat^{13}$ chord in the second and fourth measures. Figure 10.20 provides a summary of common jazz sonorities and their related chord symbols. Of note in this example are the two "**sus**" chords, C^sus4 and C^7sus4, which are quartal harmonies (i.e., harmonies generated by fourth intervals) that get their name from the common 4–3 suspension that temporarily creates a sonority with both a P5 and a P4 above the bass in common-practice tonality.

Fig. 10.19   Lead sheet of the A section to Guaraldi, "Christmas Time Is Here"

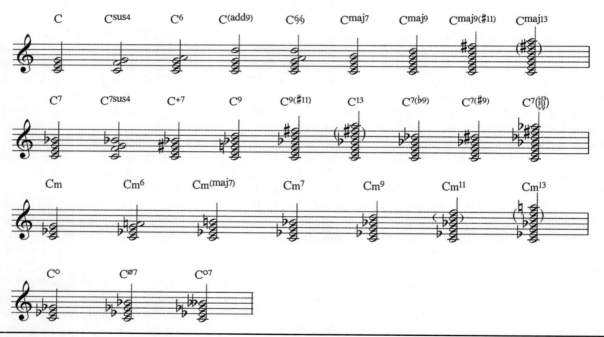

Fig. 10.20   Summary of common jazz chords

Reharmonization

One of the enduring legacies of the bebop era is jazz musicians' commitment to reworking and reharmonizing tunes from previous eras. Dizzy Gillespie and Charlie Parker, in particular, were known for reharmonizing popular show tunes with complex chord changes and then crafting new melodies to fit those changes to create **contrafacts**—pieces with familiar harmonic structures to which different melodies are added. The most well-known set of contrafacts in the jazz style are called "rhythm changes" tunes, as their harmonic progressions are derived from George and Ira Gershwin's 1930 song "I Got Rhythm" from the musical *Girl Crazy*. There are hundreds of rhythm changes tunes, many of which have become jazz standards themselves, such as Charlie Parker's "Anthropology," Lester Young's "Lester Leaps In," Sonny Rollins's "Oleo," and Thelonious Monk's "Rhythm-A-Ning."

While rhythm changes tunes tended to more or less maintain the harmonic structure from "I Got Rhythm," other contrafacts featured more extensive reharmonizations of their source material. Reharmonization is a very complex topic (indeed, jazz arranging books often dedicate several chapters to it), but generally speaking, individual chord substitutions "work" in a reharm when the original chord and substitute chord share one or, ideally, two chord tones. The tritone substitution involving dominant seventh chords that was discussed earlier in this chapter, for instance, features two common tones. A major tonic triad (e.g., C major), then, can be substituted with a number of chords that preserve two common tones, including vi^7 (Am^7, which preserves C, E, and G), iii^7 (Em^7, which preserves E and G), IV^{maj7} (Fmaj^7, which preserves C and E), ii^9 (Dm^9, which preserves C and E), $\flat$VI^{maj7} (A$\flat$maj^7, which preserves C and G), $\flat$VII$^{9(\sharp11)}$ (B$\flat^{9(\sharp11)}$, which preserves C and E), $\flat$III^{maj13} (E$\flat^{maj13}$, which preserves C and G), and several others. However, chords can also be substituted with one another based solely on one common tone, provided that the rest of the voice leading, both into and out of the substitute chord, is smooth.

MELODIC WRITING IN JAZZ

Melodically, jazz makes use of the same materials as so-called classical music, including diatonic scales, chromatic alterations, whole tone scales, and octatonic scales (though they are known as diminished scales in a jazz context, as mentioned previously). As evidenced in the previous example, sequential melodic motion is additionally characteristic of the style. Furthermore, jazz artists frequently utilized scales associated with folk and popular styles, including pentatonic scales and blues scales.

Pentatonic Scales

Pentatonic scales are five-tone pitch collections that can be thought of as rotations of the diatonic system without the tritone interval that exists between $\hat{4}$ and $\hat{7}$ in the major scale and $\hat{2}$ and $\hat{6}$ in the natural minor. While there are technically five different "modes" or rotations of a given pentatonic collection, the two that are used most often in music are the major pentatonic scale and the minor pentatonic scale. The major pentatonic scale can be thought of as representing scale degrees $\hat{1}$—$\hat{2}$—$\hat{3}$—$\hat{5}$—$\hat{6}$—$\hat{1}$ of a major scale (e.g., C—D—E—G—A—C), while the minor pentatonic scale includes scale degrees $\hat{1}$—$\hat{3}$—$\hat{4}$—$\hat{5}$—$\hat{7}$—$\hat{1}$ from the natural minor (e.g., A—C—D—E—G—A, the same pitch classes as its "relative," the major pentatonic, simply "rotated" down in pitch one position). The lack of the characteristic tritone interval in the pentatonic scales creates an extremely consonant set of pitches (as the only fourth and fifth intervals are perfect in quality) that does not have the classically tonal tendency tones that drive functional harmony. As a result, pentatonic scales have been used in a wide variety of styles, from relatively tonal folk music to that of the post-tonal avant garde. In jazz, pentatonic scales are used in the creation of composed melodies as well as improvised solos, where they are a favorite of beginning players due to their consonant sounds (which tend to "fit" a wide variety of chord progressions, making mistakes less frequent). Figure 10.21 reproduces the B section of McCoy Tyner's "Passion Dance," which exclusively uses the pitches from the E$\flat$ minor pentatonic scale in the melody (E$\flat$, G$\flat$, A$\flat$, B$\flat$, and D$\flat$) atop both B$\flat$ and E$\flat$ pedal tones. This particular collection is perhaps the easiest pentatonic scale to visualize on the keyboard, as it comprises the black keys along with its relative, the G♭ major pentatonic scale.

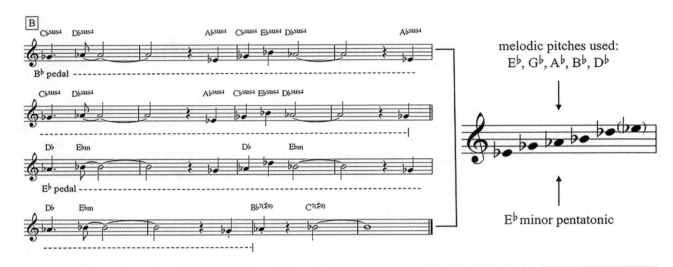

Fig. 10.21   Lead sheet of the B section to Tyner, "Passion Dance"

Blues Scale

Very much related to the minor pentatonic scale is the six-tone **blues scale**, perhaps the most characteristic melodic pitch collection in jazz (and, of course, blues). The blues scale has additionally been an important component of several other popular music styles, including rock, R&B, and hip-hop, for over a century. The only difference between a blues scale and a minor pentatonic scale is the addition of what is known as the "blue fifth" or "flat five," which is most often notated as a lowered fifth scale degree located a tritone above or below the pitch center. Thus, while an A minor pentatonic scale is spelled A—C—D—E—G—A (or $\hat{1}$—$\flat\hat{3}$—$\hat{4}$—$\hat{5}$—$\flat\hat{7}$—$\hat{1}$ from natural minor), an A blues scale is spelled A—C—D—E♭—E—G—A ($\hat{1}$—$\flat\hat{3}$—$\hat{4}$—$\flat\hat{5}$—$\hat{5}$—$\flat\hat{7}$—$\hat{1}$). In practice, this "blue fifth" is usually more of an inflection than a true scale degree, and it often appears as a "bent" note that tends downward to scale degree $\hat{4}$ (or, slightly less commonly, upward to scale degree $\hat{5}$ from the "sharp four") to create a very soulful embellishment. The blues scale is used similarly to pentatonic scales, as it sounds appropriate in a wide variety of harmonic contexts. Thus, an improviser can use a blues scale to solo over minor seventh chords, dominant seventh chords, ii—V—Is in both major and minor keys, etc. There are also many famous jazz charts whose composed melodies are derived from the blues scale, as well as successful modern pop/rock singles.

CHROMATIC COMPOSITION: POP/ROCK MUSIC

While the chromatic harmonic practices of R&B, funk, soul, and hip-hop can be traced to those of jazz and blues styles, pop/rock music largely avoids jazz's complex chord changes and frequent tonicizations, instead sticking to primarily diatonic triads within a single key. In this way, it may be tempting to compare pop/rock harmony with common-practice tonality. However, pop/rock harmony is often less traditionally functional than jazz (which is characterized by a near-constant use of ii—V[—I]s), and it possesses several unique idioms that will be explored later in this section.

MELODIC WRITING IN POP/ROCK MUSIC

Melodically, pop/rock music is very syncopated in a manner similar to jazz and blues, though its pitch content tends to be limited to major and minor scales (with relatively infrequent chromatic alterations to "fit" non-diatonic progressions), pentatonic and blues scales, and diatonic modes. Songwriters do not typically choose whole tone, octatonic, and chromatic scales when composing melodies.

Pentatonic and Blues Scales

Pentatonic and blues scales predominate in pop/rock music, which is no doubt related to the heavy influence from folk and blues styles—genres that were characterized by the near-exclusive use of such scales. Several rock styles, including "classic rock," hard rock, and heavy metal (which scholars often refer to en masse as "blues-based rock"), make use of pentatonic and blues scales in nearly every layer of a song—both within the main guitar-and-bass "riff" in the accompaniment as well as in the vocal melody. However, this is not an exclusive trait of rock music; other popular styles such as R&B can be similarly "saturated" with these scales. One such example comes from The Temptations' hit song "My Girl" (1965), which is reproduced in Figure 10.22. Note that the melody is derived exclusively from the C major pentatonic scale, while the famous guitar line alternates between C and F major pentatonic scales to follow the I—IV—I—IV plagal progression that characterizes the beginning of the song's verses.

Fig. 10.22   Lead sheet of the initial verse from The Temptations, "My Girl"

Diatonic Modes

Another set of scales used frequently in rock music is the collection of **diatonic modes**—the various "rotations" of the diatonic collection. The diatonic modes have existed for centuries and can be traced back to the melodies of the ancient Greeks, though there was a renewed interest in them for compositional purposes during the twentieth century—both in rock and jazz (hence the term "modal jazz") as well as in concert music. As you are already aware, major scales and their relative minor scales are made of the same pitch classes; they are simply rearranged to begin at two different places within the overall diatonic collection. These "relatives" represent only two of seven possible starting points for scales in the collection, however. The seven intervallically unique modes within the diatonic system are each named after tribes or regions in ancient Greece: **Ionian** (which is the major scale, viewed most easily on the white keys on the piano from C to C), **Dorian** (a minor scale with a raised sixth degree, as in the white keys from D to D), **Phrygian** (a minor scale with a lowered second degree, as in the white keys from E to E), **Lydian** (a major scale with a raised fourth degree, as in the white keys from F to F), **Mixolydian** (a major scale with a lowered seventh degree, as in the white keys from G to G), **Aeolian** (the natural minor), and **Locrian** (a minor scale with a lowered fifth degree and a lowered second degree, as in the white keys from B to B). Figure 10.23 provides a summary of the diatonic modes using the "natural" pitch classes that are visible on the white keys on the piano. Note that each mode uniquely positions the two diatonic half steps (which are indicated with a pointed bracket).

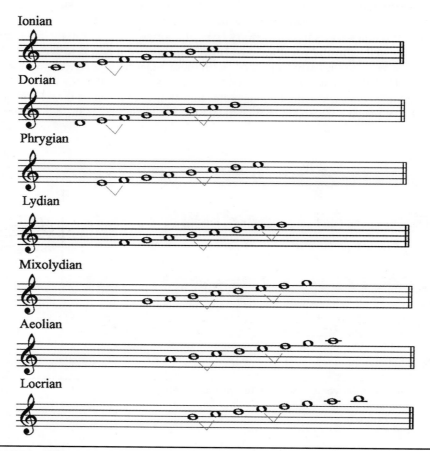

Fig. 10.23   The diatonic modes

Just as major and minor scales yield starkly different emotional qualities in music, each diatonic mode possesses its own unique affect and is thus applicable for specific dramatic contexts. For example, the "otherworldly" quality of the Lydian mode tends to make it useful in film music (particularly in the sci-fi and fantasy genres), while the bluesy subtonic of the Mixolydian mode makes it especially appropriate for major-key rock tracks.

"Darker"-sounding modes, such as the Phrygian and Locrian modes, tend to be used in the formation of riffs in the hard rock and heavy metal genres, among several other applications. One notable example of a "metal" riff that possesses a Phrygian sound comes from the repeated bass line to Tool's song "Forty-Six & 2" (1998), which is reproduced in Figure 10.24.

Fig. 10.24   The main bass riff from Tool, "Forty-Six & 2"

Perhaps the most noteworthy aspect of this riff is the alteration to the Phrygian mode that takes place at the end of the riff via the inclusion of F♯, creating an altered or "synthetic" scale that is known alternatively as the Phrygian dominant scale, the Spanish Phrygian scale, or simply the fifth mode of the harmonic minor (among several other names). Altering modes by introducing accidentals (and even additional pitches) can yield inspiring results and can help you "artificially" generate new ideas in a logical way as a composer.

HARMONIC WRITING IN POP/ROCK MUSIC

As noted earlier in this chapter, pop/rock harmony tends to employ diatonic triads with regularity, though borrowed chords, sus chords, and add chords also predominate. A primary difference between pop/rock harmony and that of the music of the common practice, however, is that it is only loosely functional relative to such centuries-old traditions. For example, the two stock pop/rock progressions discussed at the end of Chapter 9, I—V—vi—IV and its rotation vi—IV—I—V, feature plagal chord successions that would be considered retrogressions by tonal standards. In pop/rock music, though, IV—I is often used to create strong harmonic conclusions in the same manner as V—I, and blues-derived V—IV "retrogressions" are entirely normative. In addition, repetitive chord successions such as I—vi—I—vi, IV—I—IV—I and its retrograde I—IV—I—IV are not problematic (as would be the case in traditional tonality).

Modal Harmony

As many of pop/rock music's chord progressions defy the norms of standard major/minor functionality, theorists have more recently begun to understand them as representing modal harmony (progressions derived from the diatonic modes). For example, the extremely common ♭VI—♭VII—i progression that is used in songs like Bon Jovi's 1986 hit "Livin' On a Prayer" (see Figure 10.25) can be understood simply as representing a string of diatonic chords built on scale degrees $\hat{6}$, $\hat{7}$, and $\hat{1}$ of the Aeolian mode, without attempting to apologize for the lack of a dominant function chord within a traditionally functional minor key context.

♭VII as V

Given the extreme frequency with which pop/rock phrases conclude with ♭VII—i/I chord successions, however, most musicians consider subtonic chords like the one in the previous example to truly possess dominant function.

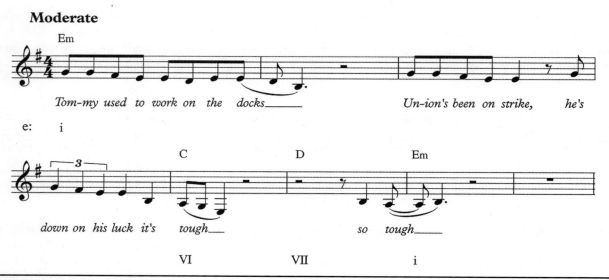

Fig. 10.25 Lead sheet of the first verse from Bon Jovi, "Livin' On a Prayer"

After all, the ♭VII chord does share two common tones with V^7 ($\hat{2}$ and $\hat{4}$, the same common tones shared by the leading tone triad). This fact was exploited by jazz musicians, who frequently used what became known as the "back-door progressions" of ii—♭VII—I and iv—♭VII—I to lead to tonic in lieu of the standard ii—V—I scheme. Generally speaking, both V and ♭VII are considered to possess dominant function in popular genres; while leading tone chords are also dominant harmonies, they are seldom used in these styles.

Power Chords

Another noteworthy aspect of many rock songs including "Livin' On a Prayer" is their consistent use of fifth intervals as primary harmonic units instead of triads or seventh chords in the guitar part, which can be indicated with chord symbols by simply adding a superscript "5" after the pitch class of the root (e.g., E^5 translates to a chord consisting only of E and B, the perfect fifth above E). These open fifths are usually performed as **power chords**, which typically consist of the root, fifth, and octave played in the lowest possible register of a distorted guitar; at times, the fifth is even doubled below the root to create the most bass-heavy, "powerful" sound possible. Power chords are used in a variety of rock genres, though they tend to be most strongly associated with the heavy metal genre. Despite their lack of chordal thirds, however, musicians still tend to analyze progressions involving power chords using Roman numerals, with chord qualities inferred based on the implied tonality of the song or formal section.

AC/DC's 1980 hit "Back in Black" extensively features power chords, which in the intro and verse sections outline the root motion of a standard major-key pop/rock progression featuring double plagal motion, (I—)♭VII—IV—I (see Figure 10.26). As you recall, plagal motion refers to the falling P4 root motion involved in a IV—I progression; thus, double plagal motion is said to take place in this progression due to the root's dual P4 descent from ♭VII to IV that is immediately followed by a normative IV to I move. The double plagal progression is open to a variety of interpretations, as it can be considered to exemplify mode mixture (in which the subtonic harmony is a borrowed chord from the parallel minor) or modal harmony (as the progression would represent harmonies from the Mixolydian mode, built on the first, fourth, and seventh degrees). Additionally, some theorists point to rock music's tendency to simply harmonize each note from a pentatonic scale with a major triad (for instance, the common, open "guitar chords" of E, G, A, C, and D all possess roots generated from the C major or A minor pentatonic scale); the double plagal progression, then, would represent the harmonization of $\hat{1}$, $\flat\hat{7}$, and $\hat{4}$ from the minor pentatonic scale with parallel major triads. While the modal ambiguity of the double plagal progression (and several other common pop/rock progressions, including II$^\sharp$—IV—I) may at first seem troubling, as it defies a single, "correct answer" or analytical perspective, it is important to recognize that this ambiguity is itself a signature trait of pop/rock harmonic practice. Furthermore, the availability of multiple approaches to understanding a piece of music should be embraced, as music—including the subfield of music theory—is, after all, more art than science.

Fig. 10.26 Main guitar riff from AC/DC, "Back in Black"

SUMMARY OF TERMS FROM CHAPTER 10

modulation	chromatic mediant	pentatonic scale
secondary dominant	planing	blues scale
secondary leading tone chord	chromatic modulation	diatonic modes
tonicization	octatonic scale	Ionian mode
pivot modulation	altered dominant	Dorian mode
mode mixture	tritone substitution	Phrygian mode
borrowed chord	add chord	Lydian mode
Picardy third	extended chord	Mixolydian mode
text painting	chord extension	Aeolian mode
Neapolitan sixth chord	sus chord	Locrian mode
augmented sixth chord	contrafact	power chord

CHAPTER 10—EXERCISES

1. **Chord Realization and Resolution.** Using the notation provided, voice the initial chord indicated by the Roman numeral analysis in SATB style and resolve it to the subsequent chord(s) appropriately, following traditional part-writing guidelines. Add a chord symbol above the staff as well, using slash chord symbols when appropriate.

a.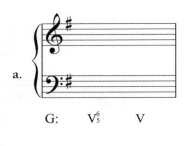

G: V^6_5 V

b.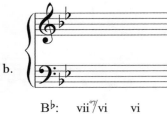

B♭:   vii°⁷/vi   vi

c.

f♯: N^6 V^7

d.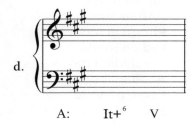

A: It+⁶   V

e.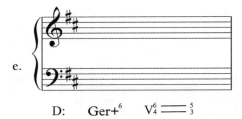

D: Ger+⁶ $V^6_4 \rule{1cm}{0.4pt} {}^5_3$

f.

G♭:   ii⁷ V^7 I
        (incomplete,
         no fifth)

g.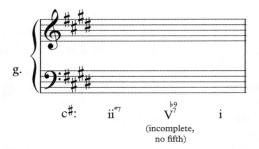

c♯:   ii°⁷ $V^{♭9}_7$ i
        (incomplete,
         no fifth)

2. **Part Writing.** Using the notation provided, complete the realization of the indicated progression in SATB style using appropriate voice leading. The first chord has been provided for you, as well as the location of the pivot chord used in the modulation. The first two measures should consist of quarter note rhythms, followed by two half notes and a whole note. After you have finished notating the realization, recreate it in a DAW of your choice. Use one virtual instrument track for each of the four parts, choosing patches that best support the mood of the composition. Once you are satisfied with the result, export the track as an uncompressed audio file (e.g., WAV or AIFF), and be prepared to deliver the session file to your instructor.

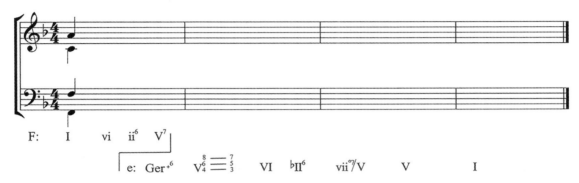

3. **Melody (Re)Harmonization.** Using the lead sheet notation provided in part a), harmonize the given melody using both root position and inverted chords as appropriate with one chord change per bar. Provide a Roman numeral analysis of the progression below the staff (complete with figured bass symbols as necessary) as well as a chord symbol analysis above the staff (complete with slash chord symbols as necessary). Then, use the notation provided in part b) to reharmonize the same melody using appropriate chord substitutions for at least four of the initial harmonies. Your chord choices should cast the most important melodic pitch(es) in each bar as chord tones, though they may be cast as appropriate chord extensions as well.

a.

b.

4. **Analysis.** Analyze the following modulating excerpts (taken from Haydn's Piano Sonata No. 50 in D Major and Mozart's String Quartet in D Minor, respectively) using Roman numerals and figured bass symbols as appropriate. The location of the pivot chord has been provided for you.

5. **Composition I.** Using the grand staff provided, compose a functional progression in SATB style that includes the following melodic and harmonic items: a borrowed chord, a secondary function chord, an augmented sixth chord, a perfect authentic cadence, and at least four melodic embellishments (chosen from passing tone, neighbor tone, anticipation, suspension, retardation, and incomplete neighbor). Be sure to include a Roman numeral analysis below the staff as well as a chord symbol analysis above the staff. After you have finished notating and analyzing your composition, recreate it in a DAW of your choice. Use one virtual instrument track for each of the four parts, choosing patches that best support the mood of the composition. Once you are satisfied with the result, export the track as an uncompressed audio file (e.g., WAV or AIFF), and be prepared to deliver the session file to your instructor.

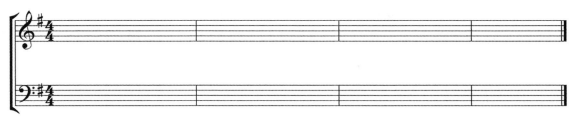

G:

6. **Composition II.** Using the notation provided below, create a lead sheet featuring an original melody that is supported by a 12-bar blues progression that features at least two chord substitutions relative to the normative blues or jazz blues schemes discussed in this chapter. While the progression will not be realized in four voices, it must be indicated using both chord symbols and a basic Roman numeral analysis. Lyrics are not required. After you have finished notating your lead sheet, realize the composition in a DAW of your choice. Use a virtual instrument track for the melody, as well as any number of virtual instrument and/or audio tracks for supporting instrumentation, choosing patches that best reflect the instrumentation of blues and jazz ensembles (e.g., guitar, bass, drums, keyboard instruments, saxes, etc.). Once you are satisfied with the result, export the track as an uncompressed audio file (e.g., WAV or AIFF), and be prepared to deliver the session file to your instructor.

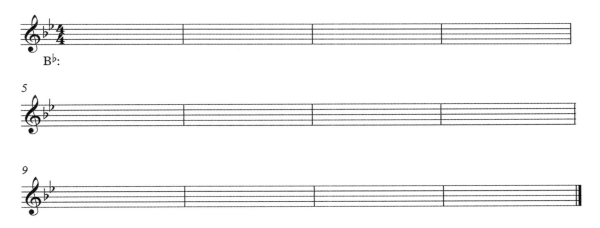

B♭:

5

9

7. **Composition III.** Using the notation provided below, create a lead sheet for a verse or chorus section featuring an original melody that is supported by an authentic-sounding pop/rock chord progression. The progression may be in a major or minor key, but you must add a key signature and the progression must include the subtonic triad, a sus chord, a borrowed chord, and an add chord. Furthermore, the progression may not repeat the first four bars exactly, and it must come to a cadence in the ninth bar on tonic. While the progression will not be realized in four voices, it must be indicated using both Roman numerals and chord symbols. Lyrics are not required. After you have finished notating your lead sheet, realize the composition in a DAW of your choice. Use a virtual instrument track for the melody, as well as any number of virtual instrument and/or audio tracks for supporting instrumentation, choosing patches that best reflect the instrumentation of pop/rock ensembles (e.g., guitar, bass, drums, keyboard instruments, vocals, etc.). Once you are satisfied with the result, export the track as an uncompressed audio file (e.g., WAV or AIFF), and be prepared to deliver the session file to your instructor.

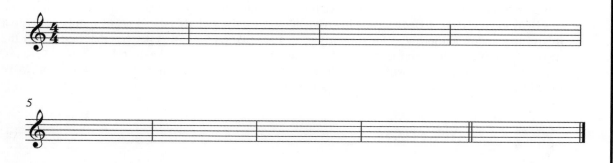

Chapter 11
Form and Development

Throughout several previous chapters, you've explored fundamental musical structures and the various ways they combine to yield complete musical ideas or phrases. Individual pitches, for example, combine to create intervals, which in turn are joined to generate chords that give rise to both chord progressions and the cadences that "punctuate" musical thoughts. To this point, though, the focus has largely been on the level of the single phrase, with Chapter 9 introducing the idea of the basic phrase (with its constituent areas of tonic, predominant, and dominant) and Chapter 10 discussing several ways to embellish the basic phrase with chromaticism. This chapter instead turns to the ways that musical ideas are developed and linked together, toward the creation of larger formal sections (or musical "paragraphs") that themselves combine to create entire compositions. First, however, it is important to delve deeper into the concept of motivic development that was first introduced in Chapter 4, as it is central to our understanding of form in music.

MOTIVIC DEVELOPMENT

Motivic development was defined earlier in this book as the process of repeating and altering a motive throughout a phrase or piece of music, which simultaneously creates both unity and variety. While true development does require some change to the initial idea, the simple repetition or recurrence of an idea can be musically impactful as well. In particular, many composers—particularly in film music—make use of the *leitmotif*, which is a short, distinctive motive or portion of a larger theme that becomes associated with a particular character, place, object, emotion, or idea by consistently recurring along with it in a dramatic setting. Richard Wagner is the composer that is most typically mentioned in discussions of *leitmotifs*, as he used them extensively in his operas, but the technique had already been in use for centuries by his time. You are already familiar with several famous film score themes that have been used as *leitmotifs* more recently, including the "Raiders March" and "Star Wars" themes by John Williams that have reappeared throughout this book.

The most common techniques for motivic development in today's music are transposition and fragmentation, both of which were introduced in the context of Beethoven's Piano Sonata No. 1 in Chapter 4 (see Figure 11.1).

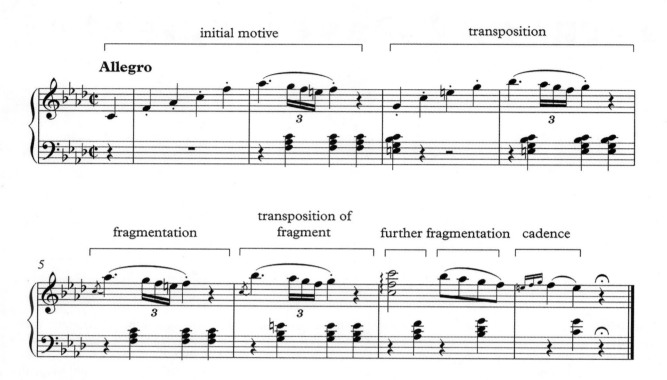

Fig. 11.1   Beethoven, Piano Sonata No. 1, Op. 2 no. 1, mvt. i, mm. 1–8

In the context of motivic development, **transposition** is the repetition of an idea at a different pitch level, such as the transposition of the initial motive from mm. 1–2 of the previous example roughly up a second to outline the dominant harmony in bars 3–4. Transposition is combined with **fragmentation** (the truncation of a motive through subtraction/deletion, the inclusion of rests, or other means) in the subsequent two measures, as the first five notes of the initial idea are deleted to create a motivic fragment in bar 5, which is then repeated up a diatonic second in bar 6 (save for the grace note on the dominant). Measure 7 is perhaps the most interesting of all, as the process of fragmentation continues in both the melody and accompaniment to the extent that the initial idea is rendered almost unrecognizable; indeed, the remaining fragments-of-fragments are often considered to be nothing but "residues" of the original motive that signal a cessation of the development process and transition into the cadential area of the phrase. The kind of systematic fragmentation encountered in Figure 11.1 is exceedingly common and represents a logical process through which composers can craft larger phrases and forms out of a single, brief idea. Indeed, most great pieces are the result of the thorough development of but a few strong themes, as opposed to the constant intro-duction of a multitude of new themes.

Several other common developmental techniques merit mention, including retrograde, inversion, augmenta-tion, and diminution. **Retrograde** refers to the recurrence of a motive in reverse, such that the first note becomes the last note, the second note becomes the penultimate note, and so on. Themes presented in retrograde order can be difficult to identify by ear, and as such composers do not use this technique with much frequency. A related type of development is **inversion**, wherein the melodic intervals of a motive are maintained while their directionality is reversed. For example, if an initial motive proceeds up a M6, then down a M2, then the inversion of this motive would proceed down a M6, then up a M2. This represents strict inversion, which is less common than free or diatonic inversion (or inversion combined with transposition), as the latter allows for logical harmonic support more readily. Figure 11.2, for example, includes an inverted form of the initial motive from Beethoven's Op. 2 no. 1 that begins on F5 instead of C4 and only follows the sequence of melodic interval sizes from mm. 1–2—as opposed to both the sizes and qualities—in order to project the same tonic harmony in the key of F minor despite descending in pitch. Figure 11.2 also includes rhythmically augmented and diminished forms of Beethoven's motive; **augmentation** in this context refers to the lengthening of a motive that is created via a systematic increase in its durational values, while **diminution** represents the opposite approach (with a motive's rhythms decreasing by a consistent durational factor). While augmentation and diminution are almost always considered as rhythmic manipulations, some theorists also speak of intervallic augmentation and diminution, in which a motive's melodic intervals are increased or decreased in size upon repetition.

Fig. 11.2 Summary of motivic development techniques

Fig. 11.2   (Continued)

PHRASE STRUCTURES

Motivic development techniques, like those shown in Figure 11.2, play directly into our notions of phrase structure, relating both to how phrases are constructed individually and to how they relate to one another in combination. The opening of Beethoven's Piano Sonata No. 1, for example, represents a classic phrase type based on its use of transposition and fragmentation known as a sentence. A **sentence** is a phrase that is dedicated to the development of a single idea in a specific pattern: first, during what is known as the "presentation phase," the basic idea is presented and then repeated in a varied form (most typically via transposition, to outline the V chord); afterward, during the "continuation phase," the basic idea is fragmented and varied further, leading to a climax and, ultimately, a cadence. Figure 11.3 presents Beethoven's initial phrase once more, this time with an analysis of the sentential form of the phrase.

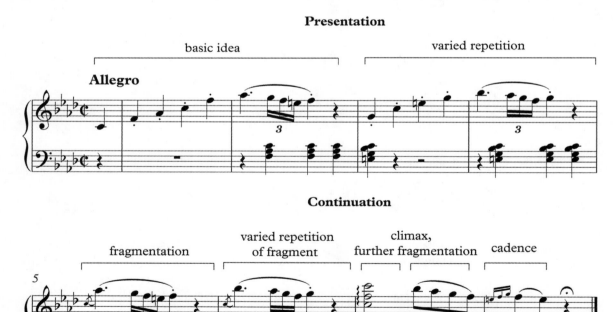

Fig. 11.3   Sentence structure in Beethoven, Piano Sonata No. 1

PERIOD STRUCTURES

Another example exhibiting sentence structure comes from the second movement to Beethoven's Sonatina in F Major (see Figure 11.4). Notice how the music sounds divided into two separate—yet very closely related—sentences, each with its own presentation and continuation phases. These phrases can be heard in terms of call and response (or question and answer) due to their melodic similarities as well as their cadential pattern: the first phrase begins on tonic and arrives at the dominant (creating a half cadence with the rolled chord in bar 8), while the second phrase follows a similar path but ends on a more conclusive perfect authentic cadence. Typically, the initial "call" (or "question") phrase is known as the **antecedent**, while the "response" (or "answer") phrase is known as the **consequent**. "Antecedent," with its prefix "ante," refers to "that which comes before," while "consequent" literally means "something that follows as a logical conclusion." The arrangement of phrases into an antecedent/consequent relationship is called a period. A **period** therefore features multiple related phrases structured such that the final cadence is the most conclusive. There are quite a few types of periods, including the **parallel period** (whose antecedent and consequent begin in the same way or in a similar manner), the **contrasting period** (whose antecedent and consequent differ), the **modulating period** (which features a change of key), the **three-phrase period** (which typically consists of a two-phrase antecedent and single consequent phrase), and the **double period** (which is composed of a two-phrase antecedent and two-phrase consequent). Each type of period is illustrated in the following set of examples (see Figures 11.4–11.8). Note that each of the examples is also a **symmetrical period** (whose phrases are of equal length), though **asymmetrical periods** (whose phrases are of unequal length) are also common. Asymmetrical periods are typically the result of three techniques: the addition of extra material at the beginning of a phrase (which is known as a **prefix**), the insertion of extra material in the middle of a phrase (which is known as **interpolation**), or the addition of extra material at the end of a phrase (which is known as a **suffix**). The most common type of suffix is the **cadential extension**, which takes place when a conclusive cadence is followed by motivically related material that reaffirms the tonic harmony or simply repeats the cadential pattern (e.g., V—I, V—I, V—I). Asymmetry can also arise due to phrase elisions, which were discussed in Chapter 9.

Fig. 11.4   Parallel period structure in Beethoven's Sonatina in F Major, mvt. ii, mm. 1–16

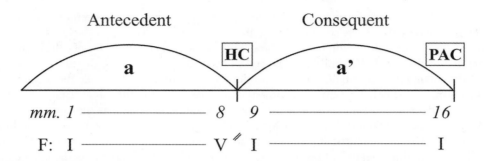

Fig. 11.5 A phrase diagram of Beethoven's Sonatina in F Major, mvt. ii, mm. 1–16

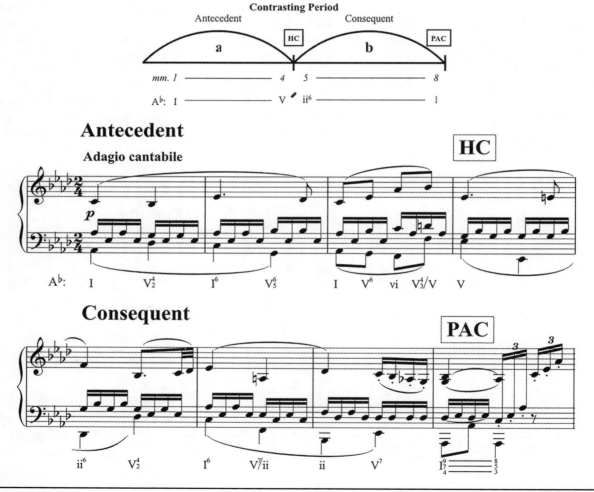

Fig. 11.6 Contrasting period structure in Beethoven, Piano Sonata No. 8 (*Pathétique*), mvt. ii, mm. 1–8

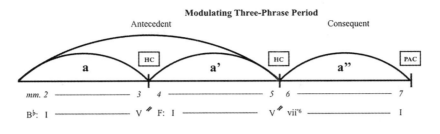
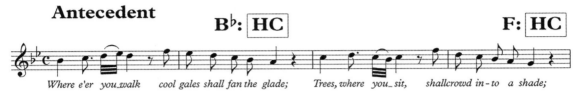

Fig. 11.7 Modulating three-phrase period structure in Handel, "Where'er You Walk," mm. 2–7

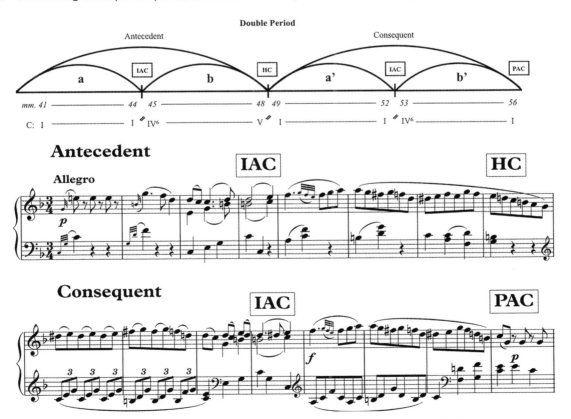

Fig. 11.8 Double period structure in Mozart, Piano Sonata No. 12 in F Major, mvt. i, mm. 41–56

Independent Phrases and Phrase Groups

Importantly, not all multi-phrase structures are periods. When phrases take place one after the other but do not relate, they are simply referred to as **independent phrases**. Independent phrases are common in the "B" sections of short rounded binary forms (which are discussed later in this chapter), as the initial phrase represents a new idea while the second phrase hearkens back to the outset of the piece; though they are temporally adjacent, they do not truly belong together. Additionally, some combinations of phrases do cohere in a manner similar to a period, yet do not conclude with a relatively strong cadence (which is a requirement of any period). These are labeled in a straight-forward manner as **phrase groups**. Figure 11.9 provides the melody and bass line of a phrase group taken from Johannes Brahms's *Variations on a Theme from Joseph Haydn*; it features a (relatively) strong-weak IAC—HC cadential pattern, which is the retrograde of the period's required scheme.

Fig. 11.9 Brahms, *Variations on a Theme from Joseph Haydn*, mm. 11–18

FORM IN THE MUSIC OF THE COMMON PRACTICE

In traditionally tonal music, musical ideas such as independent phrases, phrase groups, and especially periods combine to create larger formal sections and, ultimately, complete forms. **Musical form** is the term used to describe the overall shape of a piece, which is created via the combination of sections that contrast one another. Contrast is chiefly engendered by changes in thematic design (differing motives, themes, phrases, etc.) and harmonic structure (differing key areas and harmonic progressions), though it can truly be achieved via the alteration of any musical domain (rhythm, timbre, dynamics, articulation, register, etc.). Typically, composers clarify formal boundaries by modifying several musical parameters as a piece moves into a new section, adjusting melody, harmony, rhythm, dynamics, and more at the same time.

Up to this point, the examples in this chapter have all come from music of the common practice, with an emphasis on music from the Classical period; this style of music will continue to be the focus for the following overview of traditional forms. This is because music from the Classical era tends to exhibit clear phrase structures that combine in an orderly fashion to create well-defined formal sections that are relatively easy to understand. Strict adherence to form, order, tradition, and clarity are indeed hallmarks of all Classical art.

BINARY FORM

One of the most commonly used forms in the common practice was **binary form**, so named due to its two large, contrasting sections (A and B). The first section (or reprise) in a binary form would typically be very straightforward, with a clear harmonic progression and classic phrase structure (such as a parallel period). In contrast, the second reprise would normally begin with a period of harmonic instability leading to a half cadence, followed by a phrase or two leading back to a strong cadence in the original key. Binary forms are labeled according to two parameters: the level of harmonic closure attained at the end of the A section, and the presence or absence of the initial idea at the end of the B section. If a binary form ends conclusively on a PAC in the original key at the end of the A section, it is considered harmonically closed and is labeled as a **sectional** binary form. If, however, the A section ends inconclusively or modulates to a different key, it is called a **continuous** binary form. Binary forms featuring a return of the initial theme at the end of the second reprise—which are very common—are referred to as **rounded binary** forms, while those whose second reprise consists entirely of new material are called **simple binary** forms. J. S. Bach's famous *Minuet in G* is an example of a simple sectional binary form, as its A section ends with a PAC in the home key of G major while its B section avoids a restatement of the original theme (though it does hearken back to the theme via the artful use of motivic development techniques). Figure 11.10 recreates the melody of the *minuet* that begins the third movement from Mozart's well-known chamber work, *Eine kleine*

Fig. 11.10   Mozart, *Eine kleine Nachtmusik*, mvt. iii, mm. 1–16 (melody)

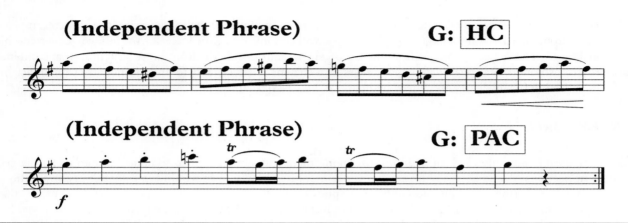

Fig. 11.10   (Continued)

Nachtmusik; this excerpt exemplifies rounded sectional binary form. Note how the consequent from the A section's parallel period returns to conclude the B section as an independent phrase that takes place after a sequential opening.

TERNARY FORM

While the previous rounded binary example can be thought of as possessing three parts (the A section, the unstable beginning of the B section, and the return of the A section), a true **ternary form** includes three complete, independent sections that each end with a conclusive cadence. The main difference between rounded binary forms and ternary forms is the contrasting section; while the beginning of the B section in a rounded binary form is typically short, harmonically unstable, and motivically related to the A section, the B section of a ternary form is usually longer, more harmonically stable, and motivically unrelated to the A section. Figure 11.11 recreates Schumann's ternary form piece *Wichtige Begebenheit*, whose A sections are in A major while its B section—which features an entirely distinct melody—is in D major. As the A section in this piece ends conclusively with a PAC in A major, it represents sectional ternary form. Some scholars use the more specific term "full sectional ternary" when analyzing pieces like this, as each section ends with a PAC without modulating.

The Schumann example can also be considered an example of **simple ternary form**, as its constituent sections (ABA) are composed of phrases and periods that do not represent larger forms. Another common type of ternary form is **composite ternary form**, in which each constituent section is itself a complete binary form, making the overall tripartite structure a "form of forms," so to speak. In fact, the earlier *minuet* example from Mozart's *Eine kleine Nachtmusik* is part of a larger *minuet* and trio scheme that represents composite ternary form: the *minuet* is the initial large A section, the trio is the large B section, and the return to the *minuet* via a *da capo* score marking (translating literally as "from the head") creates the final A section bookend. Figure 11.12 provides a form diagram for Mozart's entire *minuet* and trio movement. Note that the *minuet* is in rounded sectional binary form in the key of G major, while the trio is also in rounded sectional binary form, but in the key of the dominant, D major.

Fig. 11.11 Schumann, *Wichtige Begebenheit*

Fig. 11.11 (Continued)

VARIATION FORMS

Binary forms were additionally used as components of several other composite forms, including theme and variation movements. These became known as **sectional variations**, as the theme and each subsequent variation terminated with a conclusive cadence in the home key and thus represented a standalone formal section. Figure 11.13 recreates an excerpt first encountered in Chapter 10, the theme from the final movement of Mozart's Piano Sonata No. 6 in D Major (which is a theme and variations movement). This theme is in rounded continuous binary form, as the A section is a modulating parallel period.

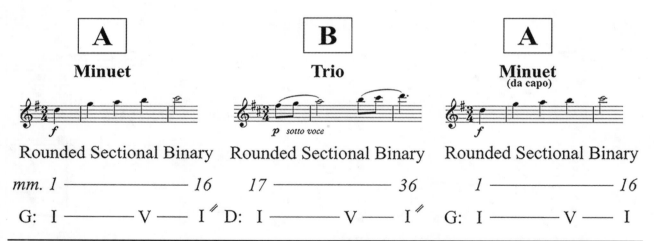

Fig. 11.12 Form diagram for Mozart, *Eine kleine Nachtmusik*, mvt. iii

Variations within Classical sectional variation forms would typically preserve the theme's binary structure while altering several other musical parameters, such as key or mode, meter, harmonic progression, rhythm, texture, timbre, register, dynamics, articulation, and tempo. Often, composers would begin with a few variations focused on rhythmic changes to the theme, followed by more structural changes to harmony, key, and meter before leading to a bombastic, fast-tempo finale. There was no set quantity of variations to be included in a theme and variations movement, though they typically numbered in the teens, allowing composers to display their command over multiple musical domains as well as motivic development techniques. Figure 11.14 provides the seventh variation in Mozart's set of 12 variations on the previously provided theme, which maintains the theme's rounded continuous binary form that involves the tonics of D and A while altering the mode and harmonic progression (among other changes).

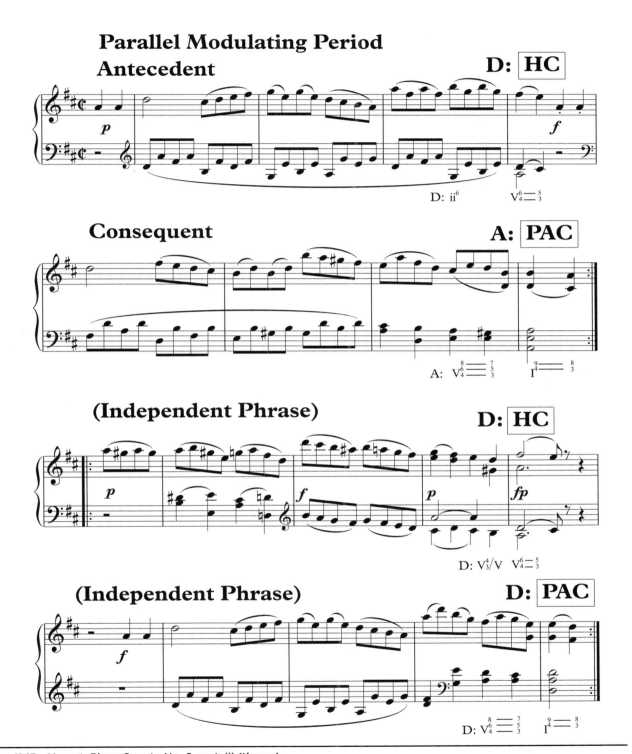

Fig. 11.13   Mozart, Piano Sonata No. 6, mvt. iii (theme)

Fig. 11.14   Mozart, Piano Sonata No 6, mvt. iii (var. VII)

In contrast to sectional variations, whose harmonic/cadential structure, repeat signs, and variation labels all clearly demarcate the beginning and ending of each variation, there are styles of **continuous variations** that feature a shorter, repeated idea that continuously flows throughout a work while variations are added in a less rigid or clearly articulated fashion. The most common type of continuous variations is the *passacaglia*, which is characterized by a repeated bass *ostinato* that anchors variations that take place in the upper contrapuntal voices. An *ostinato* is any persistently repeated musical idea; thus, the *basso ostinato* or "ground bass" that characterizes the *passacaglia* is specifically a repeated idea that persists in the bass. Similar to the *passacaglia* is the **chaconne**, which is a form that repeats a harmonic progression more generally, without strict adherence to a literal bass *ostinato* (though this difference between the *chaconne* and the *passacaglia* is often disputed). While sectional variations became more prevalent during the Classical period, continuous variations were most common during the earlier Baroque era. Figure 11.15 recreates the famous ground bass used in Bach's Passacaglia in C minor for organ, which remains one of the most well-known sets of continuous variations.

Fig. 11.15 Bach, Passacaglia in C Minor, mm. 1–9a

SONATA FORM

While the previously mentioned sectional variation and composite ternary forms made literal use of rounded binary forms as constituent elements, sonatas expanded and ornamented the rounded binary model to create a new form entirely. A **sonata** can be thought of as a rounded binary form whose A section—known as the **exposition**—consists of at least two distinct themes: the **primary theme** (or theme group), which is in the tonic key, and the contrasting **secondary theme** (or theme group), which is in a non-tonic key. These themes are usually bridged by a **transition** subsection whose function is to modulate to the secondary key area. The transition is considered **dependent** if it makes use of motives from the primary theme, while it is considered **independent** if it introduces new melodic material. (Importantly, transitions—as well as retransitions, which will be discussed shortly—are not unique to sonata form, and are used in a variety of formal structures when there is a need to smoothly move to another key area.) Another aspect of the sonata's exposition that differs from the A section in a rounded binary form is the **closing area** or section that takes place after the secondary theme and remains in the secondary key area. The closing area can feature multiple subsections, including a new **closing theme** or set of themes, as well as a **codetta** that clearly and emphatically terminates the exposition. Moreover, while rounded binary forms conclude with a brief restatement of part of the A section in the tonic key, sonata forms typically end with an altered restatement of the entire A section in the tonic key that is called the **recapitulation**. A final key difference between rounded binary forms and sonata forms regards the B section. In rounded binary forms, the B section is quite short, typically consisting of a brief sequence followed by a half cadence that leads back to the tonic key. The B section in sonata forms, on the other hand, features extensive motivic development of earlier themes (hence the section's name, the **development**), often within multiple key areas, and usually leads to a lengthy **retransition** subsection that sets up the recapitulation, often via a dominant pedal. New thematic material is sometimes introduced and explored during the development section, as well. While both B sections initially feature harmonic instability and ultimately lead back to the tonic key, a sonata's development section can be quite expansive, particularly in Romantic-era sonatas (which, following Beethoven's model, became more akin to ternary forms due to the B section's increased length). Figure 11.16 provides the general sonata form model, once again referencing Beethoven's Sonata No. 1 in F Minor.

Importantly, composers did not strictly adhere to this model, often playing with the form by moving to unexpected key areas (or by adding or subtracting sections). For example, while Classical-era sonata expositions most

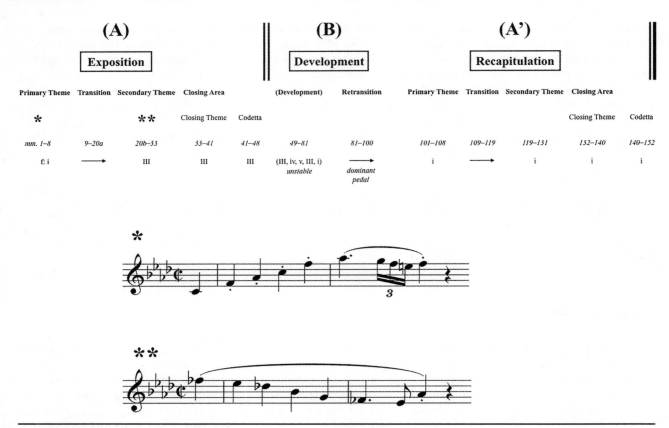

Fig. 11.16 Sonata form in Beethoven, Piano Sonata No. 1, Op. 2 no. 1, mvt. i

frequently moved from major tonic keys to dominant keys (and from minor tonic keys to relative major keys, as in Figure 11.16), Romantic-era sonatas often explored distant key relations such as chromatic mediants. Beethoven's *Waldstein* sonata, for example, features a primary theme in C major and a secondary theme group in E major. Furthermore, composers at times expanded the form by adding an optional **introduction** section prior to the exposition of themes, or, more commonly, by inserting a long **coda** after the recapitulation that at times featured additional thematic development. While the generic sonata formula itself engendered narrative significance with its contrasting themes and initial opposing key areas, the litany of formal options available for composers to adjust rendered the form extremely flexible with regard to the creation of musical meaning.

RONDO FORM

Another form that involves the reappearance of a primary theme amid contrasting ideas is **rondo** form, which is most typically presented in five main parts. The primary theme in a rondo is known as a **refrain** (or *ritornello*); the refrain can be a phrase, set of phrases, or, in the case of a composite rondo, a complete form such as a rounded binary form. The rondo's refrain is contrasted by complete formal sections that are typically in non-tonic keys; these are called episodes. In a five-part rondo, there are three appearances of the refrain (which may be altered upon reiteration), and these alternate with two episodes that contrast both with the refrain and with one another, creating a form that is labeled ABACA. Figure 11.17 provides a form diagram of the previously encountered second movement to Beethoven's *Pathétique* sonata, which is a five-part rondo. Importantly, the basic ABACA structure is embellished here, with the refrain being developed each time it reappears (creating an ABA'CA" scheme), along with the addition of both a retransition (following the second episode) and a coda.

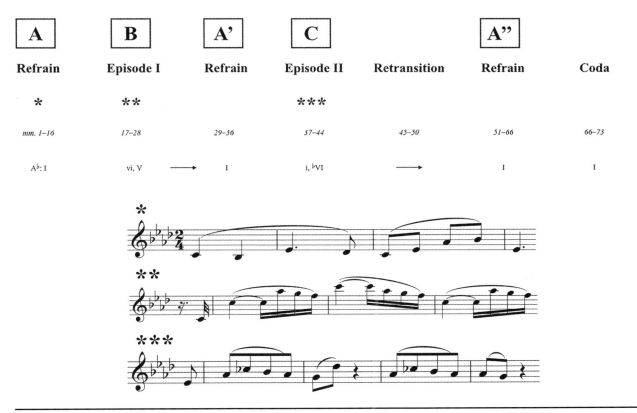

Fig. 11.17   Five-part rondo form in Beethoven, Piano Sonata No. 8, mvt. ii

Two other types of rondo form exist as well: seven-part rondo and sonata-rondo. In a Classical-era seven-part rondo, there are four appearances of the refrain that alternate with three episodes, creating a form that is labeled ABACAB'A or, less commonly, ABACADA (if the third episode represents new material). An important characteristic of the seven-part rondo is that the final episode typically sounds in the tonic key along with its surrounding refrains; this echoes the sonata standard of initially presenting the first contrasting theme in a non-tonic key before eventually assimilating it into the home key during the recapitulation. Indeed, when such a seven-part, ABACAB'A rondo possesses a second episode (section C) that is primarily developmental in nature and concludes with a retransition, it is labeled as a **sonata-rondo**. Sonata-rondo forms are almost identical to traditional sonatas, except that the closing area—which is in the secondary key within the exposition—is substituted with another reappearance of the primary theme/refrain in the tonic key. Figure 11.18 presents a comparison between the standard sonata form and sonata-rondo form.

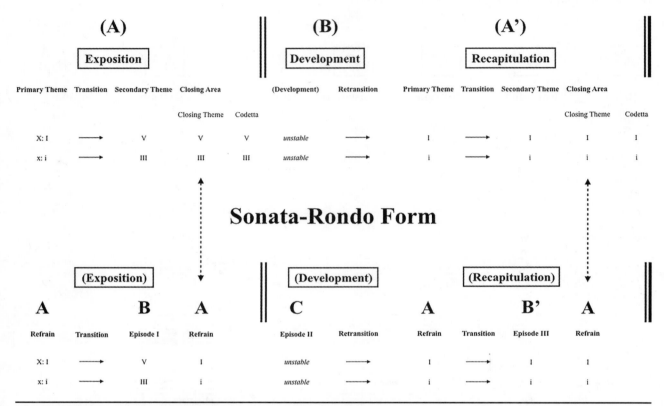

Fig. 11.18   A comparison between sonata and sonata-rondo forms

MULTI-MOVEMENT COMPOSITE FORMS

Despite their considerable length, composite ternary, sonata, and rondo forms do not represent the highest level of form in common practice music. Instead, they often function as single movements within even larger, multi-movement works that may be thought of as third-order forms (or "forms-of-forms-of-forms"). In the Baroque era (and far earlier), a common multi-movement form was known as the **suite** (which Bach also called the *partita*); this consisted of several dance movements, often preceded by a separate prelude. The Baroque dance suite came to be solidified as a four-movement piece whose individual movements were each binary-form dances: the *allemande*, the *courante*, the *sarabande*, and the *gigue*. However, other dance types, including the *minuet* and *bourrée*—both composite ternary forms—were included in suites on occasion. Another multi-movement form that originated in the Classical era was the **string quartet**, which was first established by Haydn. This was traditionally a four-movement scheme as well, but with more formal variety than the suite: the first movement was typically in sonata form, the second movement was almost always at a slow tempo (but without a specified form), the third movement was a composite ternary dance movement (most often a *minuet* and trio), and the fourth movement was usually in rondo or sonata-rondo form. Very similar to the string quartet format is that of the Classical **symphony**, an orchestral work that customarily followed the same four-movement pattern: a fast-paced sonata followed by a slow and lyrical movement, then a lively *minuet* (or *scherzo*) and trio, and ultimately a rondo or sonata-rondo form. The finale of a symphony also exhibited the standard sonata form at times, but it was almost always at a quick tempo. Yet another multi-movement work that emerged in the Romantic era was the **song cycle**, a collection of several art songs (or *Lieder*) that were presented together and shared a unifying narrative or theme. Song cycles—many of which contained over 15 separate *Lieder*—were composed of individual movements that were usually either in **strophic form** (a repeated A section despite text changes), **modified strophic form** (AA'A"A"', etc., which included slight variations to the music for each verse), **through-composed form** (ABCD, etc., without musical repetition), or ternary form (including AAB ternary form, which is uncommon outside of the art song tradition). While suites, string quartets, symphonies, and song cycles came to exhibit more or less standard formal trends in their respective musical eras, these formulas were always mere guidelines for composers, who freely modified them to create unique narratives, to support a specific text or idea, or simply to reflect individual taste. This was especially the case in the twentieth century, which featured the development, allusion, parody, and even complete abandonment of standard forms.

FORM IN JAZZ AND POPULAR MUSIC

In Chapter 10, you were first introduced to the two most commonly encountered forms in jazz: the 12-bar blues form and the 32-bar AA'BA" song form used in jazz standards. The 12-bar blues can be thought of as being composed of three 4-bar units: an initial 4-bar statement with a harmonic focus on tonic, a second 4-bar restatement that focuses on the subdominant (and often repeats the initial melodic gesture), and a final 4-bar "turnaround" section that functions as both a departure from the initial statement and a conclusion to the short form via a move from the dominant back to tonic (see Figure 11.19, which includes the jazz blues progression).

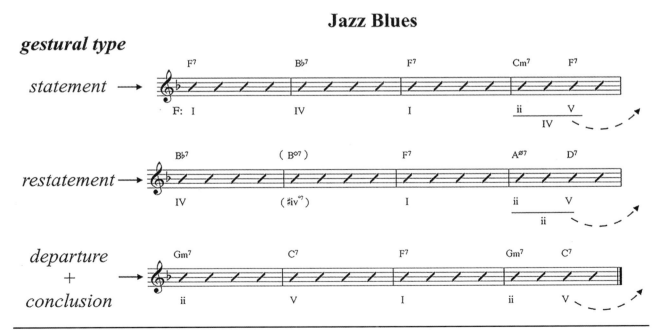

Fig. 11.19 The 12-bar jazz blues scheme

While the 32-bar AA'BA" song form—exemplified in Figure 11.20 by the jazz standard "Have You Met Miss Jones?"—is quite a bit longer than the blues scheme, it shares the same gestural pattern: an 8-bar initial statement begins the form (A, which takes the first ending), followed by an 8-bar altered restatement (A', which takes the second ending), a contrasting 8-bar departure section known as the **bridge** (B), and finally an 8-bar conclusion (A").

Fig. 11.20 Lead sheet of Rodgers and Hart, "Have You Met Miss Jones?"

Importantly, jazz musicians do not simply play through the form of a tune one time (which would be described as a single "chorus"); rather, there exists a composite form that is created via the performance of several choruses that each serve a specific formal function on a higher level. This is the case for charts that exhibit 12-bar blues form, AA'BA" form, or another type of section-level form. The composite form engendered by most jazz performances is in three main parts: the **head** (the initial performance of the tune's composed melody), the **solos** section (where individual instrumentalists take turns improvising over one or more choruses apiece), and the **head out** (the final performance of the head). Perhaps counterintuitively, the most important section within the composite form of a jazz performance is the solos section, not the head, as improvisation is prized in the style and serves as the main attraction for both the performers and audience. Note that the basic head/solos/head out structure is typically ornamented via the addition of an introduction section (known as an "intro" or "vamp") as well as a coda (known as a "tag"). A common tag used in 32-bar jazz standards (including "Have You Met Miss Jones?") features an evaded cadence: as most jazz standards terminate with a ii—V—I progression, the tag delays the final tonic by instead inserting a iii—vi after the dominant and returning to the beginning of the last four bars, creating a iii—vi—ii—V sequence that can be repeated ad infinitum until the band decides to finally deliver the terminal tonic to end the piece.

VERSE-CHORUS FORM

The standard song form used in pop/rock music also exhibits composite form, as well as the AA'BA" structure popularized during the early twentieth century. This form is known as **verse-chorus form**, and it focuses on verse and chorus sections that are paired together to form a large, repeated A section that is contrasted by a bridge section (B). The basic, formulaic pop song scheme follows the pattern of verse—chorus (A), verse—chorus (A'), bridge (B), (verse—)chorus (A"). A **verse** section in a pop song typically features different lyrics each time it recurs throughout a song, while the music remains the same (or is similar). The lyrics within verses contain most of the narrative or "plot" action in a manner similar to the *recitative* movements within an opera. In contrast, a **chorus** returns several times throughout the form, usually with the same lyrics and music each time. The chorus is more akin to the operatic *aria* in that its lyrics reflect upon, comment upon, or summarize the ideas presented in the verses. The chorus additionally tends to use the title of the song as a lyrical **hook** (or memorable motivic/thematic unit). The contrasting bridge section is so labeled when it contains new music and lyrics; a contrasting B section that is entirely instrumental (that is, without lyrics), it is usually labeled as an **interlude** instead.

While this very basic verse-chorus form was indeed used in early pop/rock music (particularly when recordings needed to be limited in duration due to phonograph technology), it became more typical to ornament the basic structure with a variety of formal sections serving specific functions—particularly transitional function. These section types include the "intro," pre-chorus, link, coda, and "outro." As in jazz, the intro is an instrumental (non-texted) section that typically serves to establish the key, meter, tempo, and progression of the song; it may contain an instrumental hook that serves as a preview to an important motive or theme to be used in the main "body" of the form. The intro usually gives way to the first verse of the song, which is optionally followed by a transitional section that is known colloquially as a **pre-chorus** (as it is formally positioned before the chorus). The pre-chorus, in a manner similar to the transition section in a sonata, often features harmonic instability and/or a progression focusing on predominant–dominant motion, which creates a dramatic sense of arrival upon the entrance of the chorus. While the second chorus section moves directly to the contrasting bridge or interlude, the first chorus in the composite AA'BA" structure is followed by the second verse that initiates the large A' section. This often features a substantial drop in energy that can be jarring, particularly when a bombastic or emotional chorus contrasts with an intimate verse that is softer in dynamics. One way that songwriters typically address this issue is through the use of a **link**, which is a short instrumental passage that, like the pre-chorus, is transitional in nature. After the second chorus and bridge, there are a variety of formal pathways that can be taken. The simplest of these is to follow the bridge immediately with another, third chorus, which may repeat a second time (or more, with a fade out used in the production process to end the song in an artificial manner). Another is to return to a third verse that leads to a third chorus (which, again, may repeat). Many songs, however, add a completely new, substantial, texted section after a third chorus, which often features a repeated refrain or lyrics that provide narrative closure to the song. This coda section creates a terminal climax within the form that can be very appealing; a famous example is the raucous, four-minute coda to The Beatles' hit song "Hey Jude" from 1968. A final formal ornament that is standard in pop/rock songs is the **outro**, which is an instrumental section that serves as a song's conclusion. The outro may introduce new material, but it more commonly repeats a prominent hook from the body of the song and/or restates the song's intro at a higher energy level, which is the case in Silverchair's 2007 hit "Straight Lines" (see Figure 11.21).

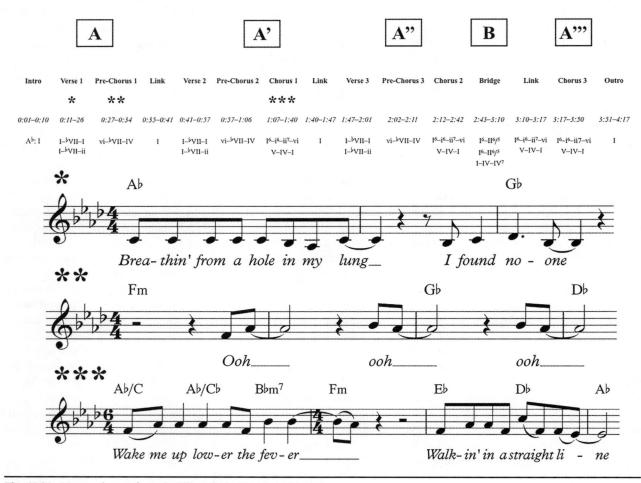

Fig. 11.21 Verse-chorus form in Silverchair, "Straight Lines"

While the form of "Straight Lines" may seem to be extremely complex and ornate, it is actually very common for the basic verse-chorus form to be embellished with several additional instrumental sections in modern pop/rock music. In fact, this type of elaborated verse-chorus form has become the stock formula for most hit songs. Most songwriters and artists in the twenty-first century use this formula loosely and alter it in inventive ways to create unique formal structures (such as Silverchair's AA'A"BA" form in "Straight Lines," which includes an "extra" verse, pre-chorus, and link at the song's outset); this echoes the way that common practice musicians played with the traditional forms of binary, ternary, sonata, and rondo in their compositions.

SUMMARY OF TERMS FROM CHAPTER 11

leitmotif
transposition
fragmentation
retrograde
inversion
augmentation
diminution
sentence
antecedent
consequent
period
parallel period
contrasting period
modulating period
three-phrase period
double period
symmetrical period
asymmetrical period
prefix
interpolation
suffix
cadential extension
independent phrase
phrase group
musical form
binary form

sectional
continuous
rounded binary form
simple binary form
ternary form
simple ternary form
composite ternary form
sectional variations
continuous variations
passacaglia
ostinato
chaconne
sonata
exposition
primary theme
secondary theme
transition
dependent
independent
closing area
closing theme
codetta
recapitulation
development
retransition
introduction

coda
rondo
refrain
episode
sonata-rondo
suite
string quartet
symphony
song cycle
strophic form
modified strophic form
through-composed form
bridge
head
solos
head out
verse-chorus form
verse
chorus
hook
interlude
pre-chorus
link
outro

CHAPTER 11—EXERCISES

True or False. Circle "true" for each statement below that is true. Circle "false" for each false statement.

1. A *leitmotif* is a theme that recurs throughout a long musical work, appearing at a new transposition level each time.

    True   False

2. A symmetrical period is a set of phrases that cohere, are equal in length, and exhibit the following structure: a relatively weak cadence terminates the antecedent, while a relatively strong cadence terminates the consequent.

    True   False

3. A phrase may be rendered asymmetrical relative to another via the use of an interpolation, which adds or repeats material in the middle of the phrase.

    True   False

4.   A *passacaglia* is a set of continuous variations based on a ground bass, while a *chaconne* is a set of sectional variations more loosely based on a repeated chord progression.

     True   False

5.   One of the main differences between a sonata form and a sonata-rondo form is that the exposition in a sonata ends with a closing area in the secondary key, while the exposition in a sonata-rondo ends with a refrain in the original key.

     True   False

6.   **Motivic Development Notation.** Using the notation below, compose appropriate variations to the given motive that individually correspond to the specific motivic development technique that is indicated in each system.

Initial Motive

Transposition

Fragmentation

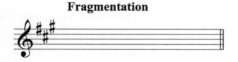

Retrograde

Inversion

Augmentation

Diminution

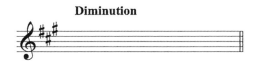

7. **Phrase Diagram Identification.** Label each diagram below according to the phrase and cadential structure that is displayed (e.g., parallel period, contrasting modulating asymmetrical period, parallel double period, independent phrases, phrase group, etc.).

a.

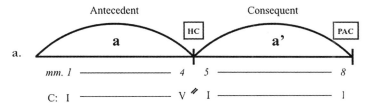

b.

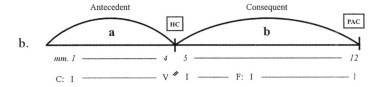

c.

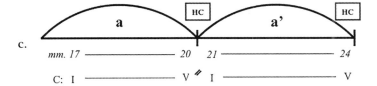

d.

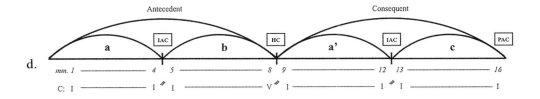

8. **Form Diagram Identification.** Label each diagram below according to the formal structure that is displayed (e.g., simple sectional binary, rounded continuous binary, sectional ternary, sonata, 5-part rondo, 7-part rondo, sonata-rondo, etc.).

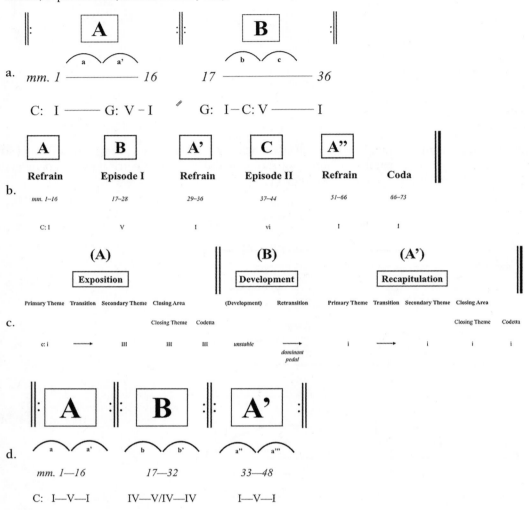

9. **Phrase Analysis.** In the space below each score excerpt, draw an arc diagram that displays the excerpt's phrase structure. Label phrases with lowercase letters (e.g., a, a', b, etc.), and label the diagram according to the overall structure that is present (e.g., parallel period, contrasting modulating asymmetrical period, parallel double period, independent phrases, phrase group, etc.). Be sure to include measure numbers, as well as Roman numerals that reflect the harmonies at the beginning and end of each phrase.

a. *Bach, Minuet in G, mm. 1–16*

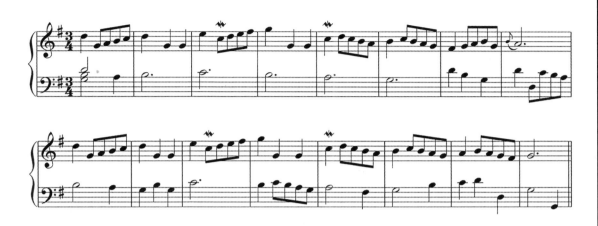

b. *Haydn, Piano Sonata No. 50 in D Major, finale, mm. 1–8a*

10. a.   **Score Analysis.** Download or stream the second movement to Mozart's Piano Sonata No. 13 in B♭ Major and listen to the piece several times while following the score (which may be downloaded from this book's companion site). Then, in the space below, complete the form diagram in a manner similar to Figure 11.16. (*Note: you do not have to include the lower portion of the diagram that includes the notation of the primary themes.*) Be sure to provide Roman numerals that reflect the main key area(s) of each section relative to the initial tonic key of E♭ major. (*Note: the transition in this piece's exposition does not modulate, which is atypical.*)

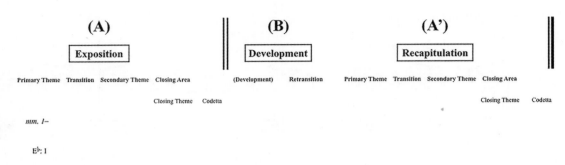

mm. 1–

E♭: 1

b.   In the space below, choose one section from the form that recurs with alteration. Then, using appropriate terminology, describe how each recurrence of the initial section differs or is developed. Consider the melody, harmony, rhythm, dynamics, articulation, timbre, and phrase structure.

11. a.   **Song Analysis.** Download or stream Katy Perry's hit single "Firework" and listen to the song several times. Then, in the space below, complete the form diagram in a manner similar to Figure 11.21. (*Note: you do not have to transcribe the melodies to create the lower part of the diagram; instead, simply write out the lyrics that characterize the beginning of each of the main sections.*) Use proper form terms for describing each section (i.e., verse, pre-chorus, chorus, link, bridge, interlude, coda, outro), and be sure to provide time stamps from the recording to indicate when each section begins and ends.

0:01–

b.   In the space below, choose one section from the form that recurs with alteration. Then, using appropriate terminology, describe how each recurrence of the initial section differs or is developed. Consider the melody, harmony, rhythm, dynamics, articulation, timbre, phrase structure, and instrumentation, as well as production techniques.

12. **Composition I.** Using the notation provided below, complete the initial antecedent phrase and add a consequent phrase to create a parallel period. Be sure to end the antecedent on melodic tones that imply the dominant triad, and end the consequent on tonic.

a.

b.

13. **Composition II.** Using the notation provided below, create a jazz lead sheet featuring an original melody that begins and ends in F major and adheres to 32-bar AA'BA" song form. While the progression will not be realized in four voices, it must be indicated using both chord symbols and a basic Roman numeral analysis. Lyrics are not required. After you have finished notating your lead sheet, realize the composition in a DAW of your choice. Use a virtual instrument track for the melody, as well as any number of virtual instrument and/or audio tracks for supporting instrumentation, choosing patches that best reflect the instrumentation of small jazz ensembles (e.g., bass, drums, piano, saxophone, trumpet, etc.). Once you are satisfied with the result, export the track as an uncompressed audio file (e.g., WAV or AIFF), and be prepared to deliver the session file to your instructor.

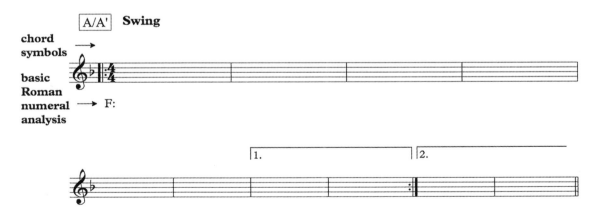

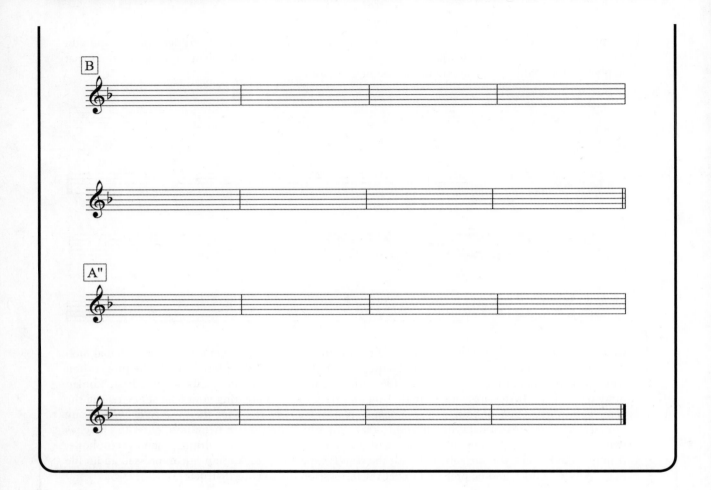

Chapter 12
Basic Orchestration

The key to a well-balanced mix lies in the arrangement and orchestration of its constituent sounds. As discussed in Chapter 7, conforming to the natural layout of the harmonics in the overtone series offers multiple frequencies the space they need to be heard clearly within an arrangement. A well-orchestrated piece will take advantage of this concept by emphasizing certain harmonic intervals in specific ranges, while avoiding those that do not adhere to the low interval limit guidelines (also discussed in Chapter 7). Indeed, the voicing of harmonic intervals is one of the most important elements of both orchestrated arrangements and professional-sounding mixes. Orchestration also involves manipulating other artistic parameters, such as coloration and amplitude. For example, doubling or layering multiple instruments within an ensemble so that they share the same harmonic or melodic material can create moments of brilliance and impact in a piece of music. With so many options to choose from, though, composers need to have a firm grasp on the timbres of all orchestral instruments and how these timbres change from region to region within their overall ranges. Once these essential composition concepts have been thoroughly practiced, MIDI orchestration can be approached with professionalism. This chapter delves into traditional orchestration methods and proceeds to discuss techniques for combining live and virtual instruments within the DAW to create realistic results in larger arrangements.

INSTRUMENTATION

Figure 12.1 provides the ranges and registral qualities of all the common orchestral instruments. Additionally, this chart illustrates the correct ordering of instruments within a score, different standard orchestra sizes, instrument transposition levels, and basic weighting/power considerations.

Instrument Order	Modern Orchestra	Large Orchestra
Piccolo(s)	flute III player doubles	flute IV player doubles
Flute(s)	I, II, III	I, II, III, IV
(Alto Flute)	flute II player doubles	flute III player doubles
Oboe(s)	I, II, III	I, II, III, IV
English Horn	oboe III player doubles	oboe IV player doubles
Clarinet(s)	I, II, III	I, II, III, IV
Bass Clarinet in B♭	clarinet III player doubles	clarinet IV player doubles
Bassoon(s)	I, II, III	I, II, III, IV
Contrabassoon	bassoon III player doubles	bassoon IV player doubles
*Saxophone(s) Horn(s) in F	I, II, III, IV	I, II, III, IV, V, VI *(VII, VIII)
Trumpet(s) in C	I, II, III	I, II, III
Trombone(s)	I, II, III	I, II, III
Bass Trombone	trombone III player doubles	trombone III player doubles
Tuba	1 player	1 player
Timpani	I, II	I, II, III, IV
Percussion	I, II *(III, IV)	I, II *(III, IV, V, VI...)
*Keyboard instrument(s) Harp(s)	1 player	2 players
Violin I Section	12 players	16 players
Violin II Section	10 players	14 players
Violas	8 players	12 players
Cellos	6 players	10 players
Double Basses	4–6 players	8–10 players

Fig. 12.1　Orchestra guide

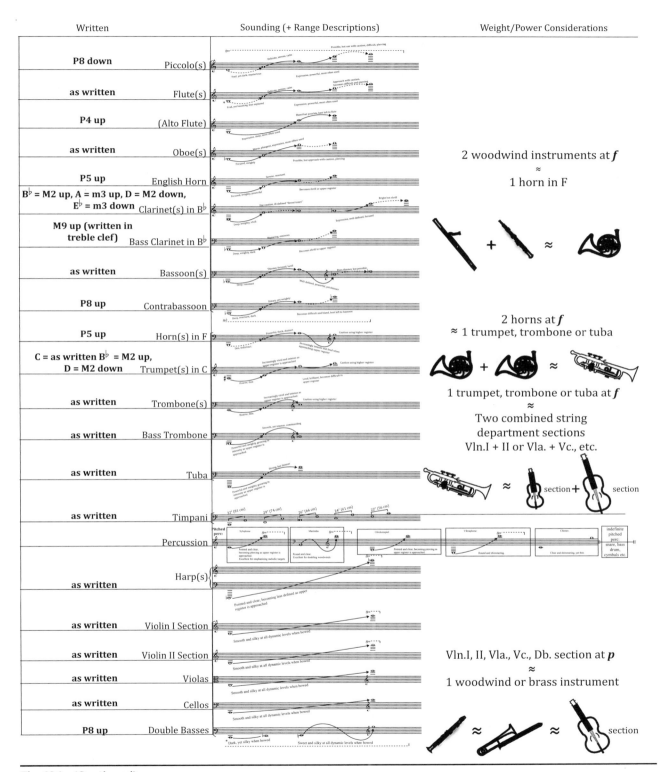

Fig. 12.1 (Continued)

TRANSPOSING INSTRUMENTS

Most instruments are non-transposing, meaning that the pitches they produce sound exactly the way they appear in a written score or part. There are, however, a variety of instruments that produce pitches a consistent interval away from those that are written; these are referred to as **transposing instruments**. The main reason why transposing instruments exist is to give performers the ability to play multiple versions of an instrument—such as clarinet in B♭, clarinet in A, and bass clarinet in B♭—using the same fingerings. This can help extend the range and coloristic opportunities of the orchestra without adding more performers to the ensemble. Indeed, performers who play transposing instruments generally "double," "triple," etc., meaning that they are able to perform on multiple instruments within a given family.

Transposing instruments are named according to keys whose tonics represent a certain interval from a frame of reference, C. The transposition level is thus indirectly provided by the name of the instrument. For example, if a performer on a horn in F played the written note C4, the resulting sound would be an F3. As F3 to C4 is a P5 interval, the horn in F therefore transposes up by a P5 from its sounding notes in notation. Similarly, a B♭ trumpet produces pitches that are a M2 interval down from notated pitches, just as B♭ is a M2 down from C. Some instruments transpose by an octave, as well, which is done to avoid excessive ledger lines in notation. The orchestral score layout is actually bordered by two such instruments: the piccolo, which sounds an octave higher than written, and the double bass, which sounds an octave lower than written. If pitches were written where they sounded for these two instruments, performers would be forced to read an exhausting amount of ledger lines.

Most notation software can help with part transposition, but it is important to understand this process, as it enables composers to study transposed scores and communicate more efficiently with performers. If one liked the sound of a particular passage in a Beethoven symphony, for example, he or she would need to reverse the transposition of the written pitches to understand what the resulting sound would be for all transposing instruments. Some scores are non-transposing, though, meaning that all pitches for all instruments are written in concert pitch. These scores are often called **concert** or simply **C-scores**, and they eliminate the need to deduce the melodic and harmonic aspects of a piece through various transpositions (though the parts for octave-transposing instruments remain transposed for the sake of legibility). Concert scores are excellent tools for the creative portion of the composition process, but they often result in excessive ledger lines (especially for instruments that transpose by a P4 or more) and fail to show how phrases will appear for the performers. Transposed scores thus excel in rehearsals, as all parts within a transposed score look identical to the parts that the players are reading. This can aid in efficient communication during short (and often expensive) rehearsals or recording sessions, where time is best reserved for conversations on musical expression. Scores in concert pitch are typically identified by the words *C-score* or *concert pitch* that appear in the top left corner of the notation; if no such description is provided, it should be assumed that the score is transposing.

EXPLORING HOMOGENEOUS AND HETEROGENEOUS TEXTURES

Understanding the general concept of score transposition allows for an exploration of each common instrument found within an orchestra. The orchestra is broken into sections of instrument families. The top portion of a score is dedicated to the woodwind instruments, followed by the brass, percussion, and finally string sections. It is common for composers to initiate their orchestration training with an introduction to the relatively homogeneous sounds that are created when scoring for a single family, a task that is less complex than blending a variety of disparate timbres. Traditional homogeneous ensembles include woodwind quintets, brass quintets, string quartets, and string orchestras. Master composers of past and present have enjoyed the textural unity and purity of sound that result from instruments constructed of like materials working together. By narrowing the instrumentation, composers are also freer to focus on the variety of timbres each instrument is capable of producing on its own, resulting in a deeper knowledge of a particular instrumental family. Moreover, it is very common for composers to shift from heterogeneous to homogeneous textures within a large orchestral work to maintain interest—indeed, this is one of the most powerful developmental tools in the composer's arsenal. It is thus recommended that students compose at least one piece for each of the traditional homogeneous ensembles before attempting to score for full orchestra.

It is also important to note that although the horn in F (or French horn) belongs to the brass family, it traditionally exists in both the woodwind and brass quintets. This is because it has a much rounder timbre than its brass counterparts, yet it possesses a weightier tone than any woodwind instrument. The horn in F may therefore be considered a "pivoting" or transitional instrument between the woodwind and brass families.

Figure 12.1 introduced different orchestral sizes. While traditional homogeneous ensembles feature a set number of players, orchestras may consist of as many players as a composer desires (depending on the budget of the project, of course). A good orchestrator, however, won't engage the entire orchestra from start to finish within a piece of music, as this tends to fatigue the ear of the listener and provides little contrast between sections of music. Instead, a piece's form tends to be shaped via the artful and judicious use of a variety of instrumental densities, from the full ensemble to homogeneous subsets to even smaller groups. To this end, composers have the option to "solo" certain instruments within a section by writing a Roman numeral above a passage that indicates the specific chair that is to perform the music. If a phrase had a Roman numeral I above it, for example, the performer in the first chair should perform alone. (Sometimes, the word *solo* is written instead, and Roman numerals are left for specific parts beyond the first chair.) When a solo section is over, an abbreviated Italian phrase *a due* (meaning "for two") or *a 2* is written above the notated melody, indicating that all players within the section are to play in unison. If three players are to return to unison playing, *a 3* may be written, and so on.

While the color of a musical passage can be adjusted on the macro level via instrumentation (that is, by choosing which instruments are performing at a given time from among all of the available options within the orchestra), it can also be manipulated on the micro level via articulation. An exploration of the unique articulations found within each family of the orchestra will thus help you shape your ideas into meaningful musical expressions.

WIND INSTRUMENT ARTICULATIONS AND EFFECTS

Wind articulations generally consist of varying degrees of *legato* and non-*legato* enunciations of pitch. To achieve non-*legato* passages, performers create a temporary break in the airflow to the instrument by forming a silent "tee" against the roof of their mouths or the reed of the instrument. This technique is called **tonguing**, and it places a slight emphasis on each note within a passage and creates separation between rhythmic values. Any time a passage of music does not include any written articulations, it is assumed that each note will be tongued separately. Wind performers are also often asked to **double tongue** passages featuring quicker rhythms that demand faster tongue movement than a series of repeating silent "tees" could produce, which is accomplished by tonguing the letters "d–k" or "t–k" in alternation. When players encounter *legato* passages, slurs tend to be used to indicate series of notes that are to be *slurred* together without tonguing each note separately. For example, the pitches in Figure 12.2 (taken from the theme of the second movement of Antonin Dvorak's famous *New World Symphony*, Symphony No. 9) are grouped into slurred units that are to be performed *legato* and within a single breath.

Fig. 12.2 Slurred notes in Dvorak, *New World Symphony*, mvt. ii

Staccato passages for wind instruments are tongued, as are *staccato* passages housed within slurs. The latter requires a tongued execution of notes that exists somewhere between a *legato* and non-*legato* performance, and is exemplified in the fourth measure of Figure 12.3, which is taken from the third movement of Mozart's Clarinet Concerto in A Major.

Fig. 12.3 Slurred *staccato* in Mozart, Clarinet Concerto in A Major, K. 622

Trilling is another important effect, though it is not limited to wind instruments. A **trill** is an excellent way to add life to a passage, and it consists of rapid alternations between two notes that are usually a half or whole step apart (see Figure 12.4, which is taken from the opening movement of Stravinsky's *The Rite of Spring*). Notice how Stravinsky extended the effect in this example by alternating it between two different clarinetists with a slight overlap, in order to allow the performers to breathe. This technique is called "dovetailing," and it is discussed with more depth later in this chapter.

concert pitch

Fig. 12.4 Trills in Stravinsky, *The Rite of Spring*, mvt. i

Another interesting articulation for winds is the *glissando*, an effect that deserves special consideration due to instrument-specific limitations (which are often disregarded by beginning students). A *glissando* is a smooth, gliding pitch transition from one note to another that proceeds through all of the intermediate microtones. Most wind instruments can "lip" a *glissando* between smaller intervals by moving their lips, rolling the instrument or moving their head slightly to alter the aim of the airflow to achieve the desired result while seamlessly changing fingerings to create smooth pitch transitions. To notate a *glissando*, a line is placed from the first notehead into the next, as in the examples in Figure 12.5. Sometimes, the word *gliss* or *glissando* may appear above the line, but this is not necessary.

The instrument most commonly thought of when discussing *glissandi* is the trombone. To understand how *glissandi* work for this instrument, one must combine an understanding of the overtone series with a comprehension of the slide positions of the instrument. There are seven slide positions, each capable of playing nine usable partials. Smooth *glissandi* are limited to the notes that fall inside the seven slide positions within each partial of a harmonic series. Tenor trombones are not transposing instruments, yet they are considered to be B♭ instruments,

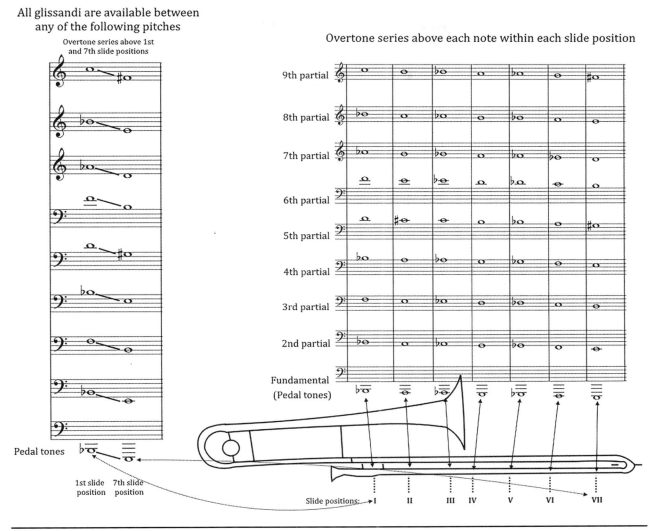

Fig. 12.5 Trombone *glissandi*

as the harmonic series in first position is based on B♭, with the lowest note in this position being B♭1. If the slide is extended to its seventh position, the lowest pitch becomes E1. Professional trombonists can therefore smoothly *gliss* between E and Bb (and vice versa), because all the intermediate pitches exist within the first partials of each slide position between positions seven and one. Put more generally, *glissandi* are possible on the trombone when they are written within a descending tritone span from any partial of the B♭ overtone series. If a composer writes a *glissando* between two pitches that are not within the tritone span of a single partial, there will be an audible, undesired break in the *gliss*. Figure 12.5 shows all possible *glissando* ranges for a tenor trombone.

Staccato, legato, slurred *staccato,* trills, and *glissandi* are certainly not the only articulations available to wind players. Other, less common effects include flutter tonguing, *tremolando* or unmeasured *tremolo* (a *tremolo* effect involving larger intervals between alternating pitches), and harmonics; each of these techniques is described in the *Additional Orchestration Concepts* section on this text's companion site.

MUTES

Mutes offer composers interesting effects, as they provide a variety of alterations to the volume and timbre of instruments. To indicate the need for a mute in a score, the term *con sordino* is added above the first note of such a passage. To indicate when the performer is to remove the mute, the term *senza sordino* is written after the last note of the muted phrase. It is important to consider the time it takes a performer to add and remove a mute, so space must be given in a composition to allow for this process. Figure 12.6 presents a list of the commonly used brass instrument mutes, along with a brief description of each mute's timbral effect.

Mute Type		Tone Quality	Associated Instruments
Straight Mutes		Bright sound when made of aluminum. Muffled sound when made of cardboard.	Horn Trumpet Trombone Tuba
Cup Mutes	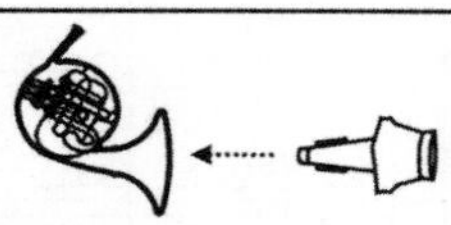	More muffled than a straight mute. Brighter sound when made of aluminum. More muffled sound when made of cardboard.	Horn Trumpet Trombone Tuba
Bucket Mutes	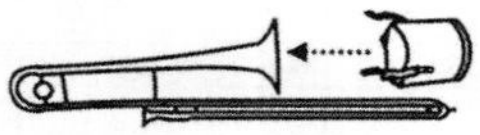	Especially muffled sound	Trumpet Trombone
Harmon Mutes		Distinctly tiny sound made famous by jazz musicians, most notably Miles Davis. The stem coming out of the first part of the mute may be inserted all the way, part of the way or completely out. Each stem position offers a slightly different tone quality. A "wah-wah" effect may be achieved by alternating between covering and not covering the end of the mute.	Trumpet Trombone
Plunger Mutes	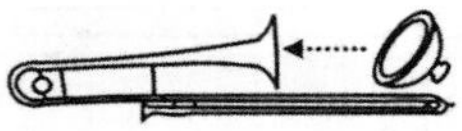	Similar to a harmon mute "wah-wah" effect, a plunger mute creates a similar sound by alternating between covering and not covering the end of the mute.	Trumpet Trombone

Fig. 12.6   Brass mutes

STRING ARTICULATIONS AND TECHNIQUES

String players may employ mutes as well, which are attached to the bridge of the instruments and muffle their timbres significantly. Although a string mute is a tool originally designed for practicing purposes, composers at times feature the restrained sound of muted strings as an effect, as in the "Venus" movement from Gustav Holst's famous suite for large orchestra, *The Planets*. As with brass instruments, the term *con sordino* is to be written above the first note that is to be muted in a score for strings, while *senza sordino* is written when the mute is to be taken away.

    As is the case with the trombone, a *glissando* is a very common effect used by all string instruments. The notation of *glissandi* is the same for string instruments as it is with trombone, which includes lines that connect noteheads, with or without the word *gliss* or *glissando* written above them. Of particular confusion is the term *portamento*, which is a playing technique wherein performers seamlessly "glide" between melodic notes that are separated by large intervals. The notation for *portamento*—which is rarely included in scores—is the same as the notation for *glissando*, except the word *portamento* may be added above the lines that connect noteheads instead of the word *glissando*. There is little to no distinction between *portamento* and *glissando*, especially considering that the notation for each may appear to be the same if the terms are omitted from the lines that connect the noteheads (which is advised). However, many modern notation software programs force composers to choose one technique or the other, with the specific terms written above the lines by default, which is likely the source of current confusion among beginning students.

On-the-String and Off-the-String Bowing

On-the-string bowing is a term representing a category of bowings that occur when the bow never leaves the string throughout the execution of a note. Off-the-string bowing, or "bouncing," instead refers to a variety of bowings that occur when the bow leaves the string or bounces momentarily. Figures 12.7 and 12.8 illustrate both categories of commonly applied on- and off-the-string bowing techniques that tend to be requested by composers.

On-the-String Bowing Techniques

Technique	Notation	Description
Down bow: - Notes are to be performed by dragging the bow downward, across the strings.	Violin 	Often used when accenting notes and closing out phrases.
Up bow: - Notes are to be performed by dragging the bow upward, across the strings.	Cello 	Often used to set up a down bow for accenting notes and closing out phrases.
Détaché: - Separately bowed notes, as in non-legato playing. - Bow direction will change for every pitch. - Each note will be accented just enough to create a clear separation between pitches but not so much as to produce a staccato articulation.	Détaché is the default stroke a string player will perform if nothing else is indicated.	Non-legato.
Staccato: - Detached bowed notes, as in non-legato playing. - Bow direction may or may not change for every pitch. - Each note will be performed as short, separate strokes.	Violin 	Non-legato, short.
Louré: - Legato bowing with slight separation between notes. - Performed in either bow direction.	Violin 	Legato with slight separation.
Martelé: - Separate, weighty, swift bow stroke. - Performed in either bow direction.	Viola  *ff*	Heavily accented notes.

Fig. 12.7   On-the-string bowing techniques

Off-the-String Bowing Techniques

Technique	Notation	Description
Spiccato: • Pitches are produced as the performer loosens the wrist of the bowing hand and the middle of the bow is dropped onto the string. • At slower tempi, performers need to move methodically to allow the bow to bounce on the string. • At faster tempi, the bouncing occurs more spontaneously, with little conscious effort.	To ensure that performers will play *spiccato* and not staccato, write the word *spiccato* above the first note of the passage in which you desire to hear the effect.  *spiccato* 	Bouncing, spring-like effect.
Jeté: • The bow is thrown onto the string producing up to six consecutive pitches in a single bow direction.		Sprightly and swift.

Fig. 12.8 Off-the-string bowing techniques

Additional String Colors

There are many additional string techniques for composers to explore that offer a multitude of coloristic opportunities. The trill was discussed earlier in this chapter in the context of wind instruments, and it is a shared technique among most instruments—including all members of the string family. As in the Stravinsky example in 12.4, trills are notated the same way for all instruments (which is also the case for *tremolando* notation). Harmonics are possible for strings as well, but they require special consideration. There are two types of harmonics available for string players: **natural harmonics** and **artificial harmonics**. Natural harmonics are produced when performers lightly press on various locations that divide an open string's length and correspond to points within the overtone series above the open string's fundamental. Artificial harmonics function similarly, but are artificially created by the performer using one finger to stop a string at some point within its length and then lightly pressing a P4 above the stop in pitch with another finger while bowing or plucking. In doing so, the performer generates a harmonic that sounds two octaves above the stopped note. The performer effectively creates a false open string with the bottom finger through this process, and generates the fourth partial above the stopped note by lightly pressing at a location that is one-quarter of the distance through the remaining string length. String harmonics are discussed in detail in the *Additional Orchestration Concepts* portion of this text's companion website. Strings also possess a collection of other interesting colors for composers to explore that involve non-standard, "extended techniques" for activating the strings. Figure 12.9 presents a list of these coloristic string effects, along with an illustration of how each is notated and a brief description of their associated timbres.

To cancel any extended bowing techniques, write *ord.*—the abbreviation for *ordinario* (Italian for "ordinary")—above the first note that is to return to traditional bowing.

String players are also capable of performing multiple pitches simultaneously on adjacent strings. To achieve a **double stop**, a performer simply fingers the two desired pitches, and then concurrently bows across the strings of the "stopped" notes. The concept is the same for **triple stops**, but this adds a third adjacent string across which the bow needs to be drawn. Although they are possible, quadruple stops will generally be arpeggiated instead, as the curvature of a bow is too straight to realistically sound four pitches simultaneously. Triple and quadruple stops are, however, easier when they involve open strings and louder dynamic levels. Instead of listing an exhausting inventory of all possible double, triple, and quadruple stops for all four instruments of the string family, it is suggested that the reader instead visit the *Additional Orchestration Concepts* section of the companion website to understand

Additional String Effects

Technique	Notation	Description
Tremolo: - Fast detaché strokes as quickly as possible for the duration of the written rhythm. - Unmeasured tremolo is the default playing technique and is notated with three slashes. To avoid an unwanted measured tremolo interpretation, the word tremolo may be added to the part. Most players will play unmeasured by default regardless. - Measured tremolo is shorthand for a series of repeating detaché notes on a single pitch. Each slash divides the rhythm into eighth notes. One slash implies eighth notes, two slashes represent sixteenth notes and three slashes denote thirty-second notes.	Viola 	Tense, uneasy, unsettling. Great for creating an anxious, apprehensive mood.
Pizzicato: - Bowing hand plucks the string instead of bowing it. - May be overpowered by heavily orchestrated *f* passages.	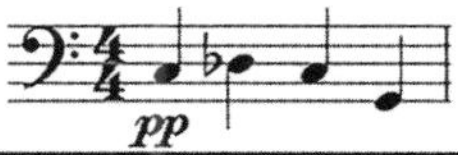 Double Bass *pizz.* *pp*	Short, percussive, pitched effect. Excellent for creating playful moods as well as darker atmospheres.
Sul ponticello: - Bow strokes occur on or near the bridge of the instrument. - Easily overpowered.	 Cello *sul pont.* *pp*	Resonates upper partials causing a thin, metallic, ominous sound. Useful for delicate or unearthly passages.
Sul tasto: - Bow strokes occur on the fingerboard. - **Flautando** may be asked instead and means to play near the fingerboard. - Easily overpowered.	 Violin *sul tasto* *pp*	Opaque, flute-like tone. Also useful for delicate or unearthly passages.
Col legno tratto: - The wood of the bow is drawn over the string instead of the hair. - Very easily overpowered.	 Violin *col legno tratto* *pp*	Very delicate effect, again useful for unearthly, eerie settings. Commonly coupled with tremolo.
Col legno battuto: - The string is struck with the wood of the bow. - Easily overpowered. - Never ask for *f* passages as it may damage the instrument and performers will likely object.	 Viola *col legno battuto* *pp*	Percussive, spiccato effect of indefinite pitch.

Fig. 12.9 Additional string effects

the mechanics of how various harmonic intervals are achieved on stringed instruments. In general, it is best to imagine performing anything one wants to compose before writing it. Double stops involving large intervals, for example, are not always possible, as they often require stretching the hand beyond what is capable. Nonetheless, samples and DAWs tend to allow such things, which gives composers a false sense of what is actually possible to reproduce live. Some samples even extend the ranges of instruments beyond what is achievable. Compounding the issue, most pieces of notation software are not equipped to identify multiple stops that are impossible to perform. If such parts were given to a live ensemble in a rehearsal, they would likely assume the parts were meant to be performed *divisi*, which divides the notated harmony into two (double stops) or three (triple stops) separate parts, resulting in a significantly thinner sound. Composers also use *divisi* purposefully, however, to extend harmonic sonorities by distributing more pitches to a fixed number of players. The marking *div* is added above the first group of pitches that are to be divided. *Unis* (unison), by contrast, is added above the first pitch that should no longer be considered as a divided part.

The tuning of a stringed instrument provides a finite collection of pitches within which a composer may work. To expand that collection, a performer may be asked to tune his or her instrument in altered ways. The term *scordatura* is used at the start of a passage that asks for an alternate tuning, while the term *accordatura* is used to signify the return to normal tuning. Performers must be given a fair amount of time to tune their instruments appropriately in either case, however, which in turn affects the rhythms that may realistically be called for in a score. Figure 12.10 is an example of how to notate *scordatura*; it is taken from the first cello passage within a suite written for a major video game release (composed by Steve Cox and Daniel McIntyre). In this example, the cello's fourth string is to be tuned a half step lower than usual, in order to make the B1 in measures 17 and 18 possible. The notation signifies this by including the term *scordatura* on the top left corner of the part, followed by the normal tuning of the first three strings and the alternate tuning of string IV in bold print.

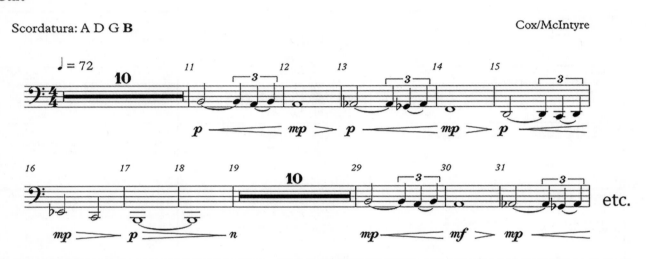

Fig. 12.10 *Scordatura* notation in Cox and McIntyre, "Hazard Suite"

    Scordatura, double and triple stops, *tremolo*, *pizzicato*, and the other string techniques that have been discussed in this section may appear numerous, but in actuality they represent only a share of the overall technical repertoire held by professional string players. Since the early 1960s, the style of scoring known as **aleatoricism** has expanded contemporary string techniques to include many new coloristic options. Aleatoricism is a popular composition technique involving indeterminacy or chance that became widespread due to the success of composers like Krzysztof Penderecki, whose music has been used in Stanley Kubrick's *The Shining*, William Friedkin's *The Exorcist*, the Quay brothers' *Mask*, and Martin Scorsese's *Shutter Island*. Many composers still exercise this technique today, as it is exciting, efficient, and powerful. Aleatoricism and chance procedures are discussed with more depth in the *Additional Orchestration Concepts* section of this book's companion website.

BLENDING INSTRUMENTS

Blending instruments from different families together to form harmonic sonorities is one of the most creatively rewarding aspects of the orchestration process. A nice instrumental blend greatly enhances the strength of a passage of music, whereas a poor instrumental blend weakens an otherwise powerful passage in an amateurish manner. When blending different instruments together, an understanding of instruments' registral characteristics is extremely important; simply placing pitches within the available range of an instrument does not necessarily result in the most appropriate sound for a given situation. The lower range of the flute, for example, would not be appropriate for f passages, as that particular register within the flute's overall range does not project very well. Likewise, placing pitches within the higher register of a trumpet part for a p passage is counterproductive, as the resultant timbres eliminate the possibility of a soft, delicate section of music. Once instruments' registral qualities are memorized, an exploration of harmonic voicings may follow. The distribution of instrumental timbres within a blended voicing may be described by one of the following three categories, each of which is demonstrated in Figure 12.11 (with special considerations listed below the figure).

Stacked voicing—Pitches are distributed between instruments that are arranged from low to high in a harmonic situation. Often, one group of instruments is exclusively given the relatively higher pitches while another group of instruments is given the lower pitches. In a four-note chord divided into two flutes and two oboes, for example, a stacked sonority might give the bottom two notes to the two oboes and the top two notes to the flutes.

Staggered voicing—The placement of instruments within a chord is staggered, such that the first and third notes of a four-note harmony are performed by one instrument type (two oboes, for example) and the second and fourth notes are played by other instruments (e.g., two flutes).

Surrounded voicing—The inner pitches of a harmony are given to one instrument type, while the outer pitches are given to others, which "surround" the timbre of the inner-voice instruments. In a four-note chord, the lowest and highest notes are often given to two different instruments (often from the same family), while the inner pitches are usually given to two performers of the same instrument.

Concert pitch

Fig. 12.11   Stacked, staggered, and surrounded voicings of a G major triad

SPECIAL CONSIDERATIONS

■ The oboe deserves special consideration. Of all the wind instruments, the oboe tends to stand out the most, drawing more attention to the notes within a sonority that it is covering. Sometimes this effect is desired, especially if those notes hold melodic value; however, when a smoother instrumental blend is preferred, it is wise to consider separating the oboes.

■ When orchestrating stacked voicings that feature a variety of instrumental timbres, it is best to space the pitches apart as much as possible, as tuning issues tend to arise between different instruments when their pitches are clustered together.

■ Harmonic voicings that exclusively feature the horn in F are traditionally staggered. This is because Classical orchestral scores included four horns that were consolidated into two staves, with each staff consisting of a *high* and *low* part (as horn players during that era tended to be specialists in either the high or low registers of the instrument). Although modern horn players excel in all registers of the instrument, the tradition of staggering the voicings of a chord remains. As such, horns I and III are almost always given the top two notes of a harmony and horns II and IV are given the bottom two.

COMMON LAYERING TECHNIQUES AND SCORE STUDIES

The following stock orchestration tips represent common coloristic choices that composers have relied on for generations. Note that the examples in this section are all taken from Holt's *The Planets*, which was used as the "temp track" (temporary score) for the original *Star Wars* film, as well as for many other films. (Temp tracks will be discussed further in Chapters 17 and 18). *The Planets* is such a significant and influential work that it is often considered to represent a standalone textbook on orchestration—particularly for film composers, as Hollywood orchestral scores have been modeling the work for decades. For clarity and efficiency, each score example that follows is condensed (*tacet* parts removed) and presented in concert pitch.

BLENDING STRINGS AND WINDS AT THE UNISON

This technique is generally used to add thickness to a strings passage. It is common to layer like-ranged instruments together when blending these instrument families (e.g., flutes play in unison with violins, clarinets with violas, bassoons with cellos, and contrabassoon with double basses). However, there is much overlap with respect to the ranges of various woodwind and string instruments; thus, many decisions are contextually based. As well, this unison doubling effect may be overused, which results in a dull or "gray" sound. Figure 12.12, taken from the opening passage to the "Mercury" movement from *The Planets*, exemplifies blending string and winds at the unison. An abbreviated set of analytical remarks related to this orchestration is provided below.

"Mercury" Score Study

■ String/wind doublings (shaded light grey) are in unison and chosen based on shared instrument ranges.
■ The main motif and accompaniment change registers frequently, making it necessary to pass the phrases between instruments possessing different registral qualities. As such, orchestral colors change frequently, resulting in a driving, playful atmosphere.
■ The end of each phrase in a given instrumental part dovetails with a continuation of or answer to that phrase that is performed by a different instrument (dovetailing is shaded dark grey). This gives each phrase an accentuated beginning and ending, which performers may definitively express.
■ For the first seven bars, the accompaniment is given to the harp part, which is doubled by different members of the orchestra at different times, generating added interest in the attacks of each harp pitch.

DOUBLING PHRASES AT THE OCTAVE

This technique is typically accomplished by the winds doubling string melodies an octave higher, which helps to emphasize the overtone series above the string section's melody line. It is very common to hear flutes playing the same melody as the first section of violins an octave higher, for example. Figure 12.13 illustrates octave doubling in Holst's "Mars" movement, with two piccolos playing an octave transposition of the melodic figure shared by the violins and flutes.

Concert Score

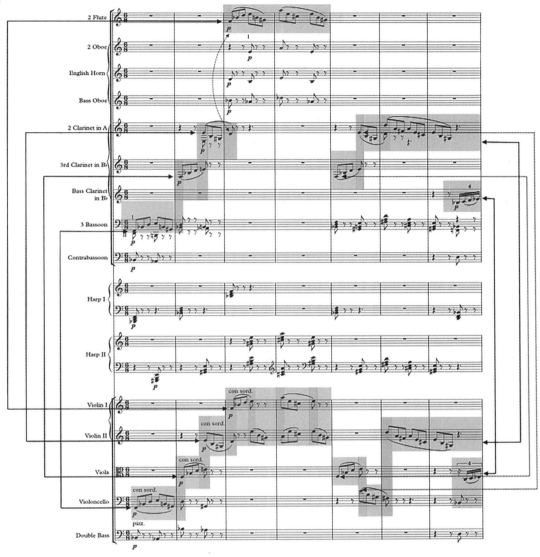

Fig. 12.12   Score analysis of Holst, "Mercury"

"Mars" Score Study

- ■ Bars 2–5: The primary melodic line (shaded light grey) is doubled at the unison by the violin I and flute players.
- ■ Bars 4–5: The piccolo doubles the violin I/flute melody an octave higher.
- ■ Bars 2–3: Another melodic line (also shaded light grey) is doubled an octave lower and shared between the violin II, oboe, and clarinet performers.
- ■ Bars 2–3: The secondary line stemming from bassoon part (shaded dark grey), which is moving in root position chords, is doubled between the viola, cello, English horn, bass oboe, bass clarinet, trombone, and bass trombone parts in piecemeal fashion. Brass parts clearly dominate the passage, overpowering the parts played by the winds and strings, which add subtle color and are largely designed to keep the parts interesting for the players.

Concert Score

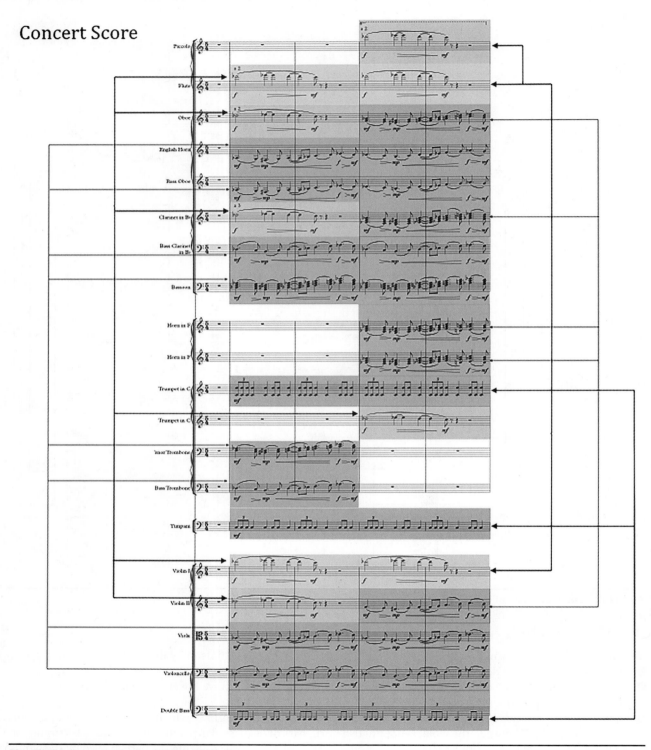

Fig. 12.13   Score analysis of Holst, "Mars"

- Bars 4–5: Horns double the secondary line. There are two horns per pitch throughout the phrase, as the horns are half as strong as other, individual brass instruments at the given dynamic level. This allows the horns to hold a dominant position within the phrase. Oboes, clarinets, bass clarinet, and violin II join the secondary line.
- Bars 2–5: An *ostinato* (also shaded dark grey, with arrows pointing into the score from the far right) is doubled over three octaves with double basses in the lowest register, followed by timpani in the middle register and two trumpets in the higher register.

OCTAVE-DOWN DOUBLING OF BASS PARTS

The **octave-down doubling** technique involves doubling lower register melodies an octave lower, usually with the double basses, to add weight and depth to the bottom of the orchestra. The double bass, after all, gets its name from the Baroque practice of playing bass parts an octave lower than they were written in the cello and/or bassoon parts, effectively *doubling* the bass parts at the octave. This technique still remains the default scoring option for double bass, though modern composers sometimes highlight the instrument by giving it a truly independent part. In Figure 12.14 (also taken from the "Mars" movement of *The Planets*), the main melodic motive carried by the cellos and doubled at the unison by two bassoons creates an unnerving atmosphere. The phrase is then doubled at the octave

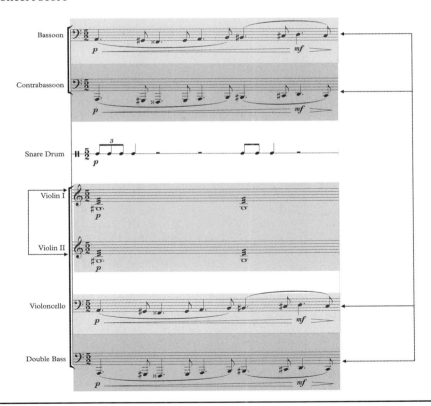

Fig. 12.14 Analysis of octave-down doubling in Holst, "Mars"

below by double basses and a contrabassoon, further enriching the depth of the passage and enhancing the ominous feel of the phrase. This excerpt is also an excellent example of percussion writing, as the snare drum part—which is a developed version of the *ostinato* that drives the entire work—helps subtly push the passage forward.

"Mars" Score Study

■ Cellos and bassoons perform a line (shaded light grey) that is doubled at the unison.
■ Double basses and contrabassoon double one another at the unison, performing the cello/bassoon line pitched an octave lower (this is shaded dark grey).
■ Violins I and II perform a contrasting line (shaded medium gray) that is doubled at the unison.

STAGGERED WIND HARMONIES

While stacked voicings create relatively salient sonorities in wind parts, staggered voicings generate smooth, balanced harmonies. This is especially the case for voicings that include oboes, as two or more adjacently stacked oboes will create a heterogeneous sound, drawing slightly more attention to a particular harmonic interval. While this may be useful in specific situations, staggered voicings that include oboes (and other instruments) are used more often to "glue together" harmonic passages in unique, imaginative ways. Figure 12.15 is taken from the "Neptune" movement of *The Planets* and demonstrates a uniquely blended, staggered arrangement of voices. The staff on the left of the figure is a score reduction that brings all parts onto a single treble clef staff. Note that the flute part is inserted between the oboes, resulting in the desired, staggered voicing.

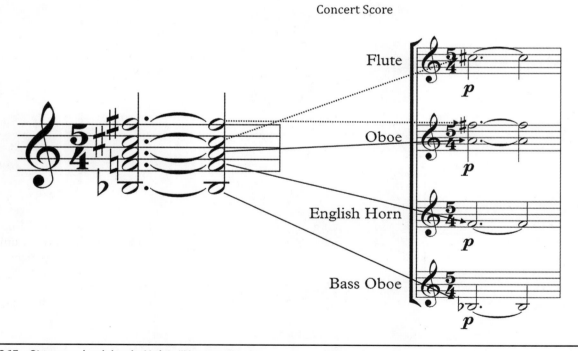

Fig. 12.15   Staggered voicing in Holst, "Neptune"

The information in the preceding section may be considered a brief introduction to the craft of orchestration. You are encouraged to study scores, attend concerts, and read other texts dedicated to the craft alone. While the study of orchestration may at first seem overwhelming, there are a few other general guidelines that should initially prove helpful in generating successful arrangements. To this end, the following list is provided; it is intended to offer further structure and direction to an initial exploration into the complex art of orchestration.

GENERAL GUIDELINES FOR ORCHESTRATION

Clarify Form: The form of a composition should be enhanced and delineated by the orchestration. New sections of music provide important opportunities for fresh instrumentation.

Avoid Listener Fatigue: An overuse of heavy layering will create a tiring experience for the listener. The best way to make a section feel powerful is to contrast it with more delicately scored sections.

Avoid Stasis: The orchestra provides many coloristic opportunities that are limited only by the imagination of the composer. If one orchestral palette is used for the entirety of a piece, it will feel stale, unimaginative, and boring.

Avoid the Overuse of Color: Changing color is an important and exciting part of the orchestration process, but it can be overdone. The form of a piece should help the orchestrator understand when changes in instrumentation, blend, or weight are appropriate. Random changes of color will take attention away from the composition as a whole and may confuse the listener by presenting too much information to process in a short period of time.

Create Distinction between Melodic, Contrapuntal, and Harmonic Content: Successful orchestrations make it clear which instruments are playing primary melodies, which instruments are performing countermelodies, and which instruments are playing accompanimental harmonic content at any given moment.

Use Percussion: Percussion parts are very often employed to accentuate important formal or melodic moments and should not represent compositional afterthoughts.

Enliven the Accompaniment: Although there are times when slow-paced, simple, sustained sonorities are a desired effect, it is important to consider when it may be more appropriate and exciting to activate the rhythms of the supporting material. This is in large part a compositional decision that becomes apparent after instrumentation choices have been made.

Use Your Imagination: Experimentation is always encouraged when orchestrating. In the world of media scoring, those who are able to create a new or fresh sound that may be uniquely married to a particular commercial, scene, or film are highly regarded and sought after. Howard Shore's score to *The Lord of the Rings* movies created such an effect, as his refreshing use of the orchestra was designed to enhance other compositional effects that combined to create a distinctly foreign and ancient sound palette.

Practice Orchestrating Previously Composed Works: Maurice Ravel, who is among the greatest orchestrators in history, consistently followed this guideline. His earlier experiments included orchestrating his own piano pieces as well as those of others (notably Modest Mussorgsky's *Pictures at an Exhibition*). This, in turn, allowed him to develop into a master of orchestral colors and textures. Orchestrating previously composed pieces allows you to concentrate solely on timbre, freeing you from many other compositional complexities.

Study Scores: Although it would be problematic to pinpoint a single composer or composition as the starting point for modern orchestral writing, the works of Nikolai Rimsky-Korsakov are generally regarded as worthy of serious study. Richard Wagner is known for expanding the size and power of the orchestra and should be studied, too, as should any composer you find particularly interesting. Rimsky-Korsakov is, however, a uniquely important individual because of his influential book on orchestration, which cites the composer's own works. Other important orchestral composers to study include Richard Strauss, Igor Stravinsky, Claude Debussy, Gustav Holst, and Gustav Mahler, among others.

MIDI ORCHESTRATION

One of the most important responsibilities held by the modern commercial composer is the ability to create realistic orchestral scores within a home studio environment. In the past, "mocking up" an orchestral score was a specialized skill that many technically apt composers used in order to break into the industry. In more recent times, this ability has become a standard part of every successful composer's skill set and is no longer considered an area of specialty. For lower-budget projects, MIDI realizations are often the final product, and they need to sound as convincing as possible, as a poor MIDI realization will quickly turn a genius composition into an amateurish outcome. MIDI orchestration is not solely used in lower-budget scenarios, however; indeed, it is involved in many major projects, particularly to create depth as well as sounds that are not always possible in a live setting. Moreover, most professional scores need to be approved by directors, game developers, or other clients before a decision to include live performers is made; thus, composers need to be able to craft mock-ups that sound as polished as possible. Put simply, demo-quality work is no longer acceptable in the industry, making MIDI orchestration techniques valuable—even mandatory—for any contemporary producer.

Creating realistic MIDI realizations begins with high-quality samples; as a result, the sample library tends to be the aspect of the project studio that requires the most maintenance. Every few months, software and sample developers put out new and innovative tools that help composers more efficiently create realistic-sounding projects. Remaining knowledgeable about recent developments in this area will ensure that your sound palette is current and relevant. Although buying every new piece of gear as it becomes available is certainly not recommended, it is important that you remain well informed on current technological trends and consistently devote time to researching new software and sample developments.

WORKING TO THE STRENGTHS OF YOUR SETUP

Many beginning composers feel overwhelmed by the variety of sample choices available, which exist within a wide price range. Although a substantial initial investment is necessary, composers should only purchase the tools they believe they need for a project they are hired to complete (or want to be hired to complete). Some larger sample packages boast a multitude of sounds, and while only a few of the included samples may be high in quality, they are often enough to get started, provided that certain strategies are employed when they are used. Composers with more modest systems should therefore utilize the following list of practical techniques when producing projects during the beginning phases of their project studio build-outs. These methods will remain useful even when one's home studio and sample library collection reach a professional standard.

Highlight Exemplary Samples: It may seem obvious, but one should always compose for the sounds they possess that are of the highest quality. If you have access to a great-sounding horn in F patch, but do not have a professional-level trombone sample, you should not be writing for trombone until you are able to update your setup. Until such time, you should rely on the horn in F patch and write for that instrument as much as possible.

Hide Inferior Samples with Layering: This technique should be used with caution, as it will not always result in successful outcomes. As described in Chapter 7, the timbre of an instrument is determined by the unique array of frequencies that are excited above its performed fundamentals. Since even low-quality patches excite the same general frequencies as live instruments, these weaker patches are, at minimum, able to be aurally identified and correlated with specific instruments by listeners. When layered with instrument patches of better quality, the poor attributes of the low-quality patches are often masked, leaving the listener with an impression of the color of the instrument without accentuating the sample's shortcomings. If the layering is done appropriately (following stock orchestration techniques), the listener will be focused on the finer characteristics of the better patches and deceived by the familiarity of stock orchestral doublings.

UNDERSTANDING THE REGISTRAL QUALITIES OF ORCHESTRAL INSTRUMENTS

One of the most common mistakes that beginner orchestrators make is ignoring the ranges and registral qualities of orchestral instruments. While DAWs do allow unrealistic phrases to come to life (which may be used for special effect), listeners tend to be confused when a mix's volume balance doesn't correlate with the acoustic realities of the instruments that are performing. For example, if a passage consists of a *p* solo clarinet part layered with three trumpets playing in unison, the clarinet part will not be heard in a live setting. The virtual mixer in a DAW will allow a producer to simply lower the faders of the trumpet parts and raise the fader of the clarinet part to rectify this issue, but the effect will be unrealistic, as the amount of energy it takes a live performer to produce f trumpet passages is felt as well as heard, creating a dominant sound that masks the parts with which these passages are layered. Careful study of the orchestra guide in Figure 12.1 will ensure that sequenced passages for orchestral instruments are realistic.

PROGRAMMING

Without articulations and dynamic variety, MIDI sequences and live performances alike sound dull and unmusical. Velocity control (dynamics), expression (*crescendos/decrescendos*), and articulation switching are, therefore, crucial aspects relating to the success of a MIDI production. While creating *staccato* articulations is relatively easy within a sequencer (one may either use a *staccato* instrument sample or create visible breaks between MIDI events by editing their lengths), *legato* passages are somewhat less intuitive. To enhance the realism of a *legato* phrase, the ends of the MIDI events within the passage should be slightly elongated so that they overlap with the initiation points of the subsequent events. By blurring the boundary between the attack and release point of two notes, the illusion of *legato* phrasing is created. Figure 12.16 demonstrates this technique with the opening of the "Neptune" movement from Holst's *The Planets*.

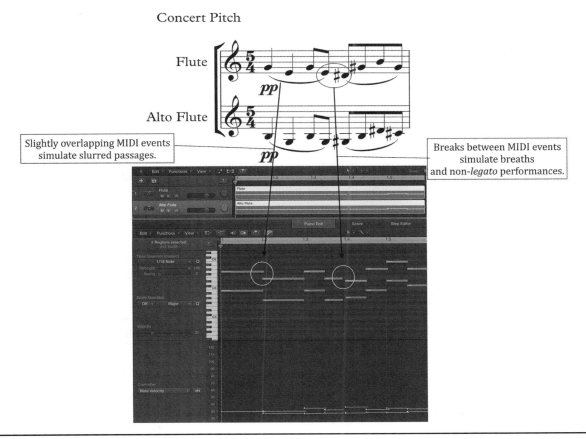

Fig. 12.16 Slurred and *legato* phrases in Holst, "Neptune"

Typically, *legato* patches consist of three adjustable samples that are combined together: a sustaining sample, a *legato* sample, and a release sample that are each crossfaded and set to different volume levels. Many modern *legato* samples additionally include **legato transitions**, which are additional samples that are joined to *legato* patches in order to create smooth transitions between overlapping MIDI events. Figure 12.17 is a screenshot of EastWest's Play engine with a *legato* violin patch loaded from the company's Hollywood Strings library. Note the three circled samples in the articulation window that combine to create this patch.

Fig. 12.17   EastWest's Play engine

Slow MIDI Attack Compensation

Even the most expensive sample libraries can be plagued with oddly slow attack speeds, causing performances to sound sloppy, even after quantization and visual editing is complete. There are two methods producers use to compensate for this issue: the first involves dragging all MIDI events slightly to the left within the piano roll editor until the passage sounds in time, and the second involves offsetting the start time of all MIDI events using batch processing. Figure 12.18 demonstrates this second process in Logic Pro X, which involves manipulating a delay feature within the Inspector window to allow MIDI events to be offset by specific durations. It is important to note, however, that all samples do not typically need to be delayed by the same amount using this procedure—even those that come from the same library packages. You should use your ears and a metronome to guide the precision of performances while feeling free to experiment with different delay settings to achieve the desired result.

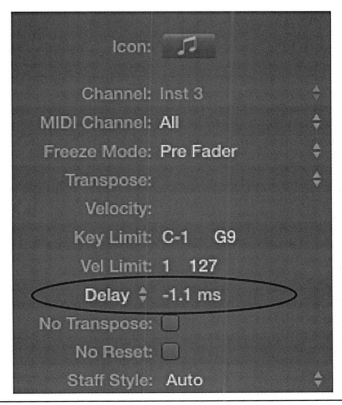

Fig. 12.18   MIDI delay compensation in Logic Pro X

Multi-Samples

A **multi-sample** is a combination patch that itself consists of multiple samples. There are many multi-sample orchestral patches, for example, that provide the entire sound of a full orchestra divided into registral regions and mapped out across a MIDI keyboard. These orchestral multi-samples (or "multis") tend to layer all sound in the lower register with double bass, cello, low woodwind, and low brass samples, for instance, to generate familiar stock sounds and doublings. Multi-samples are great for sketching ideas, as they provide immediate access to standard orchestral colors. The downside to using samples like these, however, is that composers relinquish a significant amount of orchestral control over their ideas, as multis tend to only allow for basic adjustments to volume and panning. Thus, it is advised to use multi-sample orchestral patches as a tool for sketching ideas that are later split out and re-orchestrated manually.

BALANCING LIVE PLAYERS WITH MIDI SEQUENCES

Most contemporary commercial productions include a combination of one or more live elements working concurrently with MIDI sequences, for a variety of aesthetic and financial reasons that are discussed further in Chapter 14.

When deciding which MIDI instrument(s) are to be replaced with a live recording, the most prominent melodic instrument of the piece should be the producer's first choice, as it will have more impact on the realism of the entire project than live instruments that predominantly perform the inner voices of chords or otherwise fulfill accompanimental roles. For the same reason, solo MIDI passages are great choices to replace with live instruments, even if these passages are short in duration. It is also common for composers to work with a small group of trusted studio musicians to help generate the illusion of a larger ensemble. To enhance the sound of a string ensemble, for example, producers at times record one live performance for each member of the string family, and afterward mix these performances with MIDI string samples to effectively create full sections for violin I, II, viola, cello, and double bass that each feature a live first chair player. If a project's budget only allows for one live string player, though, the section with the most prominent melody should be recorded with a live first chair performer (which is usually violin I).

It is not recommended, however, to record individual instrumentalists separately and later mix these audio recordings together to create the sound of a section or instrumental family within a string orchestra. This is because each individual sound wave won't have the ability to interact with the sound waves and reverberations that would be naturally produced by other instruments being recorded simultaneously in a truly live ensemble situation. Tuning issues may also become an issue when performances are recorded separately and then mixed together. After all, a string orchestra produces such a large sound in part due to the slight differences in intonation from player to player and the constant adjustments to intonation that performers make in reaction to those around them. If, for example, one performer is overdubbed repeatedly, effectively layering the same musician, intonation is often too precise to generate the large, chorus-like effect of a real string orchestra. For this reason, it is recommended to record the first chair of each section and blend them with the highest-quality full-section samples available when combining live and virtual instrumentalists.

GENERATING THICKNESS

The biggest complaint that film and television producers have with music submissions—especially trailer tracks—is that these productions don't sound "thick" enough. No matter how powerful a composition is, it will not likely sell if it does not have a modern, thick, "Hollywood" sound. Good orchestration will help create such an effect, but adding a few production elements that are not possible in live contexts can aid in generating the enormous sound that clients tend to crave. These production techniques are listed below.

Add Sub Bass: Sub basses can substantially strengthen the foundation of tracks, though caution should be exercised when using them, as too much low-end energy can easily unbalance a mix.

Add Cinematic Percussion: Japanese taiko drums and hybrid synth percussion instruments are often used to thicken media compositions. There are many sample libraries on the market that generate these and other similar sounds, which tend to feature patch names like *war drums*, *cinema percussion*, etc.

Add Synthesizers: the addition of synth patches can help thicken an orchestration as well as provide fresh, interesting, and particularly modern-sounding colors.

Adhere to the Overtone Series: In Chapter 7, the importance of voicing harmonies in adherence to the overtone series was demonstrated in a figure that showcased a bar taken from Holst's "Mars" movement from *The Planets*. Figure 12.19 reproduces that image in order to serve as a reminder that mimicking the natural presentation of sound will result in powerful, clear representations of harmonic events.

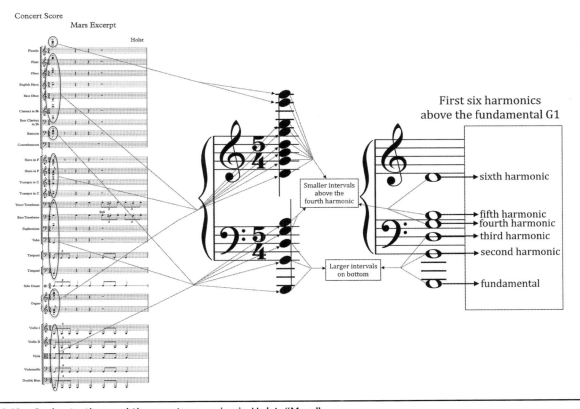

Fig. 12.19 Orchestration and the overtone series in Holst, "Mars"

A thorough understanding of the overtone series along with the instrumental timbres, registral characteristics, and articulations presented in this chapter is crucial, as these combine with knowledge of standard voicings and doublings to aid in the generation of powerful and logical arrangements of sound in orchestrations. These concepts should be considered when working with live instruments, virtual instruments, or a combination of both instrument types in your own projects. However, there is no substitute for studying and duplicating classic scores, which will further prepare you to make informed artistic choices and deliver professional-sounding orchestrations.

SUMMARY OF TERMS FROM CHAPTER 12

transposing instruments	*con sordino*	*accordatura*
concert score	*senza sordino*	aleatoricism
C-score	natural harmonics	stacked voicing
tonguing	artificial harmonics	staggered voicing
double tonguing	double stop	surrounded voicing
trill	triple stop	octave-down doubling
glissando	*divisi*	*legato* transitions
mute	*scordatura*	multi-sample

CHAPTER 12—EXERCISES

True or False. Circle "true" for each statement below that is true. Circle "false" for each false statement.

1. Concert pitch F4 to A♭4 is an expressive, well-defined range for clarinets.

    True   False

2. At a loud dynamic level, two woodwind instruments equal the weight of a single horn in F.

    True   False

3. At a loud dynamic level, one horn in F equals the weight of any other brass instrument.

    True   False

4. At a loud dynamic level, one trumpet, trombone, or tuba equals the weight of any two string instrument sections combined.

    True   False

5. At a soft dynamic level, one trumpet, one clarinet, and one string instrument section share equivalent weights.

    True   False

6. Since the English horn is performed by an oboe player, it should always appear under the oboes in a score layout.

    True   False

7. The orchestral score is bordered by octave transposing instruments; the piccolo sounds up an octave and the double bass sounds down an octave (relative to what is written in the score).

    True   False

8. Unison doubling is an exciting sound that should be maintained for as long as possible.

    True   False

9. Octave doubling is weak, since it defies the overtone series.

    True   False

10. Trombones can easily perform a *glissando* between any two notes.

    True   False

11. Orchestration Exercise

a. In any notation software, create a one-measure score for a large orchestra. Voice a single D major triad in root position at a loud dynamic level using the entire orchestra in a way that best takes advantage of the overtone series. Score the triad with a whole note in common time. Be prepared to turn in the PDF file, as well as the notation software file of your score.

b. In any DAW, realize your newly orchestrated D major triad with MIDI samples. Be prepared to turn in a bounced audio file, as well as the full DAW session of your project.

The following excerpt is taken from Maurice Ravel's solo piano piece *Le tombeau de Couperin*. A recording is available on this text's companion website. Answer the questions below the score, which are related to possible orchestrations of the passage.

12. In the space provided below, point out three measures where a change in orchestral color might benefit a possible orchestration. Describe how you came to these conclusions.

13. Would it be wise to give the melody in mm. 14–22 to a trumpet? Describe why or why not in the space below.

14. In the space below, describe why an all-brass introduction may or may not work.

15. Would it be wise to double the melody an octave higher in mm. 26–29? Describe why or why not in the space below.

16. Orchestration Exercise

   a. Chapter 9, Exercise 7 asked for a 9-bar SATB-style composition. In any notation software, orchestrate the composition you have created for a full orchestra. Be prepared to turn in a PDF score, as well as the notation software file of your project.

   b. In any DAW, realize this newly orchestrated composition with MIDI samples. Pay close attention to dynamics and phrase markings when sequencing each part. Be prepared to turn in a bounced audio file, as well as the full DAW session of your project.

17. Orchestration Exercise

   a. In any notation software, create an orchestration of the previous passage by Ravel that includes any members of a full orchestra (with a minimum of two parts per wind instrument) that you feel would best color the work. Be prepared to turn in a PDF score, as well as the notation software file of your project.

   b. In any DAW, realize your newly created orchestration with MIDI samples. Pay close attention to dynamics and phrase markings when sequencing each part. Be prepared to turn in a bounced audio file, as well as the full DAW session of your project.

PART IIB
AUDIO ENGINEERING ESSENTIALS

Chapter 13
Introduction to Mixing

The keys to a professional mix are organization and an understanding of **signal flow**, the journey an audio signal takes from its sound source to a master fader. The word "flow" within the term is appropriate, as an audio signal's pathway through various circuits can be thought of as being similar to the route that water travels before exiting a faucet. Water begins at a source in the earth and then passes through certain pipes while bypassing others. Sometimes water may pass through a water softener, adding salt; afterward, it may additionally flow through a filtration system that further changes the water's consistency and flavor before exiting a faucet. The end result—the taste of the water—will thus be affected by the specific conduits through which it travels. An audio signal travels through a similar system of avenues that may be utilized or bypassed depending on the outcome a producer desires. This chapter explores signal flow in depth, tracing the typical path of an audio signal from source to master fader. To best understand this process in the digital production world, routing is discussed in the context of outboard mixing consoles, which will help illuminate processes that tend to be hidden from the user within DAWs. Audio signal pathways originate at sound sources and enter mixing boards as balanced or unbalanced signals.

BALANCED AND UNBALANCED INPUTS

Most mixing boards have a series of **balanced** and **unbalanced inputs** that are designed to receive microphones or other inputs via cables. An unbalanced input cable contains two wires: one that carries an audio signal and one ground wire. Noise is sometimes carried along with the audio signal, so unbalanced cables should be as short as possible to minimize its presence in the signal. **RCA** (Radio Corporation of America) and **TS** (Tip Sleeve) are the two most common unbalanced cables used in audio. RCA cables are generally used to connect consumer-grade speaker systems and TS cables are typically used to connect guitars, basses, keyboards, and other electronic instruments to amplifiers or other inputs. A balanced input contains three wires: two that carry an audio signal and one ground wire. One of the signal-carrying wires reverses the polarity of the incoming audio signal at the source end of the cable; afterward, the input device (e.g., a mixing board, etc.) reverses it once more to protect the resultant audio signal from unwanted noise. If an undesired sound is picked up at some point along the length of the cable, it will be duplicated among the two signal-carrying wires, which creates a phase cancellation effect (i.e., that sound will not be heard). Since the original audio signal's polarity is reversed in one of the signal-carrying wires, though, phase cancellation involving the original audio signal is bypassed as it is reversed again when the signal enters the input source. The two most commonly used balanced cables are **TRS** (**T**ip **R**ing **S**leeve) and **XLR** (Cannon Electric's **X** series with an added **L**atch and **R**ubber compound). XLR connectors are used to connect microphones to other devices, including the balanced inputs of a mixing console.

MICROPHONE TYPES

A **microphone** is a transducer that creates an electrical image based on a detected sound signal. Different instruments and recording scenarios require different microphones, and there are a variety of microphone (or "mic") types that producers commonly utilize. For example, a loud heavy metal guitar sound from an amplifier will necessitate a different microphone type than the acoustic sound of a string quartet. Understanding the characteristics of three general types of microphones can help you choose the best tool for a given production task in your studio.

DYNAMIC MICROPHONES

A **dynamic microphone** is a versatile tool used for a variety of recording scenarios. A dynamic microphone has a diaphragm fixed to a coil that is wrapped around a magnet. When sound waves push the diaphragm, the coil of wires moves back and forth inside a magnetic field, creating voltage, which in turn forms a varying image based on the character of the incoming pressure wave. Figure 13.1 illustrates this procedure.

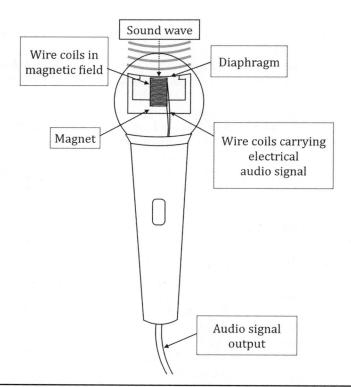

Fig. 13.1 Dynamic microphone

Dynamic microphones may be used in a variety of applications, but they are best known for their durability. High and low frequencies are not often reproduced with great clarity (as a significant amount of energy is required to move a coil of wire), but this fact also makes dynamic mics an excellent choice for picking up strong sound waves from guitar amplifiers and other loud, high-energy sound sources. For recording scenarios that require more high- and low-end frequency definition, however, a condenser microphone may be a better option.

CONDENSER MICROPHONES

A **condenser microphone** works differently than a dynamic microphone. It consists of a solid back plate and a diaphragm, which creates an electrical mechanism called a capacitor. When the diaphragm moves according to the energy of an incoming pressure wave, the distance between the plate and diaphragm changes, resulting in what is known as **fluctuating capacity**; this in turn creates electrical current, resulting in an outgoing audio signal (see Figure 13.2). A condenser microphone requires voltage throughout the capacitor to work; thus, a battery or external power supply is a necessary component of a condenser microphone.

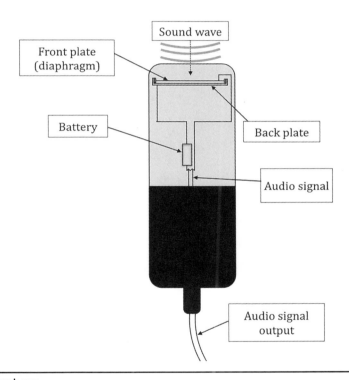

Fig. 13.2 Condenser microphone

Condenser microphones have evolved throughout the years such that there are now many subcategories that exist (e.g., cardioid condensers, electret condensers, etc.), each with their own unique qualities. Although these microphones aren't the best choice for high-energy sound sources, they very clearly capture subtleties in both low- and high-frequency spectrums; as a result, they are one of the most widely used microphone types in any studio. As a rule of thumb, loud sounds often require the durability of a dynamic microphone (which requires a good deal of energy to function), whereas large frequency ranges generally demand the use of condenser microphones, which are very sensitive and better able to capture nuances in a performance.

RIBBON MICROPHONES

Although **ribbon microphones** are not used as often as dynamic or condenser microphones (especially in home studios), they are common enough to merit mention. These microphones are designed with a magnetic plate positioned behind a metallic ribbon. Variations in electrical current are formed when sound waves cause the ribbon to vibrate, creating an audio signal. Figure 13.3 demonstrates this procedure.

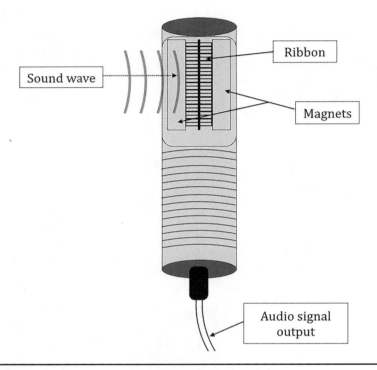

Fig. 13.3　Ribbon microphone

Ribbon microphones have the ability to pick up extreme ranges in frequency, but are particularly delicate—they are easily damaged by physical force or excessive sonic energy. Ribbon microphones are generally quite expensive, as well, making them somewhat atypical in a home studio.

MICROPHONE POLAR PATTERNS

Of equal importance to the type of microphone being used is the polar pattern (or pickup pattern) associated with the microphone. A **polar pattern** is the directional span from which sound is picked up by a microphone. For example, the sound of a room's natural reverberation is sometimes desired in a production to create realism; certain polar patterns capture a wider directional span for such purposes. In contrast, there are times when a producer wants to record no sound other than the source directly in front of the microphone; there are pickup patterns devoted to this as well. There are three main polar patterns, and understanding each of them aids in the microphone selection process for various recording contexts. Each individual polar pattern is discussed below.

UNIDIRECTIONAL/CARDIOID PATTERN

The unidirectional polar pattern is the most commonly used polar pattern in a studio. A unidirectional microphone is often referred to as possessing a **cardioid** pattern because of the heart-shaped design created by its directional span of sound absorption. Cardioid microphones exhibit excellent rejection from anything outside of the heart-shaped field, especially from the back of the microphone. Figure 13.4 illustrates a unidirectional pattern of sound absorption.

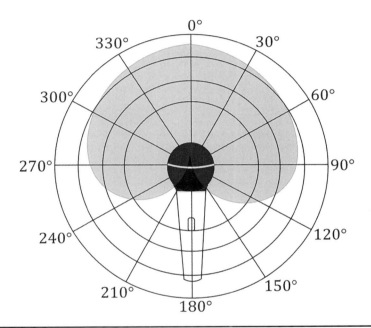

Fig. 13.4   Unidirectional/cardioid polar pattern

There are polar patterns that slightly expand the basic cardioid pattern, such as the **supercardioid** pattern (which expands the field to include a small area behind the microphone) and the **hypercardioid** pattern (which includes even more of the field behind the microphone than the supercardioid pattern). Cardioid patterns are most useful in situations where sound other than the original source needs to be rejected.

BIDIRECTIONAL/FIGURE 8 PATTERN

The **bidirectional** polar pattern picks up sound equally from the front and back of a microphone. The field of sound absorption resembles a **Figure 8** and is often referred to as such. Figure 13.5 demonstrates a bidirectional pattern's field of sound absorption.

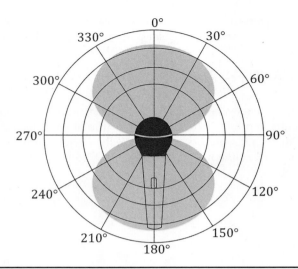

Fig. 13.5   Bidirectional/Figure 8 polar pattern

Bidirectional microphones are often used during radio interviews between two people, but can be suitable for recording any two sound sources that face one another; sound coming from the sides will be rejected.

OMNIDIRECTIONAL/BOUNDARY PATTERN

An **omnidirectional** or **boundary** microphone picks up sound from all directions. Since there are no rejection areas, care must be taken when selecting this type of pattern for use in a studio environment. Figure 13.6 illustrates the field of sound absorption of an omnidirectional microphone.

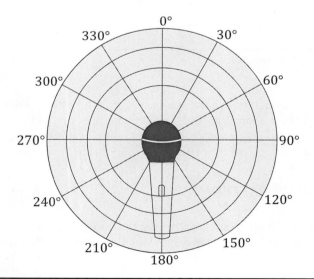

Fig. 13.6   Omnidirectional/boundary polar pattern

Boundary microphones are used for recording large choirs, string sections, or other ensembles; they are also employed when the natural sound of a room's reverberation is desired in a recording.

Understanding the polar patterns of microphones will prepare you to correctly choose the best tool for a given recording situation. Once the desired field of sound absorption has been decided, you should begin comparing frequency response charts to determine which make and model yields the best results for a given task.

FREQUENCY RESPONSE CHART

A **frequency response chart** shows how well a microphone responds to certain frequencies within a typical range from 20Hz to 20kHz (the range of human hearing). Some microphones respond better than others in specific ranges (making them particularly suitable for capturing performances on certain instruments), while others boast a flat or neutral response across a variety of frequencies. A flat response provides the closest reproduction of the original sound source as possible; therefore, microphones featuring flat responses are highly desirable. Figure 13.7 compares the frequency response charts of Shure's SM57 cardioid dynamic microphone with Shure's SM27 large diaphragm cardioid condenser microphone. Notice the expanded frequency range of the condenser microphone, which may be a better choice for more delicately nuanced recordings. Compare these findings with the frequency response chart of the SM57, which is exaggerated in the 2kHz to 10kHz area, making it a wise option to capture the "pop" of a snare drum or the high frequencies of a lead guitar. The "dips" in frequencies below 50Hz and above 10kHz also demonstrate why dynamic microphones are excellent choices for louder, more high-energy situations.

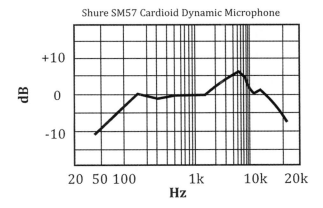

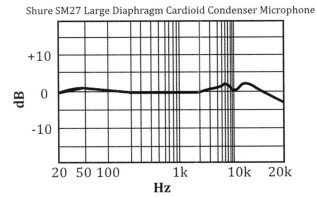

Fig. 13.7   Frequency response chart comparison

Once sound passes through a microphone, it enters a mixing console through one of its balanced inputs. A guitar or keyboard can also enter a mixing board at this point, but will do so through one of the unbalanced, quarter-inch inputs. After the sound passes through the input, it begins a journey with many different path options to follow; producers route signal down a variety of different avenues depending on the sound desired.

THE BASICS OF ROUTING

The exact layout of most mixing consoles varies from manufacturer to manufacturer, but the main components typically remain the same. Most professional mixing boards have at least eight **channel strips** and are usually expandable by increments of eight to up to 256 channels (or more). To comprehend signal flow, you must first understand the basic layout of a channel strip. Figure 13.8 illustrates the main layout you might encounter on a mixing board.

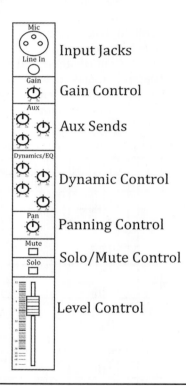

Fig. 13.8 Basic channel strip layout

Notice that multiple features are contained within some sections. Input jacks contain both balanced and unbalanced inputs, for example, and there are multiple knobs within the aux sends and dynamic control areas. A closer inspection of each stage of a channel strip will elucidate the functions and controls contained therein and help clarify the concept of signal flow.

SIGNAL FLOW

Once an audio signal passes through an input jack, it normally travels through a pre-amp that features a **gain knob** controlling the volume level at which the audio signal will proceed. Figure 13.9 demonstrates this early phase in the life cycle of an audio signal.

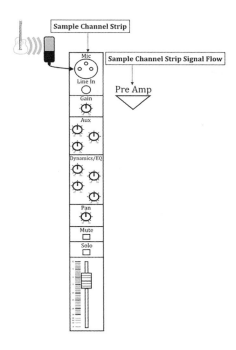

Fig. 13.9 The pre-amp section of a channel strip

Once the signal passes this point, it enters an auxiliary or "aux" section, which allows for routing to external pieces of gear known as **inserts** and back again (see Figure 13.10). This allows the producer to add effects from outboard processors (e.g., echo, reverb, etc.).

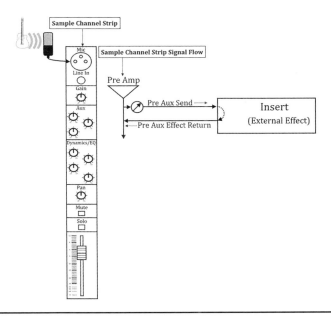

Fig. 13.10 The aux/inserts section of a channel strip

This section may be bypassed if the producer doesn't desire to add any external effects at this point. The next step is for the signal to pass through the dynamics/EQ section, which is where equalization and compression adjustments can be made using the console's onboard capabilities. Compression will be introduced in Chapter 15.

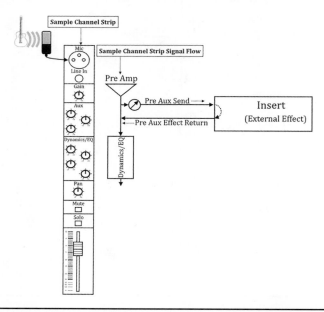

Fig. 13.11   The dynamics/EQ section of a channel strip

After the dynamics/EQ section, the audio signal travels through three more areas before reaching the channel fader. These sections include the **pan**, **mute**, and **solo** sections. The pan section allows the producer to move the audio signal left or right within the stereo field. The mute button mutes the signal such that no sound within the channel strip is heard, while the solo button allows the sound from the channel strip to be heard exclusively (see Figure 13.12).

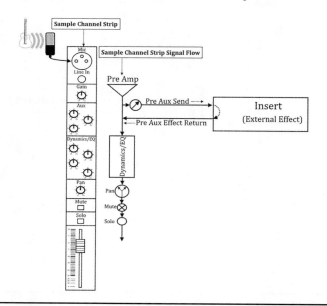

Fig. 13.12   Pan, solo, and mute sections of a channel strip

The producer does have the option of adding effects after the signal has been equalized, compressed, or otherwise processed. Adding effects at this point will result in a different sound than adding them in the aux section of the channel strip (if the sound has already been manipulated). For example, it is not uncommon to add echo or reverb later in the process using the post-aux send/return, as doing so ensures that certain frequencies will be emphasized or attenuated due to adjustments in the previous dynamics/EQ section that allow for a cleaner, more controlled sound to be further effected. Figure 13.13 illustrates this phase in the journey of an audio signal.

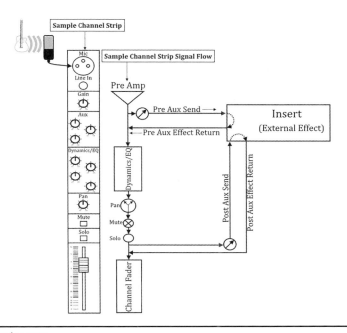

Fig. 13.13   Post-aux send and return

The audio signal finally passes through the channel fader and into a master fader, where all channel faders are joined to form the mix. The mix is typically heard by being routed through a power amplifier to a set of loudspeakers within a studio environment. Figure 13.14 demonstrates an audio signal traveling from a channel fader to a master fader and ultimately to loudspeakers via a power amp.

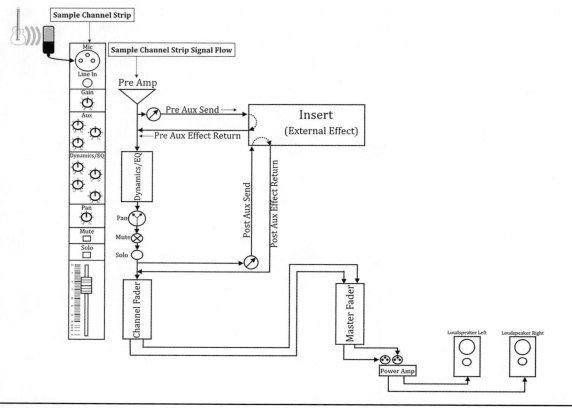

Fig. 13.14   Routing from a channel fader to a master fader and eventually to loudspeakers via a power amp

An audio signal has a variety of pathway options with regard to signal flow, with each option coloring the sound within a channel (and thus the mix) in specific ways. The conduits through which sound travels in a console have different names and purposes; these are explored with more depth in the subsequent section.

BUS AND AUXILIARY TRACKS

A **bus** is a pathway that transports signal from point A to point B; busses are often used for grouping instruments of like frequencies to create a more manageable workflow. An example would be a **drum bus**, which transports and combines the separately recorded signals of each discrete drum-set element (hi-hats, toms, snare drum, kick drum, etc.) into a single, more manageable track. In a typical situation, each drum-set component is assigned its own channel on a mixing board. Managing each drum element on its own across multiple channels is quite cumbersome; thus, producers tend to send each element through a bus and sum them together for a more organized layout. Adjustments can still be made to the individual levels of separate drum tracks, but the bus scheme additionally affords the producer the ability to raise and lower the summed volume of all bussed instruments with a single fader. Figure 13.14 shows a drum bus and related routing within Pro Tools 11.

Once the sonic elements that are to be summed have been determined, the producer sends each separate audio signal through a bus to be combined within an auxiliary or **aux track**. An aux track is best understood as a destination (albeit a temporary one in most circumstances), while a bus is a "signal vehicle" that transports signal from

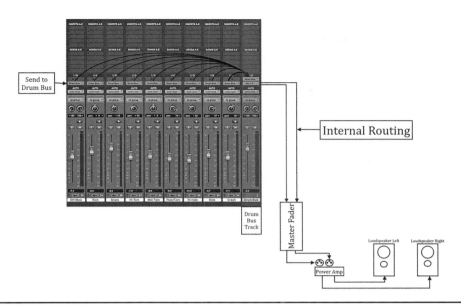

Fig. 13.15   Drum bus in Pro Tools 11

a point of origin (i.e., a normal track) to such a destination. Figure 13.14 demonstrated a common example using a drum bus, but what is often called a "drum bus" is in actuality an auxiliary track. In most DAWs, aux tracks are automatically generated when a producer creates a new bus. New busses are typically created by clicking on the stereo output of a channel, which results in the appearance of options for assigning busses and other outputs. Once the new bus has been selected, a new auxiliary track will appear. It is important to immediately name the newly created aux track to avoid confusion and maintain session organization.

AUXILIARY TRACKS FOR EFFECTS

A common function of an aux track is to add an effect (or series of effects) to multiple tracks at once. Considering the fact that it is not uncommon for professional projects to reach up to 100 or more tracks, adding effects plugins to each individual track—a technique referred to as **in-line effects**—uses CPU power inefficiently, creates a less manageable workflow, and may eventually cause performance problems for even the fastest computers. (There are, however, some effects plugins that are only used in-line; see Chapter 15 for an exploration of such channel effects.) Additionally, one of the aims of a producer is to manage listener perception, making a mix sound as if each constituent element is sharing the same acoustic space; batch processing tracks using certain effects, such as reverbs and delays, often aids in this endeavor. The most efficient way for multiple tracks to share an effect is to bus them to the same auxiliary track. As mentioned previously, this can be accomplished by selecting a new bus, which in turn creates a new aux track. At this point, the new aux track should be named based on the effect it will produce (e.g., "Long Reverb"). The desired effect plugin is added on the aux track as an insert. Recall that an insert is simply an effect that is added to a channel; it is so named because an audio signal's flow was traditionally interrupted by the insertion of a hardware effects module. Figure 13.16 reproduces Figure 13.10 from earlier in this chapter to revisit the routing related to inserts.

You may add several busses to several aux tracks, allowing for numerous effects to be shared among multiple tracks. Importantly, though, the bus routing from track to track occurs internally, making it crucial for you to comprehend and trace this hidden organization on your own. Figure 13.17 illustrates the internal routing of a Logic Pro

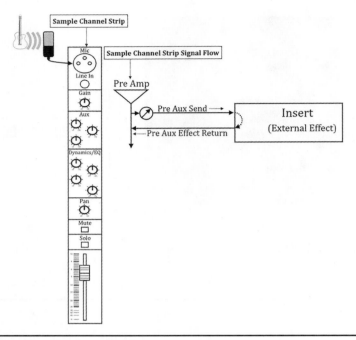

Fig. 13.16   **The aux/inserts section of a channel strip**

X project including a typical bus-to-aux track setup for several tracks sharing two different reverb types. All Bus 1 sends are routed to the auxiliary track on the right, while all Bus 2 sends are routed to the auxiliary track on the left.

In Figure 13.17, there is a knob next to each bus within each track. This knob determines how much of the audio signal from a particular track is bussed to the indicated aux track. The various signals bussed to the aux track are then combined and effected by whichever inserts are added to the aux track, with the fader of the aux track

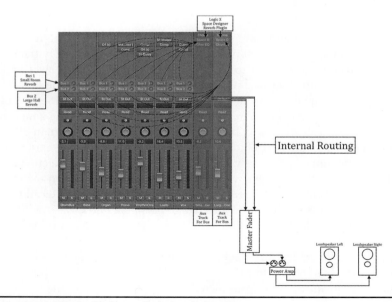

Fig. 13.17 Multiple effects shared by multiple tracks in Logic Pro X

controlling how much effected signal is routed to the **master fader**, which in turn merges all the tracks of a mix together.

In the scenario presented in Figure 13.17, there are two points within the signal flow that can serve to manage the amount of reverb perceived within the mix. The first is the send knob of the bus, which determines the amount of the original signal to be bussed to the aux track containing the effect. The second is the fader of the aux track, which determines the amount of the effected sound to be merged at the master fader with the other tracks within the session.

PRE- AND POST-FADER AUX SENDS

Once a bus's send level is set via the bus knob, the ratio between the **dry** (uneffected) audio signal and the amount of signal being sent to the aux track is established. This level, along with the volume of the aux track containing the effect insert, determines the amount of effect perceived in the mix. The wet/dry ratio can be changed, as the bus knob can be turned counterclockwise for less of the incoming signal to be sent to the aux track or clockwise for more of the signal to be sent. As the channel fader is turned up, the send level of the bus increases at the ratio previously set with the bus knob. This is called a **post-fader aux send** because the channel fader volume is directly linked to the output of the bus send. Post-fader aux sends are the most commonly used aux sends for adding effects, as they streamline workflows by eliminating any need to recalibrate wet/dry ratios each time the channel fader is adjusted. A less frequently used configuration called a **pre-fader aux send** busses the audio signal to an aux track before the channel fader enters the equation. In this situation, the channel fader only alters the volume of the dry signal. Thus, the ratio of **wet** (effected) sound to dry sound is not fixed when the signal hits the channel fader. Although less common, pre-fader aux sends are used for certain effects that require the independent manipulation of dry signal. For example, to create an atmospheric effect wherein an instrument sounds as if it is continuously moving closer to the listener, an aux track can be set up with a reverb effect and sent to the master fader at a high level while the channel fader gradually moves the dry sound up in the mix. With so many complex routing possibilities, one of the most important aspects of a mix is the organization of tracks within a session.

TRACK ORGANIZATION

It is crucial to establish a solid workflow foundation by organizing tracks at the very outset of a session. Before recording anything, many producers label tracks according to the instruments that will be used within the production. Once material is recorded, any bus groupings are usually labeled as well. Color-coded tracks further add to the visual organization of a session. Similar instruments, such as various drums, may share an assigned track color. Tracks may be colored any way a producer wants; one example in the context of a rhythm section would be to color-code drum tracks red, guitar tracks blue, bass tracks yellow, and keyboard tracks orange. There isn't a standard color-labeling scheme, but there are certain track orderings that producers tend to follow. For instance, drum tracks are often positioned to the left of a mixing board, followed by bass, guitars, keyboards, and finally vocals on the right. In a tracks overview window, the drums would therefore be positioned in the highest vertical position, followed below by bass, then guitars, and so on. Although this conflicts with the typical layout of a notated orchestral score, it is the most common way of organizing a session. Figure 13.18 illustrates a well-organized, color-coded session in Pro Tools 11 that follows this standard track layout scheme.

Whichever track ordering you favor, it is important to remain consistent with your labeling and coloring schemes. If a project session needs to be passed to another producer, for example, and the layout order doesn't conform to that producer's preferences, it will be easier to reorganize the session if the original project is presented in a

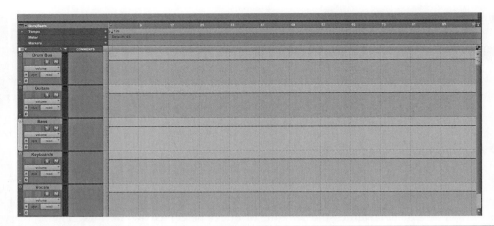

Fig. 13.18   Standard track organization example in Pro Tools 11

logical, well-organized layout. Moreover, a well-ordered project ensures an efficient workflow when a session needs to be reopened and revisited over a long period of time.

CONVERTING MIDI TO AUDIO

When musical ideas become more than sketches and truly begin to take shape, composers often decide to convert MIDI tracks to audio tracks to save CPU power and simplify the visual presentation of a session. This process, which is named differently by different DAW software companies, is labeled "bounce regions in place" in Logic Pro X. Regardless of the DAW being used, the wording of the process invariably involves the word **bounce**, which translates to "convert" in a mixing context. When a MIDI track is bounced, an audio file of that track's MIDI information appears. By default, most DAWs hide and (temporarily) disable the instrument plugin of the original MIDI track after such an audio bounce in order to avoid the confusion related to seeing and hearing two different types of tracks—a MIDI track and an audio track—that are playing back the exact same music. Should a compositional change need to be made after bouncing a MIDI region in place, though, the option to unhide the original MIDI track (and enable the associated instrument plugin) is available, and the MIDI track can be bounced again after any alterations are completed. Figure 13.19 features two separate views of the same session within Logic Pro X, with the image on the right being visually streamlined via the use of hidden MIDI tracks that result from the process of bouncing in place.

Unhidden MIDI Tracks   Hidden MIDI Tracks

Fig. 13.19   Hidden and unhidden MIDI tracks in Logic Pro X

EVOLUTION MIXING

An efficient way to remain organized is to consistently attend to the direction of a mix throughout all stages of a project. **Evolution mixing** is a strategy in which the rudimentary elements of a mix evolve alongside the musical components of a project. Put differently, with each new compositional idea, the broader elements of a mix (e.g., basic levels and layout organization) are assessed in reaction to any added sonic parts. When a project is ready for a final mix, it will already be organized, and the basic, relative audio levels will have previously been established. Evolution mixing requires the constant consideration of all sound at every stage of the development of a session, and, as a result, it allows producers to send rough ideas to clients in a more rapid, time-effective way throughout the life cycle of a project (as the components of a mix progress together in lock step). As a project unfolds, it is also of the utmost importance to continually listen to mixes of similar styles of music as points of reference. **Referencing** other, related music should take place at every stage of a project, especially during the final mix, when most compositional decisions have already been made. Consistent referencing ensures that you are fully aware of the sonic qualities required of professional work; this will influence certain mixing decisions throughout your project. **Monitor referencing** is a term used to describe the process of mix comparisons made on multiple speakers and headphones; this extremely helpful strategy is discussed in more depth in Chapter 15.

From the initial input to the final loudspeaker output, sound passes through a complex series of pathways within a mix. With so many routing possibilities and attendant sonic manipulations, it is important for you as a composer to remain organized and to consistently reference music of similar styles to ensure that your session is of high quality. A well-organized project ensures a manageable workflow and allows you to be confident that any artist or producer can navigate your session. With a tightly designed session layout, you are ready to apply more advanced mixing techniques and bring your work another step closer to being a final, professional product.

SUMMARY OF TERMS FROM CHAPTER 13

signal flow	cardioid	drum bus
balanced input	supercardioid	aux track
unbalanced input	hypercardioid	in-line effects
RCA connector	bidirectional/Figure 8	master fader
TS connector	omnidirectional/boundary	dry signal
TRS connector	frequency response chart	wet signal
XLR connector	channel strip	post-fader aux send
microphone	gain knob	pre-fader aux send
dynamic microphone	insert	bounce
condenser microphone	pan	evolution mixing
fluctuating capacity	mute	referencing
ribbon microphone	solo	monitor referencing
polar pattern	bus	

CHAPTER 13—EXERCISES

True or False. Circle "true" for each statement below that is true. Circle "false" for each false statement.

1. Signal flow is the invariable routing that an audio signal undertakes that can never be altered.

   True   False

2. TRS and XLR cables are commonly used balanced cables.

    True   False

3. A condenser microphone has a diaphragm fixed to a coil wrapped around a magnet. When sound waves push the diaphragm, the coil of wires moves back and forth inside a magnetic field, creating voltage, forming an image based on the character of the incoming pressure wave.

    True   False

4. A dynamic microphone consists of a solid back plate and a diaphragm, which creates an electrical mechanism called a capacitor. When the diaphragm moves according to the energy of an incoming pressure wave, the result is fluctuating capacity, which in turn engenders electrical current and thus an outgoing audio signal.

    True   False

5. An omnidirectional microphone pickup pattern is often called a cardioid pattern because the pattern created resembles the shape of a heart.

    True   False

6. Complete the diagram below by adding the missing arrows that would complete the signal flow described in Figure 13.14.

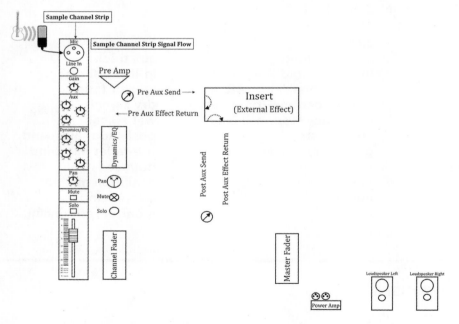

7. In the available space below, explain what an insert is and how it is used in the context of the previous diagram (see Figure 13.14).

8. In the available space below, describe the difference between a bus and an aux track.

9. In the available space below, explain what a drum bus is and why a producer might create and use one.

10. In the available space below, explain the difference between an in-line effect and an aux track effect. Afterward, describe why a producer might use an aux track effect instead of an in-line effect.

11. Do the following in any DAW:

    a. Create one MIDI bass track, one MIDI keyboard track, and one MIDI synth lead track.

    b. Sequence an 8-bar piece of music with the instrumentation described above.

    c. Color-code and organize your tracks.

    d. Bounce the MIDI tracks to audio.

    e. Hide the MIDI tracks.

    f. Create an aux track, add a reverb plugin to the aux track, and rename the aux track "Reverb."

    g. Bus each audio track to the newly created reverb aux track and apply the effect to taste.

    h. Export the session as an uncompressed audio file (e.g., WAV or AIFF) and be prepared to deliver it to your instructor along with the session file.

12. In Chapter 8, Exercise 12, you were asked to create a MIDI realization of a passage from "The Realm of Gondor" from *The Lord of the Rings* trilogy. Open the completed file and follow the instructions below. If the assignment has not yet been completed or you are unable to access it, be sure to complete it before proceeding to the instructions below.

    a. Color-code and organize your tracks.

    b. Bounce the MIDI tracks for the horn in F to audio tracks.

    c. Hide the MIDI tracks.

    d. Create an aux track, add a reverb plugin to the aux track, and rename the aux track "Reverb."

    e. Bus each audio track to the newly created reverb aux track and apply the effect such that it sounds as if each instrument was recorded in a large cathedral. Experiment with the presets of the reverb plugin you are using until you are happy with the result.

    f. Export the session as an uncompressed audio file (e.g., WAV or AIFF) and be prepared to deliver it to your instructor along with the session file.

Chapter 14
Recording and Editing Live Instruments

MIDI has enabled producers to work out their ideas in project studios, often within the comfort of their own homes. As computers and software have grown in strength, efficiency, and affordability, many professional-quality projects can now be completed without ever stepping into larger, more expensive recording studios. This, in turn, positively affects composers' profit margins, as they do not need to absorb the costs of studio time. Many successful producers use MIDI tracks the majority of the time, as they can create a professional-sounding, affordable musical backdrop to which select live instruments are added based on availability and the needs of a given project. However, even if a session consists mostly of well-programmed, high-quality samples and synthesizers, the presence of live-recorded instruments adds warmth, realism, and a human quality that is not easily programmed via MIDI. Some producers have the capability of recording every musical element live in their project studios, but more often than not, a small amount of live recorded instruments will work in tandem with programmed MIDI events to create professional, cost-effective creations. This chapter investigates the basic principles of live recording in the context of a project studio, and discusses the challenges that are faced when working with live elements.

GENERAL RECORDING CONSIDERATIONS

In a digital environment, a safe average recording level should be around -18dB, which may fluctuate between -20dB and -6dB at the extreme. One should never record signals that are consistently -6dB or louder, as this won't allow for enough headroom. (Headroom will be discussed further in this chapter.) Beyond recording level, there are many components that contribute to the overall sound quality of a recording: the sound source (the instrument and performance), the environment in which the sound source is located (the room), the particular type of microphone(s) used to capture the sound, and the placement of the microphone(s) relative to the sound source within the environment. Of these, the most important element is the recorded sound source; the quality of the instrument being used and the precision and emotional expression of the performance are paramount. With so many considerations to keep in mind, it may be beneficial to remember the following set of questions, which will create a strategic approach to live recording.

1. **What is being recorded?** Is it a lead vocal? A choir? An acoustic guitar? A string quartet?
2. **Where should it be recorded?** Inside a large hall with lots of reverberation? In an isolation booth? In a "live room" inside a studio?
3. **How should it be recorded?** How close should the microphone(s) be placed to the sound source? Is stereo or mono recording most appropriate for this sound source?
4. **What microphone type(s) should I use?** What kind of frequency response would benefit this sound source?

In order to address these questions, you first need to become familiar with the basics of microphone placement and explore a variety of instrument miking techniques. These topics are considered in the following section.

CLOSE AND AMBIENT MIKING

Close miking is a technique in which a microphone is placed as close to a sound source as possible. By doing so, the producer is able to have a high degree of control over the recording, as the reverberation of the room in which the sound source is captured does not significantly color the sound. Such reverberation is difficult to eliminate or edit at a later stage within the mix. However, if a microphone is placed too close to a sound source, a phenomenon known as the **proximity effect** occurs, which boosts frequencies under 100Hz by as much as 16dB. This is typically undesirable; however, many vocalists take advantage of the effect, as it thickens the voice in the lower registers. Care must be taken, though, as the proximity effect can cause issues with headroom, which can create a distorted signal. In audio engineering terms, **headroom** is the range between an audio signal's loudest moment and a DAW's maximum output level. **Ambient miking**, which is the opposite of close miking, places a microphone a considerable distance from a sound source in order to take advantage of the coloration provided by the environment's reverberation. Ambient recording is often desired when capturing more than one instrument (e.g., a string orchestra) in a single **take** or recording pass, when the reverberation of the room aids in sonically combining the players into a cohesive unit while providing its own character within the recording. Once close or ambient placement is determined, the next consideration regards the number of microphones that are to be used in the recording. Stereo miking opens up many sonic advantages.

STEREO MIKING

Recorded sound from a single microphone will result in a monaural or **mono** recording. Modest project studios may only have access to one microphone, and getting a quality recording from a single mono microphone is absolutely possible. Moreover, mono recording can be the most appropriate choice, even if multiple microphones are available. For example, if a producer wanted a sound to be particularly localized in a mix, like a lead vocal, a single microphone could work very well. However, the involvement of two or more microphones offers the potential of creating a stereo image by combining multiple mono signals, which can provide more coloristic sonic possibilities. The option of blending signals—or simply having more recorded signals to choose from—is usually desired, and **stereo miking** provides these possibilities. Nonetheless, the more microphones brought into the equation during stereo recording, the more complicated mic placement becomes; this is mainly due to phase cancellation issues, which result in hollow, weak sounds when signals are mixed together.

PHASE CANCELLATION

A sound wave is measured within a span of 360 degrees, representing one complete, five-step cycle of a pressure wave. This measurement begins at a pressure wave's initial climb from normal pressure, where it then leads to a maximum point of positive pressure (**compression**), back to normal pressure, then to a maximum point of negative pressure in the opposite direction (**rarefaction**), and ultimately back to normal pressure. Figure 14.1 demonstrates a complete cycle of a sound wave.

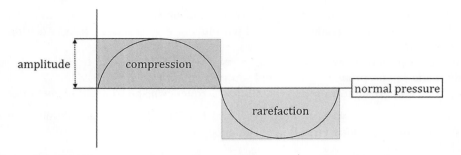

Fig. 14.1   A complete cycle of a sound wave

If two microphones recording the same sound are placed close together, the exact moment sound enters each microphone will be slightly different. If the maximum point of compression enters one microphone at the same time as the maximum point of rarefaction enters the other microphone, phase cancellation occurs and the result is silence. Put differently, the negative pressure of rarefaction captured by the first microphone "pulls down" the positive pressure of compression captured by the second microphone. Sound waves that cancel themselves out directly are said to be **out of phase**. However, if sound enters both microphones at varying points over the cycle of a waveform, the result is a weaker—but not completely canceled—sound; this phenomenon is referred to as **phase shifting**. If sound enters both microphones at the same time, the sound wave's amplitude will increase, creating a stronger sound. When this happens, the recorded signals are referred to as being **in phase**.

Figure 14.2 demonstrates a pressure wave coming from a single source that enters two different microphones at different moments.

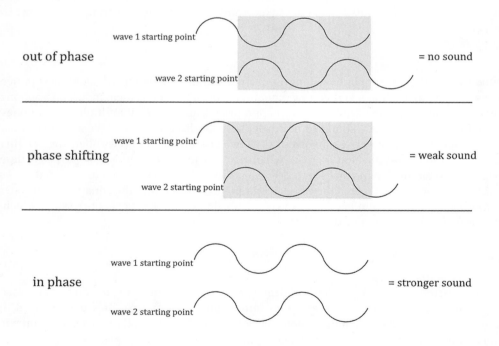

Fig. 14.2   Phase relationships between recorded signals

To prevent **phase cancellation** (or **phasing**) issues, care must be taken in the placement of each microphone. If both microphones are too close to a sound source, phasing will be very apparent, as the volume levels captured by both microphones will be nearly identical. Phasing becomes less obvious the farther the second microphone is from both the first mic and the sound source, as its captured volume is lower. The "**3-to-1 rule**" is a valuable guideline for stereo microphone placement; it is a strategy that places the second microphone far enough away from the first microphone to avoid phasing issues. The 3-to-1 rule states that when recording a sound source with two microphones, the second microphone should be positioned at least three times the distance from the first microphone as the first microphone is from the sound source. For example, if the first microphone is placed two feet from a guitar, the second microphone should be placed at least six feet from the first microphone, as is the case in Figure 14.3.

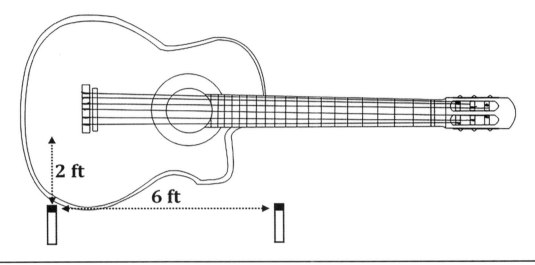

Fig. 14.3   The 3-to-1 rule

STEREO MIKING TECHNIQUES

There are many common stereo miking techniques with which every producer should be familiar. The techniques described below are no more than starting points for producers to build upon, however. Experimentation and imagination should factor into the decision of how to handle any recording situation.

COINCIDENT X-Y STEREO MIKING

The **coincident X-Y stereo miking** technique uses two matched unidirectional (cardioid) microphones facing each other along a range of angles between 90 degrees and 130 degrees. A pair of microphones is considered **matched** if they are of the same make and model and were created at the same time. This guarantees that the same parts and assembly methods were used. Matched microphones often come together as a pair. The left microphone in a coincident X-Y configuration will pick up the right side of a recording environment, while the right microphone will pick up the left side. If the microphones are as close to each other as possible and facing each other, this setup is referred to as coincident. If the microphones are facing opposite directions and are farther apart (yet still within 12 inches of each other), the configuration is called **near-coincident**. Figure 14.4 demonstrates both types of X-Y configurations.

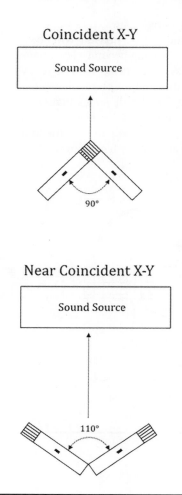

Fig. 14.4   Coincident and near-coincident X-Y configurations

Since both microphones are placed close to one another in an X-Y configuration, sound arrives at them at almost the same time, which lowers the likelihood of phasing issues. If the sound source is narrow, like a solo instrument, stereo separation is generally good. If the sound source is too wide, however, as in the case of a large ensemble, separation will likely suffer. **Stereo separation** refers to the level of audibly perceived individuality from among multiple signals that combine to form a stereo image.

BLUMLEIN (FIGURE 8)

The **Blumlein** technique, named after electronics engineer Alan Dower Blumlein, is similar to the X-Y configuration, but uses bidirectional (Figure 8) microphones at a 90° angle instead of unidirectional (cardioid) microphones. The left microphone in this setup will record the front right and back left areas of a room, while the right microphone will capture the opposite. This configuration is a good choice for capturing the sonic characteristics of a room. Figure 14.5 illustrates the Blumlein technique by coloring the right microphone's polar pattern dark grey and the left microphone's polar pattern light grey. The dotted lines depict the polar patterns associated with being behind the microphones, while the solid lines show the areas that are captured in front of each microphone.

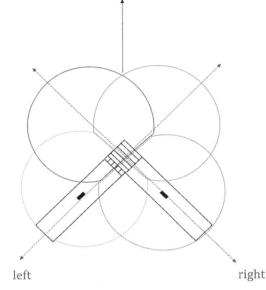

Blumlein (Figure 8)

Sound Source

left   right

Fig. 14.5   The Blumlein (Figure 8) technique

MID-SIDE (MS) STEREO MIKING

Mid-side stereo miking is a popular technique because one microphone captures the sound of the room while the other is aimed straight at the sound source. In this configuration, a cardioid mic (or mid-mic) is aimed directly at an instrument, while a Figure 8 mic (or side-mic) is aimed left and right to capture the ambient sounds of a room. Once a recording is complete, the MS signal is fed to a mixer, where the signal from the side-mic (or Figure 8) is copied and phase inverted. (In most DAWs, gain or trim plugins typically offer an option to invert the polarity of a signal.) Once the copy is inverted, both signals are then panned hard left and right with the mid-mic's (cardioid) signal panned to the center. The three signals are then mixed to taste, creating a realistic-sounding stereo environment. When the ratio of side-to-mid signal is higher, a larger stereo image is perceived. Figure 14.6 demonstrates the MS microphone technique.

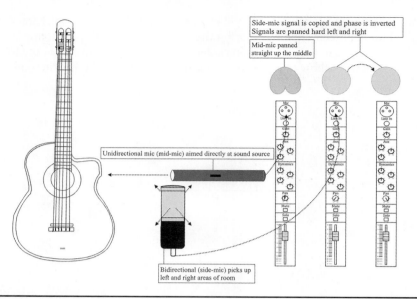

Fig. 14.6 MS microphone technique

SPACED PAIR

The **spaced pair technique** uses two cardioid microphones that are usually spaced three to ten feet apart (though they can be as close as one foot apart and as far as twenty feet apart, depending on the size of the instrument or ensemble being recorded). The left microphone is panned hard left, while the right mic is panned hard right. To avoid phasing issues, the 3-to-1 rule should be observed in a spaced pair configuration. Many producers choose to aim each microphone at a different area of the instrument being recorded, in an attempt to capture different timbres. Figure 14.7 is a reproduction of Figure 14.3, since it is an example of both the spaced pair technique and the 3-to-1 rule.

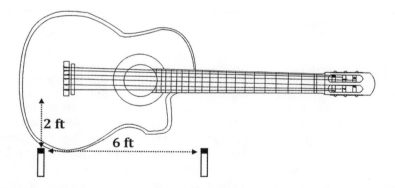

Fig. 14.7 Spaced pair technique and the 3-to-1 rule

The preceding stereo miking techniques can be applied to both ensemble and solo instrument recording situations. Experimentation with each technique will allow you to find your favorite configurations for a variety of recording environments, sound sources, and budgets. Remember, however, that the best location to place a microphone is the one your ear determines; try a variety of different locations until you achieve the sound you desire.

When choosing a microphone for use in any recording configuration, consider either a) a microphone with a frequency response that complements the sound source or b) a microphone with the flattest response possible. Also note that isolation plays an important role in recording instruments, and **sound barriers** (devices designed to limit the amount of outside noise that is captured during recording) are often used.

INSTRUMENT-SPECIFIC RECORDING TECHNIQUES

The following section provides more detailed information on recording certain instrument types. The instruction in this section will be directive, but this is only for clarity and efficiency; these techniques are solely guidelines and should be adjusted based on your individual taste.

ACOUSTIC STRING INSTRUMENTS

When recording individual acoustic string instruments, begin by aiming a large diaphragm condenser microphone with a cardioid polar pattern where the neck and body are joined at a distance of about 12 inches, moving it closer or farther away depending on where it sounds best. If two microphones are used, employ one of the previously discussed stereo miking techniques. However, if you do not have access to a large room with solid acoustic qualities, stereo miking might not be the best option; remember that professional sounding recordings are possible with a single microphone. When recording acoustic guitar with two microphones, though, it is common to use a spaced pair configuration, aiming a large diaphragm condenser at the bridge or sound hole and a small diaphragm condenser at the twelfth fret. It is important to consider the 3-to-1 rule to avoid phase issues, though both microphones should be positioned an equal distance from the guitar. The MS technique is another popular option, as it offers the ability to blend multiple timbres and creates a realistic-sounding stereo image. Yet another option for recording acoustic guitar is to place a condenser microphone over the shoulder of the guitarist (aimed down at the guitar), with a second condenser mic placed in front of the guitar, pointed at the twelfth fret. Placing a microphone over the shoulder of a guitarist will capture more high-end frequencies and pick noise. Figure 14.8 illustrates all four techniques.

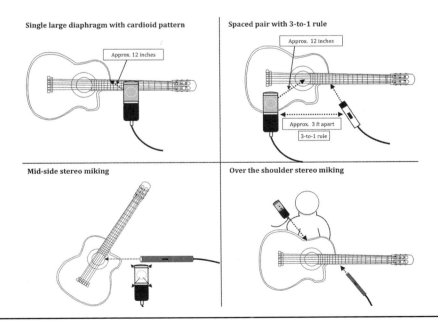

Fig. 14.8 Recording options for acoustic guitar

INDIVIDUAL VOCALS

When recording individual vocal tracks, isolate the vocalist with sound barriers and aim a condenser microphone with a cardioid polar pattern just above the lips of the singer. To avoid excessive popping sounds caused by consonants, aim the microphone slightly off its horizontal axis or use a **pop filter** (a circular device placed in front of a microphone that filters out unwanted popping sounds).

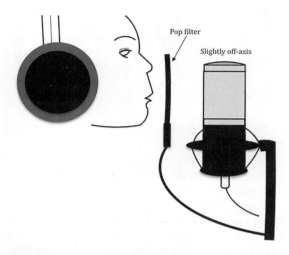

Fig. 14.9　Recording individual vocals

BRASS INSTRUMENTS

To record brass instruments such as trumpet, trombone, etc., start by placing a large diaphragm condenser microphone with a cardioid polar pattern within 12 inches of the instrument, aimed straight into the bell. This places the microphone directly into a narrow beam of intense sound. Work with the natural movements and body position of the player until he or she is comfortable and the best-sounding microphone position is found (see Figure 14.10).

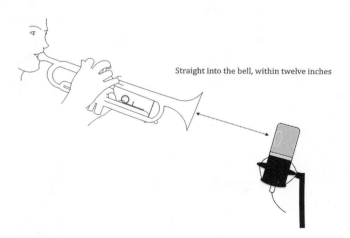

Fig. 14.10　Recording individual brass instruments

For the purposes of recording, woodwinds will be divided into two categories: woodwinds with larger bells and straight-shaped woodwinds. Examples of woodwind instruments with larger bells include all clarinets and saxophones. Straight-shaped woodwinds include all flutes, oboes, and bassoons. Although bassoons and oboes do have bells, they are not as pronounced as those found on clarinets and saxophones.

WOODWINDS WITH LARGER BELLS

When capturing performances of woodwind instruments with larger bells, begin by placing a large diaphragm condenser microphone with a cardioid polar pattern within 12 inches of the instrument, aimed between the finger holes and the bell. Aiming a microphone directly into the bell will produce a discordant, unrealistic recording for these instruments. Since much of the sound comes from the finger holes, capturing a combination of the bell and finger holes will create a more pleasant and realistic quality.

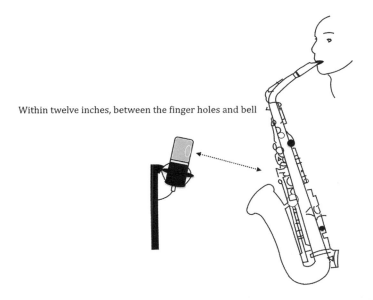

Within twelve inches, between the finger holes and bell

Fig. 14.11   Recording individual woodwind instruments with bells

STRAIGHT-SHAPED WOODWINDS

Place a large diaphragm condenser microphone with a cardioid polar pattern within eight inches of the instrument, aimed at the finger holes for a warm, inviting sound. If the microphone is pointed directly into the bell, a brighter sound will be achieved. A comparison of the two options will help you decide which placement is right for a given recording situation. To capture the breath sounds of a flute, producers sometimes aim the microphone directly at the lips of the player. For less breath, the microphone should be aimed at the finger holes (see Figure 14.12).

Within twelve inches, aimed at the finger holes

Fig. 14.12   Recording individual straight-shaped woodwinds

AMPLIFIED ELECTRIC GUITARS

Begin the process of capturing an amplified electric guitar by aiming a dynamic microphone with a cardioid polar pattern a few inches from the center of the amplifier's speaker for a bright sound. For a warmer sound, aim it on a slight angle to the left or right. If two microphones are involved, the second one should be a large diaphragm condenser microphone with a cardioid polar pattern that is placed a few feet away from the speaker and aimed directly at the sound source. In this configuration, the second microphone is used to capture the ambience of a room; it can be as far away from the speaker as necessary, even up to ten feet or more. Figure 14.13 demonstrates these three common approaches to recording amplified guitars.

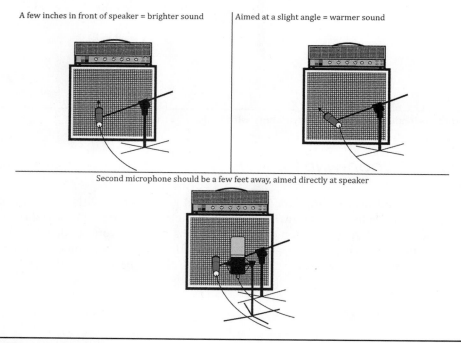

A few inches in front of speaker = brighter sound

Aimed at a slight angle = warmer sound

Second microphone should be a few feet away, aimed directly at speaker

Fig. 14.13   Recording amplified guitars

There are many ways to record amplifiers and experimentation is key. Often, the signal from the electric guitar (or any instrument with a quarter-inch output) is split into a **direct box** (DI box) that carries a clean signal to be recorded onto a separate channel. This signal can be used to experiment with different sounds at a later time. The recorded, clean sound can later be fed into an amplifier and manipulated further; this is known as **reamping**. Many contemporary DAW amp simulator plugins offer multiple realistic amplifier emulations, giving producers a lot of flexibility and realism. Another simple option is to plug the guitar directly into a pre-amp or a digital audio interface that has a built in pre-amp, which can be used to record the signal directly from the instrument. Since most project studios are equipped with converters that have built-in pre-amps, though, a separate interface pre-amp isn't typically necessary. The signal can simply be captured, and then run through virtual amplifier plugins and other effects. Amp simulation pedals are also becoming popular as they emulate expensive amplifiers with more and more accuracy at a fraction of the cost and space. Amp simulation pedals effect a signal before it enters a digital audio interface. It is wise to run a signal through any signal-boosting pedal before entering an interface to assure a powerful enough signal to work with. An amp simulation pedal set to a clean tone that may be tweaked with amp simulation plugins is a solid option for home recording.

AMPLIFIED ELECTRIC BASS

DI box recording is the most commonly used method of capturing a bass signal, and as such producers often leave bass amps out of the equation. The DI box method may, however, be combined with the recording of an isolated bass amplifier; a dynamic microphone with a cardioid polar pattern is typically used for this purpose, aimed at the center of the speaker, a few inches away, much like the first example in Figure 14.13 that demonstrates recording amplified electric guitars.

DRUMS

The process of recording drums is complicated by the fact that the producer is actually recording multiple percussion instruments (snare, kick, toms, cymbals) at the same time. Each distinct element is typically captured by its own microphone, as is the room in which the full drum kit is placed. A typical setup includes overhead microphones, a separate microphone for the top and bottom of the snare drum, a microphone inside (and sometimes outside) the kick drum, as well as separate microphones for each tom and cymbal. As you can see, recording drums is a process that requires a fair amount of equipment and space, both of which are not commonly found in project studios. For this reason, drum recording is beyond the scope of this book. More often than not, professional drummers will either be recorded at high-end studios or will have dedicated, permanent drum-recording setups in their own homes. Some contemporary studio drummers are able to import sessions into a DAW, record the drum parts on their own, and send the recordings back to the producer to be mixed. The most cost-effective process, though, is to create drum parts via MIDI and replace them with live drums in a larger studio if the budget allows.

No matter what method of capturing sound is exercised, the recording process begins with a determination of the appropriate tracking setup for the task at hand. It is important to routinely consider sample rate and bit depth options at the start of any project.

RECORDING SESSION SETUP

One of the most important steps in the recording process is determining the sample rate that will be used to record the session. Most DAWs offer a range between 44.1kHz to 192kHz to choose from. Although higher sample rates will ensure a higher quality, high sample rates also create very large files and may not always be necessary. Chapter 5 introduced the concept of the Nyquist theorem; this is where it should be applied. Multiply the frequency of the highest pitch that is to be captured by two and use the lowest available sample rate that exceeds this number.

Considerations of bit depth are also required at this stage. Most DAWs offer 16-bit or 24-bit options. More bits provide more potential measurements of each moment within a sample, which results in more dynamic range. It is therefore recommended to use 24-bit recording whenever possible, as the increase in dynamic range results in greater headroom. Moreover, 24-bit recording has become an industry standard in both the audio and video worlds, so most clients will expect this level of recording precision. Importantly, it is impossible to increase the sample rate of something that has already been captured, so care must be taken at this early decision-making stage. When working with a client, ensure that deliverable specifications are communicated promptly at the start of any project. Once the recording method has been established, the actual recording process may begin.

HEADPHONE MIXES

It is important to consider the comfort of the musicians being recorded. Performers need to be situated in positions that are natural relative to the instruments they are playing, and all distractions need to be kept to a minimum. One frustrating disruption comes in the form of **latency**, which is a noticeable delay between the moment sound is produced and the moment it reemerges through monitors or headphones. Interface buffer size settings are therefore crucial. **Buffer size** is the allocated amount of time dedicated to processing sound as it enters a computer. A larger buffer size setting is taxing on a computer and may create latency during recording, so smaller buffer sizes—which are easier on a computer's CPU and allow for less latency—are typically chosen, making for a smoother recording process. When editing and mixing, however, higher buffer sizes are advantageous, as they allow more time for a computer to process sound, which in turn allows for more plugins to be used at a given time. Therefore, it is common to record with a low buffer setting, which is then increased during the editing and mixing process to a high buffer setting. Unlike sample rates, buffer size settings can be changed at any time. Many DAWs also offer **low latency** features, which allow for higher buffer settings to be used during recording by temporarily bypassing CPU-heavy plugins. Low latency settings are available within the buffer settings window or as plugins in most DAWs.

Once latency is corrected, a **headphone mix** is needed to avoid sound from the studio monitors being picked up by the microphone(s) used in the recording. High-end studios often have expensive headphone systems costing thousands of dollars, but all that is typically necessary within a project studio is a simple headphone amplifier that is capable of outputting sound to as many performers as needed. Although the workflow may be slightly different from DAW to DAW, the basic concept remains the same: in the mix window of the DAW, the outputs of any desired elements to be heard in the headphone mix should be sent to one of the stereo outputs of the interface; once there, the balanced outputs of the interface will feed directly into the headphone amplifier. Note that a headphone mix may be sent either as a pre-fader or post-fader send. Headphone mixes featuring pre-fader sends are used when the musicians desire mixes that differ from that which is heard by the engineer, while post-fader sends provide musicians with the identical mix that is heard by the engineer.

THE RECORDING PROCESS

The next stage of production is the actual recording and editing process. It is rare for a performer to record a perfect take on a first pass in any recording situation. Even if a part is perceived as being performed perfectly, it is common and wise to record multiple back-up takes in case smaller mistakes were missed; DAWs have many tools to make this process more efficient.

COMPOSITE RECORDING

Composite recording, or **comping**, is a term used to describe the act of recording multiple takes of a single part across different tracks, followed by combining the best parts of the individual take tracks into a single, final track. In the past, producers would record new takes on individual tracks, edit them to create one composite take, and bounce them down to a single, new track. Once this was done, the original tracks that were used to record each individual take were deleted to save hard drive space and maintain a manageable session. However, modern DAWs allow composite tracking to occur within a single track by layering takes on top of one another. Once recording is finished, the parts are edited together and combined within the same track.

If a certain section of a piece of music presents significant difficulty for a performer, that section may be isolated, and a process known as "punch recording" may be employed. Punch recording, often called "punching in/out," gets its name from the traditional recording process in which a producer would choose an in and out point and "**punch-in**" the record button as the performer approached a problem section, then "**punch-out**" a bar or two later. By doing so, a new recording would replace the original for the specific amount of time the record button was "punched-in." During punch recording, it is important to give the performer a few bars to play along with the recording prior to the punch-in, so that the transition between the original recording and the new punched-in section feels natural (resulting in a much easier edit when merging the two separate recordings). In modern DAWs, punch-in and punch-out points may be programmed ahead of time, so the producer doesn't need to press anything while the performer plays through a difficult passage. Figure 14.14 demonstrates this process in Pro Tools.

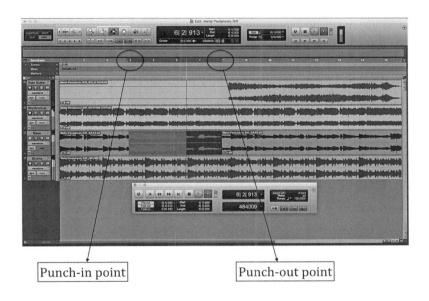

Punch-in point   Punch-out point

Fig. 14.14   Punch recording in Pro Tools 12

Although punching-in is still a feature found in modern DAWs, there are arguably more efficient ways of isolating and recording problematic sections. Cycle recording and quick swipe editing are two solutions to this end. These techniques are particularly useful for performers faced with demanding passages that benefit from isolation.

Cycle recording (or loop recording) involves setting up a section within which a recording will continually capture new takes every time it cycles or loops through its programmed start and end points. A cycle may begin and end at any point within a project. It is common to set up a cycle recording that lasts for the entire duration of a project, allowing for a performer to record multiple piece-long takes without stopping. It is wise to add a few bars to the beginning and end of a loop, however, in order to allow the performer to prepare for the subsequent take. Each DAW has a slightly different approach to cycle recording, accommodating different workflow designs. Pro Tools approaches the task by assigning takes to "playlists," which may be edited down to a single track. Logic Pro X automatically layers each take underneath the original recording in what it refers to as "take folders," while Cubase takes a similar approach but refers to individual layers as "lanes." Figure 14.15 demonstrates track-length cycle recording in Logic Pro X. Notice the three added measures to the beginning and end of the loop, giving the performer preparation time between each take.

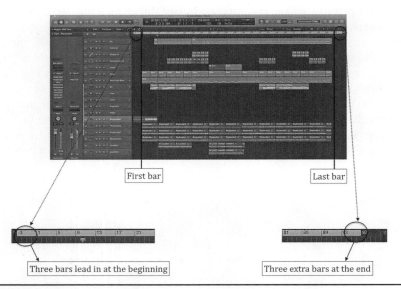

Fig. 14.15　Cycle recording in Logic Pro X

As mentioned earlier, the punch-in option still exists in modern DAWs, but cycle recording offers the same benefits while additionally allowing repeated takes of the isolated section. Figure 14.16 demonstrates cycle recording an isolated passage in Logic Pro X. In this example, the DAW is programmed to continuously record between bars 57 and 65.

Fig. 14.16　Cycle recording an isolated passage in Logic Pro X

CONSOLIDATING AND EDITING COMPED TAKES

All DAWs approach take consolidation in slightly different ways. Logic Pro X offers an especially efficient approach called **quick swipe comping**. Each additional recorded pass is listed in a separate take folder underneath the first take, allowing you to see all takes in an organized manner. You then have the option of swiping the mouse and high-lighting any section of any take within a take folder, essentially "soloing" the highlighted passage from the rest of the takes within that folder. The number of edits within a take folder is unlimited using quick swipe comping, as well, allowing for microscopic precision when editing. Moreover, Logic Pro X automatically creates crossfades between the different takes, which smoothly merges them together, and the results can be heard in real time, as soon as a swipe is completed. Crossfades are covered in more detail in the next section. It is important to note that when two takes are combined at a moment in which each waveform is at a high amplitude peak, a popping sound is likely to occur, making for an obvious and poor edit. Therefore, the best way to avoid popping sounds is to find edit points where both waveforms are at their lowest amplitudes. Once the composite track is satisfactory, all tracks can be "flat-tened and merged" together permanently to form a new waveform. Figure 14.17 shows a take folder in Logic Pro X with multiple quick swipes.

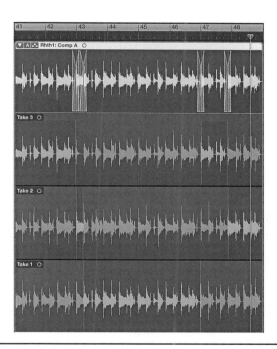

Fig. 14.17   A take folder in Logic Pro X with multiple quick swipes

FADES/CROSSFADES

A **fade in** is a measured increase of volume from silence to a signal's original amplitude. A **fade out** is the progressive decrease of an audio signal to silence. Fade ins and fade outs are almost always applied to both the beginning and end of any waveform to avoid noticeable edit points. Many producers apply fades even if popping sounds aren't overtly identifiable. Most DAWs offer multiple fade options with a variety of possible fade shapes (see Figure 14.18, which illustrates fade options in Pro Tools 12).

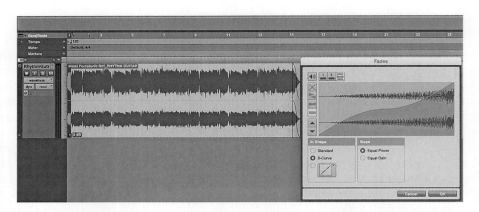

Fig. 14.18   Fade options in Pro Tools 12

A **crossfade** is an editing process that smoothly blends two separate waveforms into one. Crossfades make it possible for comped takes to be evenly joined without the popping or clicking sounds that are often the result of combining two different waveforms that possess distinct amplitudes. Figure 14.19 provides a close-up view from Figure 14.17's quick swipe function in Logic Pro X. Notice the differences in amplitude between the ends of the waveforms on the left and the starting points of the waveforms on the right. Crossfades are applied in instances like these to create seamless transitions.

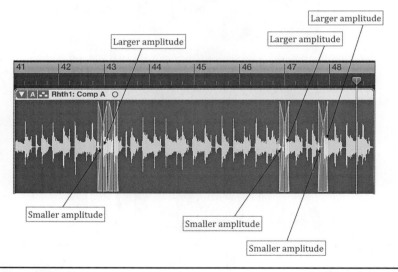

Fig. 14.19   Crossfades in Logic Pro X

An understanding of the basic principles explained in this chapter, combined with a willingness to experiment, will yield positive results during live recording. Once you understand the basic guidelines of recording and editing, you are ready to grasp the fundamental principles of mixing and processing. Before any processing may begin, however, it is extremely important to make sure that the initial recordings sound as perfect as possible. A mix can only sound as good as the raw materials that are being combined, so care must be taken to ensure that the very best performances are captured and edited. Trying to mask poor edits or performances during the mixing and processing stage will add unnecessary complexity to an already intricate task.

SUMMARY OF TERMS FROM CHAPTER 14

close miking
ambient miking
proximity effect
headroom
take
mono
stereo miking
compression
rarefaction
phasing
in phase
out of phase
phase shifting

phase cancellation
3-to-1 rule
matched microphones
coincident X-Y stereo miking
near-coincident stereo miking
stereo separation
Blumlein stereo miking
mid-side (MS) stereo miking
spaced pair stereo miking
sound barriers
pop filter
DI box (direct box)
reamping

latency
buffer size
low latency
headphone mix
composite recording
comping
punch-in
punch-out
cycle recording
quick swipe comping
fade in
fade out
crossfade

CHAPTER 14—EXERCISES

True or False. Circle "true" for each statement below that is true. Circle "false" for each false statement.

1. Modern-day project studios are only designed to handle MIDI, so all live recordings should take place in high-budget studios.

    True   False

2. Ambient miking is a technique in which a microphone is placed as close to a sound source as possible.

    True   False

3. The maximum point of positive pressure in a pressure wave is known as compression.

    True   False

4. Phase cancellation removes unwanted sound and will enhance the overall sound quality of a waveform.

    True   False

5. The 3-to-1 rule is designed to avoid phasing issues.

    True   False

6. The right microphone in a coincident X-Y configuration will pick up the right side of the room, and the left microphone will pick up the left side of the room.

    True   False

7. The left microphone in a Blumlein stereo miking configuration will record the front right and back left areas of a room, while the right microphone will capture the opposite.

    True   False

8. One benefit of mid-side (MS) stereo miking is that it strives to capture an instrument's qualities plus the ambience of the room.

    True   False

9. A condenser microphone with a cardioid polar pattern is typically aimed just above the lips of a singer.

    True   False

10. Solo brass instruments should always be recorded as far away from a microphone as possible.

    True   False

11. When recording a solo tenor saxophone, a large diaphragm condenser microphone with a cardioid polar pattern is typically placed within 12 inches of the instrument and aimed at the finger holes.

    True   False

12. When recording a solo flute performance, a large diaphragm condenser microphone with a cardioid polar pattern is often placed within eight inches of the instrument and aimed at the finger holes to create a brighter sound.

    True   False

13. If two microphones are involved in the recording of an amplified guitar, the second one should be a large diaphragm condenser microphone with a cardioid polar pattern placed a few inches away from the speaker, aimed away from the sound source.

    True   False

14. The best position to place a microphone is the one your ear determines.

    True   False

15.   Record yourself performing the melody you sequenced for the final exercise in Chapter 9 or 10 on your primary instrument (or a keyboard instrument if your primary instrument is non-pitched). If you have not completed these exercises, then compose an 8-bar melody first. Proceed in the order provided below.

    a.   Create a new audio track.

    b.   Give yourself a 1-bar count off (this is usually adjusted in the DAW's transport or metronome feature).

c.   Record four separate takes of the melody using your DAW's cycle record feature.

d.   Edit together each take to create one composite track using quick swipe editing or another take consolidation approach.

e.   Bounce and deliver the final recording to your instructor, which should possess the following specifications: 24-bit (bit depth), 48kHz (sample rate).

Chapter 15
Mixing and Processing

Once the elements of a project have been recorded and edited, the next steps of the project's development may take place: mixing and processing. Processing includes adding effects that can enhance the main parameters of a mix, which are volume, width, and depth. Controlling these attributes can only be accomplished in an environment that has been treated to appropriately present audio signals.

ROOM PREPARATION AND MONITORING

ACOUSTIC TREATMENT

Care must be taken to treat your studio room appropriately, so that it absorbs and deflects frequencies in a way that doesn't cloud the sonic atmosphere. One widespread issue related to room design is **flutter echo**, a ringing effect that is caused by sound reflecting back and forth between two hard, parallel surfaces. Flutter echo is most often heard in square-shaped rooms, and, since project studios typically exist within composers' bedrooms or living rooms (which tend to be square shaped), it is quite common. Fortunately, there are simple solutions to remedy this phenomenon. To identify flutter echo and other acoustic needs of your project studio, walk around while clapping your hands, paying close attention to the quality of the sound and how it changes from place to place. If the reflected sound is pleasing, you may not need much treatment at all (though this is not the case in most home recording spaces). However, if the sound can be described as being "tinny," a good amount of treatment will be necessary. There are three main components of **acoustic treatment**: absorption, diffusion, and bass traps.

Absorption

Absorption treatments "absorb" sound before it has the chance to reflect around the room, which can cause acoustic problems. **Acoustic foam** is a common remedy; it can be purchased online or in most music stores.

Fig. 15.1   Acoustic foam

The thicker the foam, the more frequencies it will be able to capture; however, excessive absorption may result in an unwanted dry or "dead" sound. A two-inch-thick piece of foam is only capable of absorbing sound above approximately 400Hz, which leaves many bass frequencies unabsorbed. A four-inch-thick piece of foam is able to absorb as low as 200Hz, though it still renders several low frequencies unaffected. One way to approach this problem is to separate the foam from the wall by a few inches, which enables even more low-end absorption. However, the use of separate bass traps is the most common way to handle low frequency issues.

Bass Traps

Issues related to bass frequencies are extremely common in typical project studios. When a speaker outputs wavelengths that are related to the dimensions of a room, the frequencies will either cancel themselves out or be reinforced, causing acoustic distortion. These resonance frequencies are called **room modes**, and they exist between 20Hz and 200Hz. Most room modes tend to congregate in the room's corners; thus, **bass traps** are typically placed in these locations (see Figure 15.2).

Fig. 15.2   A bass trap

Diffusion

Sound waves may also converge in specific "hot spots" throughout a room, which can cause more problematic frequency cancellation or reinforcement. **Diffusion** treatment is a solution to this issue. Objects known as diffusers are used to scatter the reflecting frequencies that remain after the absorption process (via acoustic foam and bass traps).

Fig. 15.3   A diffusion panel

In most project studios, diffusion may not be a necessity, as its effectiveness reduces when room size decreases. Indeed, bass traps may be the only treatment needed for smaller home studios, with acoustic foam panels being a supplementary option (if the budget allows). If your project studio is large, diffusion panels can help, but only after bass traps and acoustic foam are in place. Once your room is properly treated, the next consideration regards speaker monitors, which need to be placed correctly in order to get the cleanest distribution of sound.

REFERENCE MONITORS AND MONITOR PLACEMENT

The biggest challenge producers face regards whether or not their mixes translate well in multiple playback environments. Reference monitors are therefore an extremely important part of any studio, as speakers with the flattest response over the greatest frequency range typically translate best. With so many options on the market, it is important to understand a few basic principles before choosing a pair of studio monitors.

Monitors and Projection Field

The three main designs for studio monitors are **near-field**, **mid-field**, and **far-field**, with each option's name referring to the distance between the speakers and the producer. The clarity and accuracy of sound increases as the distance between the producer and the monitors decreases, and, as such, near-field monitoring is optimal. However, larger rooms—especially those with bulky recording consoles—may require mid- or far-field options, despite the fact that the natural frequency reflections within the room will interfere with the sound. Luckily, most project studios are smaller in size, and thus near-field monitoring is all that is needed to successfully produce professional work. The next important consideration concerns the manner in which the speakers receive power.

Active and Passive Monitors

With regard to receiving power, there are two main speaker types: **active** (power is received from a built-in amplifier) and **passive** (power is received from a separate amplifier). Although it is possible to create a professional monitoring environment with passive monitors and a separate amplifier, the extra gear requires space, which is limited in most project studios. For this reason, most producers benefit from the convenience of active monitors. Regardless of your choice regarding active or passive monitors, however, you must select speakers with an appropriate wattage rating.

Output Power

A common misconception about output power—which is measured in watts—is that it only contributes to loudness. In actuality, greater wattage creates greater headroom (which allows for cleaner transients, more clarity, and better dynamic range). It is therefore important to strike a balance between budget and maximum wattage. Power is distributed using three main designs: single-amp, bi-amp, and tri-amp. In a **single-amp** configuration, a crossover system divides the frequencies, sending the higher frequencies to a tweeter and the lower frequencies to a woofer; these speakers are all powered by one amplifier. In a **bi-amp** configuration, a crossover network sends the high frequencies to one amplifier and the low frequencies to a second amplifier before being routed to the speakers. A **tri-amp** configuration further separates the signal into high, low, and mid-range frequencies, with each frequency band being sent to a dedicated speaker. Tri-amp designs generally sound clearer than single or bi-amp configurations.

Low Frequency Control

Project studios are generally equipped with five- to eight-inch monitors. Many smaller studio monitors come with ported cabinets, which help extend low frequency response. Although this is somewhat helpful in the reproduction of low frequencies, ported cabinets tend to sound muddy (especially if the ports are on the back side of the speaker cabinets, facing a wall). Closed-cabinet eight-inch speakers will generally offer enough low frequency response to create high-quality work, though some composers prefer to work with a separate subwoofer for even greater control over low frequencies. Not all producers agree that a subwoofer is necessary, but it is always important to build an environment that reflects that of the listeners. For producers desiring to work in the television, film, or video game industries, a subwoofer might be a worthy consideration, as today's listeners tend to invest in home entertainment systems that include them. Composers of electronic dance music should be even more inclined to choose the subwoofer setup, as nightclubs almost always have systems featuring multiple subwoofers. Regardless of your personal choice of setup, though, it is important to position your speakers in optimal locations to produce the best results.

Speaker Placement

Monitors are positioned properly if the shape of an equilateral triangle is created between the two monitors and the producer's head, with each side of the triangle being three to five feet in length. Whenever possible, speakers should be raised on stands instead of being placed flat on a desk or other object, as this avoids sound reflecting off of hard surfaces before reaching the producer's ears. Monitors should also be placed on monitor pads, which help to absorb more sound. Figure 15.4 illustrates proper speaker placement.

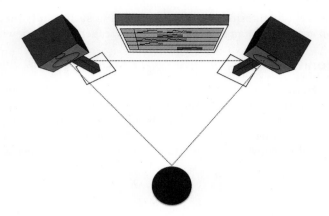

Equilateral triangle formed between speakers and head

Fig. 15.4　**Proper speaker placement**

Controlling the Weaknesses of a Monitoring System

Once you have your monitor system calibrated and feel that a mix is complete, be sure to bounce it and listen to it in multiple environments. Two important environments to test are your phone's speakers and your vehicle's audio system. Typical phone speakers do not produce much in the way of low frequencies, while car speaker systems generally exaggerate these frequencies (as they often come equipped with a subwoofer). If your mix translates well using these two drastically different speaker configurations, chances are it will translate well in most other places, too. If your mixes sound unbalanced in one or more test environments, you may need to adjust your monitor setup or even the mix environment within the DAW. For example, if your completed mixes tend to sound exaggerated in a specific frequency band, make adjustments in the DAW so that those frequencies sound less pronounced during the mixing phase. If your mixes specifically sound too bass heavy, try raising the volume on your subwoofer during the mixing phase, which will help you keep the lower frequencies in order so that they translate better over a wider variety of speaker setups.

Proper speaker selection, speaker placement, and acoustic treatment are three of the most important stages in studio design, but it is important to remember that a well-designed studio does not guarantee professional results. Regardless of the studio's treatment and monitor configuration, you must take the time to learn and adjust to the mixing environment. It is beneficial to reference mixes with a pair of quality headphones that possesses a flat frequency response; however, it is very difficult to mix solely using headphones and achieve results of the same quality as when mixing with speaker monitors. This is because the stereo image is perceived differently when mixing in headphones, as the distance between headphone speakers is extremely close to your ears. This difference tends to result in a distant sound when projects are mixed using headphones. Referencing projects with a combination of headphones and speakers will set the stage for professional outcomes.

FINAL SESSION PREPARATION

PRE-MIX LEVELING

Pre-mix leveling involves establishing a basic set of volume levels before processing and volume automation are applied to a mix. This is a vital stage in the life of a project, as any elements that appear to distort at this juncture will harm the mix at ever-greater levels during the subsequent stages of the mixing process. Pre-mix leveling can be a relatively simple task, however, if you consistently address the volume of all of the musical parts from the outset of the project. This strategy is known as evolution mixing, which was introduced in Chapter 13. Another strategy, known as proper gain staging, will additionally ensure professional results.

Proper **gain staging** involves a disciplined approach to managing the output level of any audio signal throughout all phases of its journey through a session. It requires an understanding of all of the locations within a signal's path wherein gain can be applied, and a dedication to ensuring that the signal's level is never increased near the point of clipping (distortion). Beginner producers often hastily increase individual output levels to achieve louder-sounding music. Without proper care, this can easily cause clipping, which can be compounded within the session via inserts and sends—stages wherein gain increases may not be readily visible. In analog studios, it is common to "push" a signal's output to make up for low-level hiss or other unwanted audible sounds that are caused by tape recorders; however, in digital recording, the input signals are far cleaner, rendering this technique unnecessary and even detrimental to the signal. Generally speaking, the main monitors or headphone levels should be increased if more volume is desired, not the individual track levels within the project.

Producers do tend to have individual gain staging ranges within which they feel comfortable working, but you are advised to keep volume levels as conservative as possible. As mentioned in Chapter 14, a safe recording level is between -20dB and -6dB at the extreme, with a customary average around -18dB. A conservative gain staging level is between -12 and -18dB, which ensures that clean, manageable sounds are being combined, allowing you to concentrate instead on the three main elements of the mix: volume, panning, and depth.

MIXING: THE THREE COMPONENTS OF THE "AUDIO CONTINUUM"

Three-dimensional space consists of three components: height, width, and depth. The metaphorical space of the **audio continuum** in a mix may be thought of as sharing similar parameters, with height being determined by volume, width being primarily defined by panning configurations, and depth being controlled by time-based effects. Volume may be modified in a number of ways, from simple fader movement to spectral and dynamic processing, which will be discussed in the next section. Panning may be accomplished by turning virtual pan pots (potentiometers) to the left or right, or via stereo imaging. Depth can be adjusted with time-based processing (e.g., reverb or delay), which creates the illusion of forward or backward placement within a mix. Figure 15.5 provides an illustration of the audio continuum.

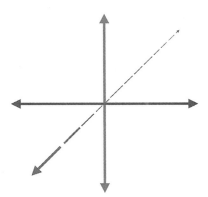

Volume - fader movement, spectral (EQ) and dynamic (compression/gating)
processing (up & down arrow)

Panning - pan pot movement and stereo imaging (left & right arrow)

Depth - time-based processing (reverb, delay, etc.) (dotted arrow)

Fig. 15.5 The audio continuum

VOLUME

High-quality compositional arrangements and mixes both share a relationship with the overtone series. A well-produced arrangement, for example, will place larger harmonic intervals between the lower-pitched instruments, leaving the smaller harmonic intervals for the higher-pitched instruments. A good engineer will emphasize these relationships by means of spectral processing, attenuating and boosting certain harmonics. **Spectral processing** is another term for equalization, which was initially covered in Chapter 7 along with the overtone series. It is important to recall that one of the distinguishing factors of an instrument's characteristic sound is the specific set of overtones that are emphasized above a given fundamental it produces. If too many overtones are cut from a signal, an instrument may begin losing its sonic profile, resulting in strange or unrecognizable sounds. For this reason, a higher Q setting (and smaller bandwidth) should be used when attenuating a frequency range, as this allows for the removal of unwanted frequencies without infringing upon the overall character of the sound. If a frequency range is to be boosted, however, a lower Q-factor setting (and thus a larger bandwidth) may be applied. Figure 15.6 illustrates the colloquial concept of "boosting wide" and "cutting narrow" within Logic's Channel EQ plugin.

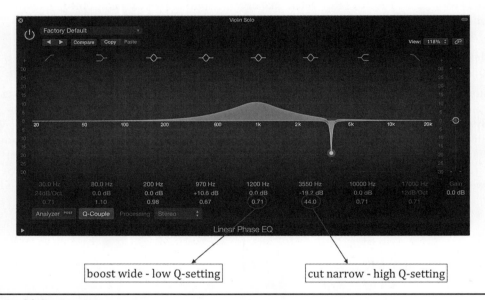

boost wide - low Q-setting   cut narrow - high Q-setting

Fig. 15.6   Boost wide, cut narrow

EQ Sweeping

Spectral processing is very useful for eliminating unwanted frequencies from an otherwise pleasant signal. Once a track is isolated from the rest of the mix, a common approach to finding undesired sounds is to sweep all frequencies.

EQ sweeping is typically done with a parametric equalizer, which affords greater control over Q-factor settings. The process begins by assigning a high Q-setting to any one of the available frequency bands within the equalizer. Once this is done, the selected band should be boosted to its highest level so that the specific frequencies are exaggerated and clearly heard. At this point, the small band should be swept through the entire frequency spectrum until the unwanted sound is pinpointed. The gain modifier assigned to the band can then be lowered until the sound adequately fades from the signal. Figure 15.7 demonstrates EQ sweeping, again using Logic's Channel EQ plugin.

Sweep through all frequencies until problem is detected

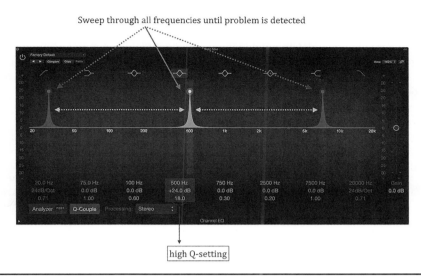

high Q-setting

Fig. 15.7 EQ sweeping

If a desired sound is not adequately audible within a mix, the EQ sweeping process can also be used to precisely locate and boost it appropriately. Care must be taken when boosting too many signals, however, as this may result in poor gain staging and/or multiple instruments "fighting for dominance" within a certain portion of the frequency spectrum. For these reasons, many producers prefer subtractive equalization to additive equalization.

Subtractive vs. Additive Equalization

Additive equalization is a process through which desired frequencies are boosted so that they sound more dominant in a mix. **Subtractive equalization**—attenuating undesired frequencies so that they do not dominate a mix—often provides a cleaner approach to accomplishing the same goal, as non-attenuated, desired frequencies appear louder and thus more dominant than those that are attenuated. A more complex method of equalization combines additive and subtractive processes and is known as **complementary equalization**. Complementary EQ is an excellent way of dealing with situations wherein multiple signals that share the same general frequency range (such as the kick drum and bass guitar) are all desired. The complementary equalization process involves metaphorically "carving out" frequency space for each desired signal to dominate within the shared band, so that there is not competition over any single frequency. In the case of the kick drum and bass guitar, there are two common options that make use of complementary EQ.

Option 1: High-pass filter the sub bass band (20–50Hz) and slightly boost the bass band (50–200Hz) of the kick drum. (It is also common to boost some of the point band frequencies [1k to 5kHz] to bring out the "slap" of the foot pedal hitting the drum.) Next, slightly boost the sub bass band of the bass guitar.

Option 2: High-pass filter the sub bass band (20–50Hz) and slightly boost the bass band (50–200Hz) of the bass guitar. (It is also common to slightly boost some of the clarity band frequencies [500Hz—1kHz] to bring out some of the harmonics of the instrument. Boost this section sparingly, however, as it often tends to add a "honky" sound.) Next, slightly boost the sub bass band of the kick drum.

Both options create a segment within the larger, shared frequency region that is dedicated to each signal. Spectral processing such as complementary equalization is an important aspect related to the volume component of the audio continuum. Compression also relates to volume, in that it modifies the dynamic range of an audio signal.

Compression

Compression involves lowering the volume of the maximum points of a waveform while simultaneously amplifying the quieter moments. In doing so, a compressor decreases the dynamic range, allowing for the details of the quieter sections to become clearer in the mix. Compression also allows the entire signal to be boosted without the louder sections becoming too loud (see Figure 15.8).

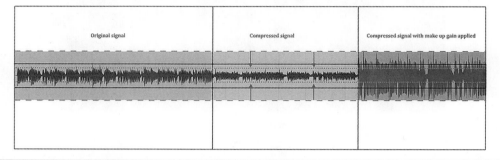

Fig. 15.8   A waveform before and after compression

Most compressors offer five main parameters: threshold, ratio, attack, release, and make-up gain (see Figure 15.9).

Threshold: The threshold knob specifies the amplitude at which compression is activated. The compressor will reduce a signal's amplitude when it exceeds the limit set by the threshold. A lower threshold setting will reduce more of a signal, while a higher setting may only affect a signal's loudest moments.

Ratio: The ratio knob specifies how much of a signal will be reduced. A ratio setting of 2:1 means that every 2dB of sound that exceeds the threshold setting will be reduced to 1dB over the threshold. A 2:1 ratio results in slight compression, while 6:1 ratios and above are considered to be aggressive compression settings. A compressor with a ratio setting of 20:1 or higher is technically functioning as a **limiter**, which is a tool that limits the output of a signal's peak level.

Fig. 15.9   The Pro Tools 12 Compressor/Limiter plugin

Attack: The attack knob relates to the speed at which the compressor will react to a signal passing over the threshold amplitude. Shorter attack settings cause the compressor to reduce a signal more quickly, while longer attack settings cause the compressor to reduce a signal more gradually.

Release: The release knob provides the duration that the signal will remain compressed after it falls back below the threshold.

Make-up gain: Once a signal has been compressed, the overall output level will decrease, as the signal's peaks have been moderated. Make-up gain provides the option to bring the signal back to its original volume, but with less dynamic range, making it stand out more in a mix.

A **multiband compressor** is a compressor that divides the frequency range into adjustable bands, allowing for specific types of compression to be applied only to specific bands. Multiband compression is typically reserved for mastering and will be explored further in Chapter 16.

A compressor may also be used to "duck" or attenuate signals in real time, creating space for other sounds to shine within the mix. This technique is called **sidechaining**, and it involves sending sound from one channel so that it can be used to alter the sound of another. The sending or "triggering" track will activate a compressor that is assigned to the receiving channel. The receiving channel then attenuates all of its incoming signals when the triggering track's audio passes the threshold set by the compressor. Sidechaining was originally used to add presence to dialogue tracks so that they could compete with background music in situations such as radio spots or infomercials (where the spoken word needed to dominate the mix). The background music in these scenarios would be "ducked" via a compressor that was triggered by the dialogue, allowing the words to be perceived clearly despite the overlapping frequencies. Figure 15.10 demonstrates the sidechaining process in Logic Pro X. Here, a kick drum's attacks trigger compression on the bass track, allowing them to sound more present in the mix. This particular use of sidechaining, when done to the extreme, creates an effect known as **pumping**, which is a common sound heard in many electronic genres.

Fig. 15.10   Sidechaining using Logic Pro X's Compressor plugin

Equalization and compression are two of the producer's most important tools. Before attempting any other processing, you should work on developing a strong command over these essential aspects of audio production. Once you are able to make audio signals fit comfortably within a mix and achieve a good volume balance, you are ready to explore further concepts.

Gating

By decreasing the dynamic range of an audio signal, compression allows a waveform to sound more defined and sit more prominently in a mix. Sometimes, however, unwanted sounds exist in the quieter areas of a signal, which become even more pronounced after compression. To reduce or eliminate such sounds, a process known as gating may be used. **Gating** is the opposite of compression: once a signal's volume falls *below* a set threshold point, the signal becomes further attenuated. This is useful for eliminating traffic sounds, studio hum, or any low volume sound that adversely affects the quality of a signal. A gate—sometimes called a noise gate—is said to be "open" when a signal passes above the set threshold, and it is said to be "closed" when a signal passes below the threshold and is attenuated.

Gates also normally include five adjustable parameters: threshold, ratio, attack, hold, and release. Conceptually, each component of a gate works in the same way as the similarly named parameter found on a compressor. On both compressors and gates, the threshold sets the level at which attenuation will begin. The threshold knob on a gate thus specifies the lowest volume level that triggers the gate to "close," causing any sound below that point to be attenuated. Any sound above the threshold of a gate will pass through the "open" gate unaffected. The ratio setting adjusts the degree to which a signal will be attenuated when the gate is "closed." Attack and release knobs determine how long it will take to transition to and from processing, just as they do on a compressor. The hold parameter, though, is unique to gates; it adjusts how long the gate will remain closed after the signal returns to a level above the threshold. The release time is therefore responsible for creating a natural gradient back to an unprocessed state (i.e., a *release* from a processed state), whereas the hold knob specifies when the release will be initiated.

Equalization, compression, and gating are three important processing components, all of which are related to the volume of an audio signal. As they each modify the entirety of a signal, though, they are most often manifested as inserts on individual channel strips, so that they affect only one signal at a time. Equalization and compression inserts are typically found one after the other within a single channel strip, with the order of the processing being an important consideration. Indeed, there are benefits and problems associated with either ordering.

The Order of Equalization and Compression

One benefit of placing equalization first in the chain is that it allows for the attenuation of unwanted frequencies before compression, which creates more headroom and a cleaner signal passing into the compressor. The problem with this ordering, though, is that any attenuated frequencies may be boosted during the compression process, essentially undoing the equalization. Moreover, if a certain frequency is boosted by the EQ, the compressor may attenuate it if it reaches a level beyond the compressor's threshold setting, again undoing the equalization previously applied. If, however, compression is applied first, it will attenuate the peaks of a signal; when equalization is applied later, boosted frequencies may recreate these peaks and render the use of the compressor unnecessary. Some producers thus place EQ before and after compression (though this can become confusing, particularly when several tracks are involved in the session). When you are processing, always choose an order of operations that suits the particular situation (as opposed to adhering to a template), and remember that some signals may blend well without equalization or compression; you should avoid applying effects unless they are solving a specific problem.

WIDTH

In a mix, width is related to the placement of sound along the left/right spectrum of the stereo field; this is accomplished through panning. Experimentation with the assignment of audio signals to one side of a stereo image or another—and the degree to which they are panned—is an important part of the creative process. Although there are no rules for where specific instruments should be positioned within a stereo image, there are a few guidelines that are commonly followed. In modern mixing, for example, the bass guitar is almost always panned in the center position, as it would be difficult to complement or properly balance the powerful low-frequency energy that the instrument produces if it were panned to one side. Some jazz recordings do pan the bass to one side, but this is to help showcase the artist as well as recreate a live sound (by assigning instruments to the relative positions in which they would sound if the listener were watching a live performance). The standard panning of orchestral instruments follows the same practice of recreating the perspective of an audience member (see Figure 15.11). For example, since orchestras traditionally place violin I players on the left of the stage, these parts tend to be panned to the left in recordings. Importantly, most sound libraries that offer orchestral section patches are pre-panned following this traditional scheme; as such, care should be taken to avoid over-panning orchestral instruments. Solo instruments, however, can generally be placed wherever they fit best in a mix, regardless of their traditional positions within a large live ensemble.

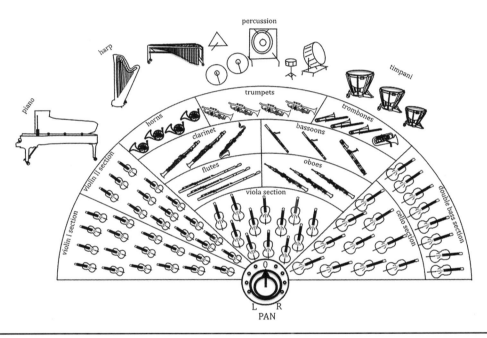

Fig. 15.11 Orchestral panning

In modern pop/rock recordings, the kick drum is usually panned to the center along with the bass guitar to allow the high-energy transients it produces to always remain in focus. Snare drums are also generally panned to the center for the same reason. Lead vocals tend to be panned to the center, too, along with any other parts that require emphasis; this helps these important parts stand out clearly. Instrument signals that are generally panned away from the center position in pop/rock ensembles include the background vocals, keyboard, guitar, and especially the cymbals, which can be panned to the left (hi-hats and crash) and right (ride) to simulate the perspective of the drummer behind the kit (see Figure 15.12).

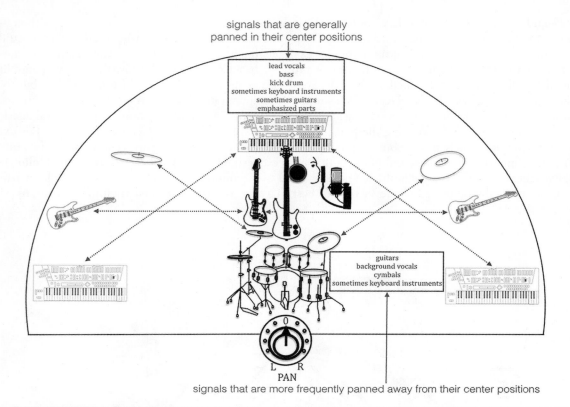

signals that are generally
panned in their center positions

lead vocals
bass
kick drum
sometimes keyboard instruments
sometimes guitars
emphasized parts

guitars
background vocals
cymbals
sometimes keyboard instruments

L   R
PAN

signals that are more frequently panned away from their center positions

Fig. 15.12   Pop/rock ensemble panning

When deciding where to pan instruments in your own mix, be sure to reference existing mixes that you enjoy, paying attention to where the parts are panned as well as to how the panning changes throughout the track. It is important that mixes in commercial music settings remain approachable, however. Common practice dictates that kick drums, basses, and lead vocals should be panned center, for example, and it is wise to at least consider doing the same in your own mixes, as the basic approaches to panning outlined in Figure 15.12 have proven successful for decades. Remember, though, that panning should always serve a purpose: to help create separation, space, and width within a mix.

DEPTH

Depth is achieved in a mix through time-based processing. By applying effects such as delay, reverb, and modulation, you can create sounds that are perceived to be closer or farther away from the listener within an illusory space. This allows a piece of music to sound as if it were recorded in a large hall or small room, for example.

All instruments that you desire to place within the same sonic space should generally share the same time-based effects; assigning these effects to auxiliary tracks—instead of adding separate instances of each effect to individual tracks—provides a clean and CPU-efficient means to this end. Individual tracks can then be adjusted with regard to the amount of each effect that is applied by modifying their send levels (or the position of the aux tracks' faders). This provides flexibility at the individual track level as well as continuity across all tracks that are fed to the same aux track(s) for processing.

Delay

Delay effects work by copying a signal and repeating it a certain number of times at a given durational interval. Short delays of between 30ms and 120ms are often used to create a doubling or thickening effect, especially for vocals. Longer delay settings create the illusion that the audio signal is being placed farther away from the listener. Most delay plugins allow users to sync the timing of the delayed copy (or copies) to the tempo of the track, creating identifiable rhythmic values within the meter of the song. Sometimes a "**tap tempo**" feature is present to this end, which allows the user to physically tap in a tempo to which the delay is synced. The delayed copies may also be panned to one side or the other within the stereo field; additionally, the percentage of dry and wet signal can be specified. Like delay, **echo** is an effect that repeats a copied version of an audio signal, but echo specifically involves repeating the signal at ever-lower amplitudes until the sound completely fades out. The terms delay and echo are often used interchangeably, but some producers use the term echo only to describe the very natural-sounding effect that was created by vintage tape machines that looped a copy of a signal at ever-lower amplitudes. Delay and echo can add interesting effects and a sense of dimension to an otherwise dry signal. Reverb plugins, too, use a similar approach and are used to create depth; indeed, delay, echo, and reverb are all different subtypes of the same effect process.

Reverb

Reverb, which is short for reverberation, involves creating a series of delayed copies of a signal that reach the ear at slightly different instants. The reverb effect is thus composed of a source signal plus the delayed "reflections" of the signal that virtually "bounce" off of the surfaces of a digitally rendered space. There are two main types of reverb plugins: algorithmic reverb and convolution reverb.

An **algorithmic reverb** uses mathematical algorithms to create a series of diminishing delays that simulate a particular acoustic space. The advantage of algorithmic reverbs is that the user may customize many parameters that affect the virtual space, including room size, room shape, and stereo control. Algorithmic reverbs are generally less expensive and more CPU-efficient than convolution reverbs, too, although they don't typically sound as realistic.

A **convolution reverb** works by taking samples of the acoustic parameters of an actual environment, which are known as **impulse responses**. The environment is excited by a sound source—usually a snare hit or starter gun—and then recorded; the convolution processor then removes the sound source, leaving behind reverberations that are used to provide a digital recreation based on the exact dimensions of the real space. Although convolution reverbs are generally more expensive and CPU-intensive, they sound more realistic than their algorithmic counterparts.

Both algorithmic and convolution reverbs create the illusion that a sound was recorded in an environment other than the one in which it was truly captured. They can add depth by expanding the perceived boundaries of the listening space, allowing individual sounds to seem farther back from the listener or farther apart from one another. The depth of a mix may be further enhanced by combining delay, reverb, and modulation effects.

Modulation

The three main types of **modulation effects** are flanging, phasing, and chorus effects. These effects were first popularized in the 1960s, and, when used liberally, tend to be associated with the psychedelic movement in music. In modern music, these effects are used far more subtly, but they remain very useful tools for creating thicker and/or more interesting sounds as well as the perception of depth within the audio continuum. Unlike reverbs and delays, modulation effects are often added locally as inserts on individual instrument or vocal tracks, rather than being added globally to aux tracks.

Flangers, phasers, and chorus effects operate based on the same basic principle: creating a copy of a signal and combining it with the original signal at a small interval of delay. In doing so, the peaks and troughs of the original waveform meet with the peaks and troughs of the delayed copy at different points, creating a "comb filtering" effect as the combined signal goes in and out of phase. These types of modulation are accomplished by an LFO (low frequency oscillator) in modern processors. The durational interval at which the copied signal is combined with the original differentiates flangers from chorus effects.

A **flanger** features a very short delay (1–10ms) between the original and copied signals that gradually changes over time. Flanging was originally created by playing back a signal on two different tape machines while applying pressure to one of the machines' flanges. By varying the pressure placed on the copied signal's flange, the sound wave would filter through the frequencies of the original sound wave, creating a unique "swooshing" effect. Examples of flangers being used in rock music include Jimi Hendrix's "Bold as Love" and Lenny Kravitz's "Are You Gonna Go My Way."

Chorus effects, on the other hand, feature a constant delay duration that is between 10 and 20ms. Two famous examples of the chorus effect are the guitar parts to Nirvana's hit "Come As You Are" and Metallica's "Fade to Black."

Phasers work a little differently, as they possess "all-pass" filters that are set to filter certain frequencies before combining the copied signal with the original. Different frequencies are then delayed by varying amounts, causing some to be canceled while others are strengthened; this in turn produces harmonically unrelated peaks and troughs. Led Zeppelin's hit "Kashmir" is an example of a phase effect being used on a drum set, whereas Radiohead's more recent song "Paranoid Android" contains examples of a phaser being used on electric guitar parts.

Delay, echo, reverb, and modulation plugins can create interesting effects, determine the backward or forward placement of a signal within a mix, or manipulate the perceived acoustic space in which a mix exists. These effects, however, can easily be overused or underutilized. A mix with too much depth can feel distant or muddled, while a mix lacking in depth may sound dry and uninteresting. The strategy of mix referencing is, as always, the best solution when finding an appropriate level of depth in your own projects.

MIXING WORKFLOW STRATEGIES

WORKING WITH PRESETS

Most processors are preprogrammed to include a number of factory settings or **presets** that allow for quick, generic sound manipulations. These are usually accessible via drop-down menus within plugins. Advanced users often prefer not to use presets, but they may temporarily reference them to gain an understanding of how an effect may alter the sound of an audio signal when determining if a certain sonic direction might be beneficial. Most preset names are quite straightforward with respect to the effect they have on signals, aiding this process. For example, an EQ preset called "Brighten" would likely boost frequencies in the higher registers. If a preset improves the signal or mix but doesn't completely bring it to taste, the plugin may be altered from the preset state, and often saved within the DAW afterward to create a new, user-defined preset. Presets thus offer quick and easy solutions for beginning producers as well as starting points for advanced users to create their own signature sounds.

GROUPING VS. BUSSING TRACKS

When track counts become high, projects easily become cumbersome or unmanageable; thus, organizational techniques are essential. Two effective DAW functionalities related to session organization are track grouping and track busses. As the name implies, track grouping involves collecting designated tracks together into groups so that edits that are made to one track affect every track within the group. For example, a fader movement made on one grouped track will move the faders of all grouped tracks, which is an efficient workflow for multi-track volume changes (see Figure 15.13, which demonstrates a similar technique using volume automation and grouped tracks). Track groups also make it possible to edit multiple waveforms simultaneously, allowing for precise edit-point uniformity.

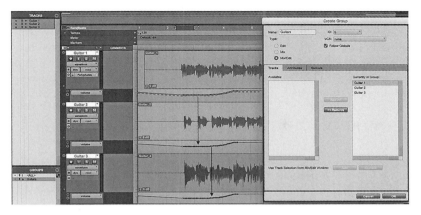

Changes made to one grouped track will affect all grouped tracks

Fig. 15.13   Volume automation applied to grouped tracks in Pro Tools 12

Moreover, this process allows an effect to be instantiated on all tracks within a group, simply by assigning that effect to a single grouped track. This doesn't allow for the management of individual track effects, however, since every added insert is duplicated across all grouped tracks. If a delay plugin were to be added to one track, for example, it would be simultaneously added to all tracks within the group. Track busses address this concern, allowing for greater control when batch processing signals. Once a collection of tracks is assigned to a bus, that bus moves a designated amount of signal from each of the assigned tracks to an aux track before arriving at the master fader. Effects inserts may then be added to the aux track in order to batch process all of the tracks being fed to it simultaneously (though the amount of signal being bussed from each individual track is customizable). A major benefit to this organization scheme is that each track assigned to a bus may possess its own individual effects inserts that do not affect any of the other tracks that are routed to the shared aux track. Figure 15.14 demonstrates both individual track effects and batch processing via track busses within Pro Tools 12.

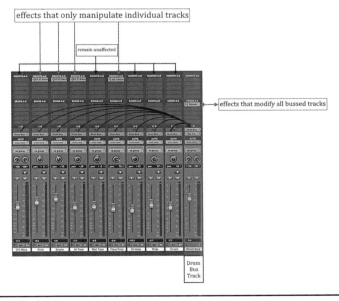

Fig. 15.14   Track busses in Pro Tools 12

The volume, width, and depth of your mix may all be adjusted by carefully manipulating parameters within the processors discussed thus far. Once all of your project's elements are contributing to a generally balanced and desirable mix, you are finally ready to "commit" and proceed to the next production stage within the DAW: the automation of volume and other parameters. At this point within your project's life cycle, it is advisable to create a separate copy of the session and retitle the file in a way that indicates its unfinished state. This will allow you to compare the developments made during both earlier and later stages of production with this preliminary mix of the project.

SUMMARY OF TERMS FROM CHAPTER 15

flutter echo	gain staging	pumping
acoustic treatment	audio continuum	gating
absorption	spectral processing	delay
acoustic foam	EQ sweeping	tap tempo
room modes	additive equalization	echo
bass traps	subtractive equalization	reverb
diffusion	complementary equalization	algorithmic reverb
near-field monitors	compression	convolution reverb
mid-field monitors	threshold	impulse responses
far-field monitors	ratio	modulation effects
active monitors	limiter	flanger
passive monitors	attack	phaser
single-amp	release	chorus
bi-amp	make-up gain	preset
tri-amp	multiband compressor	
pre-mix leveling	sidechaining	

CHAPTER 15—EXERCISES

True or False. Circle "true" for each statement below that is true. Circle "false" for each false statement.

1. Acoustic treatment is only found in high-end studios.

    True   False

2. For smaller studio rooms, diffusion is a requirement.

    True   False

3. A subwoofer is a required part of any project studio.

    True   False

4. When equalizing, it is typical to boost narrow and cut wide.

    True   False

5. Complementary equalization involves precisely matching the equalization of two instruments that possess similar frequency ranges.

    True   False

6. In the space below, specify why this speaker layout doesn't conform to the recommended arrangement described in this chapter.

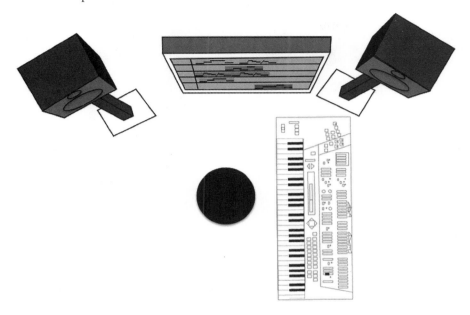

7. **Gain staging exercise.** In a DAW, create an audio signal. Then, follow the steps provided below.
    *   Open a level metering plugin and set the output of that signal so that there is -3dB of headroom.
    *   Duplicate the track.
    *   On the duplicated track, EQ to taste.
    *   On the duplicated track, compress the signal to taste.
    *   Mute the original track.
    *   Make adjustments to the EQ and compression outputs so that the duplicated track has a level of −3dB.
    *   Unmute the original track.
    *   Bounce both tracks separately so that your instructor is able to compare their levels.

8. In the space below, list the three components of the audio continuum, and provide two examples of processors that affect each component.

9. In the space below, describe if the parameters of the Logic Pro X compressor in the diagram below are set to compress or limit an incoming signal. Then, explain the differences between compression and limiting.

10. **Sidechain exercise.** In a DAW of your choice, create a session featuring four MIDI tracks, a sample rate of 48.1kHz, and a 24-bit bit depth. Then, follow the steps provided below.

   • Set up a session that is in $\frac{4}{4}$ at a tempo of 130bpm.

   • Create a kick drum pattern consisting of four quarter notes per bar. Copy and paste that bar so that it lasts for 16 bars. Choose an electronic kick patch for the channel.

   • Create a snare part consisting of two quarter notes on beats 2 and 4; again copy and paste the pattern so that it lasts for 16 bars. Choose an electronic snare patch for the channel.

   • Create a hi-hat pattern made up of eighth notes; copy and paste it so that it lasts for 16 bars. Choose an appropriate hi-hat patch for the channel.

   • Compose a 4-bar electric bass pattern that features the exclusive use of eighth notes and outlines a I—vi—IV—iv progression in the key of C major. Copy and paste the pattern so that it lasts 16 bars. Choose an electric bass patch for the channel.

   • Route the kick drum so that it triggers a compressor that is added to the bass channel (a sidechain).

   • Set the compressor so that a pumping effect is achieved.

   • Bounce an audio file from the session that includes all four tracks, and submit it to your instructor.

11. **Complementary equalization exercise.** Using a copy of the session from the previous sidechain exercise, complete the following:

   • Bypass the compression setting on the bass track.

   • Create complementary equalization between the kick and bass tracks.

   • Bounce an audio file from the session that includes all four tracks. Submit the audio file to your instructor along with a screenshot of both equalizers demonstrating the complementary equalization you applied.

Chapter 16
Final Mix Considerations

The final stages of a mix are crucial for the success of an overall project and represent the finishing touches that characterize professional work. These stages involve enhancing depth and width with advanced processing, applying final automation decisions across all parameters, and developing the master chain. Basic depth and width considerations were explored in Chapter 15, but a more advanced concept known as psychoacoustic processing merits additional attention.

PSYCHOACOUSTIC PROCESSING

Psychoacoustic processing has been around since the mid-1970s and has provided many interesting effects for producers to use. **Psychoacoustic processing** is a technique used to "excite" or "enhance" a dull-sounding audio signal by adding synthesized harmonics. Psychoacoustic processors are generally called **exciters** or **enhancers** for this reason, and they add brightness—sometimes referred to as "sparkle"—to an audio signal. There are a number of different methods that are used to create brightness in a mix via psychoacoustic processing, though the first enhancer, called the "Aural Exciter" (which was developed by a company called Aphex in 1975), operated under a specific, three-step process. First, the Aural Exciter high-pass filtered anything above a specified threshold setting; then, a small amount of distortion was added to the signal, adding high-frequency harmonics; finally, the dry (unaffected) signal was then mixed to taste with the wet (affected) signal.

Other psychoacoustic processors work by applying **dynamic equalization**, which is similar to compression in that specified frequencies become attenuated when they pass a volume threshold set by the user. **Low-frequency enhancement** is possible, too, and there are a number of techniques employed by different plugin manufacturers to this end. One technique involves adding higher harmonics to a signal that may or may not have been present to begin with; in doing so, the listener's brain perceives a fundamental below the added harmonics, even if it does not actually exist. Another method used to create low-frequency enhancement is the addition of synthesized sub-harmonic frequencies below a fundamental pitch. The addition of these very low frequencies doesn't typically create unwanted sound, as the added tones generally exist below the threshold of audible frequencies; the added tones thus create an effect that is more felt than heard.

Stereo image enhancement is yet another form of psychoacoustic processing; it creates a sound field that is perceived to be wider than it really is. Most stereo image processing tools work by means of phase shifting and MS processing, named after the MS recording technique discussed in Chapter 14. MS processing divides the information within a stereo signal into two distinct areas: the middle (M) and the side (S). Widening via phase shifting involves sending sound from one area slightly before or after it is sent from the other; the resultant delay creates a widening effect. This effect should be used sparingly, though, as phase issues and loss of definition are possible. Stereo enhancers are thus typically used on aux tracks housing the signals of certain instruments (e.g., guitars), while stereo field manipulation is otherwise controlled via panning on individual channels.

Importantly, though, panning may be automated (along with other aspects of a mix such as volume, effects, and instrument plugin parameters), breathing interest and life into a project. Automating panning and effects busses can substantially reshape the depth of a mix throughout time, while subtle alterations of volume can provide nuance, detail, and narrative trajectory.

VOLUME AUTOMATION

Automation was first introduced in Chapter 8 in the context of controlling MIDI parameters, but volume automation is also exceedingly common in audio production. Once a basic set of levels has been established (and equalization and compression at the individual track and bus levels are in place), a project is ready for the automation process. Importantly, automation is used to create nuance via the subtle attenuation or boosting of signals; compressors tend to mitigate more substantial volume changes, so more minor alterations that do not result in overcompression are typical. Compression therefore handles the broader framework of volume editing, leaving the refined, detailed work to the automation process.

In the past, projects that required multiple volume changes over time necessitated numerous real-time fader movements, which needed to be coordinated into a recorded performance. Engineers often had to enlist the help of assistants or even band members to manually move faders during a recording for this purpose. Luckily, modern DAWs allow a single producer to accomplish what once required multiple people. When automation is enabled, most DAWs present lines or lanes that represent the volume of a track over time. Automation curves within these lanes can be compared to the effects of *crescendo* and *decrescendo* symbols in music notation, though there is an important difference. By raising and lowering the volume of certain tracks, velocity levels and/or timbres aren't affected; thus, passages that were performed at a *pp* dynamic level will not sound as if they were performed at a *ff* dynamic level simply by raising the volume via automation. The effect will instead be that of a soft performance that happens to be played back at a louder volume. As true intensity levels of a performance cannot be easily fixed with automation, then, passages with incorrect dynamic levels should be re-recorded. However, passages that are intentionally recorded at *pp* levels and then boosted via compression and volume automation can maintain an intimate atmosphere while focusing the attention of the listener on specific passages of music. For vocals, volume automation can also enhance the intelligibility of certain syllables; this is achieved by increasing the volume during moments when specific vowels or consonants are unclear.

Automation for instrument tracks is also essential. For example, a guitar part featuring a hook might be automated to have an increased volume level right before a vocal part enters. Once the vocals enter, the guitar part can then be lowered so that the vocals stand out without struggling to be heard over the guitar part. Professional producers consistently shape the volume of all parts within a mix using automation in this manner, so that the dominant features of each section are heard clearly and the supportive elements do not overpower them. Figure 16.1 provides a screenshot of a mix featuring volume automation in Pro Tools 12. This example focuses on the transitional link section between the chorus and bridge of Daniel McIntyre's "Sunken Sally," a production library track that has been used in several national sports broadcasts. Note the purpose of the volume changes near the link section: the drums are boosted significantly, while the bass and guitar parts are either attenuated, faded out, or taken out entirely to create a typical "break down section" feel.

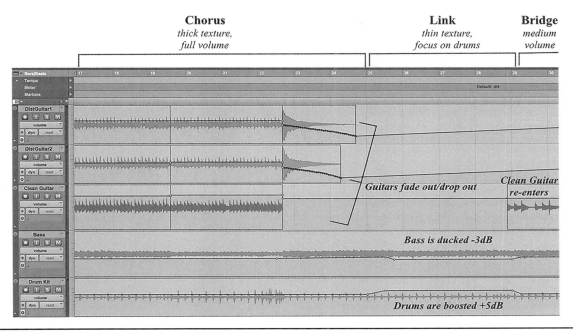

Fig. 16.1 Volume automation in McIntyre, "Sunken Sally" (Pro Tools 12)

AUTOMATION OF TIME-BASED EFFECTS

The depth of a mix may be automated as well, as adjusting the amount of reverb or delay over time can create the illusion of backward and forward movement relative to the listener. Automating time-based effects in this manner can take an element that is perceived to be in the background during a verse and bring it to the foreground during the chorus, for example. The automation of a time-based effect (or, indeed, any effect) that involves a send to an effects bus may be accomplished in one of two ways: the automation of the send knob on an individual channel basis, or the automation of the aux track's fader (which affects all signals being fed to it). While the automation of an aux track fader may help in shaping multiple elements of a mix with one move, there is a risk of oversaturating the project with one effect. Automation involving individual bus sends on a per-channel basis, then, provides a more controlled method of applying effects. Automation lanes in most DAWs allow the user to select from among many possible parameters, including the bus send level (see Figure 16.2, which illustrates this process in Logic Pro X). The white line running left to right on the grid represents the automation of the send level for the selected track. In this case, reverb is being added incrementally to a piano track, creating the illusion that the instrument is being moved farther away from the listener.

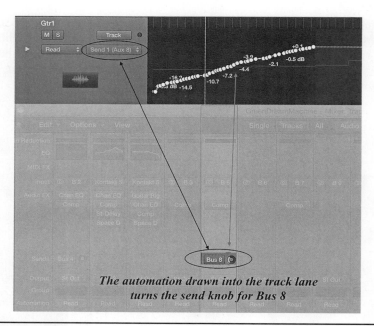

The automation drawn into the track lane turns the send knob for Bus 8

Fig. 16.2   Send level automation in Logic Pro X

The concept of gain staging that was introduced in Chapter 15 continues to be relevant during the automation process. It is wise to limit the master output volume to -6dB to allow for a conservative amount of headroom, which may be used by the mastering engineer during the final stages of the project's life cycle.

MIX STEMS

Before a project is sent to a mastering engineer, however, mix stems are often needed. A **mix stem** is a group of audio signals that are fed into a single aux track in order to help with the global organization of a project while allowing for simple batch processing. It is very common for television, video game, and other media productions to require "printed" or bounced stems in lieu of—or in addition to—a full mix; the stems are then combined together at a later date. Orchestral stems are generally organized by instrument sections, so violins, violas, cellos, and double basses would be stemmed together into a single "strings" stem; other orchestral stems include the brass, woodwinds, and percussion. Pop mixes often feature a stem for drums and percussion, a second stem that includes all guitars, keyboards and bass parts, a third stem for background vocals, and a fourth and final stem for lead vocals. When all of a mix's elements are appropriately balanced and logically "stemmed," the project is ready for mastering.

MASTERING AND THE MASTER CHAIN

While self-mastering is becoming more and more common, a mix should be sent to a specialized mastering engineer any time that the budget allows for it. Mastering engineers generally make subtle, final touches to a complete mix in order to make it conform to a number of parameters and industry standards. Equalization, for example, is used in a sparing and judicious manner to manipulate the entirety of the track during mastering, while it may be used more liberally during the mixing process to affect individual signals or groups of signals. Subtler, global changes to the sound of a project are therefore reserved for mastering, while more substantial, local changes are reserved for mixing. If major changes are being considered during the mastering process, the mix should be revisited.

Mastering—involves addressing—though not necessarily altering—five primary categories related to a mix, which are listed below.

Enrichment—Enhancing dynamics and stereo image perception.

Noise reduction—Addressing audio defects (e.g., low-end hum, pops, etc.), often using special mastering software.

Continuity—Editing all tracks within a single project (e.g., an album) in order to establish similarities in volume level and sound quality.

Metadata and ISRC—Embedding pertinent information into the digital file for each track. This typically includes the composition title, the artist/composer, the copyright information, and a unique identifier known as an ISRC (International Standard Recording Code).

Deliverables—Meeting established criteria related to the final recording submission (e.g., sample rate, bit depth, file format, etc.).

THE MASTER CHAIN

When self-mastering mixes in their project studios, producers employ a **master chain**, which is a series of plugins that is added to the DAW's master output. The enrichment stage of mastering, which is related to dynamics and image perception, takes place within the master chain. While there is not a universally accepted standard collection or ordering of plugins involved in a master chain, there are tools that tend to be present in most master chains. These oft-used tools address the following processes, which tend to take place in the provided order: (gain), equalization, single-band compression, (multiband compression), (tape saturation), (imaging/mid-side equalization), limiting, and level metering (note that parentheses around processes indicate that they are somewhat less standard). Figure 16.3 provides an annotated screenshot of a master chain in Logic Pro X that features three third-party plugins: Waves's Renaissance Compressor (single-band compression) and L1 Ultramaximizer (limiting), as well as FabFilter's Saturn (tape saturation/distortion).

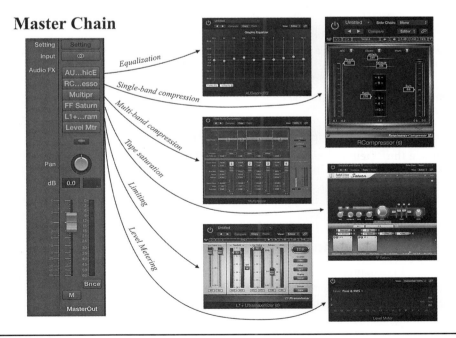

Fig. 16.3 A master chain in Logic Pro X

The Master Chain: Gain

As discussed earlier in this chapter, it is typical to maintain a good amount of headroom during the mixing process. In a master chain, a simple gain plugin is used to increase a mix's level before further processing, which uses up some of the provided headroom. Boosting signals to occupy leftover headroom may also be accomplished via make-up gain within compressors and (especially) limiters, but this can result in a dynamically flat or thin sound when overdone, despite the added loudness. It is therefore recommended to begin a master chain with a gain plugin; limiting should only be used to add a few decibels at the end of the mastering process to make up for any remaining headroom.

The Master Chain: Equalization

Equalization added at this late stage should be applied very conservatively, so as to avoid any major impact to the overall sound of the project. (Remember that mastering involves subtle alterations, with more substantial adjustments reserved for mixing.) Typically, EQ added to the master chain is either corrective (if there is a very slight issue with a particular frequency band) or in service to consistency (if there are several tracks that need to share a particular sonic signature). As discussed in Chapter 15, the practice of boosting wide and cutting narrow should still be followed in this equalization context.

The Master Chain: Single-Band Compression

The purpose of a single-band compressor in the context of a master chain is to unify all of the elements within a mix by processing them collectively using the same plugin. Single-band compression in this context is thus an "adhesive" tool that is used to metaphorically "glue" the various pieces of a mix together. As with other processing involved in a master chain, compression should be applied sparingly; the compressor's virtual gain reduction meter should show minimal movement.

The Master Chain: Multiband Compression

In a master chain, a multiband compressor allows for compression to be applied uniquely to specific frequency ranges, which may prevent overuse of the effect. If only a small region within the frequency spectrum requires compression, a multiband compressor is an appropriate choice, as it is flexible enough to precisely shape the small area without affecting the entirety of the mix.

The Master Chain: Tape Saturation

Tape saturation is a type of psychoacoustic processing that involves adding a small amount of digital distortion to a signal, which in turn generates high-frequency harmonics that provide a sound similar to that of a tape recording. As discussed in Chapter 15, it is common to boost or "push" signals during analog recording to make up for low-level hiss or other unwanted audible sounds that are caused by tape recorders. As signals are pushed, the analog gear produces signals that are often described as sounding "warm." In a digital context, signals will clip if pushed too hard; thus, tape saturation plugins offer a modern solution for achieving the warmth that characterizes analog recording without producing any clipping in the DAW.

The Master Chain: Imaging and Mid-Side Equalization

As discussed earlier in this chapter, imaging involves manipulating the perceived width of a mix through phase shifting or MS processing. For example, a project can be made to sound wider by perceptually expanding the stereo image, while MS equalization adds the ability to filter specific areas within the image without processing the entire signal. Stereo imaging should be approached with great caution, however, as the clarity of a mix can easily be degraded using this type of processing—particularly within the center of the stereo field, which typically hosts important, focal material. As such, many producers do not include stereo imaging plugins as part of their master chains, instead using these processors during the mixing phase (where more specifically tailored stereo manipulations may take place solely at the instrument or group level).

The Master Chain: Limiting

Limiting may be the most important stage of a master chain. It is used to boost a project's overall signal level while preventing the output from clipping. It is recommended to place a limiter in the penultimate position within the ordering of master chain plugins; however, the limiter should be the first plugin added to the chain. Put differently, the signal should flow through gain, equalization, compression, and any other added processing before hitting the limiter, but the limiter should be added to the master chain before anything else in order to prevent clipping. While opinions do vary regarding the position of certain plugins within the flow of a master chain, the use of a limiter at or near the end of the chain is rarely debated. As with all processing in the context of mastering, limiting should remain subtle, adding only a few dB to make up for any leftover headroom.

The Master Chain: Level Metering

A level meter should be the final plugin of any master chain, and it should be carefully monitored throughout the mastering process. The faders on a level meter are based on **dBFS**, which stands for "decibels relative to full scale." This relative scale orients the producer to the maximum output level, 0dBFS, at which clipping may occur. A signal that is -6dBFS is therefore 6dB below the point at which clipping may occur. A level meter typically turns red as a signal moves past 0dBFS, indicating that the output level of a track, group of tracks, or plugin is too high and needs to be adjusted.

Importantly, most modern DAWs allow users to save an entire master chain as a preset that can be used as a template for mastering. These user-defined, multi-plugin presets promote efficient, organized workflows and additionally allow users to easily manage the continuity of multi-track projects that may require several sessions.

MASTERING SUITES

Some pieces of software are designed to combine all of the processing involved in mastering into a single **mastering suite**. While there are several mastering suites on the market, iZotope's Ozone 7 has become an industry standard, allowing higher-quality productions to be accomplished in home studios. Ozone 7 may be used as a standalone program (allowing the user to focus solely on mastering with "fresh ears," outside of the DAW environment), or as a plugin that can be applied directly to the master chain of a project within a DAW (creating a more efficient workflow). Whether in standalone or plugin mode, Ozone 7 and other mastering plugins offer gain matching functionality for comparison purposes. **Gain matching** allows the user to bypass any processing that is added during the mastering phase while boosting the signal to a level equal to that of the processed mix. This allows the producer to impartially evaluate whether the addition of processing has actually improved the mix's quality (as the false impression of improvement often results from the presentation of a mix at a louder volume).

NOISE REDUCTION

Often, compression and EQ plugins raise the volume of the **noise floor**, or base level of unavoidable background noise that is created by the various electronics participating in a mix environment. The noise floor can be easily lowered via **noise reduction**—the process of eliminating clicks, hums, clips, and other unwanted noises from a mix. There are many industry-standard noise-reduction software tools on the market today, including iZotope's RX6, Waves's W43 Noise Reduction, and Sonnox Restore—all of which are designed to address the unwanted artifacts found in otherwise well-produced projects.

METADATA AND ISRC

Metadata is digitally encoded information about a piece of music, such as the artist(s) involved in its creation. Although it is not necessary, it is recommended to use a software program that adds metadata to audio files, especially in the context of an album; embedding metadata is important for exposure and royalty collection, and the required software is low in cost and readily available. Another consideration is to acquire an ISRC, or International Standard Recording Code. An **ISRC** is a unique code that is generated to function like a digital fingerprint in identifying a specific recording of a piece of music. Anyone using an audio file that features properly embedded metadata and an ISRC will be able to identify its creator(s) and other pertinent copyright information via the display window in a media player, thus promoting international exposure while assuring that royalties are distributed properly.

DELIVERABLES

The final stage in the mastering process—whether the project is handled by a mastering engineer or self-mastered by the producer—regards the delivery medium. It is critical to check with the client or distributer to get all deliverable requirements before taking any steps at this stage. Generally, most digital distributors accept CD-quality WAV files, which are 16-bit WAV files with a sample rate of 44.1kHz. Some distributors, however, are beginning to accept 24-bit WAV files at sample rates higher than 44.1kHz. One benefit of higher-quality files is that they may be converted to lower-quality formats, such as a WAV file being converted to a compressed MP3 file. While this results in some quality loss, "up-converting" a lower-quality file to a higher-quality format does not actually increase quality at all. As such, it is advised to export mastered deliverables at the highest resolution acceptable for the format in which it will be distributed.

Though mastering itself requires five separate processes and can be quite involved, it represents the final stage in the life cycle of a music production. This chapter has been devoted to this final step, with the previous three incorporating the earlier stages of session and room setup, live recording, editing, mixing, and processing. While the subsequent chapters in this book address the integration of composition and production topics in the specific context of music for media, understand that the essential techniques covered throughout Part II will allow you to create professional-quality productions in any musical setting.

SUMMARY OF TERMS FROM CHAPTER 16

psychoacoustic processing
exciter
enhancer
dynamic equalization
low-frequency enhancement
stereo image enhancement

mix stems
mastering
master chain
tape saturation
dBFS
mastering suite

gain matching
noise floor
noise reduction
metadata
ISRC

CHAPTER 16—EXERCISES

True or False. Circle "true" for each statement below that is true. Circle "false" for each false statement.

1. The two most common psychoacoustic processors are enhancers and enrichers.

    True   False

2. Low-frequency enhancement may be applied by adding high harmonics or sub-harmonic frequencies.

    True   False

3. Panning is usually accomplished on aux tracks, while stereo enhancers tend to reside on the individual track level.

    True   False

4. Mix stems for pop/rock recordings typically feature a stem for vocals, a stem for drums and percussion, a stem for guitars and basses, and a stem for keyboards.

    True   False

5. **Automation Exercise.** Realize the following notated excerpt from Mozart's Symphony No. 14 in A Major as a four-track MIDI production within a DAW of your choice, using volume automation to approximate the changes in dynamics that are indicated by the score. When you are finished, bounce an audio file from the session that includes all four tracks. Submit the audio file to your instructor along with a screenshot of the automation lanes within the DAW's arrange window demonstrating the automation you applied.

6. In the space below, describe why the volume automation used in the previous exercise cannot realistically reproduce the score's dynamic changes in the same manner as live performers. What other type(s) of editing would need to be involved to aid in a more realistic recreation?

7. In the space below, describe the spatial effect that is created by automating a gradual decrease in the send level of an instrument track into an aux track that contains a reverb insert. How does this automation affect the perceived distance between the listener and the instrument?

8. In the space below, list the following effects in the order in which they typically appear within a master chain: equalization, limiting, tape saturation, multiband compression, single-band compression, gain, level metering, imaging.

9. In the space below, describe one advantage and one disadvantage of sending a project to be mastered professionally (instead of self-mastering in the DAW using a master chain).

PART III
PRODUCING MUSIC FOR MEDIA

Chapter 17
The Client/Composer Relationship

The music industry is just as much about personal relationships and business acumen as it is about musical skill. One of the most important talents a composer can have, for example, is the ability to make connections and maintain relationships so that they blossom into sustained business interactions. Every person that you meet in the industry has the potential to be an individual in a position to launch your career (or at least be one or two people removed from such an individual). As such, this chapter will briefly explore some practical steps you may take to develop relationships and business techniques to begin—and maintain—a career in the music business.

INTERPERSONAL SKILLS

SMALL TALK

It may seem quaint, but the ability to initiate and sustain a conversation with someone you have never met is an extremely important skill for a successful composer to have. It is therefore wise to stay informed and possess at least a rudimentary knowledge of current events. Conversations about sports are often good "small talk" icebreakers, but they should be approached cautiously, as some sports fans are legitimately turned off by people who do not support their favorite teams (or support their favorite teams' rivals). The same can be said about discussions of politics, though these conversations are far riskier, as they can quickly turn into emotionally charged debates with certain clients. While it is therefore advised to "play it safe" and engage in small talk that is centered on relatively benign subjects, such discussions quickly begin to feel stale, awkward, and impersonal as time progresses and should therefore only be used to introduce more meaningful topics; indeed, conversations should be quickly directed toward common interests—especially musical ones—as soon as they become apparent. For example, if a client mentions that she plays guitar or another instrument that you play for a living, this represents a fantastic opportunity to continue the conversation. The key to initial exchanges with clients is to get them talking about things they enjoy and are passionate about, contributing to the discussions in meaningful ways while always being cognizant of the place that music may have in the conversations. This strategy may seem cold and calculated, but a client will be more likely to contact you for work if he or she enjoys talking with you. In other words, you need to sell yourself before you can sell your music. Even if the conversation does not immediately yield a contract or "gig," you may end up making a friend—and most friends take care of each other professionally when they are able. Achievement in the industry is thus directly related to the number of strong, positive relationships one has; friendships go a long way in the field, and one can never have too many of them.

NETWORKING

Developing contacts and relationships requires as much energy and attention as making music. Freelance work, in particular, requires an artist to look far ahead into the future to ensure that the amount of time that goes by without a paying gig is as small as possible. A freelance composer should ideally strive to have gigs lined up six months into the future. Thus, whenever you are not actively working on a project, you should be seeking out new relationships and looking for the next job (or the job after that). That said, let the quality of your work be your primary networking tool. Each successfully completed project will almost always lead to more work if the product is exemplary. Indeed, if past clients are happy with your music and enjoyed working with you, they are more likely to call you for their next projects *and* more likely to recommend you to other clients in need of your skill set.

The Freelance Tree

Thus, a freelance composer's career may be thought of as being similar to a tree, with its roots representing early contacts and gigs, its trunk representing career-launching mentors and opportunities, and its branches signifying additional contacts and jobs. Early opportunities help composers establish themselves in the industry. These early projects do not often generate much income, but they do help legitimize their abilities in the eyes of more reputable connections. Composers' careers are established, however, through the people and opportunities that are signified by the trunk of the tree, which is, of course, the thickest part of the tree that supports all of the branches. These connections are the metaphorical center—though not necessarily the chronological center—of composers' careers, as connections made at this level often result in clients who will grow with them over substantial periods of time, generating a series of job opportunities. There are many famous examples of sustained client/composer relationships in film and multimedia. Director Steven Spielberg and composer John Williams are a particularly famous case: they have collaborated on several film projects over a decades-long span following the release of *Jaws* in 1975. Director M. Night Shyamalan and composer James Newton Howard share a similar relationship, as do director J. J. Abrams and composer Michael Giacchino. It is advised that you research these and other similar client/composer relationships, attending in particular to how these famous artists evolved over multiple projects with the same director, honing their voices and sharpening their expressive abilities.

The career "limbs" that follow in the freelance tree metaphor all stem from recommendations generated within the trunk; similarly, the branches stem from recommendations originating within each limb, and so on. Figure 17.1 illustrates this type of growth in important clients and opportunities in the career of Don Davis, a successful film composer most famous for his score to *The Matrix* trilogy (among other films). The figure does not represent Davis's entire artistic output; rather, it provides a career overview, showing how his education and orchestration skills led to early composition opportunities that in turn led to more established connections and more substantial composition projects. The early orchestration gigs represent the roots of Davis's career and served as "proof of concept" that demonstrated his ability to successfully complete work. These opportunities were successes, making it easier for clients at a higher level in the industry to trust in Davis's professionalism, which in turn yielded higher-paying work with more exposure that corresponds with the trunk of his freelance tree. Names of important directors with whom Davis has fostered sustained creative relationships are provided in bold print within Figure 17.1.

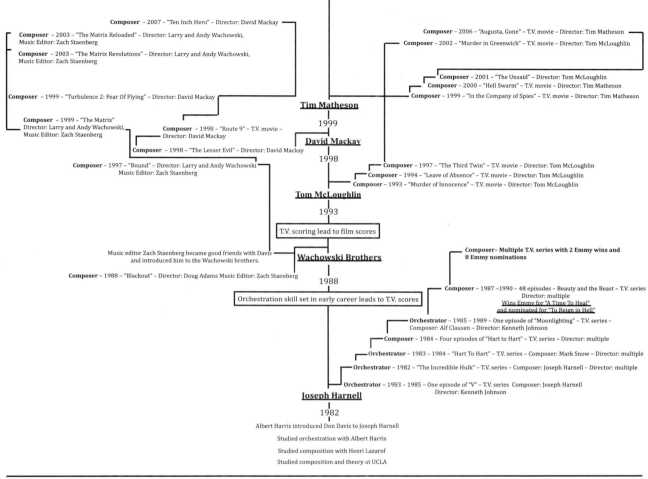

Fig. 17.1   Career overview of Don Davis

As this figure demonstrates, success sometimes comes from impressing the right teachers. Davis studied orchestration with Albert Harris, who later introduced him to composer Joseph Harnell. This important link in turn provided Davis with several valuable orchestration opportunities, including work for the 1982 television series *The Incredible Hulk*. After years of proving his worth as an orchestrator, Davis was able to fulfill his aspirations and attain a new phase in his career as a film and television composer. Davis's career soon flourished, as he garnered two Emmy awards and eight nominations for television scores, and he provided incredible, memorable film scores for projects such as *The Matrix* trilogy and the award-winning *Bound*.

LEVERAGING PERIPHERAL SKILLS

Many successful media composers began their careers in specialized areas, serving as orchestrators, sound design artists, post-production engineers, performers, etc. Any of these peripheral skill sets have the potential to open doors and make connections in the realm of composition, particularly when success is demonstrated in these other areas. Herbert W. Spencer is another example of a noteworthy composer who, like Don Davis, spent a substantial portion of his career orchestrating the music of other artists, including many of John Williams's high-profile film scores such as *E.T. the Extra-Terrestrial* and the original *Star Wars* and *Indiana Jones* trilogies. While you should devote the majority of your time to refining your composition and production skills, it is advised that you maintain your other industry-related interests, as they may ultimately serve your composition endeavors in addition to being fulfilling on their own.

BUSINESS SKILLS

MAINTAINING A WEB PRESENCE

The importance of maintaining an Internet and social media presence cannot be stressed enough in the composition field. Facebook, Twitter, and LinkedIn are just a few current examples of social media sites that composers use ubiquitously. Generally speaking, media composers in today's industry should plan to invest the time needed to update all social media platforms a minimum of once per week. Not all social media posts need to be industry related, however; composers, after all, need to sell themselves as individuals first and musicians second.

Working composers must also maintain professional-looking, easy-to-navigate websites that demonstrate their skill sets, enumerate past and current projects, and, crucially, provide contact information. Personal pictures are generally kept to a minimum on composition websites, though a few well-chosen and well-placed images can go a long way toward establishing the composer's personality and artistic identity. While website images—which are often headshots taken by trained photographers—tend to be professional in nature, showing one's personal side can make a composer seem more approachable.

UNDERSTANDING THE COMPOSER'S ROLE IN THE PROJECT

There are many facets to the music business, and the roles of artists differ dramatically depending on the subfield within which they work. A pop star, for example, must know the target demographic of his or her genre and cater to the current trends within that area of the industry. In this case, the client is the collective group of people who purchase records and attend live concerts. While it is always important for commercial musicians to maintain a degree of integrity regardless of their chosen artistic subfield, it is equally important for them to satisfy their clients. In the world of media composition, the role of the composer is significantly more restricted, as the principal task when creating a sonic brand, trailer, production track, or film score is to unwaveringly support someone else's vision. If, for example, a client requests "dark" music that lasts for 45 seconds with a "sting" (musical emphasis) at 30 seconds, then that is precisely what the composer needs to create. Often, clients will provide reference tracks on which composers are to model their ideas. In a sense, the client is truly the composer in these situations, and the composer is the medium through which the client's ideas pass in order to bring them to fruition in a professional and artful manner. Most clients will tolerate (and even appreciate) composers who add their own artistic voices to media projects, but deviating substantially from the project specifications (or "spec") is always a poor decision. Indeed, composers with business acumen understand that the priority is to satisfy the client (and do so to the extent that future recommendations and gigs may result from the experience) while creating work they can be proud of; these goals need not be mutually exclusive.

It is also crucial to understand the hierarchy at play in every project, especially when the client is a team of individuals (such as a business). Directors, producers, and—in the case of video games—developers tend to be the individuals that make final choices related to the appropriateness of media compositions. However, while they may love particular composition submissions, music editors generally do not factor into final musical decisions. As such, it is imperative to learn early on whose vision you are truly supporting in a media project. With multiple opinions and ideas at play, a composition gig can become overly complicated and frustration will tend to follow. Simplifying this process as much as possible through clear communication will help avoid such issues; knowing who has the final say when dealing with a collective client allows you to strategize and move forward more efficiently.

MUSICAL SKILLS

REFERENCE TRACKS

The ability to emulate a reference track is extremely important in the field of commercial composition. If a client provides a reference track in a country style, for example, and the composer responds with a submission that features techno characteristics, the composer will likely lose the gig and not be paid. Part of the modern producer's skill set is therefore the ability to extract the essence of a piece of music and employ it in a similar-sounding work without illegally copying the source material. Indeed, as a fine—and continuously moving—line exists between copying a work and creating an original, yet audibly influenced, work, it behooves composers and artists to familiarize themselves with current copyright statutes and recent infringement cases.

A famous example that represents a composer's success in handling a reference track is John Williams's *Star Wars* score. As mentioned in Chapter 12, Steven Spielberg used Gustav Holst's *The Planets* as a temp track for the film. (Temp tracks, which are recordings of existing works that are temporarily used to score scenes and convey the atmospheric support that is desired for the composer to provide, are compiled by music editors and often include multiple pieces of music; these pieces are typically chosen from film scores whose rights are owned by the studio producing the project.) John Williams brilliantly captured the essence of *The Planets*—especially the "Mars" movement—in an original way, creating a classic score that is still used in more recent *Star Wars* movies.

REVISIONS

No matter how well a reference track is handled in the creation of an initial submission for a particular project, though, most clients do suggest revisions to first drafts upon reviewing them. Revision notes can be as simple as a request for an added cymbal hit at a specific time point or as complex as a complete rewrite. Regardless, prompt and strict adherence to revision requests is key for your success as a media composer. Most of the time, revisions are minimal to moderate, assuming that appropriate attention has been given to all notes and reference tracks in the formation of the initial submission. Sometimes, however, it takes a few drafts for a client to arrive at a clear understanding of what they truly want to hear. This can be extremely frustrating, but it is a reality of the industry; asking specific questions that require clear communication on behalf of the client often aids in avoiding such a drawn-out revision process. It may seem difficult, especially during the earlier stages of your career, to alter any part of a piece of music into which you poured so much energy, passion, and detail. Mature composers understand, though, that success is only achieved when both the client and the composer are satisfied; the client ultimately has the final say regarding what will and will not work for a project.

The music industry is an ever-changing, complex world that may at first seem unapproachable from the surface. However, you should feel empowered knowing that many of the most famous media composers came from humble beginnings (often engaging in specialized, limited, uncredited projects), and that career-launching opportunities are often only friendly conversation away.

Chapter 18
Scoring for Short-Form Media

In recent years, the field of "film scoring" has expanded to include so many different areas that it is more appropriate to refer to the act of creating supporting dramatic music as scoring for media. Music for media refers to any composition that is designed to support the dramatic atmosphere of any medium, and the creation of music for media includes production track writing, scoring for television and radio commercials, film scoring, video game scoring, and more. Music for media is thus all around us; wherever there is technology, there is generally a need for music to operate within and through that technology, from tablets to smartphones, wearable devices, and beyond. Accordingly, there are many opportunities for composers to be active within the media scoring sector, and it represents an excellent place to find work—and even base a career—within the industry. Project studios hold an especially important position in this area of the music business, as even the higher-budget projects usually begin within them.

SESSION PREPARATION FOR VIDEO SCORING

The first step involved in scoring for media is to manipulate settings within the DAW so that it can play back video and sync with newly composed music. This stage of the production process is usually referred to as "session prep," short for DAW session preparation. The most common video format that clients provide to composers in media scoring situations is QuickTime, which offers multiple settings to which the session must conform. As such, a common initial step in preparing a scoring project is ascertaining the frame rate, sample rate, and bit depth of a QuickTime video file; this should be done before opening the DAW.

FRAME RATE, SAMPLE RATE, AND TIMECODE

The first step toward this end is to determine the frame rate or FPS of the file. **FPS** stands for frames per second and indicates the number of still images that are presented within the duration of a second in a video. The frame rate determines the perceived "fluidity" or naturalness of a motion picture, so a higher FPS will appear more realistic than a lower frame rate. In videos, frames are **interlaced**, or divided into odd and even partitions of alternating, horizontal lines, which are called fields. The first field presents the odd divisions of an image and the second field presents its even counterparts. The fields are then played back-to-back at a rate that is so fast that the mind perceives the alternating images to be joined into a singular, complete frame. To avoid interference, television stations have based frame rates on electrical standards. In the United States, for example, 60Hz is the standard alternating current frequency, and so a rate of 60 interlaced fields per second (or 30 FPS) became the standard. Similarly, the electrical standard throughout most of Europe is 50Hz, so 25 FPS became the standard in those nations. Without interlacing, the images appeared to have phasing issues with the electrical current, causing the picture to wobble back and forth. In 1953, the National Television Standards Committee (**NTSC**) was established in the United States, and a new standard FPS rate was put into effect in order to compensate for the added color carrier signal in television, which created phasing issues with the audio carrier signal. To compensate for this unwanted interference, frame rates were slightly lowered, by .03 FPS; the result was the current NTSC standard (which is followed in the U.S., Japan, and many other countries) of 29.97 FPS.

As technology progressed, video producers needed a way of labeling each discrete frame to allow for more detailed editing capabilities. In the 1960s, **SMPTE timecode** (named after the Society of Motion Picture and Television Engineers) was adopted, which presented two detailed duration labeling options for both 29.97 FPS and 30 FPS videos. Both options, called drop frame and non-drop frame, present timecode in hours, minutes, seconds, and frames—HH:MM:SS;FF and HH:MM:SS:FF, respectively. Aside from the semicolon separating the seconds and frames in drop frame timecode, both timecode options appear to be the same; however, they are in fact different, and the distinction is important. For **drop frame** timecode, 00 and 01 are dropped from the counting scheme for every minute (except when the minute number is divisible by ten); this periodic skipping of timecode seconds addresses the disparity between the timecode (which runs at 30 FPS) and the NTSC video (which runs at 29.97 FPS). It is important to note that no frames are altered or dropped in the video, despite the name "drop frame"; what is dropped is simply the numbers within the timecode to compensate for the slower frame rate.

Fig. 18.1 SMPTE timecode within a Pro Tools 12 session

Interlaced formats are standard for video/television broadcasts, while **progressive-scan** formats are standard for film. Film is typically shot at 24 FPS, though progressive-scan formats are expressed by the lone letter *p*; accordingly, film that includes 24 non-interlaced frames per second is labeled as 24p. Higher frame rates are possible, and these provide even smoother motion. Regardless of the format used, composers must check the FPS rate to ensure that their DAWs remains in sync with the videos they are scoring.

SCORING WITH QUICKTIME VIDEOS IN THE DAW

In the past, composers needed to set up complicated syncing schemes to ensure that their DAWs would work properly with the videos they were scoring. In today's industry, however, videos are delivered as QuickTime files, which play back at the same frame rate as the source material. Thus, composers using these files simply need to check the settings within QuickTime and match their DAW session preferences to adhere to the video's parameters before importing the file; this process will result in a successfully synced session. The following list provides a summary of the steps that need to be taken in order to properly set up a scoring session with QuickTime video. (To find the frame rate [in FPS] and sample rate [in kHz] of a QuickTime video, open the file within a video player and search for an "inspector" or "information" menu item. In QuickTime Player, for instance, the pertinent menu item is *Show Movie Inspector*.)

- Note the frame rate of the QuickTime video (24p is the standard).
- Note the sample rate of the QuickTime video (48kHz is the standard).
- Ensure that 24-bit recording is enabled within the DAW.
- Correctly select input and output devices in the DAW.
- Match the frame rate in the DAW to the frame rate of the video.
- Match the sample rate in the DAW to the sample rate of the video.
- Import the video.

HIT POINTS AND PACING

Once the video and hosting DAW are synced, the next phase of preparation, which involves marking important time points within a scene, may begin. Before initiating this next step, it is important to view the scene multiple times in order to get a feel for its general pacing, emotional content, and atmosphere. Once the scene has been thoroughly inspected, **markers** (visual indicators that are added to a session in order to emphasize important moments) may be added. Often, scenes are given to composers with **spotting notes** (spreadsheets that include specific timings and descriptions), which call for certain moments within a scene to be musically emphasized; these moments should be assigned markers in the DAW. The director and the media composer sometimes create spotting notes together, though it is also common for music editors to generate these documents after meeting with the director. In higher-budget situations, however, the composer, music editor, director, and producer are often present for a **spotting session** to collectively generate notes for the composer while viewing the video production. Spotting notes are crucial, because they provide specific start and stop times for each cue, along with the precise length and brief description of each scene. In essence, spotting notes are the detailed instructions that the composer must follow in order to succeed on a scoring gig.

Once the spotting notes are thoroughly read and markers have been added, they need to be locked to the time-code to prevent any "video drift" that results from altering the tempo of the music. By default, markers will be labeled numerically as *Marker 1*, *Marker 2*, etc. While this represents a logical scheme, it is usually best to provide shorthand descriptions for each marker to keep sessions organized and maintain an understanding of the scene and its important moments. In Figure 18.2, for example, the first marker within the Logic Pro X session is called "This is Kim," as it reflects the introduction of a character named Kim in the scene in the imported video.

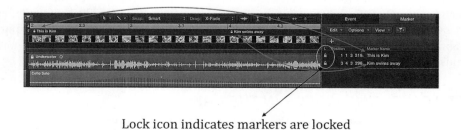

Lock icon indicates markers are locked

Fig. 18.2   Locked markers in Logic Pro X

For workflow efficiency, most DAWs are equipped with scene cut detection functions, such as Logic Pro X's "Create Marker Set from Scene Cuts" function (see Figure 18.3). This feature scans the imported video and automatically adds markers every time a scene cut is detected. Once these markers are added, it is important to review the scene again and delete unnecessary markers (or add missed markers where they are required), as well as label the markers using scene descriptions.

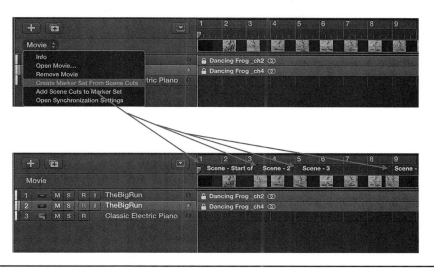

Fig. 18.3   Create Marker Set from Scene Cuts function in Logic Pro X

Many beginning media composers tend to musically overemphasize scene cuts without regard to the purpose of introducing musical emphasis. Not all scene cuts need accentuation, and to add a **hit point** (or marked location of musical emphasis within a production) to every cut will likely result in a jarring experience for the viewer. Although important moments often do occur at scene cuts, sometimes cuts are provided simply to provide continuity or as a natural part of a conversation.

Hit points sound most natural when they occur on downbeats. Oftentimes, this happens naturally, with the video requiring emphasis at the same time as a downbeat occurs within the flow of the music, without the need to manipulate anything. Most scores for media, however, will require some form of rhythmic adjustment to ensure that hit points are articulated at appropriate times and in musical ways. Tempo changes and *fermatas* are common items employed for this purpose, as the score is simply sped up, slowed down, or made to linger on a specific moment in order to fulfill the need for a hit point to take place on a downbeat. *Fermatas* are particularly useful, as they can allow the tension of a moment to build dramatically before being released on a hit point's downbeat. However, these strategies do not always make sense within scenes; often, the overall tempo and pacing needs to be preserved for dramatic purposes. In these cases, metric changes (resulting in what is referred to as **changing meter**) tend to be quite useful. For example, if a visual hit point lands on the second beat of a bar of an established quadruple meter (e.g., $\frac{4}{4}$), the previous bar could instead be changed to quintuple meter ($\frac{5}{4}$), which would allow the hit point to land on the subsequent downbeat. Non-standard meters such as simple quintuple (e.g., $\frac{5}{4}$), sextuple ($\frac{6}{4}$), and septuple ($\frac{7}{4}$) tend to take place with more regularity in music for media for this reason, and, since they maintain the same beat units as their more standard counterparts (e.g., $\frac{3}{4}$ and $\frac{4}{4}$), they often avoid an excessively unnatural or jarring experience for listeners. In situations where visual hit points take place between established beat units, though, changing the meter to an **asymmetrical meter** (a meter whose beats are of different lengths) may be needed to create downbeat accentuation. Following the previous example, this might involve altering a bar of $\frac{4}{4}$ (four equal beats, or 2+2+2+2 divisions) to become $\frac{7}{8}$ (three unequal beats, or 2+2+3 divisions) in order to allow a hit point that arrived an eighth note "too early" to instead represent a strong downbeat. Incorporating asymmetrical meters into scenes can cause an audible "hiccup" in the established flow of the music, however, particularly if they are deployed infrequently (which may attract unwanted attention and disrupt the scene's atmosphere). This may not be as aesthetically pleasing as a subtle tempo change, which could accomplish the same purpose. Figures 18.4 and 18.5 provide examples of both types of rhythmic adjustments that are used to force markers (and hit points) to take place on downbeats within Digital Performer; Figure 18.4 demonstrates how changing meter can be used for this purpose, while Figure 18.5 shows how a tempo change could be employed to the same end.

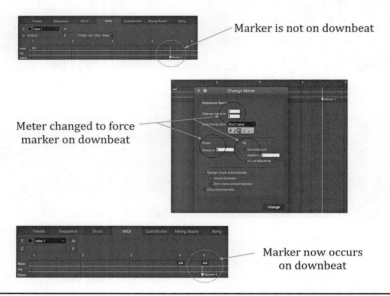

Fig. 18.4   Using changing meter to force a marker to a downbeat in Digital Performer 9

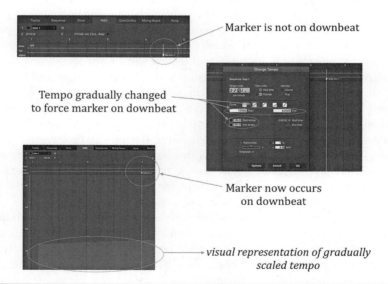

Fig. 18.5   Using a tempo change to force a marker to a downbeat in Digital Performer 9

It is important to note that musical hit points should take place within one to three frames *after* a visual hit point occurs. If musical emphasis arrives slightly late, the mind will correct the temporal disparity instantly, and perceive the events to have taken place at the same moment. If, however, musical emphasis arrives early, it can soften the impact of the hit point or be perceived as a mistake. This psychological approach to hit point placement is widespread in the industry, as it is generally understood that the audience needs a split second to process a visually important cue before it can be emphasized with musical expression and perceived clearly. This is especially the case in situations when revealing or important spoken moments represent the hit points, as the dialogue needs to be processed for meaning in order to be understood in the context of a musical accompaniment.

PUNCHES AND STREAMERS

Digital Performer offers a useful set of tools called punches and streamers for the purpose of preparing for hit points. A **streamer** is a superimposed visual cue—usually a white vertical line—that works its way from left to right across the screen over the course of a predetermined amount of time prior to a hit point. Streamers generally last between two and three seconds and are used to visually anticipate an approaching hit point. Once the hit point arrives, a **punch** (or circular flash) visually articulates it. Punches and streamers are especially important for conducting live ensembles to record with locked picture. Conductors often prefer to work without a sounding click track, and punches and streamers allow them to express a more fluid, fluctuating tempo while staying synchronized with visual cues from within the scene. Punches and streamers also help composers musically prepare for important scene locations, and allow them to ensure that their hit points are led to and arrived at in appropriate ways. Figure 18.6 adds a streamer and punch to the changing meter example from Figure 18.4.

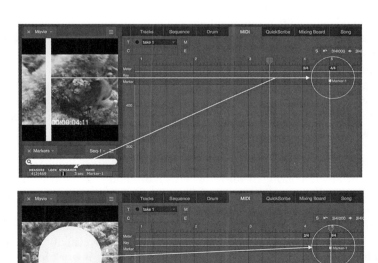

Fig. 18.6 A streamer and punch in Digital Performer 9

RISERS, STINGERS, AND BUTTONS

Risers are also used as a way to prepare hit points, and they create the musical tension that is often released at the hit point. A **riser** (or rise) is either a synthesized sound or composed instrumental passage that builds tension leading up to a hit point. There are many contemporary sample and synth libraries that come with—or are solely dedicated to—risers. Generally, risers tend to incorporate *crescendos* while getting higher and higher in pitch until the impact of the hit point. Risers range in style from simple filter sweeps over white noise through aleatoric, rising clusters for orchestra. In scary scenes, risers often lead to **stingers**, which are sudden bursts of musical emphasis that are designed to surprise the audience. Stingers are also deployed abruptly, without an added riser, which can add to the element of surprise. Another technique used to emphasize hit points is to incorporate what is known as a button. **Buttons** function similarly to stingers, but are generally used outside of thriller or horror genres and at the ends of musical sections; often, they mark logos at the ends of commercials, or wrap up scenes by adding one final musical gesture.

SCORING COMMERCIALS

Scoring for commercials often involves more hit points within a shorter span of time than scoring for longer forms such as documentaries and films. Commercials are frequently fast paced with several scene cuts, constantly demanding the attention of the audience. As such, it is important for the composer and director to communicate thoroughly about which scene cuts should be regarded as musical hit points and which should not. Sometimes the music heard in a commercial score may be nothing more than a consistent harmonic **bed** with a few hit points, while other times, hit points, risers, and buttons dominate the musical landscape. Although not always present, sonic branding is another important element in scoring for commercials. A **sonic brand** is an audible counterpart to a visual branding, which helps a company conjoin a memorable soundbite with a product or service. Sonic brands can be composed of a few short notes or even a single sound effect and are rarely more than a few seconds in duration. Most of the time, they will follow the animation of a visual logo and articulate any hit points that may naturally arise from such movement. A common first step in creating a sonic brand is to assign a different rhythm or sound to each syllable of a product's name. This will allow simple, memorable connections to be made between the product and the music by listeners. The national television station NBC, for example, has a famous sonic brand that consists of three separate pitches—one for each letter of the company's name—that outline a second inversion major triad. While it may seem boring or artless to score a brand in this fashion, such simplicity is often the most important (and most difficult) element to achieve, and has resulted in sonic brands that have stood the test of time. After all, the more complicated the sonic brand, the easier it is to forget.

Sonic brands generally remain married to a product from commercial to commercial, though the surrounding music may change. One typically encountered form for both radio and television commercial "spots" is the ABA form, which begins with a sonic branding (A) and is followed by a bed that supports a voiceover (B), ultimately ending with a restatement of the sonic branding (A). A **jingle**, which can be thought of as an expanded version of a sonic brand, is still encountered today—especially in radio—despite being commonly associated with earlier eras. Jingles once dominated television commercials and tied products with short, catchy songs that audiences often had trouble getting out of their heads. Radio jingles remain an excellent source of work for media composers, especially in local markets. A well-made jingle or sonic brand will function as an **earworm**, which is a colorful, yet somewhat disturbing industry term used to describe a memorable audible concept that "infects" the mind of listeners after entering through their ears.

Scoring for short-form commercial media is similar to long-form dramatic scoring in that the appropriate musical atmosphere must be created in order to support the scene. In the case of commercial scores and jingles, that atmosphere must be musically resonant with the product that the client is attempting to sell. Communication with clients regarding the appropriate atmosphere is therefore paramount, especially at the outset of the project, and reference tracks can be particularly useful in establishing the desired tone of the composition. As with any project involving scoring for media, though, composers should expect to work through a few rounds of revisions before ultimately achieving the final, accepted version of the project.

SUMMARY OF TERMS FROM CHAPTER 18

FPS	spotting notes	riser
interlaced	spotting session	stinger
NTSC	hit point	button
SMPTE timecode	changing meter	bed
drop frame	asymmetrical meter	sonic brand
progressive-scan	streamer	jingle
marker	punch	earworm

CHAPTER 18—EXERCISES

1. **Sonic Brand Composition.** In a DAW, create a sonic brand for an imaginary product called the *Dream State System*, which is a standalone video game platform designed for educational entertainment. The target market is young children between the ages of three and six years old. The sonic brand should be three to five seconds in length, and should use musical materials (melody, harmony, rhythm, timbre, production effects) that are appropriate for the target demographic. Be prepared to deliver a bounced stereo file and full DAW session to your instructor.

2. **Commercial Spot Composition.** Create a piece of music to be used in a *Dream State System* commercial that follows the ABA commercial form. The music should be 30 seconds in length and should use musical materials (melody, harmony, rhythm, timbre, production effects) that are appropriate for the target demographic. Be prepared to deliver a bounced stereo file and full DAW session to your instructor.

3. **Short-Form Composition with Hit Points and Risers.** Create a composition in any style that is two minutes in length and includes at least one of each of the following harmonic items: modulation, borrowed chord, extended chord, and sus chord. The composition must also use exactly one riser, which should be used to lead into one of the three required hit points at 0:50, 1:10, and 1:45. Add markers for each of these hit points in your session and use at least one meter change *and* one tempo change to align your hit points with downbeats. Be prepared to deliver a bounced stereo audio file to your instructor, along with a full DAW session that clearly demonstrates the meter and tempo changes.

Chapter 19
Scoring for Longer-Form Media

Commercials and other short-form media scores need to create and maintain a suitable sonic environment for the product being advertised. By contrast, long-form scores—such as films, television shows, documentaries, web series, video games, etc.—need to set an appropriate mood and then capture emotional changes that occur over a longer period of time. This chapter will explore techniques for setting appropriate atmospheres, maintaining continuity and interest, altering emotional content, developing ideas, and creating final deliverables for more complex media scores.

SETTING THE APPROPRIATE ATMOSPHERE

Most long-form media projects begin with a **title sequence** (opening credits sequence) that includes a **main title**, which displays the title of the work; this is one of the most important moments of a media score. Title sequences generally display white or light-colored text (credits) over a black background, sometimes accompanied by images. It is therefore almost entirely up to the composer to set the appropriate atmosphere in the absence of substantial imagery or dialogue. Themes are often presented at this point, but the biggest task is setting the tone for the entire film to follow. Action movies tend to start big and fast, as is the case with John Ottman's opening to *X-Men: Apocalypse* (2016): a rapid eighth-and-four-sixteenths pattern performed by the orchestra in 6/8 time immediately lets the audience know they are in for a fast-paced adventure. In contrast, Kyle Nixon's title sequence score for the Netflix original series *Stranger Things* moves relatively slowly, with an all-synth atmosphere featuring slow-moving arpeggiators to create a mysterious feeling of uncertainty. Title sequences are both the introduction to the world in which a story operates and an overview of the emotional arc through which the film will work. As such, it is important for composers to understand how to set an appropriate musical landscape—not just for title sequences, but also for any scene that needs to conform to a specific emotional arc.

DIATONIC MODES

The diatonic modes were presented in Chapter 10 along with brief descriptions explaining how they could be used to create certain musical atmospheres. Figure 19.1 continues this discussion, with specific examples taken from film scores, television series, and video games that represent specific moods or emotions. An important note to consider is that a scale or mode is a starting point from which composers may begin exploring fresh sounds, but at no point should a mode be considered to directly (or exclusively) represent a particular mood. Scales, modes, and other compositional tools might be excellent springboards into general atmospheres, but shouldn't be relentlessly adhered to.

Ionian	Dorian	Phrygian	Lydian	Mixolydian	Aeolian	Locrian
General descriptions of each mode						
Happy, positive	Exotic, darker, but with uplift. Can sound ancient.	Exotic, dark, foreign. Can sound ancient.	Happy, nostalgic, innocent	Powerful and noble. Can sound ancient.	Dark, very frequently used. Can sound ancient.	Dark, foreign. Rarely used.
Examples taken from film scores, television series, and video games						
"Test Drive" from the film *How to Train Your Dragon* (John Powell)	Discretion from the film *The Second Best Exotic Marigold Hotel* (Thomas Newman)	"Scent of Death" from the film *Argo* (Alexandre Desplat)	"Define Dancing" from the film *Wall-E* (Thomas Newman)	"Riots" from the film *American Pastoral* (Alexandre Desplat)	*A Gift of a Thistle* from the film, Braveheart (James Horner)	"Dance of Jethro's Daughters" from the film "The Ten Commandments" (Elmer Bernstein) *Locrian with a raised 2nd
"A Call To Arms" from the film *Glory* (James Horner)	"Cheyenne's Theme" from the film *Once Upon a Time in the West* (Ennio Morricone)	"Lothlórien" from the film *The Lord of the Rings, The Fellowship of the Rings* (Howard Shore)	Main title from the film *To Kill A Mockingbird* (Elmer Bernstein)	"Wallace Courts Murron" from the film *Braveheart* (James Horner)	"Thorin" and "Misty Mountain" from the film *The Hobbit* (Howard Shore)	
	"Morning in Karthal" from the video game *Might & Magic X: Legacy* (Roc Chen)	"Vision of Beasts" from the video game *Far Cry Primal* (Jason Graves)	"Kelpcake" from the film *Finding Dora* (Thomas Newman) *Lydian with a lowered 7th		"The Den" from the docudrama *Bears* (George Fenton)	
	"Main Theme" from the video game *Assassin's Creed 4: Black Flag* (Brian Tyler)	"The Prince Of Persia" from the film *The Prince of Persia: The Sands of Time* (Harry Gregson-Williams) *Phrygian with a raised 3rd	"First Generation" from the video game *The Sims 3: Generations* (Steve Jablonsky)		Main title from the television series *Game of Thrones* (Ramin Djawadi)	
		"Xerxes' Tent" from the film *300* (Tyler Bates)			"Let Us Quest!" from the film *Your Highness* (Steve Jablonsky)	
					"Main Theme" from the video game "Gears of War 4" (Ramin Djawadi) *Aeolian with a raised 4th	
					"Nascence" from the video game *Journey* (Austin Wintory)	

Fig. 19.1 Examples of modes and corresponding emotional content

NON-WESTERN INFLUENCES

Non-Western instruments and scales can further the potential for exoticism or culturally specific musicality. For example, Figures 19.2 and 19.3 show Westernized notations of traditional scales used in Japan and China. Much like the diatonic modes, many of the scales used in Asia are rotations of a set intervallic structure; additionally, they tend to be derived from certain instrument tunings. Like the modes, each rotation of the original scale has its own name, but a detailed exploration of these rotations can quickly become confusing and thus is beyond the scope of this book. For the purpose of simplicity, each rotation will simply be assigned a mode number.

Hirajoshi

The Japanese scale that is most familiar to Western ears is the **Hirajoshi** scale. This scale is derived from the tuning conventions for the koto, which is a 13-stringed zither that is used in many traditional Japanese musical contexts. Figure 19.2 demonstrates the Hirajoshi scale and two of its commonly used rotations. The intervallic structure of the scale is W, H, 2W, H, 2W (2W simply means two whole steps, or a M3). As Hirajoshi modes do not typically begin with major third intervals above the tone center, only three of the five potential rotations tend to be used.

Modes based on Hirajoshi = rotations of the original scale (mode 1)

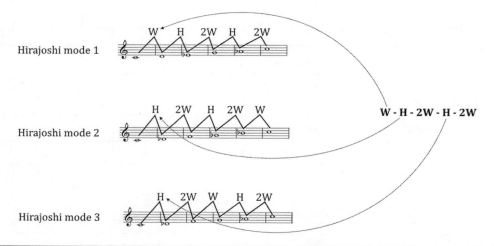

Fig. 19.2 Modes based on Hirajoshi

Gong

The principal scale used in Chinese music is called **Gong** and has an intervallic pattern of W, W, W+H, W, W+H. Each of the modes or rotations of this scale—which is equivalent to the major pentatonic scale—starts and ends on a different starting point from the original scale, just like the diatonic modes. Figure 19.3 illustrates the modes based on Gong.

Modes based on Gong = rotations of the original scale (mode 1)

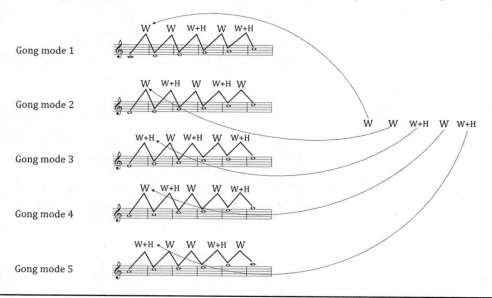

Fig. 19.3 Modes based on Gong

You are encouraged to research other non-Western scales to gain further inspiration. Indian classical music, for example, consists of **ragas**, or intervallic combinations designed to color an atmosphere and create specific moods. There are thousands of ragas to explore, creating a surplus of unique sounds to consider. Understanding the musical differences between distinct cultures is important in scoring for media and should not be ignored. If a scene takes place in ancient Japan, for example, listeners expect a certain sonic palette. The use of ethnic instruments such as the koto or shakuhachi (a traditional Japanese flute) in this setting would be appropriate, but the atmosphere would be confused if an Indian tabla (a traditional Indian percussion instrument) or sitar (a traditional Indian stringed instrument) were introduced. Basic research generally provides enough information to score a scene appropriately and is an important step in the compositional process, as it is the responsibility of a media composer to create a fitting and supportive musical setting.

THE 80:20 RATIO

While media scores should incorporate suitable material for the purpose of defining region (or the general location where the scene is taking place), the main thrust of any score is to support the scene's emotional content. Most scores for media will assign approximately 80% of its expression to the drama and emotional atmosphere of the scene, while the remaining 20% is used to define the region, typically through the musical domains of instrumentation and pitch. The resultant 4:1 ratio of drama and region in effective scores for media can be considered more directly as the **80:20 ratio**. A good example of drama and region working together to create clear emotional content is Hans Zimmer's score to *The Last Samurai*. During the "Battle in the Fog" cue, Zimmer uses gong and taiko instruments to situate the scene within Japan while painting an atmosphere of terror through the use of a driving rhythmic force. As the scene progresses, the orchestra dominates, as aleatoric string passages give way to a driving *ostinato* and, eventually, a romantic melody in the brass section. As the scene ends, traditional Japanese sounds subtly reemerge with shakuhachi, gongs, and taiko accompanied by the high strings. Listening to the score (even without the visual element present), it is easy to know where this scene takes place, and, most importantly, the type of action and emotion being portrayed. The list below provides other film score examples that feature ethnic sounds that are used to color scenes in a subtle way for the purpose of signifying region. The composer for each cue is in parentheses.

- "I Remember Everything" from the film *Jason Bourne* (John Powell): This cue combines the use of the fifth mode of the harmonic minor—for example, C, D♭, E, F, G, A♭, B♭, and C—with percussion to express an unusual Icelandic location. The use of this exotic-sounding pitch collection is particularly noteworthy, as most of the score consists of a typical Western orchestral palate.
- "Scent of Death" from *Argo* (Alexandre Desplat): This excerpt paints a frenetic, fearful, abstract Middle Eastern landscape by combining unnerving, fast-paced, breathy vocal repetitions, a relentless driving rhythmic figure that is accompanied by low strings and Middle Eastern instruments, and occasional wailing Phrygian phrases sung by a woman.
- "Impossible Waves" from *Kubo and the Two Strings* (Dario Marianelli): A Western orchestral sound palette with harmonic swells moving by chromatic mediant between Fm and Am create a mysterious fantasy atmosphere that is subtly colored by Japanese instruments.

The 80:20 ratio is not a strict rule, but it is a good place to start when deciding how much of a scene should be colored by the location in which a scene is taking place. Importantly, the 80:20 ratio needn't be applied only to situations located in exotic lands; rather, it can apply to any setting, even basic urban or rural environments. Gustavo Santaolalla's score to the film *Brokeback Mountain* is an excellent example of how one might suggest a rural setting with the understated use of acoustic guitar mixed with harmonic and melodic orchestral palates that generate a sense of struggle. Moreover, the classic Lalo Schifrin score to the film *Dirty Harry* sets an urban scene by creating a groove with a rhythm section that is mixed with a chamber orchestra that produces an overall sensation of tension through a series of dissonant chords and intervals.

USING HARMONIC AND RHYTHMIC MOVEMENT TO CREATE ATMOSPHERE

Scales and modes are excellent ways to help define a region or atmosphere, but harmony and rhythm should not be ignored. Slow-moving rhythms tend to fit slower-moving scenes, while quicker rhythms fit more fast-paced action. The pace of movement on screen should help determine tempo and meter. Mixed meters can aid in the creation of uneasy environments by constantly defying listeners' expectations, while consistent meters usually do the opposite. Straying from traditional harmonic motions can also trigger emotional responses. Hans Zimmer's "Dream Is Collapsing" cue from the film *Inception* is an excellent example of how harmonic motion can generate an unsettling atmosphere. The basis of this cue is the repeating harmonic progression Gm—F#/A#—D#—B, which contains familiar chordal structures that are combined in atypical ways—often generating chromatic mediant relationships—in order to create tonal instability. This instability in turn supports the ambiguity within the scene—the audience is meant to feel uncertain about what is reality and what is a dream.

Kyle Nixon's title sequence from the Netflix series *Stranger Things* is both an excellent example of the 80:20 ratio and an example of the use of harmonic language to create atmosphere. This score uses retro-sounding synths to create a nostalgic, early 1980s feel. A constant sixteenth note/sixteenth note/eighth rest pattern creates a heartbeat-like backdrop for a simple harmonic progression that moves between Em and Cmaj⁷. An arpeggiating synth constantly outlines a Cmaj⁷ chord as synth pads and bass notes move between the chords' roots, creating a dark, yet stable tonality heard as i—VIᴹ⁷ in the key of E minor. This repeated, non-functional succession of chords echoes the traditional sci-fi practice of vacillating between chords whose roots are a third apart to create an atmosphere of uncertainty.

THEMATIC CONTINUITY AND LEITMOTIFS

Scales, modes, rhythms, and harmonic motion can all be used to create continuity throughout a score. Composers can also generate continuity thematically, and often do so using *leitmotifs*. A *leitmotif*, as explained in Chapter 11, is a short motive used to represent a character, place, emotion, or other important element throughout an entire storyline, often developing thematically along with the dramatic element it signifies. Famous examples of *leitmotifs* include most of John Williams's output throughout the 1980s. Film series like *Star Wars*, *Indiana Jones*, and *Superman* are classic examples of how *leitmotifs* can be used in film, as the main characters in all of these films have their own *leitmotifs*. In *Star Wars*, "the Force" is such an important component to the story that it, too, was given its own music. Howard Shore's scores to *The Lord of the Rings* films and *The Hobbit* used *leitmotifs* as well, to help connect characters and places and drive the storyline. Shore created a *leitmotif* for the Shire, the location in the stories where the hobbits originate, which he called upon many times throughout the films to help create a feeling of longing for home. The final scene from *The Fellowship of the Ring*, for example, involves the main character Frodo saving his longtime hobbit companion Sam from drowning. As the two characters embrace, a tin whistle plays the Shire *leitmotif*, sonically representing their friendship and shared history dating back to the Shire.

The use of *leitmotifs* is an excellent way to make deep connections that may not seem obvious, especially between different works by the same composer. For example, John Williams uses shades of Darth Vader's *leitmotif* "The Imperial March" from *Star Wars* episodes IV, V, and VI as Anakin Skywalker's theme in episodes I, II, and III, which delightfully plays on the audience's knowledge of future events to create musical and dramatic foreshadowing.

Once a *leitmotif* has been established, the composer can repeatedly rely on it to help carry ideas through multiple scenes. The literal recurrence of a *leitmotif* may often be suitable, but slight changes in tonality, harmonization, and rhythm can provide freshness and a developmental component that is appropriate when the character(s) associated with a particular *leitmotif* undergo(es) certain emotional transformations. Thematic development is also an essential tool for custom scoring, providing an efficient way for composers to align the characters of a story with the plot in consistent ways. This concept is used in the long-running television series *The Simpsons*, which presents a clear theme in the title sequence that is often referred to and transformed in a variety of ways throughout hundreds of episodes. *The Simpsons* has a dedicated composer, Alf Clausen, who provides custom scoring for every episode, while the producers also license ready-made "production tracks" to provide fresh sounds and specific genres. This series, like many other projects, thus combines the continuity of *leitmotifs* and custom scoring with the modularity of ready-made composition.

CUSTOM SCORING VS. READY-MADE COMPOSITION

Custom scoring and ready-made composition are the two large categories into which most long-form media compositions fall. **Custom scoring** refers to music that is created "from scratch" according to the specific requests of a director, producer, or other client for the purpose of filling the needs of a specific project. This is the area of the industry most commonly associated with the term "film scoring." Spotting notes and conversations about long-form development separate this field from **ready-made composition**, which consists of music that is made to generically fit a multitude of situations. A publisher working for a production house typically contracts ready-made music; the production house then curates a library of this type of music in order to fill a variety of needs for its clients.

PRODUCTION TRACK CREATION

As with all areas of scoring for media, understanding the role the music plays in a project is the most important thing a composer needs to comprehend. Scores for media play a supportive role; as such, the music must set an appropriate atmosphere, follow the drama and pacing of the situation, and leave enough space for dialogue and sound effects. **Production track** composers rarely have the luxury of working with *leitmotifs* or thematic development techniques; instead, the sonic atmosphere tends to be consistent within a track and must be reinvented with each new track. Production tracks are used in a very wide variety of projects in the industry; as such, a brief list of scenarios that tend to involve production tracks is provided below, which may help you better understand the range of functions these tracks fulfill.

- Reality TV: providing emotional beds and generic action scoring
- Sitcoms: providing genre-specific needs
- Sports TV: providing emotional beds for feature stories, generic action scoring, show opens, and **bumpers** (brief pieces of music that are used to transition between sections of programming, such as into and out of commercial breaks)
- Radio and TV "spots": providing emotional beds for dialogue within commercials
- Live events: providing show opens and bumpers

MODULAR COMPOSITION

On the surface, production track creation seems simple in that it primarily consists of creating beds with appropriate emotional settings, without the stresses of working with locked picture (such as hit points or specific timing requirements). In reality, however, most composers find that specific timings and hit points take away a lot of questions, providing a clear protocol or blueprint to follow. Production track writing consists of creating full pieces of music with memorable beginnings, middle sections, and endings that need to be modular in design so that editors can easily take out certain sections, rearrange sections, or otherwise edit as they see fit to appropriately match the situation for which they need music. Sections of a **modular composition** therefore need to be strong enough to exist on their own—and they must each end convincingly, given that any section may need to function as the final segment of the work. Some producers desire extremely short introductions (or no introductions at all), though others are willing to edit accordingly if a piece's form needs to be rearranged to meet the needs of the project. There are a number of different styles of production tracks, and most production houses present their libraries in an organized fashion, grouping certain styles together. Production tracks generally eschew vocals, although there are exceptions. The list below catalogues some of the most common genres found in production house libraries.

- *Storytelling*: Tracks that are emotionally charged with an obvious dramatic arc. These tracks can be in major or minor keys, but most producers prefer a certain amount of uplift at some point within the music so that the music can end positively.
- *Tension*: Compositions that contain a fair amount of dissonance, but are not necessarily atonal. Mixed meter can be useful in these tracks, but can also draw too much attention to the music.
- *Horror/Thriller*: Tracks containing even more dissonance, aleatoric-sounding passages, and even atonal sections.
- *Romance*: Compositions that may reflect any genre, from R&B to soaring orchestral styles, but are focused on creating a sweet, heartfelt sound.
- *Comedy*: Tracks that are light, quirky, and silly.
- *Military*: Brass-driven compositions that often utilize drum corps sounds.
- *Action*: Big, *ostinato*-driven, orchestral tracks that are often hybrid scores in that they additionally feature electronic elements such as synth lines and/or sub basses.
- *Rock*: Tracks reflecting styles ranging from classic rock to heavy metal, usually without vocals.
- *Electronic*: Compositions that incorporate elements of electronic styles ranging from house through techno, usually without vocals.
- *Hip-hop*: Tracks reflecting a variety of hip-hop subgenres, usually without vocals.
- *Funk*: Groove-oriented tracks without vocals that make use of standard funk ensemble instrumentation, including horns.

Staying Clear of Dialogue

An important consideration when scoring to media—especially production track writing—is careful attention to the melodic domain. Even though most production tracks consist of musical beds, some melodic elements are generally present. Since dialogue is so important, though, it is essential that melodies are strong enough to maintain interest yet supportive enough to avoid drawing an unnecessary amount of attention (to the detriment of the dialogue). Production track melodies therefore generally avoid the higher registers and include enough space for the spoken word to remain in the foreground.

Maintaining Interest

The overall atmosphere of a production track must be immediately apparent to the listener. Many producers race through libraries looking for an instant match to the project at hand, so the music must stand out and express the emotion it advertises within seconds. While generating interest is crucial, maintaining that interest is just as important. This can be particularly difficult, as many production track styles come from the pop world, which consists mostly of music with vocals and lyrics. A typical Top 40 song will, for example, have a bed of music over which a vocalist develops melody lines and lyrical themes. If the vocals were taken away, the music would not likely stand on its own. Since production tracks do not generally include vocals, though, other aspects of the music must develop in place of vocal lines and lyrics. As a general rule of thumb, some aspect of the track should change every four bars. This can be as simple as an added shaker loop or as complex as a newly added section of music. Compositional development is therefore an essential aspect of production track creation; simply looping ideas together rarely works in today's industry, as competition and production track quality have increased substantially.

Although production track creation fits under the umbrella term of ready-made music, customization is very common. Clients often reach out to the publisher who has licensed a piece of music to the production house's library in order to ask for a few changes to be made so that the composition can better fit their project. Music editors can often adjust tracks to this end, but sometimes the client's requests are beyond what music editors can realistically handle. At this point, the publisher will contact the composer and the three parties will work together until the composition fits the required specifications. Often, a few simple modifications are requested, but more substantial "rewrites" do occur. Sometimes the composer will even work with a rough cut of the video, and specific timings and hit points begin to enter the conversation, turning what was once a ready-made composition into a custom score. This is especially true in the trailer track industry.

TRAILER TRACKS

A **trailer track** is a piece of music that is used to support a movie or video game trailer. In the 1980s, composers began creating ready-made scores that could be used to support movie trailers. The challenge was to create music that was as powerful and effective as the score that was used in the actual film, but on a much smaller budget. This compositional genre still exists today, but on a much larger scale now that home studios are capable of producing high-quality work and trailers for video games have become commonplace. To complicate things, some trailer track composers hire live musicians—even live orchestras with full choirs—and create compilations that studio executives license, following the model used for production tracks by composers, publishers, production houses, and television producers. The result is that trailer tracks, in order to compete in this industry segment, must sound extremely thick and contain album-quality audio. There are two general formal schemes that trailer tracks generally exhibit, and both follow an A–B pattern, with the B section representing an explosive, dense, thematic formal unit characterized by a definitive conclusion (see Figure 19.4).

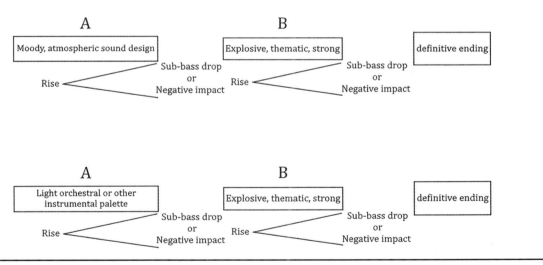

Fig. 19.4 Two common A–B trailer forms

The first general trailer track form begins with a sound design atmosphere, while the second is initiated with an orchestral/instrumental sonic palette. **Sound design**, in its most simple form, is the act of modifying a sound source in some way to create a new sound. In the synth world, sound design entails manipulating LFOs or other synthesizer parameters to create original sounds. **Organic sound design**, however, involves recording live sounds and manipulating them by way of computer processing (e.g., time-stretching, adding effects, editing waveforms, etc.). Sound design is a term that is often used to describe the creation of sound effects (or SFX) used in a film, but it can also be used to describe a compositional approach that entails creating innovative sounds for musical purposes. The distinction between the actual film score and the SFX can be blurred when sound design is used as a compositional device, so communication between directors, sound effects teams, and the composer is important. A trendsetting example of a musical sound design element is Mike Zarin's explosive, brass-like, percussive sound that is used to help define the dream state in the trailer for the film *Inception*. The sound was so effective that it was further developed by Hans Zimmer and used as a *leitmotif* throughout the movie's score.

Track counts are generally very high to account for the large, epic sound that most modern trailers require in their B sections. However, a consistently dense, loud score is less dramatic than one that includes a wide dynamic range. For this reason, at least one riser tends to occur within a trailer track, and it typically lasts anywhere from three seconds to a full minute. Risers usually end on either a bass drop or a negative impact, as opposed to a further dynamic increase with the same instrumentation, which aids in the delineation of the two main sections of the trailer's form and allows space for the dialogue to create a moment of impact. A **bass drop** is a sub bass sound that sonically articulates an important hit point. A **negative impact** is a termination of a rise that never delivers the full impact that was implied or expected. Often, this lack of a sonic "payoff" results in a stronger effect than the powerful climax that was anticipated.

VIDEO GAMES

Creating an appropriate emotional atmosphere is the most important element of scoring video games, as it is for the other forms of media. The most difficult element of scoring video games is that it is essentially aleatoric by nature: since the score is effectively interactive, and depends on how the game is played, the music needs to fit certain compositional requirements in order for it to unfold properly in a variety of scenarios. There are two main techniques used for game implementation: horizontal re-sequencing and vertical layering. **Horizontal re-sequencing** consists of multiple loopable sections of music that can alternate back and forth at given points without creating discontinuities. Each loopable section has a series of markers embedded in the audio file that may be used to trigger a change to a different section of music. If, for example, a player moves to a new area within a game's level, this triggers a marker in an audio file, and the game will change to a different loop of music. Some games' audio files have a relatively low number of markers, where other games may have markers on every downbeat, allowing for more musical possibilities and a higher degree of interaction. The challenge of horizontal re-sequencing is that every section of music must work with every other section of music at each marker point; the loopable sections' tempos and keys should therefore be related or equal to one another. Figure 19.5 illustrates the concept of horizontal re-sequencing.

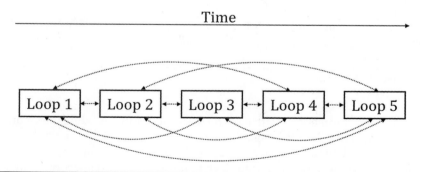

Music progresses from one loop to any other loop

Fig. 19.5   Horizontal re-sequencing

Transition cues are often used to help create smoother connections between loops in a horizontal re-sequencing scheme. A **transition cue** is a small audio file—often a short stinger or atmospheric clip—that is used to bridge together the larger looping sections.

Vertical layering takes a different approach to interactive game composition. **Vertical layering** effectively breaks a large composition into autonomous units that can function both individually as well as with any combination of the other parts. Certain parts will join into or drop out of the texture as time progresses according to the intensity of game play, creating a continuous development and re-orchestration of a passage. Vertical layering is sometimes referred to as vertical remixing or vertical re-orchestration, since the thickness or density of sounds interacting with one another changes from loop to loop. Figure 19.6 demonstrates vertical layering.

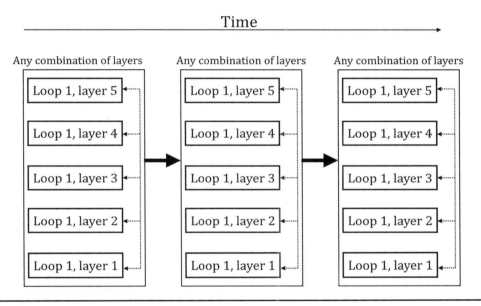

Fig. 19.6   Vertical layering

DELIVERABLES

It is extremely important to communicate with clients about specific deliverable requirements, as there is not a prevailing, industry-standard set of deliverable needs across all forms of media (and there are even discrepancies within the same forms of media). Some clients might ask for simple stereo WAV files, for example, while others may require full DAW sessions. With constantly changing technology, the deliverable needs of scoring for media occupy an ever-larger range; however, it is quite common for stemmed sessions to be requested. A **stemmed session** or "stem session" is an organized version of a larger session that records similar sounds (and/or those related by instrument family) into groups to create a more manageable session that can be easily recreated by other producers in different DAWs. These new recordings are referred to as **stems**. Most stem sessions are created in a DAW (such as Digital Performer, Cubase Pro, or Logic Pro) and prepared for final mixes to be completed in Pro Tools, which is an industry-standard program that is very frequently used for final mixes. Final mixes can be professionally completed in any DAW, but for higher-budget projects, it is standard practice to submit stem sessions for use in Pro Tools. The list below, corresponding to Figures 19.7A–L, demonstrates a step-by-step approach to preparing stems in Logic Pro X and importing them into Pro Tools for a final mix session.

IN THE ORIGINAL DAW (E.G., LOGIC PRO X)

- Bounce a fully mastered demo mix.
- Click Save As and add the word "Stems" to easily indicate that this session is a stem prep session.
- Join MIDI regions by selecting unjoined MIDI regions within each MIDI track and pressing J. (If MIDI regions are not joined, Pro Tools will create a track for each separate MIDI region, creating far more tracks than needed.)

Press "j" to join MIDI Regions

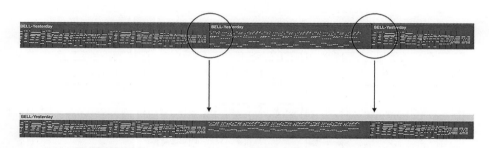

Fig. 19.7A   Stem session prep for Pro Tools

- Mute or delete the master chain plugins.
- Check that levels for all tracks are not clipping and adjust accordingly if clipping is present. Level decreases and increases should be made at the grouped bus level to ensure that the relative balance of the mix is unaltered. Importantly, volume will be addressed again in the final mix phase, and quieter volumes are much easier to work with than mixes with clipping.
- Fold all reverb and delay effects into each stem. Soloing busses will bypass reverb and delay; therefore, each bussed instrument needs to be soloed in accordance with the stem being bounced in order to preserve reverb and delay effects.

Soloed for stem group

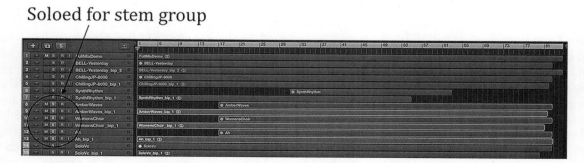

Fig. 19.7B   Stem session prep for Pro Tools

- Cycle select the exact length of the project. This should match the length of the fully mastered demo mix.
- Bounce each group of instruments as stems into a premade stems folder. Settings: PCM (WAV or AIFF), 48kHz (sample rate), 24-bit (bit depth), interleaved with no dithering, offline bounce, include audio tail, no normalization.

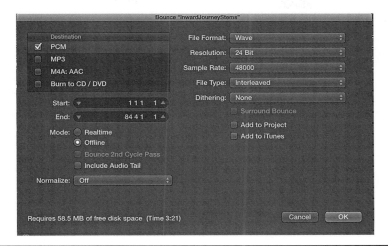

Fig. 19.7C   Stem session prep for Pro Tools

- Select and solo all MIDI tracks, then Export Selection as MIDI File into the stems folder. This will create a MIDI file that can be imported into Pro Tools to recreate all MIDI tracks in the project.

Fig. 19.7D   Stem session prep for Pro Tools

IN THE FINAL MIX DAW (PRO TOOLS)

■ Create a new session in Pro Tools. Settings: 48kHz (sample rate), 24-bit (bit depth). You will be prompted for a save location and file name, which will need to be specified.

Fig. 19.7E   Stem session prep for Pro Tools

■ Select Import MIDI from the File menu, and then select New Tracks/Instrument Track, Import tempo map from MIDI File, and Import Key Signature from MIDI File.

Fig. 19.7F   Stem session prep for Pro Tools

■ Hide all MIDI tracks that have been created. It is wise to include MIDI tracks in stem sessions in case they are needed at some point during the final mix (samples may need to be replaced, for example), but they should be hidden to prevent clutter.

Clicking the gray colored circles on the left of the track names will hide tracks

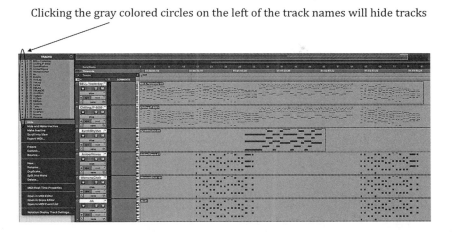

Fig. 19.7G   Stem session prep for Pro Tools

■ Select Import Audio/Stems from the File menu to add the audio stems to the session. Be sure to click Copy instead of Add within the subsequent menu so that the audio files are automatically copied to the session folder location, making file management simpler.

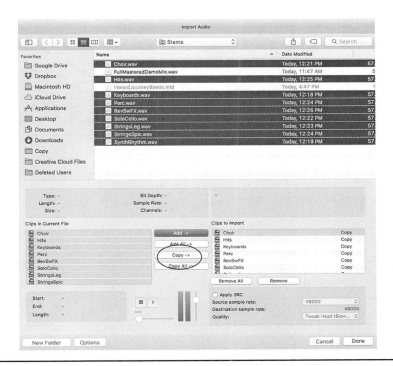

Fig. 19.7H   Stem session prep for Pro Tools

■ Press Done, then choose New Track as the Destination and Session Start as the Location in the Audio Import Options menu.

Fig. 19.7I Stem session prep for Pro Tools

■ Reorder tracks if necessary.

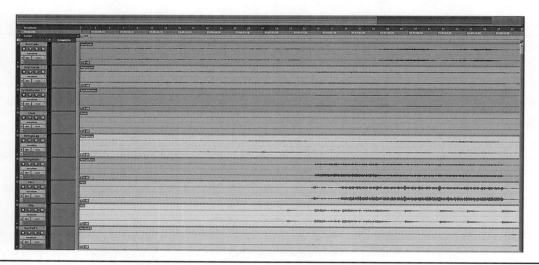

Fig. 19.7J Stem session prep for Pro Tools

■ Add a master fader by selecting New from the Track menu. Settings: Create 1 new Stereo Master Fader in Ticks. After the master fader has been added to the session, select and drag it to the bottom of the session within the Arrange window.

Fig. 19.7K Stem session prep for Pro Tools

■ Add the fully mastered demo mix to the session and drag it to the top of the session within the Arrange window.

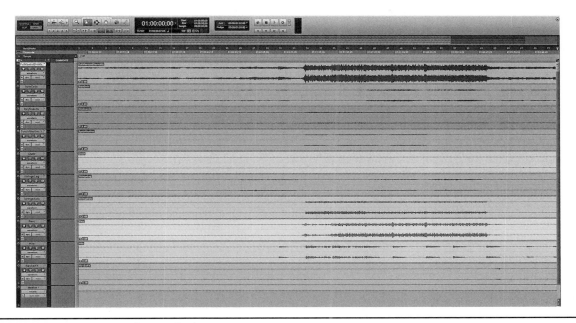

Fig. 19.7L Stem session prep for Pro Tools

■ At this point, the stem session is ready for the final mix.

Scoring for longer-form media is a complex yet rewarding undertaking that requires close attention to atmosphere, pacing, hit points, time requirements, and the role of the music within the larger project. Compositional focus must be balanced between maintaining both continuity and interest, and deliverables must be generated that adhere exactly to previously communicated specifications. Command of the materials presented in this chapter will prepare you for the everyday life of a professional media composer, which is at once challenging and extraordinarily fulfilling.

SUMMARY OF TERMS FROM CHAPTER 19

title sequence	production track	horizontal re-sequencing
main title	bumper	transition cue
Hirajoshi	modular composition	vertical layering
Gong	trailer track	stemmed session
ragas	sound design	stems
80:20 ratio	organic sound design	
custom scoring	bass drop	
ready-made composition	negative impact	

CHAPTER 19—EXERCISES

1. **Production Track Composition.** In a DAW of your choice, compose appropriate music for the title sequence of a television series that takes place in late nineteenth-century Kansas City. The show is about a former Union soldier who abandoned his post during the Civil War and assumed the identity of a soldier he killed in battle. The soldier is also the acting sheriff in a rough town. The plot pivots between the sheriff's newly found pacifism and his natural ability to violently keep the local criminal element in check. The track should be exactly one minute and twenty seconds in length. Be prepared to turn in a stereo bounce of your music, along with the full project session.

2. **Scoring for Emotion and Region.** In a DAW of your choice, compose music that appropriately sets one of the emotions and one of the regions listed below. Be sure to assign approximately 80% of the composition to the chosen emotion and roughly 20% to define the region. The track should be roughly two minutes in length. Be prepared to turn in a stereo bounce of your music, along with the full project session.

Tension	Japan
Fear	China
Nostalgia	Medieval English Countryside
Hope	Modern New York City
Suspense	Appalachian Mountains

3. **Film Scoring Practice.** In a DAW of your choice, compose appropriate music for a scene within a sci-fi film about the negative effects of long-term space travel. The music should be subtle, yet disorienting. Create a simple progression that moves primarily in thirds, set to a sound-design atmosphere of instability. At exactly forty-seven seconds, the music should slowly begin to develop into a fast-paced action scene that spirals out of control until a big hit point at exactly two minutes and fifteen seconds. Give enough space at the end of the piece for reverb tails to naturally fade out after this hit point. Be prepared to turn in a stereo bounce of your music, along with the full project session.

4. **Trailer Track Composition.** In a DAW of your choice, create a trailer track for a film about a girl who is rescued by a band of Knights Templar after her town and family are destroyed. The Knights raise the girl, educating and training her in the art of war. The girl eventually grows up to be a powerful force that seeks revenge on the bandits who killed her family. The score should be based on one of the modes that most appropriately support a twelfth-century atmosphere. The track should begin with dark sound-design elements that accompany a simple instrumental part that represents the girl's innocence and misfortune; it should then thicken in instrumentation and intensity as the score progresses. The following hit points should be emphasized:

    - 0:22
    - 0:53
    - 1:05 (bass drop)
    - 1:35 (negative accent)
    - After the negative accent at 1:35, music from the introduction should be brought back subtly, with a minimal palate.

    Be prepared to turn in a stereo bounce of your music, along with the full project session.

5. **Video Game Composition I.** In a DAW of your choice, create a series of five looping 8-bar passages that could be implemented as a horizontal re-sequencing score for a video game. The game is about an ancient Chinese kung fu master who must defend his village against imperial tyranny. Be sure to use one of the modes of Gong that creates a darker atmosphere. Be prepared to turn in a stereo bounce of each individual loop as well as the full project session.

6. **Video Game Composition II.** In a DAW of your choice, create a single passage with five distinct layers that could be implemented as a vertical layering score for a car-racing video game. The music for this setting builds in intensity the closer to first place the player gets; thus, the layers should combine to reflect moving in position from fifth through first place.

7. **Stem Session(s).** Using the same session from the trailer track composition project (Exercise 4), create a stem prep session in your original DAW and, optionally, a full stem session in Pro Tools (if you have a copy). Be prepared to turn in the full project sessions of both the prep session in the original DAW and the full stem session in Pro Tools. If you do not have access to Pro Tools, only turn in the project session from the original DAW.

PART IV
THE BUSINESS OF MUSIC COMPOSITION

Chapter 20
The Business of Music Composition

The ever-changing landscape of the modern music industry can often seem difficult to navigate, especially for beginning composers. A key to protecting yourself against unforeseen financial and legal difficulties is to develop an understanding of the common types of contracts that composers tend to encounter. This chapter will explore these contract types in the context of the American music industry and provide you with basic business strategies that will allow you to legally protect and successfully sell your music.

COMMON BUSINESS ENTITIES IN THE MUSIC INDUSTRY

Once you begin earning money as a musician, you have officially entered the music business. Many composers, however, make the mistake of waiting until well after they have created streams of income for themselves to consider forming an official business entity. This can lead to unnecessary taxation and, ultimately, lower net profits (among several other issues). It is therefore important to plan ahead and consider the variety of business entity options that are available. Note, however, that each of the options makes you and your business responsible for different levels of **liability**. Liability refers to the responsibility of individuals or businesses for any unpaid debt or legal actions taken against them. Understanding the levels of liability associated with each type of business entity is therefore crucial in determining the best option for your career.

A **sole proprietorship** is the easiest business entity to establish, as there are no costs associated with its creation. One must simply declare as a sole proprietorship when filling out a state-required business registration. Business taxes pass through sole proprietorships to their owners (hence the term **pass-through** taxation), making the owners accountable for recording and paying them on their individual tax returns. Although it is easy to initiate a sole proprietorship, this structure does not offer any liability protection. A **partnership** is essentially the same as a sole proprietorship, except that liability is equally shared between multiple partners. Partners can also choose to be **limited partners**, releasing specified individuals from liability and, in turn, offering them restricted control over the business.

A **limited liability company** (LLC) alleviates many liability concerns for the owner by creating a separate entity, though there are some important caveats. First, an LLC owner remains responsible for defaulting on loans, outstanding tax debt, or engaging in any illegal conduct. Second, the owner must open a separate business checking account and acquire a distinct tax ID number. Third, there are typically costs associated with establishing an LLC, which vary from state to state and can be quite costly. There are usually annual costs for maintaining this type of business entity, as well. Moreover, **articles of organization** and an **operating agreement**, each of which identifies the governing members of the LLC and describes their financial and managerial responsibilities, must be filed with the secretary of state within the state in which the LLC will operate. LLCs are additionally subject to pass-through taxation, following the model for both sole proprietorships and partnerships. When an LLC begins to generate profit, however, it may instead elect to be taxed as a corporation, which typically results in lower rates. Despite the additional paperwork and operating costs, LLCs are the most flexible in terms of structure, while optionally retaining the same tax benefits as corporations within a far less complex archetype.

There are two types of **corporations**: S corporations and C corporations. **S corporations** are subject to pass-through taxation, which can alleviate some administrative confusion, but they are also subject to several intricate regulations and require substantial managerial attention. Corporations issue shares of stock (either publicly or privately), meaning that income profits and losses are divided among its shareholders, who are each responsible for reporting these profits and losses on their individual tax returns. An **articles of incorporation** must be filed with the appropriate secretary of state to establish any corporation, and stock certificates must be issued to the initial shareholders. Some states require annual reporting fees as well, and the structures and protocols within corporations can become rather complex (e.g., adopting bylaws, maintaining records of director and shareholder meetings, etc.). A **C corporation** is similar to an S corporation, but on a much larger scale, as C corporations have more than 100 shareholders; as this type of business is atypical in the media composition world, a detailed explanation of C corporations is beyond the scope of this chapter.

From among the variety of business entity options, most successful musicians chose to form either an LLC or an S corporation. An LLC tends to be a better fit for solo musicians, since decisions regarding attribution of credit and distribution of profit are clearly evident in these situations, requiring no complex bylaws or protocols. A popular band, however, may have multiple members (including rotating members), and the legal establishment of each individual's specific role within the collective with an articles of incorporation can be very helpful for avoiding legal disputes. Moreover, the easy transferability of shares can be beneficial when band members join or leave the group. As such, an S corporation often provides a better structure for situations such as these. However, it is strongly advised that you seek professional legal advice before making any decisions regarding the establishment of your personal business entity. The information provided in this section of the chapter is simply designed to help you discuss music business matters from an informed position.

COPYRIGHTING YOUR WORK

Copyrighting music is the best way for you to protect your work against plagiarism. The U.S. government's copyright website makes it easy to find and complete copyright forms, and the submission process can often be handled completely online (i.e., when the composition exists in a digital format). There are two copyright forms with which composers should be familiar: **Form SR (Sound Recordings)** and **Form PA (Performing Arts)**. Form PA will protect the composition and any included lyrics from infringement, but not necessarily a recording of the piece. For this purpose, Form SR is used. However, Form SR can be used to protect both a recording and a composition (including lyrics) in cases where the composer also serves as the recording artist. Copyright protection is not free (the current cost is $35 per composition), but multiple works may often be submitted within a single SR form, offering a cost-effective way to protect your musical output.

ROYALTIES

Media composers tend to earn income via a combination of two types of business transactions: buy-outs and royalties. A **buy-out** is a situation in which a client purchases the right to use a composition without owing any further compensation or royalties to the composer, regardless of the extent of usage. **Royalties**, on the other hand, is the umbrella term used to describe usage-based payments that, in the music industry, are categorized into mechanical royalties and performing rights royalties.

MECHANICAL ROYALTIES

The term **mechanical royalties** comes from the act of mechanically reproducing a piece of music in the form of a physical recording (e.g., a vinyl record), which contains compositions that are entitled to royalties. Composers, for example, would often receive a royalty for every copy of a record that was pressed containing their music. Some contracts only offered royalties for records that were pressed *and* distributed, while others offered royalties for records sold (after a certain amount were freely distributed for promotional purposes). **Mechanical licenses**, which grant permission to reproduce and distribute copyrighted music on a variety of media, are distributed by groups like the Harry Fox Agency in the United States and the Mechanical-Copyright Protection Society (MCPS) in the U.K.; these entities in turn distribute mechanical royalties at a set rate to registered composers for registered compositions. Currently, the Harry Fox Agency's mechanical rate for physical recordings is 9.1¢ per composition, or, for pieces over five minutes, 1.75¢ per minute. Digital downloads yield the same rate as physical copies, but the rates for streamed music involves many complicated factors. The reader is encouraged to research the websites for both MCPS and the Harry Fox Agency for further details.

Musicians often equally share mechanical royalties if they belong to a band or other ensemble, regardless of who wrote the music; however, other groups reserve different allotment percentages to individual members based on a variety of factors, including authorship. These situations can easily become problematic, and thus it is advised to create a clear agreement in writing before registering any compositions with any royalty distribution agencies. Regardless of the decision that is made, the music should always be copyright protected.

PERFORMING RIGHTS ROYALTIES

A **performing rights royalty** is a royalty paid for a live or recorded performance of a composition, either in concert or in conjunction with some other media format. A **synchronization royalty** is a specific type of performing rights royalty that applies to situations in which a composition is synchronized to some form of media, as is the case with **background music** for a television show, movie, or commercial. **Sync fees** are sometimes paid in place of—or in addition to—synchronization royalties, for the limited use of a composition.

Performing rights fees and royalties are collected from music venues and other users and distributed to musicians by **Performing Rights Organizations (PROs)**. As with mechanical royalties, each country has their own PROs that serve to protect the interests of musicians. In the United States, there are three main PROs: ASCAP (the American Society of Composers, Authors, and Publishers), BMI (Broadcast Music, Inc.), and SESAC (originally the Society of European Stage Authors and Composers, an acronym that holds no significance today). In the U.K., PRS (the Performing Right Society) is the leading PRO that distributes royalties to composers and songwriters; PRS is partnered with PPL (Phonographic Performance Limited), which specifically protects the interests of performers and record companies.

Almost any venue that plays recorded music must legally apply for a **blanket license**, which allows it to transmit a specific PRO's entire catalogue of works that is generated from its membership. Although it is rarely enforced, a venue is technically not permitted to play any PRO-registered music for which it has not paid a blanket license fee. For instance, if a restaurant played music from an album of music composed by an ASCAP member, and that restaurant only paid for a blanket license with BMI, the restaurant could be liable for copyright infringement. There are also other, more complex stipulations regarding the use of PRO-registered music in restaurants that are based on restaurant size and the medium through which the music is transmitted, but these specific details are beyond the scope of this chapter.

Each PRO has its own proprietary methods for tracking performances, but most tracking comes from television cue sheets, which are submitted to each PRO on a quarterly basis by television networks. A **cue sheet** is a list of all music used in a televised broadcast that includes the program title, episode title, episode length, and specific details about each composition used, including its usage type (background music, theme music, etc.) and usage duration. In 2016, ASCAP and BMI agreed on a standard cue sheet template for all networks to use, which aids in streamlining the complicated process of reporting music "plays." Once all cue sheet data is collected, each PRO processes the information in order to determine royalty rates for its membership. Each PRO has a different system, but they all consider the number of network affiliates and ratings systems, such as the Nielsen ratings in the U.S., to determine the size of the audience reached by a composition; in turn, this data allows the PRO to generate a "weight" for each performance that determines how much money the composer should earn for a particular usage. Once all cue sheets are compiled and royalty amounts are calculated, money is paid out to composers and publishers, typically on a quarterly basis.

To join most PROs, composers must simply apply and pay a fee to one of the societies serving the country in which they're working (though SESAC membership additionally requires a referral from a current member). However, while publishers are free to join multiple PROs, composers are only allowed to be active members of one PRO at any given time. In the U.S., PROs require minimum membership term lengths from one to three years, and leaving a PRO for another can only take place within a narrow window of time; thus, choosing the right PRO is an important consideration. Each PRO offers its own unique benefits, which should be thoroughly researched before a membership decision is made; however, there are also other considerations. For example, many professionals suggest waiting to join a PRO until a publisher recommends one, because some production houses prefer to have all of the musicians with whom they work represented by the same PRO to streamline paperwork; additionally, production house executives often build important relationships with PRO administrators.

50/50 Split

Royalties for each registered composition are usually split evenly between the composer and publisher. This is referred to as a **50/50 split**, although composers and publishers are free to alter this standard as they see fit (and music that is co-composed or co-published will further divide the royalty allotment). Some production houses additionally divide royalties with complicated **sub-publishing agreements**, in which one publisher allows another publisher to represent its body of work. On the publishing side, royalty portions are typically negotiated down in these circumstances to where a single composition will not generate much income for the individual publishers. However, sub-publishing agreements are generally created to promote and sell larger volumes of music to wider audiences than typical publishing agreements would allow, which, in turn, can generate more substantial earnings.

NEGOTIATION

A troubling component of early PRO negotiations is that they resulted in a lack of royalties for any movie theater performance of a composer's music in the United States (e.g., a transmission of a film score), a problem that remains to this day. In the early years of PRO involvement in American movie theaters, ASCAP collected seat taxes, and in the 1940s, it attempted to triple them. Film companies fought back and won, making it impossible for composers to collect any royalties for their music when it is synced to picture in American movie theaters.

Situations like this speak to the necessity of negotiation in the music business. Many composers—especially young composers—find business conversations to be awkward, but they are simply too important to avoid. Music is both an art and a commodity in the industry, and to not negotiate for fair compensation is to devalue one of the most important facets of modern media. Composing and producing music takes time, and composers—just like businesspeople in any other facet of the economy—should be justly paid for their efforts. After all, while producing music is a labor of love, it is labor nonetheless.

When faced with an impending negotiation with a client, prepare to enter the discussion with a compensation range in mind with which you would feel comfortable. Then, decide whether to let the client steer the conversation or steer it yourself. If you choose the latter option, simply offer your services for an amount you deem acceptable (while allowing for some negotiation into a lower figure that you would also accept). If you would prefer to let the client direct the negotiation, a common icebreaker is to simply ask about the budget for the project and see if the client provides an offer. If the client offers less than you think you are worth in this situation (or any other), simply—yet kindly—apologize for not being able to take on the work for that figure and be prepared to walk away. It may be tempting in such a situation to accept a lower figure than you deserve, but keep in mind that the further you undervalue your musical efforts, the more you contribute to a global devaluation of the art for all composers. Understand your important role as a composer within the industry and know that every project needs you as much as you need the job. Music is an extremely valuable piece to many larger collaborative, artistic efforts; most clients understand this and, accordingly, offer fair compensation.

SUMMARY OF TERMS FROM CHAPTER 20

sole proprietorship
partnership
limited liability company (LLC)
corporation
S corporation
C corporation
liability
pass-through
limited partners
articles of organization

operating agreement
articles of incorporation
Copyright Form SR (Sound
    Recordings)
Copyright Form PA (Perform-
    ing Arts)
buy-out
royalties
mechanical royalties
mechanical license

performing rights royalties
synchronization royalty
background music
sync fee
Performing Rights Organiza-
    tion (PRO)
blanket license
cue sheet
50/50 split
sub-publishing agreement

CHAPTER 20—EXERCISES

1. In the space below, choose the business entity (sole proprietorship, partnership, LLC, S corporation, or C corporation) that you feel best fits your current or planned professional music career, and describe why this is so.

2. In the space below, identify which copyright form(s) should be filed in the following situation: an artist is attempting to protect a recording she completed of an original composition that she composed.

3. In the space below, describe the basic differences between mechanical royalties and performing rights royalties.

4. In the space below, describe what a cue sheet is and how it factors into the royalty distribution process.

5. In the space below, describe how much of a royalty portion a director will receive in a typical 50/50 split.

Appendix A
List of CC Messages and Their Associated Functions

CC Message	Function
0	Bank Select
1	Modulation Wheel
2	Breath Controller
3	Undefined
4	Foot Controller
5	*Portamento* Time
6	Data Entry
7	Channel Volume
8	Balance
9	Undefined
10	Pan
11	Expression
12	Effect Control 1
13	Effect Control 2
14	Undefined
15	Undefined
16	General Control 1

CC Message	Function
17	General Control 2
18	General Control 3
19	General Control 4
20	Undefined
21	Undefined
22	Undefined
23	Undefined
24	Undefined
25	Undefined
26	Undefined
27	Undefined
28	Undefined
29	Undefined
30	Undefined
31	Undefined
32	Bank Select
33	Modulation Wheel
34	Breath Control
35	Undefined
36	Foot Control
37	*Portamento* Time
38	Data Control
39	Channel Volume
40	Balance
41	Undefined
42	Pan
43	Expression Controller
44	Effect Controller 1
45	Effect Controller 2
46	Undefined
47	Undefined
48	General Purpose Controller 1
49	General Purpose Controller 2
50	General Purpose Controller 3
51	General Purpose Controller 4

CC Message	Function
52	Undefined
53	Undefined
54	Undefined
55	Undefined
56	Undefined
57	Undefined
58	Undefined
59	Undefined
60	Undefined
61	Undefined
62	Undefined
63	Undefined
64	Damper Pedal (on/off)
65	*Portamento* (on/off)
66	*Sostenuto* (on/off)
67	Soft Pedal (on/off)
68	*Legato* Footswitch
69	Hold 2
70	Sound Controller 1 (Sound Variation)
71	Sound Controller 2 (Timbre)
72	Sound Controller 3 (Release Time)
73	Sound Controller 4 (Attack Time)
74	Sound Controller 5 (Brightness)
75	Sound Controller 6
76	Sound Controller 7
77	Sound Controller 8
78	Sound Controller 9
79	Sound Controller 10
80	General Purpose Controller 5
81	General Purpose Controller 5
82	General Purpose Controller 5
83	General Purpose Controller 5
84	*Portamento* Control
85	Undefined
86	Undefined

CC Message	Function
87	Undefined
88	Undefined
89	Undefined
90	Undefined
91	Effects 1 (Reverb) Depth
92	Effects 2 (*Tremolo*) Depth
93	Effects 3 (Chorus) Depth
94	Effects 4 (Detune) Depth
95	Effects 5 (Phaser) Depth
96	Data Entry +1
97	Data Entry -1
98	Non-Registered Parameter Number LSB[1]
99	Non-Registered Number MSB
100	Registered Parameter Number LSB
101	Registered Parameter Number MSB[2]
102	Undefined
103	Undefined
104	Undefined
105	Undefined
106	Undefined
107	Undefined
108	Undefined
109	Undefined
110	Undefined
111	Undefined
112	Undefined
113	Undefined
114	Undefined
115	Undefined
116	Undefined
117	Undefined
118	Undefined
119	Undefined
120	All Sound Off
121	Reset All Controllers

CC Message	Function
122	Local Control on/off
123	All Notes off
124	Omni Mode off (+ all notes off)
125	Omni Mode on (+ all notes off)
126	Poly Mode on/off (+ all notes off)
127	Poly Mode on

APPENDIX B
Glossary

3-to-1 rule   a recording strategy used to avoid phasing issues during stereo miking. The 3-to-1 rule states that the distance between the first and second microphones should be at least three times the distance between the first microphone and the sound source.

50/50 split   a common type of contract agreement used in the music industry that equally divides royalties between the composer and publisher.

80:20 ratio   a compositional guideline used in media scoring, assigning approximately 80% of the expression to the drama and emotional atmosphere of the scene, while the remaining 20% is used to define the region in which the scene takes place.

A

AAX   shorthand for Avid Audio eXtension, this is a more recent plugin type used by Pro Tools software that is available in native and DSP formats.

absorption   a category of acoustic treatment that absorbs sound before it has the chance to reflect around the room, which can cause acoustic problems.

accelerando   a score marking that tells the performer(s) to gradually increase the speed of the music.

accented passing tone   an embellishment that is approached and left by step in the same direction and takes place in an accented metrical position.

accent mark   a notational symbol that tells the performer to emphasize a note with a sudden increase in volume.

accidental   a symbol used to alter the pitch of a note in a given direction without changing its letter, typically creating a chromatic alteration.

accordatura	a score marking indicating a cancellation of *scordatura* and return to standard tuning, usually in a score for stringed instruments.
acoustic foam	a type of acoustic paneling that absorbs non-bass frequencies within a studio room.
acoustic treatment	the application of physical paneling and other devices to a studio room so that it absorbs and deflects frequencies in a desired way.
active monitors	studio speakers that receive power from a built-in amplifier.
add chord	a triad to which a note is added that creates an interval of a major sixth or major second above the chord's root in some octave.
additive equalization	a process through which desired frequencies are boosted so that they sound more dominant in a mix.
ADSR	the four stages of an amplitude envelope: attack, decay, sustain, and release.
Aeolian mode	a diatonic mode that is equivalent to the natural minor scale, with a step pattern W—H—W—W—H—W—W.
Alberti bass	a particular style of bass arpeggiation that is characterized by a pitch contour sequence of low-high-medium-high.
aleatoricism	a composition technique involving indeterminacy or chance procedures that was popularized in the twentieth century by composers such as John Cage, Kryzstof Penderecki, and several others.
algorithmic reverb	a type of reverb that uses mathematical algorithms to create a series of diminishing delays that simulate a particular acoustic space.
aliasing	sonic distortion caused when a frequency is recorded that exists above one-half of the sample rate.
altered dominant	a dominant triad or seventh chord that possesses either a diminished or, more commonly, an augmented fifth.
alto clef	a C clef that assigns middle C (C4) to the third line of the staff.
ambient miking	the opposite of close miking, this technique involves placing a microphone a considerable distance from a sound source in order to take advantage of the coloration provided by the environment's reverberation.
amplitude	the intensity of energy in a given pressure wave, which is perceived by the human ear as loudness and expressed in dB or decibels (with 0dB representing the lower threshold for human hearing).
amplitude envelope	a way of describing how a sound unfolds over time from its first transient to the point at which it fades out. Amplitude envelope is described according to four stages, abbreviated as ADSR: attack, decay, sustain, and release.
anacrusis	an incomplete "pick-up" measure that takes place before the initial downbeat of a section or piece of music.
antecedent	the initial phrase or set of phrases within a multi-phrase structure that ends in a relatively inconclusive manner, leaving space for the more conclusive consequent phrase(s).
anticipation	an unaccented embellishment that is approached by stepwise motion and left by common tone.
appoggiatura	a very expressive dissonance that is preceded by leap—typically an ascending leap—and followed by step in the opposite direction.

arpeggiating $^6_4$	an apparent second inversion triad formed when the bass line of a piece arpeggiates up or down between chord tones to embellish a root-position harmony.
arpeggiation	a melodic and rhythmic figure involving a succession of leaps between chord tones.
articles of organization	a document that legally establishes a limited liability company in the United States.
artificial harmonics	false harmonics that are created when the performer uses one finger to stop a string at some point within its length and then lightly presses a P4 above the stop in pitch with another finger while bowing or plucking. In doing so, the performer generates a harmonic that sounds two octaves above the stopped note.
asymmetrical meter	a meter whose beats are of different lengths.
asymmetrical period	a period whose phrases are of unequal length.
attack	in acoustics, the point of a waveform's transient initiation. In mixing, a real or virtual knob within a compressor that specifies the speed at which the compressor will react to a signal passing over the threshold amplitude.
attenuate	to decrease the intensity of a certain range within the frequency spectrum during equalization.
audio continuum	a metaphorical three-dimensional space used to describe the fundamental parameters of a mix, which are volume, width, and depth.
Audio Warp	the audio quantization mode within Cubase Pro software.
augmentation	the lengthening of a motive via a systematic increase in its durational values.
augmented sixth chord	a chromatic predominant that features an augmented sixth interval between the lowered submediant in the bass and the raised subdominant in an upper voice, along with tonic and potentially one other scale degree ($\flat\hat{3}$ or $\hat{2}$).
automation	a manner of recording modifications to a musical parameter over time by means of fader or knob movements that are generated from a mouse or control surface, either during live playback or via asynchronous manipulations of a graphic display.
AU	shorthand for Audio Units, this is a popular native plugin format created by Apple.
aux track	an auxiliary track within a mix to which (and from which) signal is bussed, typically for the purpose of adding effects and/or grouping tracks.

B

balanced input	a connection point in an audio device that accepts three-wire noise-canceling cables such as XLRs.
bandwidth	frequency range, typically adjusted by the Q factor within an equalizer.
bar	a single, complete instance of a metric pattern that is also known as a measure.
bar line	a vertical line serving as the notational boundary of a measure.
bass	the lowest-sounding contrapuntal voice within a musical texture.
bass clef	a clef used for the notation of music for lower-pitched instruments. The bass clef is a stylized F featuring dots placed on either side of the fourth line of the staff

that identify it as an F (specifically, F3). As such, the bass clef is also known as the F clef.

bass drop a sub bass sound that sonically articulates an important hit point in a piece of music.

bass traps a type of acoustic treatment that prevents the reflection of bass frequencies and room modes within a studio.

beam a thick, horizontal line used to connect stems in music notation for the purpose of demonstrating rhythmic grouping.

beat a perceived stress in music that may also be called a pulse, though beats are more specifically considered as the primary, orienting pulses within a metric pattern.

beat division a pulse that is felt at two or three times the speed of the primary pulse within a meter.

beat subdivision a pulse below the level of the beat division. There are typically two beat subdivisions per beat division, regardless of whether the meter is simple or compound.

bed in music for media, a consistent-sounding instrumental background accompaniment for dialogue and/or sound effects that does not draw attention to itself.

bell curve EQ an equalizer that boosts or attenuates a band of frequencies unevenly in a bell curve pattern around a single peak frequency.

bi-amp a type of speaker system featuring multiple speakers that are powered by two separate amplifiers, with higher frequencies sent to one amp and lower frequencies sent to the other.

bidirectional/Figure 8 a polar pattern that picks up sound equally from the front and back of a microphone.

binary form a two-part form, with contrasting sections that are labeled A and B.

bit depth the number of bits used in each sample of an analog signal, corresponding to sample resolution.

blanket license a license that a music venue or other user purchases from a PRO that allows it to transmit that specific PRO's entire catalogue of works.

blues scale a characteristic scale used in blues and jazz styles that can be considered a minor pentatonic scale with an added half step between scale degrees $\hat{4}$ and $\hat{5}$.

Blumlein stereo miking a recording technique named after electronics engineer Alan Dower Blumlein that is similar to the X-Y configuration, but uses bidirectional (Figure 8) microphones at a 90° angle instead of unidirectional (cardioid) microphones.

boost to increase the intensity of a certain range within the frequency spectrum during equalization.

borrowed chord a non-diatonic chord that exists in the parallel key.

bounce to export a mix from the DAW and convert it into an audio file, such as an AIFF or MP3.

breath mark a notational symbol that instructs a performer when to breathe while playing.

bridge the main contrasting section within a song form.

buffer size	the allocated amount of time dedicated to processing sound as it enters a computer.
bumper	a brief piece of music that is used to transition between sections of programming, such as into and out of commercial breaks.
bus	a pathway within a mixing board through which one routes a signal to a particular destination.
button	in music for media, a concluding musical gesture used to wrap up a scene or mark a logo at the end of a commercial.
buy-out	a contract situation in which a client purchases the right to use a composition without owing any further compensation or royalties to the composer, regardless of the extent of usage.

C

C clef	a clef that assigns middle C (C4) to a specific line on a staff using a distinctive symbol that can appear to be a stylized letter C.
C corporation	a relatively large type of corporation that has more than 100 shareholders and is subject to taxation as an individual legal entity.
C score	a non-transposing score, meaning that all pitches for all instruments are written in concert pitch.
cadence	a point of rest that signals the completion of a musical idea.
cadential $^6_4$	an apparent I$^6_4$ sonority that embellishes the dominant at or near a cadence.
cadential extension	an elongation of a phrase that takes place when a conclusive cadence is followed by motivically related material that reaffirms the tonic harmony or simply repeats the cadential pattern.
cardioid	a heart-shaped, unidirectional polar pattern.
CC messages	shorthand for continuous controller messages, which are the pieces of musical information that are sent via MIDI. All CC messages fall into one of two main categories: channel messages and system messages. Channel messages have to do with an instrument's patch, timbre, and velocity, whereas system messages have to do with information and synchronization between multiple devices. There are 128 different types of CC messages, numbered 0 through 127.
cents	divisions of a semitone in equal temperament, of which there are 100.
chaconne	a continuous variation form that generally repeats a harmonic progression, without strict adherence to a bass *ostinato* (as in a *passacaglia*).
changing meter	a type of meter whose cardinality (number of beats) and/or beat division type (simple or compound) is not consistent.
channel strip	one of several units within a mixing console that typically consists of input jacks, a gain control, aux sends, dynamic control, panning control, solo/mute control, and level control.
chord extensions	chord members that create compound intervals above the root.
chorus	a section in a pop song that returns several times throughout the form, usually with the same lyrics and music each time; the chorus often includes the song's

main hook. In jazz, however, a chorus describes one complete instance of the tune's form. Additionally, in audio engineering, chorus is a type of modulation effect that features a constant delay duration between an original signal and a copy of that signal that is between 10 and 20ms.

chromatic alteration a colorful modification to a melodic line that is created by the addition of an accidental and results in a non-diatonic pitch.

chromatic mediant any non-diatonic harmony or key area whose root or tonic is a third interval away from the original tonal center, such as the major mediant in a major key.

chromatic modulation a change of key (often to a distantly related key) that makes use of a chord or voice-leading pattern that is not diatonic in both the home and target keys.

chromatic scale an ordered series of half step intervals encompassing an octave.

clef a notational symbol used to orient the reader or performer to a specific note on the staff as a point of reference.

clipping digital overload distortion.

close miking a technique in which a microphone is placed as close to a sound source as possible.

close position a voicing that involves chord tones placed as close as possible to one another in pitch space.

closing area a subsection within a sonata that takes place after the secondary theme and remains in the secondary key area.

closing theme a new theme introduced within the closing area of a sonata, after the secondary theme yet within the secondary key area.

coda a substantial, post-cadential subsection within a musical form that clearly and emphatically terminates the larger formal section while often introducing new thematic material or developing earlier themes.

codetta a short, post-cadential subsection within a musical form that clearly and emphatically terminates the larger formal section without introducing any new, substantial thematic material.

coincident X-Y stereo miking a recording technique that uses two matched, unidirectional (cardioid) microphones facing one another and positioned as close together as possible.

common tone a repeated note within a single contrapuntal voice.

comping short for composite recording, a term used to describe the act of recording multiple takes of a single part across different tracks, followed by combining the best parts of the individual takes into a single, final track.

complementary equalization a complex method of equalization used when multiple signals share the same general frequency range; this technique combines additive and subtractive processes to create a unique segment within a larger, shared frequency region that is dedicated to each signal.

composite recording a term used to describe the act of recording multiple takes of a single part across different tracks, followed by combining the best parts of the individual takes into a single, final track.

composite ternary form a three-part form whose constituent sections are complete binary forms.

compound intervals intervals that are larger than an octave.

compound meter	a pattern of stress in which each beat possesses three equal beat divisions.
compression	in acoustics, a region within a sound wave wherein air molecules are closest together, creating positive pressure. In mixing, a process that involves lowering the volume of a waveform's maximum amplitude peaks while simultaneously amplifying the waveform's amplitude troughs in order to decrease the perceived dynamic range.
concert score	a non-transposing score, meaning that all pitches for all instruments are written in concert pitch.
condenser microphone	a highly sensitive type of microphone that captures sound and creates an audio signal via a capacitor and voltage supplied by a battery or power supply.
conjunct	melodic motion by step.
consequent	the final phrase or set of phrases within a multi-phrase structure that ends in a relatively conclusive manner.
consonance	the perceptual sensation of stability engendered by certain intervals, notably those whose frequency ratios are relatively simple.
con sordino	a score marking used to indicate that a passage is to be played with a mute.
continuous	a term used to describe a form whose first large section terminates inconclusively in the original key or modulates to a different key.
continuous variations	a set of variations that features a short, repeated idea that continuously flows throughout the work; variations are added in a less rigid or clearly articulated fashion than with sectional variations.
contrafact	a piece whose harmonic structure is similar to another well-known work, despite its melody being unique.
contrapuntal motion	a description of the manner in which two melodies progress with respect to one another.
contrapuntal voices	melodically independent layers in a piece of music that combine in a coherent fashion.
contrary motion	a type of contrapuntal motion that exists when two parts progress in opposite directions.
contrasting period	a period whose antecedent and consequent differ significantly.
control surface	a piece of hardware that connects to a computer—usually via a MIDI or USB cable—to control various software functions.
corporation	a type of business that is owned by shareholders and operates as an individual legal entity, apart from its owners.
counterpoint	a technique that involves combining two or more melodies such that both harmonic unity and melodic independence are achieved.
convolution reverb	a type of reverb whose signal copy delay times are based on actual impulse responses from real spaces.
crescendo	a dynamic marking signifying the need for a gradual increase in volume.
crossfade	an editing process that smoothly transitions between two adjacent or overlapping waveforms by simultaneously fading out the initial waveform while fading in the subsequent waveform.

cross relation	an objectionable contrapuntal situation that takes place when different pitch classes sharing the same note letter (e.g., C and C♯) are used in adjacent temporal positions within different voices.
cue sheet	a list of the music included in a televised broadcast that is used by a PRO for usage tracking, royalty calculation, and royalty distribution purposes. A cue sheet includes the program title, episode title, episode length, and specific details about each composition used, including its usage type (background music, theme music, etc.) and usage duration.
custom scoring	a type of composition for media that involves pieces that are created "from scratch" and based on the specific requests of a director, producer, or other client for the purpose of filling the needs of a specific project. This is the area of the industry most commonly associated with the term "film scoring." Spotting notes and conversations about long-form development separate this field from ready-made composition.
cycle recording	also known as loop recording, this is a recording process that involves setting up a section within which a recording will continually capture new takes every time it cycles or loops through its programmed start and end points.

D

DAW	an acronym for digital audio workstation, which is a piece of recording software designed to consolidate the workflows related to the many stages of production into a single location.
dBFS	shorthand for decibels relative to full scale; this relative scale orients the producer to the maximum output level, 0dBFS, at which clipping may occur.
deceptive cadence	a cadence that involves a harmonic move from V to vi (or VI in minor keys) at the end of a phrase, wherein the submediant chord serves as a tonic substitute.
deceptive resolution	harmonic motion from V to vi (or VI in minor keys), wherein the submediant chord serves as a tonic substitute (but not at the very end of a phrase).
decibels (dB)	units of measure for amplitude, with 0dB representing the lower threshold for human hearing. In the relative dBFS context (decibels relative to full scale), 0dB represents the maximum output threshold of an audio device.
delay	an effect that involves copying a signal and repeating it a certain number of times at a given durational interval from the original.
dependent	a term used to describe a transition section within a sonata that makes use of motives from the primary theme.
development	the B section in a sonata form that often features the extensive motivic manipulation of earlier themes (though some developmental sections develop new material that is not necessarily associated with any previous theme).
DI (direct box)	a device used in recording studios that receives unbalanced signal (usually from a guitar or bass) and converts it to balanced signal before it enters a mixing console.
diatonic collection	a collection of seven different notes (plus a repeated note, creating an octave interval above the first) arranged in such a way that five of the adjacent notes are separated by whole steps while two are separated by half steps; these half step

intervals are additionally spread apart from one another as evenly as possible within the collection.

diatonic modes	the seven intervallically unique scales that represent individual rotations of the diatonic system.
diffusion	a category of acoustic treatment that is used to scatter reflecting frequencies within a studio room.
diminuendo	a dynamic marking signifying the need for a gradual decrease in volume.
diminution	the reduction of a motive's length via a systematic decrease in its durational values.
direct fifths/octaves	an objectionable contrapuntal situation that involves a leap in the soprano creating a perfect fifth or octave above the bass that is approached by similar motion.
disjunct	melodic motion by leap.
dissonance	the perceptual sensation of tension engendered by certain intervals, notably those whose frequency ratios are relatively complex.
divisi	a score marking that divides the total number of players within a single instrumental section into two or more distinct parts.
dominant	the very stable fifth degree within a major or minor scale; also, a primary harmonic function that lends an opposing force to tonic function and represents the fundamental source of harmonic tension or instability within a piece of tonal music.
Dorian mode	a diatonic mode that is similar to a natural minor scale with a raised sixth degree and features a step pattern of W—H—W—W—W—H—W.
dot	a notational symbol also known as an augmentation dot that increases the duration of a note by 50%.
double flat sign	an accidental that lowers a note by two half steps (or a whole step).
double neighbor	a melodic embellishment figure featuring consonance between the two parts in the first and fourth metric positions and dissonance between the two parts in the second and third positions. The melody featuring the embellishment proceeds by step, leap of a third in the opposite direction, and finally step in the original direction.
double period	a period composed of a two-phrase antecedent and two-phrase consequent.
double sharp sign	an accidental that raises a note by two half steps (or a whole step).
double stop	a string technique that involves plucking or bowing two pitches simultaneously on two different strings.
double tongue	a technique that wind players use to perform passages featuring quicker rhythms that demand faster tongue movement than a series of repeating silent "tees" could produce; this is accomplished by tonguing the letters "d–k" or "t–k" in alternation.
downbeat	the first beat in a metric pattern, which receives the most accentual weight.
drop frame	one type of SMPTE timecode that involves the periodic skipping of timecode seconds in order to address the disparity between the timecode (which runs at 30 FPS) and NTSC video (which runs at 29.97 FPS).

drum bus	a commonly used bus scenario that transports and combines the separately recorded signals of each discrete drum set element (hi-hats, toms, snare drum, kick drum, etc.) into a single, more manageable track.
dry signal	signal that does not have added effects.
DSP	shorthand for Digital Signal Processor, a plugin that requires the use of a separate outboard interface for processing.
duple meter	a meter possessing two beats.
dynamic equalization	a type of processing that is similar to compression in that specified frequencies become attenuated when they pass a volume threshold set by the user.
dynamic microphone	a durable type of microphone that captures sound and creates voltage via a coil-fixed diaphragm that is wrapped around a magnet.

E

earworm	a colloquialism used in music for media that describes an extraordinarily memorable segment of music.
echo	an effect that repeats a copied version of an audio signal in a manner similar to delay; however, echo specifically involves repeating the signal at ever-lower amplitudes until the sound completely fades out.
eighth note/rest	a note or rest that lasts for half of one quarter note or rest in common time.
Elastic Audio	the audio quantization mode within Pro Tools software.
embellishment	a melodic ornament used to decorate a structurally significant tone.
enhancer	a psychoacoustic processor that adds brightness—sometimes referred to as "sparkle"—to an audio signal, often by way of frequency-specific distortion.
enharmonically equivalent intervals	intervals that sound the same and possess the same number of half steps but are labeled differently (and function differently), as their constituent pitches are spelled differently.
enharmonic equivalents	notes that sound the same but are spelled differently.
episode	a contrasting formal section within a fugue or rondo that is typically in a non-tonic key.
EQ sweeping	a technique used to troubleshoot problematic frequencies within an audio signal, which involves passing a narrow, boosted band throughout the entire frequency spectrum in order to locate specific issues.
equalization	the act of shaping a signal by attenuating and/or boosting specific frequencies.
escape tone	an incomplete neighbor embellishment that is preceded by step and left by leap in the opposite direction into a chord tone.
event (MIDI)	a unit of information housed within a region (typically experienced as a musical "note").
evolution mixing	a strategy in which the rudimentary elements of a mix evolve alongside the musical components of a project, as opposed to starting the mixing process after all recording and editing has been completed.
exciter	a psychoacoustic processor that adds brightness—sometimes referred to as "sparkle"—to an audio signal, often by way of frequency-specific distortion.

expression controller (MIDI CC11)	a commonly automated CC message that works as a sub-volume, allowing for volume adjustments to be made within the boundaries set by CC7 (volume controller) at any given moment.
extended chord	a seventh chord with one or more compound intervals added above the root to create a large tertian sonority of four or more consecutive thirds.

F

fade in	a measured increase of volume from silence to a signal's original amplitude.
fade out	a progressive decrease of an audio signal's level from its original amplitude to silence.
far-field monitors	speakers that are designed to be placed a large distance away from the producer within a studio.
figured bass symbols	Arabic numerals added below a staff that indicate the intervals above the notated bass line that are to be added (typically to form chords in various inversions).
filter envelope	a timbral adjustment setting on a synthesizer that allows for some frequencies to be attenuated, while others pass through unaffected.
first inversion	a chord position featuring the chordal third in the bass.
fixed EQ	a basic equalizer that typically features three knobs adjusting high, mid, and low frequencies, with the high and low ranges controlled by low-pass and high-pass shelving EQs, respectively.
flag	a notational symbol that is added to a stem to indicate a note of relatively short length (when beams are not used).
flanger	a modulation effects processor that features a very short delay (1–10ms) between the original and copied signals that gradually changes over time, creating a "swooshing" effect.
flat sign	an accidental that lowers a note by a half step.
Flex mode	the audio quantization mode within Logic Pro X.
fluctuating capacity	the mechanism of audio signal generation within a condenser microphone, which is created when a sound wave causes a diaphragm to move relative to a back plate when voltage is between them.
flutter echo	a ringing effect that is caused by sonic reflections between two hard, parallel surfaces.
foldover	a type of aliasing or sonic distortion that is caused when a frequency is recorded that exists above one half of the sample rate.
Follow Tempo	the tempo-matching functionality within Logic Pro X.
form	*see musical form.*
Form PA (Performing Arts)	a form used to register a composition, including any lyrics, with the U.S. copyright office for the purposes of infringement protection.
Form SR (Sound Recordings)	a form used to register a particular recording of a composition with the U.S. copyright office for the purposes of infringement protection. This form may be used to protect both a recording and a composition in instances where the composer also serves as the recording artist.

forte	a dynamic marking signifying the need for a strong or loud performance.
fortissimo	a dynamic marking signifying the need for a very strong or loud performance.
FPS	short for frames per second, a frame rate that indicates the number of still images that are presented within the space of a second in a video.
fragmentation	the truncation of a motive through subtraction/deletion, the inclusion of rests, or other means.
frequency	the number of times per second that air molecules involved in a pressure wave vibrate back and forth in one complete cycle, which is in turn based on how quickly the source is vibrating. Frequency is perceived as a sound's highness or lowness, similar to pitch in music.
frequency response chart	a technical readout that demonstrates a microphone's capacity to respond to certain frequencies within a typical range from 20Hz to 20kHz.
fundamental	the base frequency or lowest-sounding tone resulting from a sound wave, which is also the first harmonic in the overtone series.

G

gain knob	a volume control for each channel of a mixing console that specifically adjusts the level at which an input signal will proceed into a channel.
gain matching	a software functionality that allows the user to bypass any processing while boosting the signal to a level equal to that of the processed mix for comparison purposes.
gain staging	the management of the output level of any audio signal throughout all phases of its journey within a session, which requires an understanding of all of the locations or "gain stages" within the signal's path wherein gain can be applied.
gating	the use of a noise gate to eliminate unwanted sonic elements within a signal that are present at levels below a user-defined threshold volume.
glide	a sonic adjustment setting on a synthesizer that creates a *glissando*—a smooth, sliding effect that passes through all of the notes between the specified starting and ending pitches.
glissando	a smooth, gliding pitch transition from one note to another that proceeds through all of the intermediate microtones.
Gong	the principal scale used in traditional Chinese music, which has an intervallic structure of W, W, W+H, W, W+H.
grand staff	a combination staff that covers a very large pitch range by joining the treble clef and bass clef staves together with a bar line and a brace. The grand staff is also known as the great staff.
graphic EQ	an equalizer displaying several sliders that control the boosting or attenuation of specific frequency bands, arranged from lowest to highest in frequency in a left-to-right format.

grid	the visual demarcation system for duration used within a DAW's main tracks view window or piano roll editor, which can be calibrated by the user to show specific rhythmic durations as vertical slices for editing purposes.

H

half cadence	a cadence characterized by resting on the dominant triad at the end of a phrase.
half note/rest	a note or rest that lasts for two beats in common time.
half step	the smallest distance between two different pitches in equal temperament. Also known as a semitone, a half step is the interval between adjacent keys on the keyboard.
harmonic minor	the minor scale that is similar to a natural minor scale but possesses a raised seventh degree, creating a leading tone. The harmonic minor scale has the interval pattern W—H—W—W—H—W+H—H, with "W+H" corresponding to the interval of an augmented second.
harmonic rhythm	the rate of harmonic change per unit of musical time.
harmonics	also known as overtones, these are frequencies heard along with a fundamental that are multiples of the fundamental pitch's frequency.
harmonic sequence	a series of non-functional chords that are bonded together by repeated voice-leading patterns.
harmony	a primary component of music relating to pitch combinations such as chords.
head	the composed melody of a jazz composition.
head out	the final performance of the head in a jazz form.
headphone mix	a customizable mix that is typically delivered from the recording interface through a headphone amplifier into headphones that are worn by the performing musicians in a session; a headphone mix is used instead of speakers for the purposes of real-time monitoring to prevent the microphones in the recording room from picking up sound that would be emitted by the studio monitors.
headroom	the range between an audio signal's peak level and the maximum output level of an audio device (such as a DAW).
hemiola	a rhythmic phenomenon that takes place when the established accentual pattern of a piece of music that is in two groups of three temporarily becomes regrouped into three groups of two or vice versa, typically at the end of a section leading into a point of conclusion.
Hertz (Hz)	a measure of frequency, with one Hz equaling one vibration per second.
high-pass shelf	an equalizer that does not affect any frequencies above a designated cutoff point, instead boosting/cutting frequencies below the threshold.
Hirajoshi	a traditional Japanese scale derived from the tuning traditions of the koto instrument that features the intervallic structure of W, H, 2W, H, 2W (2W simply means two whole steps, or a M3).
hit point	a marked location of visual and/or musical emphasis within a production.

hook	a memorable motivic/thematic unit in a popular song.
horizontal re-sequencing	a compositional technique used for video game implementation that consists of multiple loopable sections of music that can alternate back and forth at given points without creating discontinuities.
hypercardioid	an expanded supercardioid polar pattern that captures an even larger area behind the microphone, in addition to the cardioid (heart-shaped) region in front of the microphone.

I

IAC	short for imperfect authentic cadence, a cadence that includes harmonic motion from the dominant to the tonic, but is less conclusive than a PAC. The IAC may feature one or both of the harmonies in inversion, or, more commonly, may have scale degree $\hat{3}$ or $\hat{5}$ in the soprano upon the arrival to the final tonic.
impulse responses	the acoustic parameters that are recorded in a physical environment within which an impulse is introduced (such as a starter pistol); impulse responses are used to calibrate delay times in a convolution reverb.
incomplete neighbor	a general type of embellishment that is so named because it features stepwise motion on one side of the dissonance and a leap on the other. Two incomplete neighbor types are the *appoggiatura* and the escape tone.
independent	a term used to describe a transition section within a sonata that does not make use of motives from the primary theme.
independent phrases	temporally adjacent phrases that do not relate to one another motivically or structurally.
in-line effects	the use of effects plugins that are added to each individual track within a mix.
in phase	a term used to describe identical sound waves that create constructive interference by being perfectly aligned such that their peaks and troughs take place at the same time.
insert	an external device to which (and from which) signal is routed within a channel strip.
interlaced	a term that refers to frames within a video that are divided into odd and even partitions of alternating, horizontal segments and are played back-to-back at a rate that is so fast that the mind perceives the alternating images to be joined into a singular whole.
interlude	a contrasting section within a popular song that is similar to a bridge but is entirely instrumental.
interpolation	the insertion of additional material in the middle of a phrase, usually yielding an atypical phrase length.
interval	a distance between two pitches.
interval inversion	a change in the pitch ordering of an interval's constituent tones, such as when the lower note of an interval becomes the higher note by being placed in a higher octave (or vice versa).
interval quality	a secondary indication of the specific distance between pitches that form more general interval sizes, expressed as a letter.

interval size | an indication of the general distance between pitches expressed as a number reflecting the sheer number of letters within the musical alphabet A–G that are involved in the span from the first note to the second note.

introduction | a formal section that takes place at the outset of a piece, prior to the exposition of the piece's primary themes (or, in the case of pop/rock music, prior to the song's first verse).

inversion | a motivic development technique wherein the melodic intervals of a motive are maintained while their directionality is reversed.

Ionian mode | a diatonic mode that is equivalent to the major scale, with a step pattern W—W—H—W—W—W—H.

ISRC | shorthand for International Standard Recording Code, a unique code that is generated to function like a digital fingerprint in identifying a specific recording of a piece of music.

J

jingle | a short, catchy song that functions as an expanded version of a sonic brand in tying a memorable piece of music with a product or service.

K

key signature | a patterned arrangement of accidentals in music notation that signifies the key of a given section or piece of music (by including the related scale's accidentals).

key switching | a MIDI editing process that allows the user to trigger articulation changes by pressing specified keys on a keyboard controller that correspond to pitches outside of an instrument's playing range.

L

latch mode | an automation editing mode that overrides automation data in the areas that are changed during playback. Once the user lets go of the fader during playback, the adjusted parameter will "latch on" to the most recent value and remain at that level for the rest of the passage.

latency | a noticeable delay between the moment sound is produced and the moment it reemerges through monitors or headphones after being routed through circuitry.

lead sheet | a concise, score-based overview of a song that includes a basic representation of the melody on the staff along with chord symbols above the staff that indicate the progression.

leap | any melodic distance that is greater than a step. A leap is always indicated by noteheads that are more than one position apart on the staff.

ledger lines | lines that extend the staff vertically and allow for a range of multiple octaves to be notated using a single clef.

legato | a smooth and connected type of articulation that is indicated by a slur in music notation.

legato transitions | samples that are added to *legato* patches within virtual instruments in order to create smooth transitions between overlapping MIDI events.

leitmotif	a short, distinctive motive or portion of a larger theme that becomes associated with a particular character, place, object, emotion, or idea by consistently recurring along with it in a dramatic setting.
LFO	shorthand for low frequency oscillator, which is a device or plugin used to rhythmically modify a sound's low frequencies in order to generate unique *tremolo* or *vibrato* effects.
liability	a term that refers to the responsibility of individuals or businesses for any unpaid debt or legal actions taken against them.
limited liability company (LLC)	a flexible business entity that alleviates many liability concerns for the owner(s). An LLC is established via articles of organization and directed by an operating agreement. It may be taxed as a corporation or via pass-through taxation.
limited partners	members of a business partnership who, in exchange for agreeing to restricted control over the business, are released from legal liability.
limiter	a processor used in audio engineering that limits the output of a signal's peak level, usually to prevent clipping.
link	a short instrumental passage within a popular song that is transitional in nature.
Locrian mode	a diatonic mode that is similar to a natural minor scale with a lowered fifth degree and lowered second degree; this mode features a step pattern of H—W—W—H—W—W—W.
low-frequency enhancement	a type of psychoacoustic processing that involves adding synthesized harmonics to a signal in order to increase the perceived bass and sub bass frequencies; the harmonics are either added above an illusory fundamental or below an actual fundamental.
low interval limit	the lowest useful register for a given harmonic interval.
low latency	a type of DAW functionality that bypasses CPU-heavy plugins to restrict the latency that typically results from high buffer sizes.
low-pass shelf	an equalizer that does not affect any frequencies below a designated cutoff point, instead boosting/cutting frequencies above the threshold.
Lydian mode	a diatonic mode that is similar to a major scale with a raised fourth degree and features a step pattern of W—W—W—H—W—W—H.

M

main title	the portion of the title sequence in a film or other media production that displays the title of the work.
major scale	a rotation of the diatonic collection featuring a W—W—H—W—W—W—H step pattern; the generative seed from which the outgrowths of both melody and harmony in major keys develop.
make-up gain	gain applied to a compressed signal to increase its output level (usually to the original volume of the signal prior to the application of compression).
marker	an indicator that is added to a DAW session in order to visually emphasize an important time point. In game music, a marker is an embedded prompt used to trigger a change to a different section of music in a horizontal re-sequencing implementation.

master chain	a series of plugins that is added to the DAW's master output for the purpose of digital mastering.
master fader	the primary summing point within a mixer, where all tracks are combined and may be adjusted en masse.
mastering	the final stage of production, which involves making large-scale adjustments to a complete mix or set of tracks (including noise reduction), embedding digital identifiers to audio files, and meeting established criteria related to the final recording deliverable(s) (e.g., sample rate, bit depth, file format, etc.).
mastering suite	a standalone program and/or plugin that is designed to combine all of the processing involved in mastering into a single virtual location.
matched microphones	microphones that are of the same make and model and were created at the same time.
measure	a single, complete instance of a metric pattern that is also known as a bar.
mechanical license	a license that grants permission to reproduce and distribute copyrighted music on a variety of media. Mechanical licenses are distributed by groups like the Harry Fox Agency in the United States and the Mechanical-Copyright Protection Society (MCPS) in the U.K.; these entities in turn distribute mechanical royalties at a set rate to registered composers for registered compositions.
mechanical royalties	royalties that are paid to musicians when pieces of music are reproduced, distributed, and sold in a variety of recording formats.
melodic minor	the minor scale that is similar to a natural minor scale but with raised sixth and seventh degrees in its ascending form, such that its final ascending tetrachord is the same as that of the major scale. The ascending melodic minor scale has the interval pattern W—H—W—W—W—W—H. The descending version of the scale is the same as the natural minor scale.
melodic sequence	a patterned repetition of a melodic segment at different pitch levels.
melody	a primary musical parameter related to the unfolding of pitches in a linear fashion through time. A melody can also be thought of as a combination of pitches and rhythms that is perceivable as a single musical unit.
metadata	digitally encoded information about a piece of music, such as the artist(s) involved in its creation.
meter	a perceived grouping of strong and weak stresses in music.
meter signature	a fraction-like notational symbol containing numbers that refer to amounts of rhythmic units in order to indicate a meter within a score.
mezzo forte	a dynamic marking signifying the need for a moderately strong or loud performance.
mezzo piano	a dynamic marking signifying the need for a moderately soft performance.
microphone	a transducer that creates an electrical image based on a detected sound signal.
middle C	the pitch performed nearest the center of the 88-key keyboard, labeled as C4 according to the Acoustical Society of America standard.
mid-field monitors	speakers that are designed to be placed a medium distance from the producer within a studio, farther away than near-field monitors and closer than far-field monitors.

MIDI	an acronym for Musical Instrument Digital Interface, which is a protocol that allows two or more devices to connect and communicate with one another.
MIDI polyphony	the ability of certain MIDI devices to produce multiple notes or sounds simultaneously.
mid-side (MS) stereo miking	a recording configuration in which a cardioid mic (or mid-mic) is aimed directly at an instrument, while a Figure 8 mic (or side-mic) is aimed left and right to capture the ambient sounds of a room. The side-mic signal is then copied, phase inverted, and panned during mixing, such that it occupies both the left and right areas of the stereo field, with the mid-mic signal panned center to create a complete stereo image.
Mixolydian mode	a diatonic mode that is similar to a major scale with a lowered seventh degree that features a step pattern of W—W—H—W—W—H—W.
mix stem	a group of audio signals that are fed into a single aux track in order to help with the global organization of a project while allowing for simple batch processing.
mode mixture	the practice of using borrowed chords from the parallel key to enliven the harmonic landscape of a piece.
modified strophic form	a scheme used in art songs wherein the music generally repeats the same A section material for each stanza or verse of text, but with slight variations (AA'A''A''', etc.).
modular composition	creating full pieces of music with memorable beginnings, middle sections, and endings that are designed such that editors can easily take out certain sections, rearrange sections, or otherwise edit as they see fit to appropriately match the situation for which they need music. Sections of a modular composition therefore need to be strong enough to exist on their own—and they must each end convincingly, given that any section may need to function as the final segment of the work.
modular synthesis	a type of sound design wherein multiple sound modules (oscillators) are connected to create patches.
modulating period	a period that features a change of key within its duration.
modulation	a change of key within a composition.
modulation effects	effects (flanging, phasing, and chorus effects) that operate by creating a copy of a signal and combining it with the original signal at a small interval of delay. In doing so, the peaks and troughs of the original waveform meet with the peaks and troughs of the delayed copy at different points, creating a "comb filtering" effect as the combined signal goes in and out of phase.
momentary configuration	a MIDI controller configuration that will send an *on* message when a certain apparatus is depressed and an *off* message when the apparatus is released.
monitor referencing	a term used to describe the process of mix comparisons made on multiple speakers and headphone systems.
mono	short for monaural, this term describes audio that is heard from one channel or position (as opposed to stereo, which incorporates two channels and creates a field of perceived sonic positions).

motive	a salient, identifiable combination of pitch and rhythm that is shorter than a theme yet still represents a musical idea. Also known as a motif or melodic cell.
motivic development	the process of repeating and altering an initial idea throughout a phrase or piece of music, which simultaneously engenders the traditionally desired aesthetic attributes of unity and variety.
multiband compressor	a compressor often used in mastering that divides the frequency range into adjustable bands, which allows for specific types of compression to be applied to certain regions within the spectrum.
multi-sample	a combination patch that itself consists of multiple samples, often from different instruments, to recreate full sections or ensembles within a single patch.
multitimbral device	a MIDI device such as a sampler or synthesizer that is able to create sounds using up to 16 or 32 different instruments simultaneously.
musical form	the term used to describe the overall shape of a piece, which is created via the combination of sections that contrast one another due to changes in thematic design, harmonic structure, and/or other parameters.
mute	a button within a mixing board's channel strip that, when pressed, silences the signal such that no sound within that specific channel strip is heard. A mute is also a device placed on or inside an instrument to change its timbre, usually creating a muffled sound or wah-wah effect.

N

native plugin	a plugin that uses the processor within a host computer.
natural harmonics	flute-like tones that are produced when performers lightly press on various locations that divide an open string's length and correspond to points within the overtone series above the open string's fundamental.
natural minor	the minor scale that is generated by a traditional key signature, sharing all of its pitches with a relative major scale. The natural minor scale has the interval pattern W—H—W—W—H—W—W.
natural sign	an accidental that typically directs the performer to perform one of the "natural" notes (A, B, C, D, E, F, or G).
Neapolitan sixth chord	a non-diatonic major triad in first inversion that is built on the lowered supertonic.
near-coincident stereo miking	a recording technique that uses two matched, unidirectional (cardioid) microphones facing in opposite directions yet positioned relatively close to one another (within 12 inches).
near-field monitors	speakers that are designed to be placed a short distance from the producer within a studio.
neighboring $^6_4$	an apparent second inversion triad that is created when a harmony is expanded with a $^5_3$—$^6_4$—$^5_3$ interval pattern taking place over a static bass.
neighbor tone	a melodic embellishment that is approached by step and left by step in the opposite direction, returning to the original note that preceded it.
negative impact	a termination of a rise that never delivers the full impact that was implied or expected. Often, this lack of a sonic "payoff" results in a stronger effect than the powerful climax that was anticipated.

noise floor	the base level of unavoidable background noise that is created by the various electronics participating in a mix environment.
noise reduction	the process of eliminating clicks, hums, clips, and other unwanted noises from a mix, typically during the final mastering phase.
non-functional IV/iv	a IV chord that does not possess predominant function, instead moving directly to tonic.
nota cambiata	a melodic embellishment figure featuring consonance on the downbeat, followed by a dissonance that is a step above or below that consonance, a leap of a third out of the dissonance in the same direction as the previous step, and finally two steps in the opposite direction into consonant pitches.
notehead	the ovular part of a note in music notation, which is placed on the staff to indicate pitch. The notehead may be open or filled in, which aids in the specification of the note's duration.
NTSC	short for the National Television Standards Committee, which was established in the United States to standardize frame rates in television broadcasts and ensure that broadcasts did not suffer from interference.
Nyquist theorem	a principle related to sampling stating that a sample rate should be set to at least two times the value of the highest frequency one wants to capture in order to create an accurate reproduction of an analog signal.

O

oblique motion	a type of contrapuntal motion that occurs when one voice changes pitch and the other repeats the same note.
octatonic scale	an eight-note scale that features a consistent, symmetrical pattern of alternating half and whole steps.
octave	the interval from one pitch of a given letter name to another with the same letter name that is heard in a different register.
octave designations	labels applied to pitch letter names that relate to the specific octave in which they reside.
octave-down doubling	an orchestration technique that involves doubling lower register melodies an octave lower, usually with the double basses, to add weight and depth to the bottom of the ensemble.
octave equivalence	the musical principle related to the consideration of pitches separated by one or more octaves as equals in many musical contexts, due to their very similar sounds.
offbeat	a traditionally unaccented pulse within a meter, such as the second and fourth divisions within simple duple meter.
omnidirectional/boundary	a polar pattern that is characterized by equal sound absorption from all directions.
open position	a voicing that involves chord tones placed relatively far apart in pitch space, such that the chord spans more than an octave.
operating agreement	a legal document that identifies the governing members of a business entity (such as an LLC) and describes their financial and managerial responsibilities.

organic sound design	a process that involves recording live sounds and manipulating them by way of computer processing (e.g., time-stretching, adding effects, editing waveforms, etc.) to generate new sounds.
oscillator	a sound wave generator within a synthesizer.
oscilloscope	a device used to graphically represent the frequency of an electronic signal over time.
ostinato	any persistently repeated musical idea.
out of phase	a term used to describe identical sound waves that create destructive interference by being misaligned by 180 degrees such that one wave's peaks take place at the same time as another's troughs and vice versa.
outro	an instrumental section that serves as a popular song's conclusion.
overtone series	a succession of simultaneously sounding harmonics stemming from a fundamental pitch.

P

PAC	short for perfect authentic cadence, a cadence that features root position dominant and tonic chords, specifically, and stepwise motion into tonic in the soprano.
pan	a section of a channel strip that allows the producer to place an audio signal left or right within the stereo field. Placing a signal within the stereo field is called "panning."
parallel fifths/octaves	an objectionable contrapuntal situation involving consecutive perfect intervals of the same type that are connected by parallel motion.
parallel keys	keys that share the same tonic but possess different key signatures and different modes.
parallel motion	a type of contrapuntal motion that exists when two voices move in the same direction and in the same way, preserving the interval size that is created harmonically between the parts.
parallel period	a period whose antecedent and consequent begin in the same way or in a similar manner.
parametric EQ	a flexible equalizer that features several customizable bands whose Q factor can be adjusted by the user.
partnership	a business entity that is similar to a sole proprietorship, with the primary difference being that liability is equally shared between multiple partners.
part writing	a very common manner of working with harmonies on the staff in composition training that traditionally involves composing individual parts for each member of a choir, which combine on a single grand staff to create chordal textures in the manner of a chorale.
passacaglia	a piece of music that is characterized by a repeated bass *ostinato* that serves to create coherence amid a set of continuous variations (which take place in the upper contrapuntal voices).
passing $^6_4$	a second inversion triad that harmonizes a passing tone in the bass between more structurally significant chords.
passing tone	a melodic embellishment that is approached by step and left by step in the same direction, filling in the melodic interval of a third.

passive monitors	studio speakers that receive power from a separate amplifier.
pass-through	a type of taxation applicable to certain business entities that "passes through" to the business owner such that the business's taxes are filed via the owner's individual tax return.
patch	a term used when referring to a specific sound within a synthesizer, as oscillators were traditionally connected via quarter-inch patch cables to create new sounds during modular synthesis.
pedal point	a type of embellishment featuring a dissonance (usually in the bass voice) that is preceded and followed by a common tone, resolving only when other voices in the texture move.
pencil tool	an editing function within a DAW that has the ability to add MIDI events to a region. In certain DAWs, the pencil tool may also be used to "draw in" other items, such as velocity curves, fades, and more.
pentatonic scale	a five-tone pitch collection that can be considered as a rotation of the diatonic system without the two tones that form a tritone interval.
period	a multi-phrase structure that features related ideas structured such that the final cadence is the most conclusive.
Performing Rights Organization (PROs)	an organization that serves to protect musicians' interests by monitoring the usage of members' compositions, collecting performing rights fees and royalties from music venues and other users, and distributing these earnings to musicians and their publishers.
performing rights royalties	royalties that musicians are paid for a live or recorded performance of a composition, either in a concert or in conjunction with another media format.
phase cancellation	also called phasing, this is the destructive interference caused by identical sound waves that are misaligned.
phaser	a modulation effects processor possessing "all-pass" filters that are set to filter certain frequencies of a signal copy before combining it with the original signal at varying intervals of delay.
phasing	also called phase cancellation, this is the destructive interference caused by identical sound waves that are misaligned.
phase shifting	a term used to describe the interference pattern that takes place when the same sound enters multiple microphones at varying points over the cycle of a waveform, resulting in a weaker—but not completely canceled—sound.
phrase	a complete musical idea that terminates with a cadence.
phrase elision	also called phrase overlap, a unique hypermetrical phenomenon that occurs when the end of one phrase takes place simultaneously with the beginning of another. A phrase elision is additionally known as an elided cadence.
phrase group	a set of phrases that cohere in a manner similar to a period, yet do not conclude with a relatively strong cadence.
Phrygian half cadence	or Phrygian cadence, a cadence that features descending half step motion from $\flat\hat{6}$ to $\hat{5}$ in the bass and harmonic progression from a first inversion iv chord to a root position V triad.

Phrygian mode	a diatonic mode that is similar to a natural minor scale with a lowered second degree and features a step pattern of H—W—W—W—H—W—W.
plagal cadence/plagal motion	harmonic motion from the subdominant to the tonic, such as in the traditional plagal "Amen" cadence (I—IV—I).
planing	the process of transposing a sonority to a different pitch level with all voices moving in parallel motion.
pianissimo	a dynamic marking signifying the need for a very soft performance.
piano	a dynamic marking signifying the need for a soft performance.
piano roll editor	a MIDI sequencing window that presents a piano keyboard (located on the left side of the window) rotated 90 degrees such that the bottoms of the keys are facing right. Immediately to the right of the keyboard image is a graph made up of vertical and horizontal lines. The horizontal lines aid in the representation of pitch and run parallel to the keys of the keyboard. The lines running vertically across the graph relate to duration or rhythm and are divided into time segments that can be calibrated by the user.
Picardy third	a type of mode mixture wherein the chordal third of the final tonic harmony in a minor-key piece is raised by a half step to create a major I chord, lending an uplifting sound to an otherwise dark harmonic landscape.
pitch	a musical sound occurring at a point along the continuum of audible frequencies from low to high.
pitch class	a group of pitches possessing the same letter name and similar sounds that are separated by octaves.
pivot modulation	also called common chord modulation, a seamless key change that is made using a chord that exists diatonically in both the original and target keys.
pointer tool	a DAW function with the ability to move MIDI events up or down (changing pitch) as well as left or right (altering their rhythmic positions) in the piano roll editor, among other applications.
polar pattern	a microphone's directional span of sound absorption.
pop filter	a circular, screen-like device placed in front of a microphone that filters out unwanted popping sounds.
post-fader aux send	a mixing scenario that involves signal being sent to an aux track after it is routed through the channel's fader, such that the channel volume is directly linked to the output of the bus send, eliminating the need to recalibrate wet/dry ratios each time the channel volume is altered.
power chord	an open fifth sonority characteristic of hard rock and metal styles, typically consisting of the root, fifth, and octave played in the lowest possible register of a distorted guitar.
pre-chorus	a transitional section that is formally positioned before the chorus in a popular song.
predominant	a harmonic function that is so named because the chords possessing this function tend to be followed by dominant function chords. Predominants signal a move away from the tonic area and into the dominant area, initiating the building of tension that ultimately resolves at the end of an idea or piece.

pre-fader aux send	a mixing scenario that involves signal being sent to an aux track before it is routed through the channel's fader, such that the channel volume is not linked to the output of the bus send, resulting in the need to recalibrate wet/dry ratios each time the channel volume is altered.
prefix	additional material at the beginning of a phrase (such as an extended anacrusis) that usually yields an atypical phrase length.
pre-mix leveling	establishing a basic set of track volume levels before processing and volume automation are applied to a mix.
preset	a preprogrammed factory setting, usually accessible via a drop-down menu within a plugin, that allows for quick, generic sound manipulations.
primary theme	in a sonata form, the initial theme or group of themes that exist(s) within the tonic key area.
production track	ready-made compositions for television, radio, and live events that feature a consistent sonic atmosphere and are used to support specific emotions or situations. Production tracks are curated by production houses to generate production libraries that are used by directors and other media executives.
progressive-scan	a standard format for film, which involves non-interlaced still images that are typically presented at a rate of 24 frames per second or higher.
proximity effect	an audio phenomenon that takes place when a microphone is placed too close to a sound source, boosting frequencies under 100Hz by as much as 16dB.
psychoacoustic processing	a technique used to "excite" or "enhance" an audio signal by adding synthesized harmonics.
pulses per quarter	a measure of durational resolution within a DAW in terms of the number of ticks or segments within a single quarter note.
pumping	an effect common in electronic dance music that involves sidechain compression that is triggered by a kick drum track.
punch	a circular flash that visually articulates a hit point when added in Digital Performer software.
punch-in	a term used to describe the point at which recording begins when destructively re-recording or comping a segment within a track.
punch-out	a term used to describe the point at which recording ends when destructively re-recording or comping a segment within a track.

Q

Q factor	short for quality factor, this is the ratio of the core frequency to bandwidth. By lowering the Q factor, a producer expands the bandwidth of affected frequencies during equalization. Raising the Q factor does the opposite.
quadruple meter	a meter possessing four beats.
quantization	a MIDI editing process that snaps (or pulls) the starting points of selected events to the closest user-defined rhythmic value.
quarter note/rest	a note or rest that lasts for one beat in common time.
quick swipe comping	a type of composite recording that places each take within an organized, easy-to-view take folder below the initial take in a DAW. The user may then swipe the

mouse to highlight a particular section within a particular take, which places it within the composite track that is heard upon playback.

R

ragas intervallic combinations in Indian classical music (and other types of music) that are designed to color an atmosphere and create specific moods.

rarefaction a region within a sound wave wherein air molecules are farthest apart, creating negative pressure.

ratio a real or virtual knob within a compressor that specifies the amount that a signal will be reduced in dB when it exceeds the given threshold amplitude.

RCA connector shorthand for Radio Corporation of America, a connector used in a type of unbalanced speaker cable that is common in consumer-grade speaker systems.

read mode an automation playback mode that simply follows any previously recorded automation without creating new parameter adjustments.

ready-made composition a type of scoring that involves creating music that needs to generically fit a multitude of situations. A publisher working for a production house typically contracts ready-made music; the production house then curates a library of this type of music in order to fill a variety of needs for its clients.

reamping the process of routing a recorded signal (usually from a guitar or bass) out of the editing environment and into an amplifier for further sonic manipulation.

recapitulation an altered restatement of a piece's exposition section (such as in a sonata or fugue) in the tonic key.

referencing the practice of comparing one's mix to other completed, professional mixes in related genres.

refrain the primary, recurring theme or lyric in a rondo or song form.

region a unit within a track that contains either audio or MIDI information.

register a pitch region within the continuum of audible sound.

relative keys keys that share the same key signature but possess different tonics.

release a real or virtual knob within a compressor that specifies the duration that a signal will remain compressed after it falls back below the threshold amplitude.

rest a notational symbol signifying a duration of silence in music.

retardation an embellishment that is essentially an inverted suspension, in that it is an accented dissonance that is prepared by the same pitch (often featuring a tie) and resolves by ascending stepwise motion instead of descending stepwise motion.

retransition a subsection within a musical form that sets up the return of the tonic key, often via a dominant pedal.

retrograde a motivic development technique that refers to the recurrence of a motive in reverse, such that the first note becomes the last note, the second note becomes the penultimate note, and so on.

reverb short for reverberation, an effect that involves creating a series of delayed copies of a signal that reach the ear at slightly different instants, creating the perception that the signal is reflecting off of a room or space's surfaces.

rhythm	a general term used to describe the time-based or temporal organization of music. Rhythms can also be defined more specifically as musical durations of sound and silence.
rhythm clef	a clef also known as the percussion clef that is used to notate non-pitched music such as percussion parts.
ribbon microphone	an expensive, delicate type of microphone that captures sound and creates signal via a metallic ribbon that vibrates within a magnetic field.
riser	a synthesized sound or composed instrumental passage that builds tension leading up to a hit point.
ritardando	a score marking that tells the performer(s) to gradually slow the music down.
Roman numerals	analytical symbols used to identify chords' root scale degrees, qualities, and functions within a key.
rondo	a musical form that involves the reappearance of a primary theme (or refrain) amid contrasting ideas known as episodes.
room modes	resonance frequencies that are created within a room and typically congregate in its corners; room modes are usually between 20Hz and 200Hz.
root position	a chord position featuring the root as the lowest-sounding note.
rounded binary form	a two-part form featuring a return of the initial theme at the end of the second reprise.
royalties	the umbrella term used to describe usage-based payments for music compositions, performances, and recordings.
RTAS	shorthand for Real Time Audio Suite, this is the native version of Pro Tools's Time Division Multiplexing format.
Rule of Threes	a compositional guideline stating that one should deviate from the literal repetition of a motive upon its third iteration in order to create interest and avoid monotony.

S

sampler	a virtual instrument that plays back recordings of actual sounds.
sample rate	the rate at which an analog-to-digital convertor takes samples or digital snapshots of an analog signal, measured in Hertz.
scale	an ordered series of notes arranged in a specific pattern of intervals that encompasses an octave.
scale degree	a member of a scale that is indicated by a caret-topped number reflecting its position relative to tonic.
scordatura	a score marking indicating that a passage is to be played in an alternate tuning.
S corporation	a relatively small type of corporation that has fewer than 100 shareholders and is subject to pass-through taxation.
secondary dominant	a $V^{(7)}$ chord from a non-tonic key that is used to tonicize a target harmony.
secondary leading tone chord	a diminished, half-diminished, or fully-diminished chord built on the leading tone of a non-tonic key that is used to tonicize a target harmony.

secondary theme	in a sonata form, the theme or group of themes representing a non-tonic key within the exposition.
second inversion	a chord position featuring the chordal fifth in the bass.
sectional	a term used to describe a form whose first large section terminates conclusively in the original key.
sectional variations	a variation form whose theme and subsequent variations each terminate with a conclusive cadence in the home key and thus represent standalone formal sections.
semitone	the smallest distance between two different pitches in equal temperament. Also known as a half step, a semitone is the interval between adjacent keys on the keyboard.
sentence	a phrase that is dedicated to the development of a motive in a specific pattern of presentation and continuation.
senza sordino	a score marking used to indicate that a passage is to be played without a mute, thereby canceling any previous *con sordino* marking.
sequencing	the process of entering and editing MIDI information in a DAW or sequencer.
seventh chord	a tertian harmony composed of four pitch classes.
sforzando	a score marking indicating the need for a sudden, forceful accent on a specific note.
sidechaining	a type of effects processing (typically used with compressors) that involves sending signal from one channel so that it can be used to trigger sonic alterations to the signal on another channel.
signal flow	an audio signal's pathway from a sound source through various circuits.
similar motion	a type of contrapuntal motion that takes place when two voices move in the same direction, but in different ways (e.g., one voice moves by step and the other moves by leap in the same direction).
simple binary form	a two-part form whose second reprise consists entirely of new material.
simple meter	a pattern of stress in which each beat possesses two equal beat divisions.
simple ternary form	a three-part form whose constituent sections (ABA) are composed of phrases and periods that do not represent complete forms themselves.
single-amp	a type of speaker system featuring multiple speakers that are powered by a single amplifier.
sixteenth note/rest	a note or rest that lasts for one quarter of a beat in common time.
sharp sign	an accidental that raises a note by a half step.
slur	a notational symbol that is typically used to indicate that a passage is to be performed with a *legato* articulation. Slurs are similar in appearance to ties, but connect two or more different pitches as opposed to connecting equal pitches.
SMPTE timecode	a standard timecode used in audio and video production that was developed by the Society of Motion Picture and Television Engineers in the 1960s to allow producers, editors, and engineers to reference extremely specific time points within a project.
snap	to displace a MIDI event to a user-defined temporal location, as in quantization.

sole proprietorship	an easily established business entity without liability protection that is subject to pass-through taxation.
solo	a button within a mixing board's channel strip that, when pressed, silences the other channels such that no sound except that specific channel strip is heard (although any other soloed channels' signals will also be present).
solos	a term used in jazz to describe the main body of the common head/solos/head out form, wherein individual instrumentalists take turns improvising over one or more choruses apiece.
sonata	a musical form featuring the exposition of contrasting themes and key areas, the development of themes, and the recapitulation of themes (typically within a single key area).
sonata-rondo	a seven-part, ABACAB'A rondo that possesses a second episode (C) that is primarily developmental in nature and may conclude with a retransition subsection.
song cycle	a collection of several art songs (or *Lieder*) that are presented together and share a unifying narrative or theme.
sonic brand	an audible counterpart to a visual branding, which helps a company conjoin a memorable soundbite with a product or service.
sound barriers	devices designed to limit the amount of outside noise that is captured during recording.
sound design	the act of modifying a sound source in some way to create a new sound. Sound design is a term that is often used to describe the creation of sound effects (or SFX) used in a film, but it can also be used to describe a compositional approach that entails creating innovative sounds for musical purposes.
spaced pair stereo miking	a recording technique in which two cardioid microphones are used to capture a sound source; these mics are spaced according to the 3-to-1 rule to avoid phasing issues.
species counterpoint	a centuries-old training regimen in counterpoint that is graduated in nature, proceeding incrementally by level or species.
spectral processing	another term for equalization, which involves processing or filtering specific regions within the frequency spectrum.
spectrum analyzer	a DAW plugin that shows the exact frequencies that are excited during playback, along with the decibel levels for each frequency within the spectrum.
spotting notes	spreadsheets or other documents that are used in commercial scoring scenarios in order to provide specific start and stop times for individual cues, along with the precise length and a brief description of each scene.
spotting session	a collective viewing of a video project by the director, composer, and potentially other individuals involved in the production with the purpose of generating spotting notes for the composer to use while scoring the project.
staccato	a short and detached type of articulation that is indicated by a small dot above or below a notehead (usually on the opposite side of the stem).

stacked voicing	a chord voicing for multiple instruments that features pitches being distributed among instruments such that one group is exclusively given the relatively higher pitches while another group is given the lower pitches.
staff	a graph-like notational tool for music that is composed of five parallel, horizontal lines that are equally spaced.
staggered voicing	a chord voicing for multiple instruments that features pitches being distributed among instruments such that instruments of the same type do not play adjacent chord tones.
static motion	a lack of true contrapuntal motion, wherein neither voice changes pitch.
stem	the thin vertical line connected to the notehead in music notation, which may point upward or downward depending on the notehead's positioning within the staff. A stem also refers to a sub-collection of tracks within a mix sharing similar instrumentation or function; stems are typically combined for a final mix within a stemmed session (or "stem session").
stemmed session	also called "stem session," an organized version of a larger session that records similar sounds (and/or those related by instrument family) into groups to create a more manageable session that can be easily recreated by other producers in different DAWs, often for the purpose of a final mix.
step	a relatively small interval that is indicated either with noteheads that are on adjacent lines and spaces, or with noteheads on the same line or space with one or more chromatic alterations.
step progression	a large-scale melodic motion between adjacent, structural scale degrees.
step sequencing	also called step entry, a type of asynchronous MIDI sequencing that allows the user to input one note at a time.
stereo image enhancement	a form of psychoacoustic processing that incorporates phase shifting and MS processing to generate a sound field that is perceived to be wider than it actually is.
stereo miking	the involvement of two or more microphones in a recording of a single sound source, which offers the potential of creating a stereo image by blending and positioning multiple mono signals.
stereo separation	the level of audibly perceived individuality from among multiple signals that combine to form a stereo image.
stinger	in music for media, a sudden burst of musical emphasis that is designed to surprise the audience.
streamer	a superimposed visual cue in Digital Performer software—usually a white vertical line—that works its way from left to right across the screen over the course of a predetermined amount of time prior to a hit point.
string quartet	a multi-movement form that originated in the Classical era and is performed by an ensemble of the same name that features two violins, a viola, and a cello.
strophic form	a scheme used in art songs wherein the music repeats the same A section material despite the text changing in each stanza or verse.
subito	a score marking signifying a sudden change in dynamic level.

sub-publishing agreement	a type of agreement in the music industry in which one publisher allows another publisher to represent its body of work, typically in exchange for a portion of the publisher's royalty share.
subtonic	the seventh degree of a scale that is positioned a whole step below tonic.
subtractive equalization	a process through which undesired frequencies are attenuated so that they do not dominate a mix.
suffix	additional material added at the end of a phrase, usually yielding an atypical phrase length.
suite	a multi-movement form common during the Baroque era, which consisted of several dance movements that were often preceded by a separate prelude.
supercardioid	an expanded cardioid polar pattern that additionally captures a small area behind the microphone.
surrounded voicing	a chord voicing for multiple instruments that features pitches being distributed among instruments such that the inner chord tones are given to one instrument type, while the outer chord tones are given to others, which "surround" the timbre of the inner-voice instruments.
sus chord	a quartal harmony featuring both a perfect fourth and fifth above the bass and no chordal third.
suspension	an accented melodic embellishment that is approached or "prepared" by a consonant common tone and resolves down by step into another consonance.
swing quantization	a MIDI editing process that works by quantizing every other instance of a selected rhythmic value ahead or behind its position in a standard duple division by a fixed amount, giving a performance a loose quality that can emulate the swing feel.
symmetrical period	a period whose phrases are of equal length.
symphony	an orchestral work that customarily follows a four-movement pattern of fast tempo—slow tempo—dance movement—fast tempo; the multi-movement symphony form is typically performed by a large orchestra of the same name.
sync fee	a payment made to a composer—sometimes in addition to synchronization royalties—in exchange for the limited use of a composition that is synchronized to some form of media.
synchronization royalty	a specific type of performing rights royalty that applies to situations in which a composition is synchronized to some form of media, as is the case with background music for a television show, movie, or commercial.
syncopation	a rhythmic phenomenon that takes place when an accent (or group of accents) conflicts with the underlying meter's expected pattern of stress.
synthesizer	a piece of hardware or software that generates one of four types of sound waves using oscillators: sine waves, square waves, sawtooth waves, and triangle waves.

T

take	a single recording pass.
tape saturation	a type of psychoacoustic processing that involves adding a small amount of digital distortion to a signal, which in turn generates high-frequency harmonics

	that provide a simulation of the "warm" sound that is often attributed to tape recording.
tap tempo	a feature of many delay plugins/pedals that allows the user to sync the timing of the delayed signal copy (or copies) to the tempo of the track by tapping a button or key on a device, creating identifiable rhythmic values within the meter of the song.
TDM	shorthand for Time Division Multiplexing, a DSP plugin in Pro Tools software that requires a separate, dedicated processor.
tempo	the speed of a piece of music or rate at which its beats are perceived.
tempo matching	a DAW function that alters the tempo of an audio file to match the tempo of a project.
tenor clef	a C clef that assigns middle C (C4) to the fourth line of the staff.
tenuto	a smooth and connected articulation that is indicated by a horizontal line placed above or below a notehead.
ternary form	a form that includes three complete, independent sections that each end with a conclusive cadence.
text painting	the process of reflecting the meaning of a word or phrase using musical parameters such as harmony.
texture	the manner in which the parts or layers of a piece of music relate to one another. Texture is often considered to be synonymous with density, too, which is simply a consideration of the total number of layers within a piece.
ticks	durational segments measured as partitions of a quarter note within a DAW.
tie	a notated arc used to link and combine the durations of equally pitched notes, often from one measure to the next.
timbre	also known as tone color, this is the unique set of characteristics that differentiates the sound of one instrument from another. Timbre consists of two main components: the sound's amplitude envelope and the array of excited harmonics that are created above each sounding fundamental.
title sequence	an opening credits sequence in a film or other media production that includes the main title (the portion of the production that displays the title of the work).
third inversion	a chord position for seventh chords featuring the chordal seventh in the bass.
three-phrase period	a period that possesses three phrases, typically consisting of a two-phrase antecedent and single consequent phrase.
threshold	a real or virtual knob within a compressor that specifies the amplitude at which compression is activated.
through-composed form	a musical form that does not feature the repetition of large sections of thematic material (e.g., ABCD, etc.).
toggle configuration	a MIDI controller configuration that will send an *on* message when a mechanism is depressed and remain in the *on* position until it is pressed down again, like a button.
tone	*see whole step.*

tonguing	a technique that wind performers use to create a temporary break in the airflow to the instrument in order to place a slight emphasis on each note within a passage and create separation between rhythmic values; tonguing involves temporarily forming a silent "tee" against the roof of the mouth or the reed of the instrument with the tongue.
tonic	a focal note that serves as a key's gravitational center within a piece of tonal music.
tonicization	a progression that allows a target harmony to be heard fleetingly as a new tonic, due to the use of a chord or chords with secondary function.
touch mode	an automation editing mode that overrides automation data in the areas that are changed during playback. Once the fader is released, the parameter will jump back to its previously recorded value(s), as opposed to "latching" on to the final value and remaining at that level (as in latch mode).
tracks	editable lanes of information that are displayed horizontally and stacked on top of one another in a digital audio workstation.
trailer track	a piece of music that is used to support a movie or video game trailer.
transient	a sudden, temporary interruption in output level that takes place at the beginning of a waveform.
transient analysis	a DAW-based examination of an audio file's attack points, which is needed to inform the computer of the specific moments that are to be adjusted during audio quantization.
transition	in a sonata, a subsection whose function is to modulate to the secondary key area within the exposition.
transition cue	a small audio file—often a short stinger or atmospheric clip—that is used to bridge together the larger looping sections within a horizontal re-sequencing scheme in a game composition.
transport control window	a view or toolbar within a DAW that allows the user to view and adjust parameters specifically related to rhythm such as tempo, time signature, and the visualization of rhythmic values on the grid.
transposing instruments	instruments that produce pitches at a consistent interval away from those that are written in notation.
transposition	the repetition of a musical idea at a different pitch level.
treble clef	a clef used for the notation of music for higher-pitched instruments. The treble clef features a spiral around the second line of the staff that identifies it as a G (specifically, G4). As such, the treble clef is also known as the G clef, and it looks like a stylized letter G.
triad	a tertian harmony composed of three pitch classes.
tri-amp	a type of speaker system featuring multiple speakers that are powered by three separate amplifiers, with higher frequencies sent to one amp, mid-range frequencies sent to a second amp, and lower frequencies sent to a third amp.
trill	a score marking that signifies the need for a rapid alternation of pitches.
triple meter	a meter possessing three beats.

triple stop	a string technique that involves bowing or plucking three pitches simultaneously on three different strings.
triplet	a note value that is used to divide into three parts that which is normally divided into two.
tritone	a dissonant interval that spans six half steps (or three tones) and may be spelled as an augmented fourth or diminished fifth.
tritone substitution	a harmonic substitution used in jazz featuring a dominant seventh chord that can be thought of as replacing a more normative dominant seventh chord (whose root is located a tritone away) that would create root motion by falling fifth in a manner similar to a ii—V(—I) progression. The result of a tritone substitution is half step root motion (e.g., D♭⁷—C).
TRS connector	shorthand for Tip Ring Sleeve, a connector used in a type of balanced instrument cable that is common for guitars, basses, and keyboards.
TS connector	shorthand for Tip Sleeve, a connector used in a type of unbalanced instrument cable that is common for guitars, basses, and keyboards.
tuplet	a rhythmic grouping also known as a "borrowed division" that evenly divides other rhythms in ways that conflict with established metrical patterns.

U

unbalanced input	a connection point in an audio device that accepts two-wire cables such as TSs that are more susceptible to picking up noise.
unison	an interval of zero distance between pitches sharing the exact same sound and letter name.
upbeat	the final beat within a meter, which usually possesses the least accentual weight of any beat.

V

velocity	a MIDI CC message parameter that correlates with intensity or dynamic level on a scale from 0 to 127.
velocity switching	a MIDI editing process that allows the user to trigger articulation changes by assigning sample layers to specified velocity ranges.
verse	a formal section in a pop song that typically features different lyrics each time it recurs, while the music remains the same (or is similar).
verse-chorus form	the standard form in popular music, featuring primary verse and chorus sections that are paired together to form a large, repeated A section that is contrasted by a bridge section (B).
vertical layering	also referred to as vertical remixing or vertical re-orchestration, this is a common approach to interactive game composition that effectively breaks a large composition into autonomous units that can function both individually as well as with any combination of the other parts. Certain parts will join into or drop out of the texture as time progresses according to the intensity of game play, creating a continuous development and re-orchestration of a passage.

virtual instrument	a piece of software that emulates the sound of an instrument and can be accessed as a plugin within a DAW.
voice crossing	an objectionable contrapuntal situation in which a relatively lower voice (e.g., the alto) is written in a higher register than a higher voice (e.g., the soprano) or vice versa.
voice exchange	a melodic scheme in which contrapuntal voices swap pitch classes via contrary stepwise motion.
voice leading	the manner in which contrapuntal voices progress from note to note (individually) and chord to chord (collectively).
voice overlap	an objectionable contrapuntal situation wherein the higher voice (e.g., the soprano) leaps to a lower position than the previously used note in the lower voice (e.g., the alto) or vice versa, despite the voices not technically crossing.
voicing	the specific arrangement of a harmony in pitch space, pertaining to the spacing, doubling, and/or omission of the chord tones.
volume controller (MIDI CC7)	a commonly automated CC message that controls the overall maximum volume of a track that may or may not include any expression control.
VST	shorthand for Virtual Studio Technology, this is a popular native plugin format created by Steinberg.

W

well-tempered (tuning)	a tuning system that divides each octave into 12 equal semitones, which is slightly out of tune with some of the harmonics present in the overtone series.
wet signal	signal to which effects have been added.
whole note/rest	a note or rest that lasts for four beats in common time.
whole step	the second-smallest distance between two different pitches in equal temperament. Also known as a tone, a whole step is equal to two half step intervals.
whole tone scale	an ordered series of whole step intervals encompassing an octave.
write mode	a destructive automation mode that records parameter adjustments in real time while overriding any alterations that may have been made previously.

X

| XLR connector | shorthand for Cannon Electric's X series with an added Latch and Rubber compound, a connector used in a type of balanced cable that is common for connecting microphones to devices such as mixing consoles. |

PERMISSION ACKNOWLEDGMENTS

Every effort has been made to locate and secure permission from all copyright holders. Thanks to the following authors, composers, publishers, and agents for permission to use the material indicated.

MUSIC

STAR WARS (MAIN THEME). Music by JOHN WILLIAMS. © 1977 (Renewed) WARNER-TAMERLANE PUBLISH-ING CORP. and BANTHA MUSIC. All Rights Administered by WARNER-TAMERLANE PUBLISHING CORP. All Rights Reserved. Used by Permission of ALFRED MUSIC.

IMPERIAL MARCH, THE ("DARTH VADER THEME") (from "Star Wars: The Empire Strikes Back"). Music by JOHN WILLIAMS. © 1980 WARNER-TAMERLANE PUBLISHING CORP. (BMI). And BANTHA MUSIC (BMI). All Rights Administered by WARNER-TAMERLANE PUBLISHING CORP. (BMI). All Rights Reserved. Used by Permission of ALFRED MUSIC.

Symphony of Psalms by Igor Stravinsky. © 1931 by Hawkes & Son (London) Ltd. Revised version: © Copyright 1948 by Hawkes & Son (London) Ltd. U.S. copyright renewed. Reprinted by permission of Boosey & Hawkes, Inc.

The Rite of Spring by Igor Stravinsky © Copyright 1912, 1921 by Hawkes & Son (London) Ltd. International Copyright Secured. All Rights Reserved. Reprinted by Permission of Boosey & Hawkes, Inc.

IMAGES

Screen shots from Logic Pro X used by permission of Apple Inc.
Screen shots from Avid Pro Tools ® used by permission of Avid Technology, Inc. ®
Screen shots from PLAY and Hollywood Strings used by permission of EastWest Sounds, Inc.
Screen shots from FabFilter Saturn used by permission of FabFilter V.O.F.

Screen shots from Digital Performer courtesy of MOTU, Inc.

Screen shots from Kontakt used by permission of Native Instruments GmbH

Screen shots from Waves PAZ Analyzer, Waves L1+ Ultramaximizer, Waves Renaissance Compressor, and Waves Renaissance Equalizer used by permission of Waves Audio Ltd.

Screen shots from Cubase used by permission of Steinberg Media Technologies GmbH. Steinberg, Cubase, Dorico, HALion, Nuendo, WaveLab, VST, ASIO and other Steinberg product and technology names are trademarks or registered trademarks of Steinberg Media Technologies GmbH, registered in Europe and other countries.

INDEX

Note: Page numbers in italic indicate a figure or table on the corresponding page

Taylor & Francis eBooks

Helping you to choose the right eBooks for your Library

Add Routledge titles to your library's digital collection today. Taylor and Francis ebooks contains over 50,000 titles in the Humanities, Social Sciences, Behavioural Sciences, Built Environment and Law.

Choose from a range of subject packages or create your own!

Benefits for you

» Free MARC records
» COUNTER-compliant usage statistics
» Flexible purchase and pricing options
» All titles DRM-free.

Benefits for your user

» Off-site, anytime access via Athens or referring URL
» Print or copy pages or chapters
» Full content search
» Bookmark, highlight and annotate text
» Access to thousands of pages of quality research at the click of a button.

REQUEST YOUR FREE INSTITUTIONAL TRIAL TODAY

Free Trials Available
We offer free trials to qualifying academic, corporate and government customers.

---

eCollections – Choose from over 30 subject eCollections, including:

Archaeology	Language Learning
Architecture	Law
Asian Studies	Literature
Business & Management	Media & Communication
Classical Studies	Middle East Studies
Construction	Music
Creative & Media Arts	Philosophy
Criminology & Criminal Justice	Planning
Economics	Politics
Education	Psychology & Mental Health
Energy	Religion
Engineering	Security
English Language & Linguistics	Social Work
Environment & Sustainability	Sociology
Geography	Sport
Health Studies	Theatre & Performance
History	Tourism, Hospitality & Events

For more information, pricing enquiries or to order a free trial, please contact your local sales team:
www.tandfebooks.com/page/sales

Routledge
Taylor & Francis Group

The home of
Routledge books

www.tandfebooks.com